State Systems

About the Author

The author has for some years been professor at the University of California, Santa Barbara. He received a master's degree at the Fletcher School of Law and Diplomacy and a doctorate at Columbia, where he attended the Russian Institute. His twelve previously published books deal with foreign relations, Soviet politics, and related topics. His effort to analyze communist authoritarianism, however, led him into a wide-ranging historical study of autocratic rulership, the conclusions of which were set forth in *The Imperial Order*. But the compressive political and intellectual effects of universal empire suggested the opposite, the stimulative effects of a competitive international system; and in this book the author presents the fruit of many years of fascinated study of the effects of international division.

State Systems

International Pluralism, Politics, and Culture

Robert G. Wesson

THE FREE PRESS
A Division of Macmillan Publishing Co., Inc.
NEW YORK

Collier Macmillan Publishers
LONDON

Copyright © 1978 by The Free Press
A Division of Macmillan Publishing Co., Inc.

All rights reserved. No part of this book may be reproduced or transmitted in any form or by any means, electronic or mechanical, including photocopying, recording, or by any information storage and retrieval system, without permission in writing from the Publisher.

The Free Press
A Division of Macmillan Publishing Co., Inc.
866 Third Avenue, New York, N.Y. 10022

Collier Macmillan Canada, Ltd.

Library of Congress Catalog Card Number: 77-84945

Printed in the United States of America

printing number
1   2   3   4   5   6   7   8   9   10

Library of Congress Cataloging in Publication Data

Wesson, Robert G.
   State systems.

   Bibliography: p.
   Includes index.
   1. Pluralism (Social sciences)   2. Comparative government.   3. Creative ability.   4. Civilization, Occidental.   I. Title.
JC325.W49   321'.009   77-84945
ISBN 0-02-934940-0

Contents

Preface vii

Introduction 1

   The Study—Pluralism—States and Empires

Part One The Pre-Western World 19

Chapter 1   Conditions of State Systems 21

   Historical Examples—Preconditions—International Practices—Downfall

Chapter 2   The Open Society 41

   Republicanism—Sumerian Experience—Chinese Monarchy—Republican India—Greek Pluralism: *Commercial Society, Greek Democracy, Constitution of Athens, Hellenistic Aftermath*

Chapter 3   Creativity 61

   Sumeria—China of the Hundred Schools—Indian Enlightenment—Greek Success—Hellenistic Civilization

Chapter 4   Effects of Pluralism 80

   Size—Interaction and Variety—Movement—Contention—Generality: *Ancient Civilizations, Phoenicia, Araby, Partial Division: Japan and China*

Part Two The West — 98

Chapter 5   International System of the West — 101

Independence: *The Two Swords, Feudal Europe and Free Towns, The Nation-states, Defeat of Empire*—Community of the West: *Shared Heritage, International Practices*

Chapter 6   The Western Political Achievement — 128

Medieval Freedoms and the Towns—Italian Republics—Nation-states: The Authoritarian Tide—Nation-states: The Libertarian Drift—England and Parliament—France, Revolution, and the Rights of Man

Chapter 7   The Western Creativity — 153

Rise of Europe—Florescence of Italy—Eclipse of the Towns—Nation-states and Science—Prosperity of the Netherlands—Britain and the Industrial Revolution

Chapter 8   The Nation-state System: Interaction and Development — 181

Competition—The Open Society—Movement and Comparison—Commerce—Nonsovereign Divisions and Federalism—Inferior and Superior Powers: Imperial States—Size—State Systems

Part Three   From the Old to the New World — 212

Chapter 9   The Passing of the European System — 215

Nineteenth-century Indian Summer—Time of the Wars

Chapter 10   The New World System — 228

Emergence—The World Divided: *Marxist-Leninist States, Poor versus Rich*—The World as State System—Problems of the New World Order: *Morale, Government, International Order*

Epilogue — 264

References — 266

Index — 287

Preface

The present book, begun over a decade ago in connection with *The Imperial Order*, studies the decentralized as opposed to the centralized world. *The Imperial Order* dealt not with colonial empires, like those of recent memory, but with a different species: the universal or near universal empires of history, of which the Roman may be taken as prototype. The central theme was that overwhelming political power generates intellectual, economic, and ultimately political weakness. It is the central theme of the present book that the checking of political power by its division among competing states has permitted the opposite; namely, intellectual, economic, and political growth.

Something of these themes has also been explored in *The Russian Dilemma*, which treats Russia as a near universal empire subject to the competition of the more liberal and technologically more progressive state system of the West. Russia has suffered from the fifteenth century and continues to this day to suffer a profound dilemma: the contradiction between the necessity for authoritarian rule to hold its domain together and the necessity to adapt to the ways of the Western state system sufficiently in order to keep up in technology and productivity. The idiosyncrasies of Russian and Soviet-Russian political development are interpretable in this framework.

The present book focuses on the divided international order, the state systems—this phrase being used not for any international structure, as is often the usage in writing on international relations theory, but to designate a group of closely interacting independent sovereignties that collectively dominate their world. In a sense, this is a negative thesis of *The Imperial Order*; the virtues of the one condition correspond to the vices of the other, although the state systems, being more diffuse, less orderly, and less clearly defined, are more difficult to treat. They are, however, more important to us because our civilization is largely the product of a state system or several state systems, and because the present international structure is much more like a classic state system than a universal empire. In this latter respect, moreover, the present study goes beyond the previous. *The Imperial Order* halted short of the modern age, although various aspects of its conceptions are obviously relevant to latter-lay totalitarian states. *State Systems*, to the contrary, undertakes briefly to apply this paradigm to the complex modern congeries of sovereignties in the hope of shedding some light on its peculiarities.

Introduction

The Study

For Western thought, which has grown up in a seemingly eternal world of many independent sovereignties, each with its own laws, loosely joined and at the same time chronically at odds, it is easy to forget that this has not been the only or even the historically predominant condition of mankind. Humans have mostly lived in large or middling empires, hardly recognizing external powers and certainly not accepting independent sovereignty or a balance of power in principle. That independent polities should have interacted closely with a considerable number of other independencies has been the peculiar fortune—presumably good fortune—of Western Europe for over a thousand years. Similarly, Europe has been exempt, even in the seventeenth century when kings were claiming to govern by grace of God, from anything close to the despotic government that has been frequent in most of the world. Since the Middle Ages it was assumed in what may be called the Western world that civilized men were ruled by law-bound governments. It has likewise been the fortune of the West to have been mechanically more progressive and more innovative in many ways than neighboring peoples for the past millennium, a fact that has long been taken for granted but that has been little explored.

It is the thesis of this book that these three antitheses—loose international system as against large empires, constitutional as against arbitrary government, and innovative against traditional societies—are closely related and interdependent, and that, while cause and effect are inevitably reciprocal, the international situation can usefully be treated as a major independent variable, a cause from which many other things derive. International relations studies in recent years have given much attention to the effects of domestic politics, attitudes, and values upon foreign policy, the "linkage problem" (Rosenau, 1969). Scholars of international relations, however, are primarily interested in foreign policy and conflict; and they have given little attention to the reverse influence of the international system on domestic affairs. It has been noted, to be sure, that domestic politics may be "penetrated" by external powers, and the effects of war are so patent that general study has perhaps seemed unnecessary. But the broader aspects of the influence of the international milieu upon the individual states, though perhaps decisive as the influence of climate on vegetation, have been only marginally considered.

There is much in such relations that is rather obvious and familiar. Long ago, Machiavelli (*Discourse on the First Decade of Titus Livius*, 2.2) and other Florentine writers knew well the inverse relation between unification and creativity in Italy, from Etruscan times of many creative city-states through the torpor of the Roman Empire to the rise of independent towns in the Middle Ages and the accompanying cultural upsurge. Montesquieu and others have likewise commented on the stimulating effects of international interaction and on the propensity of overlarge and centralized states toward despotism and demoralization. It is widely enough known, although it has been disputed for partisan purposes, that loosely structured societies are more creative and usually more productive than more tightly controlled ones. It is readily apparent that there must be some linkage between scientific discovery and political structures; for a contemporary example, Soviet science, despite very large resource inputs, is gravely hampered by secrecy, isolation, and bureaucratic rigidities. It is even more apparent that the imperatives of such centralized states as the Soviet Union and China choke literary and artistic expression, and this has also been true of continental empires of the past.

Yet studies of scientific creativity or the rise of modern science seldom take seriously into account the political background, even to the extent of noting that the Netherlands and England, the leading centers of science in the seventeenth and eighteenth centuries, were relatively laxly governed societies. The basic background of the open society is assumed, and there is a large and informative literature on the social relations of science, but not on the political prerequisites. Similarly, analyses of the causes of invention take the political background for granted. Cultural history likewise may take note of many factors in the progress of civilization, from natural resources to techniques and channels of distribution, without mention of the political universe. The fact that periods of war and strife have been times of major cultural and economic upsurge—in classic Greece, in preimperial China, and in medieval and Renaissance Italy as well as in the modern West—has been pointed out usually as paradoxical rather than as an expectable and logical relation. The historian of ideas is likely to express surprise that the chaotic nation-state system has been the backdrop for what he admires.

Some reasons for this neglect may be suggested. One is that division, except in harmless and controlled form within the constitutional state, is hardly a respectable political principle. In a world in which war between major powers would be madness, it is not easy to think of the often violent contentions of nations as healthy and productive. Unity promises order, harmony, peace, and purposeful guidance; division means disorder and war; and war, long hateful, has become a mental abomination. It is not easy to accept the view that a divided world is in many crucial respects better, from the point of view of generally accepted values, than a unified one. The negative effects of division—especially frequent wars but also barriers to trade, the disorder of different systems, and the weakness of disunion—are all too evident; the benefits are long-term, indirect, and less obvious. Toynbee, considering the eighteenth-century thesis that division was essential for creativity, rejected its value as outweighed by the unhappiness of wars—although it is not provable that life was happier even under the best of Roman emperors than in more hazardous and turbulent Greece. Unification gives strength and so is inherently desirable; political forces bless it. Belonging to nations that pride themselves on united order and power, we approve tranquility and peace; a brutally imposed unity is something "achieved." German historians assume that Bismarck conferred a blessing when he welded together the fragments of Germany into a mighty nation, although united Germany never recovered the cultural productivity of fragmented Germany. Some sociologists—Durkheim, for example—see no antithesis between authority and freedom (Giddens, 1972). The making of an awe-inspiring political unity looms as a glorious and virtuous triumph, whereas its decomposition is historically tragic. Overweening empires represent conquest and grandeur; they win battles, erect great buildings, and fill the historical record. They have left the biggest monuments, if not the most artistic, and the bulk of documents. Nor have they been diffident in extolling themselves, and we incline to accept their word. The collapse of the Roman Empire has been lamented as though it had been maker instead of stifler of classical civilization. The breakup of the huge Abbasid Islamic empire is called decay, although this political decline ushered in the cultural flowering that made Arabic civilization memorable (Lewis 1954; Hitti, 1967). The success of empires is their perdition.

Another reason for the neglect of the principles and consequences of international division is the gap between historical and political studies. Our age likes to stress the uniqueness of its problems, and modern political science is focused on contemporary problems and conflicts. It has also, in the search for incontestable facts, strongly favored quantitative data and scientifically structured research. But quantitative data about the past are scarce and often shallow, and important relations are refractory to quantification. Political science has, thus, made little use of the chief potential data bank relating to the organization and uses of political power—that is, the historical record. Modern political science, it must be admitted, is not historically attuned. It does not even much favor comparative studies; thus little effort has been made to generalize regarding such a lively topic as the causes and morphology of military rule, or the reasons for resemblances and differences of various Marxist-Leninist states.

Modern historians, on the other hand, are inevitably impressed with the unmanageable volume of evidence and the overwhelming complexity of events;

unlike those of the eighteenth century, such as Vico and Gibbon, they have generally resisted the seductions of political generalization. This leads to a further reason for neglect of the principles developed here: the difficulty, in the age of specialization, of painting such a broad picture as is required. A modern scholar will probably, perhaps wisely, confine his creative attention to a manageable corner of the universe of information—say, Tudor England. To venture far is to defy the demands of expertise and to risk superficiality or error. That risk certainly exists here, and it is to be expected that inaccuracies may creep in, either because the facts as reported by secondary sources (on which such a work must rely) have not been checked, or because mistakes have arisen in the process of compilation. It can only be hoped that whatever such errors there may be do not invalidate conclusions based on a large number of facts. The area being a large part of the total historical panorama, it has been possible to do little more than skim the measureless mass of data, endeavoring to make the selection realistic and indicative of reality. An encyclopedic study in the style of Toynbee, however, might well drown the subject rather than clarify it.

An additional reason that scholars have paid little attention to the characteristics and results of pluralistic state systems is possibly that this in effect singles out the Western experience and sets it apart from the rest of the world. It has not been alone in the record, of course; and our study makes use of non-Western systems of the past approximately so far as permitted by the scanty historical record, focusing on the West only because this region is both best known and is responsible for the civilization that made it possible for such a book to be written. But for many centuries the Western has been the only state system, and it has been enormously more successful than any other; indeed, it has virtually overcome all competing cultural traditions. With admirable repugnance for ethnocentricity, modern scholars are and must be reluctant to seem to find in it peculiar virtues. Yet it must be recognized that it has had special qualities or a special fortune, and the fact that Western civilization has been responsible for the gestation and fruition of modern science and industry requires accounting. Unless causes can be found in the accidents of geography and history, the leadership of the West in inventiveness, science, and political freedom seems all too miraculous. And it should be much more encouraging to the countries that lag in the application of technology to production if the success and power of the West are attributed not to special genius, the Greek background, the deep effects of Renaissance and Reformation, or a particular cultural or religious heritage, but to factors that no longer avail.

It may also be doubted whether one may realistically hope to illuminate the present by the past. There may be less continuity from the eighteenth to the late twentieth century than from the eighteenth century B.C. to the eighteenth A.D. We do not really know how far the essence of international society has been altered or how deeply the strains and opportunities of the electronic-nuclear age have touched human nature. The means by which states are organized and through which they act are quite transformed. International relations and politics, communications, and all the conditions of human affairs have so changed in recent generations that it is bold even to describe societies of two thousand years ago and today by the same word, "civilization."

Yet means have changed more than ends, and Aristotle's comments on politics have not entirely lost validity. Moral maxims of two thousand and more years ago are still quoted. Many writers have seen contours of our disruptions in older civilizations; comparisons of the decadence of modern America with that of classical Rome are frequent and sometimes persuasive. It may well be—as is here contended—that the conditions favoring or frustrating science have been essentially the same in eighteenth-century England, in Confucian China, or in Moslem Mesopotamia of the Middle Ages as in modern Europe (Feuer, 1963).

The central fact of society is human nature, and fundamental relations of human existence are much as they were in the days of Hammurabi.

Long before Christ, men produced and traded on a large scale, paid taxes and were conscripted into armies, settled domestic disputes by laws and lawsuits and international ones by diplomacy or fighting, believed in gods and doubted them. The character of the state, claiming ultimate power over the lives and property of its subjects and uniting them against other states, is fundamentally as it was in the dimmest antiquity. From the beginnings of city life, society has faced the basic and still unsolved problems of control and freedom of thought and actions, the organization of production and distribution, the relation of rulers to ruled (Moore, 1958), and of independent powers to each other. Despite their changing expression, international relations have remained remarkably constant in basic drives, as autonomous sovereignties have jostled for improvement or security. The first account of dealings between states—the arbitration of a boundary dispute between two city-states of Sumeria, Lagash and Umma, by the titular king of Kish—indicates that they were more civilized in outlook than many affairs of five thousand years later.

Extreme caution must be used in extrapolations from past to present. But if society is to be made understandable, it must be possible, with caution, to draw principles of relationships between social organization and motivation. It is the hope here to discern certain regularities of pluralism and the division of power, especially on the international arena, in the historical record. So far as valid, these may be deemed, with due regard for altered circumstances, to be permanent and applicable to the present, perhaps helpful for its understanding.

Pluralism

In the conventional wisdom of political affairs, there are antithetical kinds of societies, the open and the closed: the former represented by the democracies, hopefully including the United States; the latter by authoritarian and dictatorial countries, such as Nazi Germany or Communist states, especially the

Soviet Union and China. It is ordinarily accepted that the differences between the two extremes of the political spectrum are fundamental, including presence or absence of freedom of speech, civil rights, representative government, free movement of persons, and the like. Less emphasized is the contrast between the basically private economy (although subject to regulation), guided primarily by individual decisions, and the state-owned and -planned economy. Broadly, the open society is given to variety, division, disorder, perhaps anarchy; the closed society bespeaks compulsion, more uniformity and order, perhaps more discipline and purposefulness. This is equivalent, for most purposes, to saying that the open society is multicentered or pluralistic, while the closed is centralized, monolithic, or monistic.

Pluralism is not precisely to be defined. It means the coexistence of a number of competing and self-sustaining groups: economic, cultural, religious, political, or other. Pluralism to the political scientist is close to interest group politics, wherein numerous organizations demand as a right to be heard in the deciding of policy. In the pluralistic society, many persons have a share of authority by some title other than appointment, directly or indirectly, by a central power. Feudal barons, labor leaders, religious eminences, elected officials, corporate executives, and so on, have status in their own right and through independent institutions, not because of position relative to the ruler.

Pluralism is characterized by reciprocity of relations. It is close to complexity, with multiple causation and a large number of interactions and inputs to the political process (McFarland, 1969). Simplicity of lines of control and uniformity of directions are attained only by the fiat of a single center, such as in an army. The subdivisions of a pluralistic society can go in different, even conflicting directions and so disperse power and limit the authority of the rulership and of one another (Lijphart, 1968). Robert Dahl (1971) sees pluralism as "polyarchy," the multiplicity of rulers. Dahl, however, notes no relation to the international situation except (chap. 9) that foreign domination is unfavorable. The pluralistic society is also close to Almond and Verba's (1963) "civic culture," which implies a broadly based "participant culture" of shared decision making.

The groups that constitute the makings of pluralism run a full gamut in at least three dimensions: in size, in control of members, and in independence of higher forces or capability of making private values. They may include not only the economic interests that are conspicuous in their interaction with government in representative politics, but others as diverse as racial groups (so far as coherent), castes like those of India, and the components of a federal system. They may be clearcut or overlapping. It is essential, however, that they should not be excessively unequal; in the often-cited words of Thucydides (book, 89), "Right, as the world goes, is only in question between equals in power." Dominance means order and organization, but it may also imply pride and contempt on one side, awe and subservience on the other. Superiority and inferiority reduce autonomy; politically and socially they imply relative fixity and conservatism, as in a military hierarchy, or in a caste or racially dominated society. Relations among equals, with mutual respect, imply competition and a fluid order, with the detriments of contention balanced by advantages of independence.

The dichotomy of pluralism versus monism has extensive implications running through the entire social fabric. It is nearly equivalent to that of democracy versus dictatorship (or, in the language of earlier days, despotism). In theory, democratic government might be absolutist, à la Rousseau, without subgroups within the state. In practice, however, this does not occur. The masses may hail a magnified figure, such as Mussolini, Hitler, or Stalin; but the self-proclaimed leader of the people has hardly been so bold as to permit freedom of choice and expression. If humans are allowed to press their own desires, they will differ, stake out conflicting claims to the limited valuables available, and organize to forward different interests.

If there is no democracy without freedom, neither, in practice, is there much freedom without democracy. Freedom is practically definable as the latitude for formation, functioning, and expression of independent organizations. On the one hand, if there is freedom there will be many organizations to fulfill varying needs; on the other, if there are multiple independent organizations, there will necessarily be some freedom for individuals among the offsetting powers. Pluralism does not necessarily mean democracy, however. Aristocratic elites, as in seventeenth-century Venice or eighteenth-century Netherlands, may manage a constitutional and pluralistic order defending many private interests without spreading power beyond the favored circles. But at its most illiberal, pluralism implies moderation and restraint of authority and its fixation by law.

The open society also implies the competition of differing ideas and ways, hence the mutual stimulation of independent interacting groups. The greater number and variety of interactions make a fertile intellectual environment. Since there is no single source of truth, it is to be tested in practice; dissent and confrontation of opinions produce rationality. Combined with the drives of competition, this suggests that pluralism may be important, possibly indispensable in the long term, for material or technological progress—if this is not undone by confusion and internecine conflict.

Pluralism goes deep into the structure of society, and pluralism in one aspect reinforces that in another. For example, the pluralism of a private enterprise economy is of prime importance for political pluralism. Fractionated control of the economy is a basis for fractionated political power. Checking of power at the top of the political edifice promotes checking of power throughout; the parliamentary state ordinarily has considerable local self-government. In the United States the constitutional structure of the federal government and the autonomy within their spheres of the fifty states are reflected in the partial autonomy of towns, counties, school boards, water districts, and the like, as well as in the multiplicity of private economic and cultural entities. Pluralism, giving scope for individual self-assertion, practically denotes individualistic philosophy; and it is reflected in the entire mentality and cultural product of the society. In various ways, the pluralism-monism antithesis coincides with contrasts found by political scientists between modern and traditional societies—as in achievement versus ascriptive criteria, contractual versus familial relationships, rationality versus faith, and high versus low innovation (Palmer, 1973).

The basic antithesis of pluralism-monism corresponds to a whole series of parallel antitheses: democracy-autocracy, persuasion-coercion, freedom-order, equality-hierarchy, variety-uniformity, self-will-submission, individual-social, and division-unity. More abstractly, the dichotomy is closely akin to that of spontaneity-direction, uncertainty-security, inquiry-faith, truth-power, and fact-myth. Multiple centers imply different versions of truth; and an open society, though it may have many myths, can with difficulty impose a single compulsory interpretation of the universe. Dynamically, the pluralism-monism antithesis relates to that between struggle and conformity, since independent powers almost by definition oppose one another, and to that between change and stability, because change can be checked only by the noncompetitive order. Pluralism is dynamic, because power relations are uncertain. Monism is normally static, not only because the rulership becomes satisfied with the status quo, but because attempting change means discarding carefully built-up myths and forms of control and probably stirring up divisions within society.

In these and parallel respects, the pluralism-monism dichotomy corresponds to the two basic sides of human nature, the individual and the collective, the self-directed and the socially determined, that are always somewhat at odds in every person and in every social order. Individual welfare stands always partly, sometimes sharply, at odds with the well-being of society, and it is a task unsolved by the best government fully to reconcile the twain. An increase of freedom usually implies a decrease of social order.

Both aspects are obviously essential. The more totally controlled society requires some initiative and spontaneity, and heterogeneity must be embedded in homogeneity. Whatever a pluralistically inclined society may feel to be the virtues of pluralism, it suffers defects of weakness and purposelessness unless purposeful attitudes are somehow imposed by shared necessity. Division has to be set aside in emergencies, and emergencies are chronic in the lives of nations. There must be a balance of freedom and order; indeed, some overriding order is indispensable for the health of pluralism, just as social welfare, the health and prosperity of the community, is a precondition for the welfare of the component individuals. Without a legal order moderating if not adjudicating conflicts of interest, the groups that make up the free order would inevitably collide and presumably destroy one another. A central government guarantees the rights of municipalities and of private property, while limiting these rights and prohibiting banditry. In emergencies or where central direction is more necessary, as in the management of large-scale irrigation works, pluralism recedes. For this reason, too, in times of uncertainty, pluralistic societies may tend to forget the virtues of diversity and call for a "new unifying philosophy." Order and convention, even conventional understandings that must be considered in a sense irrational or mythical, are an indispensable foundation for the liberal pluralistic order.

Nonetheless, the balance commonly swings farther in the direction of control and centralization than would seem necessary for the effective functioning of society: that is, control, which is necessary for productivity, frequently, perhaps usually, goes so far as to hamper productive capacities. This has been observable for a wide range of strongly governed societies. In large part, this occurs because authority is exercised not merely to serve the needs of the community, but also to serve the inevitable personal interests and ambitions of the controllers. Because of this intrinsic bias in favor of rulership, it is not easy to find convincing examples of states breaking down or degenerating from overgrowth of pluralism, while countless nations have been ground down by overcontrol. Although the chief reproach to the open order has been weakness, it is probably uncommon that states have been seriously handicapped by excessive openness in confrontation with more strictly governed states. To the contrary, the suffocation of independent thinking and initiative has indubitably led huge empires to an extraordinary degree of decrepitude and incapacity.

For such reasons, it can hardly be doubted that one of the most important facts about any society is the degree and ways in which power is claimed and shared. In view of this, it is remarkable that very little scholarly attention has been devoted to the theoretical and historical analysis of pluralism. The chief cause of neglect is perhaps that pluralism is an abstract. Attention goes to the concrete issues, but "freedom" is much more a slogan than an object of research, a matter of ethics and philosophy, not of social science. Such discussion of pluralism as has appeared relates mostly to political questions of democratic states, economic pluralism, and pressure groups as political factors, leading to byways of power structure, elitism, and racial and social conflict. The perhaps excessively broad questions of the origins and results of pluralism have not seemed to demand attention.

Still less attention has been given to the highest level of pluralism, the division of sovereign states. Yet of the groups into which humans are divided, the state has preeminent significance. Mankind is a group-territorial species, and the sovereign political units form the primary framework of cultured existence. The state is the compulsory form of association; people have usually been subjects or citizens of the city-state or nation more than they have been adherents of a religious or cultural group; sovereign states have often determined the other affiliations. It was exceptional when in the early Middle Ages political allegiance was rather loose, perhaps divided between the local lord and the distant king or emperor and overshadowed by allegiance to the Church. The sovereign political unit has almost always been dominant. Nations like France, England, or China have largely fixed the national language. The success of religious movements, such as the Reformation, has usually required support of the state. The territorial unit stands out also because it is clearcut. One belongs to one state or to another, and there is no standing between. Mexico and the United States hardly intermingle as entities, however much Mexicans and Americans may come into contact. The state encompasses nearly all of ordinary existence, and its laws bind. A man spends his days earning the legal tender of his state, learns in its schools, serves in its army, pays its taxes, and may be punished by its justice. Practically all of his dealings are likely to be with fellow citizens. Political frontiers have become cultural and often linguistic or religious boundaries. While religious wars have usually been at least half nationalistic, national or state conflicts have been incomparably more numerous than any other. In the development of culture and institutions, the sovereign states have played a far larger role, at least a much more visible role, than any other organization. The nation is the political reality, in victory or defeat, and the heritage is passed on to children. Hence, so far as the states form a single political universe, their division must be considered the most important aspect of pluralism.

States and Empires

If pluralism is ordinarily viewed only within the state, not in the international community as a whole, this is presumably partly because the international framework, as remarked earlier, has been taken for granted in the Western experience. It is also attributable to the very importance of the state; assuming the competitive state as fundamental, one considers only the divisions internal to it. Pluralism implies the fractioning of a political order; hence it seems applicable within the state, not on the disorderly international stage. War and the dangers of war are the most salient forms of interaction of independent states and those that have most occupied scholars.

Yet the state system does form a larger political whole. Interest groups in a nation operate within a fixed system that limits their goals and means; the sovereign states of an international community operate within constraints that are less well defined but quite real. Just as private bodies need the blanketing authority of law to coexist without mutual destruction, likewise members of a state system must have a wide range of understandings in order to coexist and engage in extensive commerce and political relations. It is true that states sometimes destroy one another, but the long-term coexistence of independent states implies that this is exceptional. State systems, for all their conflict, have lasted roughly five hundred years, as did those of classic Greece and preimperial China, and the nation-states of Europe. Contending states exist within the framework of a single culture encompassing local variations, a civilization that forms a coherent whole. It follows that their pluralism is the basic pluralism of the civilization.

A state system, as treated here, is a pluralistic civilization. The degree to which a civilization is fractioned or pluralistic runs, of course, through a continuum, from the most totally integrated or totalitarian to the most divided. There have been innumerable gradations from the dominion of "all under Heaven," in the Chinese phrase, to a much divided patchwork of scores, even hundreds, of contentious states, as in classical Greece or Renaissance Europe. China, land of empire par excellence, has been essentially under a single rulership during most of the three thousand years for which its history is tolerably known. But at times, as following the Han dynasty, it has been split between two or three or briefly several independent polities, while before the Ch'in unification (221 B.C.) there was a large but gradually shrinking number of contending states. Similarly, the Near East was held by a succession of larger and smaller variously interacting empires for two millennia before the advent of Rome.

It is instructive, however, to leave aside intermediate situations and to contrast state systems with imperial centralizations, wherein a single power has eliminated all serious rivals and feels itself master of its world. Among the best examples of the latter are the empires of the Romans, the Chinese under the strong dynasties, and the Incas. Numerous others, such as the Achaemenid Persian empire, the Byzantine empire in its days of glory, the Turkish, and the Moghul empire of India, although not enjoying such fullness, have nonetheless been filled with the spirit of universal dominion. Such realms, although perhaps receiving the homage of small client states or annoyed by barbarians along the frontiers, have lived practically to themselves, with minimal international relations. For example, the limited contacts of Rome with the distant Parthians in Iran had little significance for ordinary life; men lived in a single, Roman universe.

A state system, on the other hand, may be defined as a group of closely interacting and therefore competing sovereignties for whom interrelations are comparable in importance to domestic affairs. This implies that the group is essentially self-contained and subject to no stronger power. For relative stability there must be a fair number of states, probably at least half a dozen, with no generally acknowledged leader, so that there is open competition and some latitude for secondary powers. Familiar examples are the city-state system of ancient Greece and the nation-state system of Europe from about the end of the fifteenth century to the world wars. There have been others in India and China roughly contemporary with the Greek system, and in Mesopotamia (Sumeria) in the third millennium B.C.

Of these opposite types, the universal empire is the more amenable to analysis, just as orthodoxy is easier to describe than heterodoxy. The empire is clearly defined and bounded, comprising the area under the control of the imperial government. State systems represent nothing so definite, no single entity but a quarrelsome family, an uncertain constellation with a number of more or less affiliated units around the periphery. The empire has a history; the state system has an indefinite number of histories. One can perhaps fairly well describe the Roman world of the time of Constantine; to do as well for the Greece of the time of Pericles or the Europe of the eighteenth century, one would have to investigate a dozen individual states.

State systems are also more difficult to treat because they represent disorder or freedom against the order of the empires. The imperial power imposes uniformity with greater insistence, as in the Chinese case, or with less, as in the case of Rome during the first centuries of rule. Within a state system, the sovereign units are free to differ. Athens stood poles apart from Sparta, not merely because each had its own life, but because each had different political and economic needs. Whereas in the universal empire autocratic power is nearly unqualified and pervades all public life, freedom in the state system is varyingly shaded by motifs of domination; no state system has avoided considerable oppression. Even in Greece, the least imperial of civilizations, the drive to empire entranced and nearly ruined both of the leading cities—Sparta on land and Athens on the sea. Over medieval Europe stood two universal powers, both claiming the heritage of the Roman Empire, the papacy, and the Holy Roman Empire; and Germany was infected with the imperial tradition of the latter until modern times. Spain in its sixteenth-century season of greatness and France in the seventeenth century regarded themselves as potential if not actual world hegemons and endeavored to act the part. England, Holland, Portugal, Sweden, and even Switzerland built what they could of empire and were correspondingly affected, although never able to isolate themselves from the contentions of the nations; the European state system has been a jumble of unifying-authoritarian drives countered by divisive-libertarian ones. Hence only in limited aspects does it seem possible to treat it as a whole.

Moreover, state systems differ from one another more than do the universal empires. Emphasis on power imposes a certain similarity on all of the universal continental (as distinguished from overseas) empires.* They all face the same problem of controlling and exploiting the vast realm; this is their overriding concern, sometimes almost their sole concern; and the ways in which they meet it bear some resemblance through all differences of geography, culture, and technology. A state system cannot be imposed but can only grow up as a result of favorable conditions; and the factors supporting the independence of contentious states are never entirely clear and are probably different in each case, whether primarily geographic (as was apparently the situation in ancient Greece) or political (as with the Italian city-states). Lacking any single unifying purpose, the state systems must be expected to be heterogeneous not only internally but as a class, just as free societies are more varied than authoritarian.

Yet the antithesis between state systems, representative of decentralization, and universal empires, representative of maximum centralization and unified

---

*It must be emphasized that the acquisition of colonies does not make a state into an empire in the sense used here. Britain did not remove itself from the contentions of nations by overseas hegemony but remained an integral part of the European system. Britain acquired an empire; Rome became one. The difference is also characterized by the fact that British expansion was based on technological superiority, Roman on military and organizational capacity and drive. Nationalism within the state system merges into imperialism, but only as it reached for universality does it cease to be state centered and expand into a broader ideal transcending local loyalty.

power, is striking. Nearly everything to be noted of the former stands in opposition to something observable of empires. The primary fact is that big empire means strong government, ordinarily a unified rulership, for the two reasons that strong rule, with no openings for opposition, is necessary to keep the overly large and probably diverse realm together, and that arbitrary rule is more difficult to check in the huge state. The larger and more cumbersome the realm, the more necessary it seems to be that authority come to a focus in a single will without restraints or divisions, and at the same time the easier to overawe or repress divergent movements by the weight of the empire and its apparatus. Hence the government of the empire is all executive with little or nothing of a separate legislative or judicial authority. The emperor personally may be inactive or practically a puppet, but no other authority can legitimately challenge him. All great universal or near universal empires—Chinese, Inca, Mongol, Turkish, Persian, and so on—have been utterly autocratic, with a monarch whose will was supreme law and whose glory was that of an earthly god. Whatever freedom such empires have permitted has been a byproduct of their incapacity or decay. The states of a system, on the contrary, may be republican and more or less democratic, or oligarchic, or more or less monarchic. They may be tyrannical; but the tyrants, as in classic Greece and Renaissance Italy, pretend to follow republican forms and to rule by popular consent. Law for the empire is the pronouncement of the ruler or perhaps divine commandment; for the pluralistic states, it has more the nature of the right of the community.

From this basic reality there follow many consequences. The empire is characterized by rule of men, the states of the system more or less by rule of law. (Differences of "Oriental" and "Western" political patterns are summarized in this fashion by Treadgold, 1973.) The strong imperial government raises a bureaucratic ruling elite, the principal desire of which is to maintain its own position. Success and social position derive not from ownership or any independent standing but from relation to the governing power. Any traditional aristocracy is reduced or absorbed into the state machine, while private business is subject to extortion or regimentation and commercial classes are scorned and usually able to prosper only by official connections. In the free states, on the other hand, officialdom is much less pervasive, merchant capital enjoys some freedom and security, and money-making is more a means to political power than vice versa. The class structures differ correspondingly; practically speaking, the more pluralistic the state system, the larger the role of middle or commercial classes. Somewhat less obviously, the hereditary principle is much weaker in the imperial society, which is likely to decree division of inheritances instead of primogeniture. Since the empire is more given to political power, it is more exploitative and taxation is limited mostly by graft and inefficiency. The politics of the empire are of little interest to ordinary people, except in the storm of revolution, which renews the state and is the climactic happening; for the small states, politics are of incessant concern, and the climactic event is war and victory over fellow states.

The monopolistic universal power, self-righteously seeking to convert force into legitimacy, endeavors to control the minds of its subjects by the suppression of undesirable or subversive opinion, by propaganda and the inculcation of respect for the rulers, and through official doctrine, usually supported by a religious orthodoxy and a controlled church. In the looser but more naturally coherent society of state systems, it is much more difficult to attempt a monopoly of information and regimentation of opinion; orthodoxy yields to heterodoxy, if not skepticism. The characteristic ideal of the empire is conformity and obedience; of the competitive state, valor. Achilles, the arch-hero of the Greeks, chose glory with early death over a long life without glory. It is typical that Homer's heroes are mortals, while the gods cut a poor figure. The empire promises peace and concord; the states bespeak contention and hopes of victory through struggle. The political theory of the empire seeks harmony in accordance with a superior scheme of things; that of the pluralistic society seeks reconciliation of conflicting interests.

In the unicentered order, the government dominates society; in the multicentered, the state is secondary to the social order. The people of the empire are mobilized to build grandiose monuments, palaces or pyramids, and public works, such as the Great Wall of China. The people of plural states are much freer to enrich themselves by trade or to experiment with art and science. For such reasons empires have been culturally sterile, conserving, perhaps spreading civilization while creating little new; and their art has tended to the formal, while that of the contending states tends to the naturalistic-representational. (The distinction drawn by Pitirim Sorokin, [1957a], between "ideational" and "sensate" cultures corresponds roughly to the empire-state dichotomy.) In the empire, the artist becomes a functionary (Kavolis, 1972); in the free state, he can be a fighter in a cause. Roman unity was as unfavorable to culture as Greek disunity had been favorable. Not only did the Roman Empire fail to build higher on the classical achievements that it annexed; it was unable to maintain the old standards. Science, literature, and even craftsmanship were imitative and progressively decayed for centuries.

The imperial society is more inclined to resignation and cynicism in the face of the unreachable authority above; ambition is less to produce something than to rise in status and in the favor of higher authority. Cleverness takes precedence over truth. Excess of control, discouragement of initiative, and the parasitism of the powerful press upon the economy until it is reduced to stagnation and impoverishment. The great political order also decays politically, as officialdom grows corrupt and self-willed. Lacking a sense of community, hating the regime rather than feeling themselves a part of it, those who cannot climb the official ladder tend to retreat to little areas of privacy and freedom that the state is unable to penetrate, such as family, clan, gang, or esoteric religions. Old empires, such as the Roman in its last century or the Chinese in the decadence of each great dynasty, sink into a dull morass of fatalism and apathy much like the culture of the depressed in modern society. Those oppressed by poverty and the people of the empire alike tend to be conformist, intolerant, and fatalist, because they feel they have little control over their lives (O. Lewis, 1966; Sarbin, 1970). State systems wear themselves out by warfare; empires choke themselves by unity.

To say that all the vices belong to the empires and all the virtues to freer states is unjustified. Youthful imperial powers have been able to act effectively, build grandly, and improve political and philosophical discipline. But the empire represents power as near absolute as human conditions permit, and Lord Acton earned fame by remarking in a letter to a friend in 1887, "Power tends to corrupt and absolute power corrupts absolutely."

If the themes of competitive states and universal empire, corresponding to the dichotomy of pluralism versus monism, are opposites, they are only ends of a spectrum and forever mingled, like the colors of reality. A competitive state may rapidly or slowly turn itself into an empire, and no date can be fixed when Rome the city-republic became the universal Roman state. The rulership is ever more elevated, the apparatus swells, and pretensions grow to absolutism. On the other hand, controls of the empire eventually tend to come unjointed; for this reason, although the imperial state may grow bigger and bigger relative to rivals, its expansion comes inevitably to an end. Julius Caesar could overrun Gaul with his semiprivate army; Hadrian, master of a far larger domain, struggled to hold the border; and his successors hired Germans to defend the Roman patrimony. At the same time, an empire such as the Roman, which must continually fight to defend itself, must be less complacent and stiff than a relatively secure empire, such as the Chinese. Contrariwise, any country, perhaps any large organization, may become, especially as it ages and takes on some sacrosanct authority, a little of an empire, in which men use power of position to enhance their own standing and impose themselves beyond the wishes of those whom they theoretically serve. Just as there are at least a few rebels in every empire, in every pluralistic society there are authoritarians, whose ideals derive from the state system.

State systems can also be interpreted as a phase of historical process. The nearest thing to cyclical movement in history may be the alternation between strong control and its breakdown. There are at various levels waves of firmer and troughs of laxer government, smaller and shorter or larger and longer. France, for example, went from sixteenth-century religious strife and disunity to the harsh centralization of Richelieu; then the anarchy of the Fronde was followed by the near despotism of Louis XIV; the relaxed Regency and easygoing reigns that came after were climaxed by the breakdown, briefly anarchic, of the Revolution, which led to the autocracy of Napoleon. Somewhat similarly, empires have swung irregularly from tight and effective rule to more or less breakdown of authority. The Roman Empire every few decades had episodes of civil conflict, and seemed in the middle of the second century to have broken apart; a man could grow to maturity and raise his children without knowing stable government. Chinese dynasties eventually descended to disorder, usually after a century or two, and rebellions of some kind were legion; in intervals between dynasties, chaos prevailed.

The times of firmer rule, when energies and resources are more organized and mobilized, are better for material construction and for the imposition of social order. Conceivably, they have been times of relative happiness, at least for the many persons who find burdensome the uncertainties and necessity for choice in looser societies. But in times of breakdown of authority, of decentralization and uncontrol, logjams are loosened and traditional ways and ideas are brought into question. Such times, despite relative disorder, are at least potentially more favorable for innovation and creation. For example, the "molten society" that came out of the collapse of Rome was much more receptive to innovation than the empire had been (L. White, 1963). If the period of uncontrol is brief, its effects may really appear afterward, when a new authority has cleared the air but not yet settled into despotism or crushed independence of spirit. It may be guessed that the time of the Fronde stimulated the French mind; but the results, if there were any, appeared under and glorified the reign of the Sun King. Similarly, the scientific achievements of the Stuart Restoration may be regarded as the flowering of seeds planted in the ferment of the Puritan Revolution. This is somewhat as empires may gather fruits of preceding independent states. Rome's Augustan Age of literature, a reflection of Hellenistic creativity, was better preserved and is better known than the original.

A few times in history there has been extensive and stable decentralization, enduring decontrol without anarchy. This could occur when a fairly extensive people with a common culture and tradition, perhaps coming out of the breakup of a large realm, has become organized in a large number of local powers, as in the aftermath of the fall of Rome. If no one can restore the empire and frictions and contests between neighbors do not lead to the early extinction of independence, their growing interactions bring technical and intellectual progress, prosperity, and more confidence, in an upward spiral. Probably the rising states expand beyond their original sphere, thereby building their prestige and strengthening their political system. They may develop commercial and republican institutions that tend to moderate aggressivity. The loose political system creates its vested interests, traditional modes of thought, and practices of interstate behavior that operate to stabilize it. Means of peaceful intercourse improve, even as intermittent warfare continues.

But whatever conditions permitted the growth of independence are transitory. Political systems that encourage the application of intelligence, like those that discourage it, wear themselves out. By raising the level of technology, the state systems undermine themselves. The system becomes unstable and somewhat artifical, as one may judge from the fact that, once overcome, it is likely to yield, not to units of two or three times as large, but to a giant empire. Thus, the midget classical city-states gave way not to small territorial states, like Rhodes or Pergamum, but to the Hellenistic powers the size of European nations, and then to the Roman Empire of continental proportions. The Sumerian city-states, the small Contending States of China, and the states of Buddhist India were replaced by empires thirty or a hundred times larger. Except in the unusual geography of the West, when the dam to unification broke, it gave way entirely.

The greatest and most successful empires have been built directly on the state system that they overcame, as the Chinese and the Roman. In a sense, the universal empire may fulfill the state system over which it climbs to glory, and the united military power may spread civilization more effectively than the independent states. Thanks to the achievements of the Greeks, first Macedonians and then Romans could appropriate a world far beyond the Greek sphere. Similarly, the unifiers of Sumeria, China, and Buddhist India gathered up a region enormously larger than the previous area of their culture. By the same token, the empires standing atop state systems are far more civilized than their imperial predecessors, as Han China was ahead of Chou China and the Roman empire was an improvement over the Assyrian, and as a new universal empire, if the world is to see one, will be immensely more sophisticated than any heretofore.

There are elements of tragedy in the submergence of the turbulent society by the vast organization, wherein values of freedom and creativity are replaced by those of obedience and faith. Possibly it has been necessary; as Hobbes had it, authority can be created only by a powerful will, and monarchy saves us from anarchy. It may have been impossible to consolidate a social order and build a new civilization at the same time. But the freer pluralistic state systems are more delicately balanced than empires, less readily established, and difficult to replace when overthrown. Were this not true, history would be less a record of frustration; indeed, nuclear weapons might have been invented many centuries ago.

The contemporary international system lingers in an uncertain and unstable balance between the fears that deter war and the stupidities and passions that might ignite it. The most likely outcome of a conflict between the major powers would be, of course, the collapse of the shakily based system and its replacement by a universal rulership dedicated first to securing the peace, and second to preserving its own power. To judge from the historical record, this would almost surely imply an end to intellectual progress and major innovation, although some technological progress might continue for a time. This exchange of invention for tranquility might be widely welcomed—a fact that of itself bespeaks the decay of the state system—but it is difficult to imagine how the problems of humanity are to be solved without maximum creative thinking. It might then be the hope of some future generation that the decadent world empire would, after a severe reduction of the earth's population, again give birth to a new division of power capable of unfolding the potentialities of intelligence.

The old Western, Europe-based system has been moribund since the first part of this century, half dying, half expanding to cover the world stage through the strength and vitality of the scientific capacities. The present international order is not a state system in the historical sense because war can no longer serve its classic functions. It remains to be seen whether the world system can function without the sharpness of dangerous competition and the plasticity of acceptable violence, or whether there may be found better ways to substitute for force, while squaring national sovereignty with world needs.

This macrohistorical view thus coincides with the widespread feeling that humanity is at or near a crisis point. Many or most of the legion of problems besetting this contemporary world may be associated with the decline of the old state system that has generated science and industrial civilization, or to the painful birth of a new and necessarily differently based world order.

Part One

The Pre-Western World

1 Conditions of State Systems

Historical Examples

Of the state systems that are available for consideration, the Western is the most complex and by far the best known. It has also been exceptionally long-lived, beginning to take shape about 900 A.D. and come to an end, or at least to a major transformation into a world system, a thousand years later. This long development divides into two halves, about as clearcut as historical periodization ever is. The first was marked by the power of the papacy, the Holy Roman Empire, and the independent or semi-independent towns or city-states, and lasted half a millennium. The subsequent European world of nation-states endured another half millennium. This state system has made our world-enveloping civilization; because of its unique importance and because of the overwhelming volume of information on it, consideration of it is deferred until the latter part of this book. In the first part, the pre-Western state systems are analyzed and principles are developed to apply to the Western state, our main subject of concern.

Of pre-Western state systems, that of the Greeks is at once by far the best documented and the most significant for us, because the Greek achievement, taken over by the Romans, became the basis for the Western construction. Greek civilization began emerging on the wreckage of Mycenaean culture from a troubled dark age not long after 1000 B.C. The new growth appeared first on the western fringe of Asia Minor, with its many finger-like peninsulas and offshore islands, where the invaders found a niche between the older areas of civilization and the sea. As seafarers and traders, the Greeks grew greatly in numbers (Andrewes, 1956), and planted colonies, trading posts, and farming settlements far around the Mediterranean; and colonization helped trade, just as trade promoted colonization (Burn, 1960). By the sixth century, when the expansion came nearly to a halt, there were Greeks in southern Italy and Sicily, in southern

France, on the Bosphorus, and on the coast of the Black Sea. But the heart of Greece remained the Aegean, with its multitude of islands, bays, and peninsulas.

The rise of the Greeks was facilitated by turmoil in the Near East; in their formative period they were left to themselves (Starr, 1961). Until the rise of Persia, they held virtually for their own this corner of the Mediterranean, wedded to the sea that made Greece and held it together. There they fashioned the characteristic Greek political form, the city-state or polis, superseding the clan or tribal organization that had become irrelevant for the new way of life. Extraordinarily divided by geography, they enjoyed and cherished their dividedness, the independence of as many as a thousand city-states (W. Hale, 1970), which felt themselves kindred but passionately treasured their particularistic freedom: to be a worthy human was to belong to a free city and to live by laws made by the citizens (J. Jones, 1956).

The sense of belonging was very strong; when a man from tiny Miletus was away from home, every Miletan was a friend and ally. Socrates preferred death to flight from the Athens that unjustly condemned him. The polis, with its own laws, money, calendar, historical traditions, duties, heroes, and special pride, even its own gods (Botsford, 1939), was like a club, an association of people with a common destiny, a team always contending with other teams, whose members, Plato said, should love it more than father and mother (V. Martin, 1940). Pindar eulogized the victors at the games less as individuals than as representatives of glorious poleis. The Greeks' chief ideal was freedom and they thought more of the freedom of the state than of that of the individual—but the two were intertwined.

It was difficult to appropriate much territory. The many colonies sent out did not subject native peoples, nor were they governed by the metropolis (Woodhead, 1962). Militaristic Sparta, in many ways un-Greek, had an area a quarter the size of Belgium or about 3,000 square miles; Athens had some 1,000, Argos about 500, and others ranged down to 30 or 40 (Ehrenberg, 1960). Athens was the giant in population, with 250,000 to 275,000 inhabitants in the fifth century, including slaves; it was exceptional in assimilating the neighboring communities of Attica. Corinth had about 90,000, several others 40,000 to 60,000, and the remainder trailed down to the size of villages (Finley, 1967). It was usually possible to see foreign land from the Acropolis. There was some amalgamation through the centuries. A strong center like Athens brought various neighbors together and for a time had a small maritime empire, Thebes formed a league, and Sparta forged a miniature land empire. But the free polis remained the ideal, and the Greek state was not a territory but a group of citizens; the leading city was called not "Athens" but "the Athenians." Such was the feeling for the rights of the city-state that even in the Spartan-dominated Peloponnesian league each little town had an equal vote (Larsen, 1955). Neither by the force of any Greeks nor by voluntary federation could the cities be brought to submerge themselves. As Plato stated in his *Laws*, (626) "Every state is by a law of nature engaged perpetually in an informal war with every other state."

Yet the Greeks felt themselves Greek together, treating mostly with other Greeks and looking down on those whose speech sounded like "bar-bar," the "barbarians." The Greek state system was never so self-contained as geographically larger state systems have been, having to deal with various important neighbors, such as Lydia, Persia, Macedon, and Egypt; but Greek cultural superiority and economic and military strength sufficed, from the repulse of the Persian invasion (479 B.C.) until the rise of Macedon under Philip (reigned 359–336 B.C.), to permit the Greeks to feel supreme in their world, however divided politically, while Greek culture spread around the Mediterranean.

Because of the vitality and expansiveness of Greek culture and because the Macedonian conquerors were its converts and admirers, the suppression of Greek independence by Philip and Alexander was the prelude to the Hellenization of the Near East. Then, perhaps largely because Alexander did not live long enough to solidify his empire, the Greek state system, instead of giving way forthwith to a universal empire, was in effect expanded into a broader phase, the Hellenistic world. In it, the leading roles were played by powers comparable in size to modern European nation-states, especially Ptolemaic Egypt, Seleucid Syria, and Macedonia. These formed a triangular balance of power, flanked by numerous secondary powers, such as Rhodes, Syracuse, Judea, Pergamum, and a host of city-states left over from classic times, more or less independent of the major powers. An interesting development of the century and a half between the ascendancy of Macedon and that of Rome was the growth of federal leagues uniting most of the Greeks in defense of their freedoms. The Hellenistic state system was more than any other similar to the modern situation; and the cosmopolitan Hellenistic culture, of the time when Roman power was first coming on the scene, was suggestive of the modern in its uncertain ferment and abundance.

Approximately contemporaneous with classic Greece, there was a poorly known constellation of independent states in northern India, with a population of 15 to 20 million (Davids, 1903). Traditionally the major states were sixteen, but there were numerous smaller ones. In the fourth century B.C., when many independent states had been annexed by the Maurya empire, the Greek ambassador Megasthenes listed 118 kingdoms (Russell, 1936). Of their interactions, next to nothing is known; it is typical of the Hindu mentality, with its preference for the general and formal over the particular and factual, that practically all that is recorded of this large and important state system is in the form of theory and laws setting forth how rulers ought to behave.

The outstanding source is the *Arthasastra,* dated about 300 B.C. and attributed to Kautilya, chief minister of the conqueror who imposed the Maurya empire (c. 325 to 184 B.C.). This work is somewhat similar in purpose and spirit to Machiavelli's *Prince*; offering instruction in the overcoming of competing powers, it advises all manner of trickery or treason. It is systematic and stylized, with discussion, for example, of "seven expedients" of diplomacy: conciliation, gifts, sowing of dissension, limited warfare, isolation or nonalignment, deception, and stratagem. In its acceptance of any means to power, it belongs to the death throes of the state system; on the other hand, it takes for granted the existence of numerous independent rulers.

The fertile centuries shortly before the Christian era also saw a well developed state system in China. In the second half of the second millennium B.C., the Shang dynasty, the earliest of historical China, had been a rather loose agglomeration of more or less independent city-states and political units of small or moderate size with only a fraction of the area of present-day north China. The Chou dynasty, which came to power in the twelfth century B.C., set up a semifeudal order, with large areas assigned to retainers and relatives. As the imperial authority weakened, feudatories became more independent. In 771 B.C., the Chou emperor, defeated by a barbarian incursion, took refuge in the eastern part of his realm; thereafter control of his nominal vassals diminished to vanishing, and thereupon began the time known (especially in its latter part) as of the Contending States.

After his removal to the east, the emperor was a source of legitimacy but not of power. His chief role was ritual, carrying on the necessary sacrifices and rites. This enabled the fiction of the empire to survive as something like the medieval papacy mixed with the Holy Roman Empire, but with less power than either (R. Walker, 1953). Theoretically subject to the emperor, there were close to two hundred states of varying sizes early in the period. Their numbers shrank as more and more were annexed as a result of the continual wrestling for advantages, until in the third century B.C. only seven remained. There were cities of over one hundred thousand population, with much movement of people and commerce among states (Dun, 1965) and well developed diplomatic and political relations. This state system has been found sufficiently characteristic to be used as an example for modern international relations theory (Holsti, 1967).

The state systems of Greece, India, and China laid the basis for the respective civilizations in their corners of the world. Much of the credit for the foundations on which they built goes to the earlier Sumerian state system. In the centuries before 3000 B.C., there had been consolidation of villages, with improving agriculture based on irrigation, in the valley later known as Mesopotamia (Hole, 1966). Subsequently, cities grew up; thirteen are known from literary sources and remains of others have been found. They were by no means small; Lagash in 2400 B.C. seems to have had 80,000 to 100,000 inhabitants, including the outlying settlements, and in all of Sumeria there may have been 750,000 (D'iakonov, 1959). The Sumerians assumed a supreme sovereignty over the whole land, but the cities were self-governing and imbued with local independence. Each city-state had its own supreme divinity, although all shared a common pantheon, in much the same manner as the Greeks (Hawkes, 1973). Local patriotism seems to have been strong, and independence must have been soundly based because it lasted for many centuries. But city-states came increasingly into conflict, and ambitious rulers tried to dominate as widely as possible, until Lugalzagezzi of Umma about 2300 B.C. was able to make himself supreme.

There have been numerous other constellations of small sovereignties, but they have mostly been too feeble to stand against larger powers. Such were the Phoenician city-states, subjected to Assyria and Persia, or various groups of medieval towns, which fell under the domination of territorial monarchs before they could play out their potential roles. In central and northern Italy, scores of independent Etruscan towns formed a cultural community, approximately 750 B.C. to 350 B.C. Never long or firmly allied, they produced much art and grew wealthy, briefly powerful in their sector of the Mediterranean, before the more aggressive Romans overthrew them one by one (Banti, 1973; Hamblin, 1975).

There may have been something like state systems elsewhere, as in pre-Inca Peru (discussed below, chap. 4) and pre-Aztec Central America. The geography of Southeast Asia, the most dissected region of the globe, would seem to be propitious. There never seems, however, to have been a reasonably stable system of smallish independent states, but usually middling to small empires with weak states around (Cady, 1964; Hall, 1964). There have been numerous well organized states in Africa but they have seldom had much contact with other well organized states (Murphy, 1972; Hallett, 1970).

Beyond these, how many state systems of antiquity and prehistory may have been erased one can only guess. There have also been feudatory authorities that never felt able to claim full independence, as in Japan and the Middle East at certain periods. But these outlined herein, along with the unique Western system, are the state systems of history.

Preconditions

Competitive sovereignties with the right to destroy one another require quite special conditions to arise and endure. The inevitable conflicts must be somehow restrained, the group must be free of intrusively strong neighbors, and there must be obstacles to the dominion of any member of the community.

To secure these difficult conditions, geography may be important, as in the dissection of Greece. It is much the most divided and sea-washed area within the sphere of any major civilization, with many small islands and peninsulas, and rugged terrain impeding movement overland. Independence became more feasible with the rise of commerce between Europe and Asia, for which Greece was admirably situated, the islands of the Aegean serving as multiple bridges for sailors who feared to get out of sight of land. The trading and farming settlements could build walled towns and so form separate nuclei.

The importance of geography for the Greeks appears in the relative instability of city-states where they were less sheltered. In southern Italy and Sicily, where climate and most conditions were similar to the Greek homeland, but the land was not so dissected and the towns were correspondingly less isolated, Greek culture underwent a change. Wars there, far more than in Greece, were of annihilation. Many cities had territories well over a thousand square miles

(Littman, 1974), and little empires were built up; tyranny and violence, which became outmoded in Greece, became the rule in the West. The western Greeks did not lose their capacities but turned them to different ends. They particularly advanced military techniques and siegecraft, neglected by the Ionians who hardly hoped to capture cities (Woodhead, 1962).

While divided by geography, the Greeks shared culture, language, religion, and traditions. The classic Greece of free cities was successor of the Mycenaean Greece of great kingdoms and powerful rulers, who were buried in grandiose tombs with regal wealth of gold and ornaments. As Mycenaean Greece declined, in sterility and impoverishment, into a dark age (1100-800 B.C.), cultural unity fell away and the world became more localized (Haywood, 1964). But much of the older tradition remained. Homer tells of a king of all the Greeks mobilizing his vassals for a raiding and revenge party; and many Greek legends, as of Oedipus and Theseus, came down from Mycenaean times. Most of the classic divinities, from Zeus to Dionysius, were venerated under the great kings (Chamoux, 1963). Basic ideas of Greek religion, such as the importance of ceremonial purity in the eyes of the gods, and fear lest the happiness and pride of mortals offend the "Happy Ones," seem to reflect a preclassic authoritarian outlook.

The framework of Greek life, intellectual as well as social, was religious. The symbols of the polis and its festivals were religious, as were the sacrificial banquets in which citizens delighted. Oaths, the breaking of which was a dangerous insult to the god sworn to, were used as a guarantee of loyalty and rectitude by soldiers, jurors, and officials; and the first pledge of the Athenian oath was to defend the sanctuaries of the city (Chamoux, 1963). Tragedy and comedy grew out of rituals, and the place of religious themes in Greek literature is familiar. Many contests, like athletic games, were held in a religious setting. The Olympic games, which dated back at least to 776 B.C., and other sporting festivals were typical of the old pan-Hellenic institutions. When heralds went around announcing forthcoming games, hostilities would cease and tens of thousands flocked from far and wide to compete, trade, and exchange ideas. Gods, shrines, oracles, and festivals were essential in keeping alive the feeling of Hellas as a nation; foreign Greeks but not barbarians were allowed to share the cults. Many cities could join in a common enterprise, such as the construction in the fifth century of the temple of Zeus at Olympia, a building quite as magnificent as the Parthenon (Robinson, 1959). Thus, the Greeks came to regard their conflicts somewhat as factional fights and to accept as normal that independent states should live in peace (J. Jones, 1957).

There were several all-Greek organizations, known as amphictyonies, which sought to forward the common interests, political as well as religious, of their members, or at least to reduce conflict among them. That of Delphi, including most of Greece, was most important, and the only one whose organization is known. Its council met twice yearly (Bury, 1958; Phillipson, 1911), with two representatives from each of the tribes, which antedated the polis. Sometimes it attempted to impose sanctions against offenders; it might decree exclusion from temples, a money fine, or, as when the Phocians refused to pay, a "sacred war"; but it mostly served as a meeting place.

The Greeks were quite conscious of belonging together in opposition to Italians, Persians, or Phoenicians whose way of life was rather similar but who had different languages and gods. There was no moral obligation to keep a promise to barbarians, and wars with Phoenicians were far more savage than those between Greeks. Herodotus stressed the underlying unity of the Greeks— of blood, beliefs, and manners. Aristides, in rejecting a Persian offer, said, "The Hellenic race being of one blood, speaking one language, having the same gods, temples, sacrifices and customs, it would be shameful of the Athenians to betray it" (Russell, 1936, p. 55). After the Peloponnesian wars, eminent orators, such as Lysias and Isocrates, eloquently promoted pan-Hellenism in opposition to Persia (Adcock and Mosley, 1975).

Other state systems seem to have enjoyed a similar community of speech, religion, and traditions, which mitigated their differences, facilitated understanding, and set them apart from the outside world. Their essence is fragmentation within a basic unity.

The independence of the Sumerian city-states was favored by geography in that irrigation centers were separated by stretches of wasteland in contrast to the natural unity of the Nile valley. But Sumerian culture covered a well defined area, over which it was remarkably uniform, details of the script being the same in the various cities (Saggs, 1962). Like the Greeks, the Sumerians sometimes set aside their quarrels to join in the common defense. Since they shared gods, the king of Kish could arbitrate the boundary dispute between Lagash and Umma in the name of a generally recognized deity, Enlil. There was a common shrine at Nippur to Enlil, whose recognition gave legitimacy to kings; and rulers of Kish, Ur, Uruk, and other cities at times held a vague hegemony over the whole (Hawkes and Wooley, 1963). But the cities seem to have formed only a loose league, owing some loyalty but not tribute; and at times rival royal centers existed simultaneously.

The rivalries of Indian states were subdued not only by common religious heritage but by the exceptional power of the priestly or Brahmin caste, cutting squarely across political lines. The Chinese Contending States, sharing language, literature, rituals, and culture, felt very strongly their common superiority to the barbarians to north, west, and south. The ritual suzerainty of the Chou emperor was important for the stability of the system of local independencies, because they were respected as vassals of the emperor within the accepted socioreligious order. Even when much of that order had disintegrated, wars were represented as punishment of rebels against the Son of Heaven (Duyvendak, 1963); and it was felt wrong to annex another state because princely houses were responsible for keeping up traditional rites. In an interstate conference of the seventh century B.C., the rulers agreed to respect the authority of the emperor, to cooperate against barbarian invasion, to join against usurpers, not to aggress against one another, and to let the leading state arbitrate disputes (Li, 1965).

International Practices

If a state system requires favorable circumstances to come into existence, it must also develop practices of coexistence in order to prosper. Legitimacy makes a stable international order, but a stable international order likewise gives legitimacy to its components, as these become accustomed to beneficial dealings with one another and develop customs or rules of interaction, international comity or what is generously called international law.

Among the Greeks, conflict was tempered by community, and the existence of the loser was usually not in question. Imperialism sought rather to gain subordinates than to engulf neighbors (V. Martin, 1940). Except in the grim Peloponnesian wars, there was some feeling that battle was a sport, a contest of champions, like the duels of the *Iliad*. Beginning for some some trivial offense, wars often ended after a battle and the erection of a trophy, made of wood, not bronze or stone, that hatred be not permanent (Glotz, 1929). Citizen armies, anxious to get back to their occupations or to gather the harvest, were loath to undertake sieges, which were seldom successful (Zimmern, 1931; Burn, 1960), unless the attackers had partisans within. It was sometimes agreed to decide the issue by a single battle (Adcock and Mosley, 1975).

Issues were usually local, such as contested borders or rights of access or transit. Ideology was a secondary consideration, as democratic states allied themselves with oligarchies when it suited them. Consequently, it was easy to pass from hostilities to friendship as former enemies found common interests. Before the Peloponnesian wars, according to Thucydides, sea power was often used to plunder and to colonize, "whereas by land, no conflict of any kind which brought increase of power occurred; what wars they had were mere border feuds" (book 1, chap. 15). Thucydides regarded the disastrous clash of Athens and Sparta as abnormal and tragic; and although atrocities were committed, they troubled the Athenian conscience. Aristophanes could raise a public antiwar protest; as he said, "Panhellenic forces rally—now if ever—for release/From the grilling grind of warfare and from military fuss," and "If any merchant, selling spears or shields, would fain have battles to improve his trade, May he be seized by thieves and eat raw barley" (*Peace*, 302-303, 447-49).

There were conscious efforts to regulate war, in the spirit of Plato, who urged that the victor should not loot and burn, but take only the year's crop, for the Hellenes were like a family, discordant but not at war, natural enemies of the barbarians and natural friends among themselves (*Republic*, 470 seq.). Since law was near to divine command, the common pantheon made it easy to develop conventional practices concerning such matters as access to shrines, the right of asylum, and the burial of the slain. Crops might properly be destroyed but wells should not be poisoned; captives should be given the opportunity of ransoming themselves; a defeated city ought not be razed (Cary and Haarhoff, 1940). There was a "truce of God" during major festivals, and roads to chief shrines were kept open in wartime. Heralds, whose primary functions were religious (Adcock and

Mosley, 1975), and usually ambassadors were protected even among enemy forces.

Peaceful settlement was sometimes sought through arbitration by outside parties, third states, or the Delphic oracle. This might be refused, as Sparta rejected Athenian offers at the beginning of the Peloponnesian wars. But the practice was useful, especially because in the multiplicity of independent states it was always possible to find a neutral. There is historical record of eighty-one arbitrations, mostly by a neutral city (Bozeman, 1960). Outside arbiters were also sometimes called to judge between internal factions (Glotz, 1929). There was some feeling that refusal of arbitration was improper and risked divine anger (Adcock and Mosley, 1975).

Diplomacy was elaborate and sophisticated, although it differed from that of modern times in concern with ceremonial questions of the common religion and the protection of shrines. There being no permanent envoys, negotiations were usually carried on by committees of respected citizens instructed, in the democratic cities, by the popular assembly. They would plead their case with the host assembly, which would then hear its own speakers and reach its decision. Inviolability of ambassadors was accepted, although they were sometimes abused as a taunt. There were also proxenoi, permanent officials somewhat like modern consuls. Citizens of their state of residence, they were originally recognized to represent aliens in court before these gained judicial standing (J. Jones, 1956). In time they came to look after the interests, political as well as commercial, of a foreign state. Nomination as proxenos was also an honor that cities bestowed on eminent men abroad. Carthage and other Phoenician towns had a similar institution (Phillipson, 1911).

The Greeks were loosely tied by many treaties sanctioned by oaths to the common deities, covering such matters as trade, intermarriage, the common athletic games, and political relations. (For examples, see Adcock and Mosley, 1975.) Early treaties were frequently mutual commitments to refrain from piracy, and there were many for abstention from reprisals, for the protection of merchants and their goods, and the orderly collection of debts. The right to trade was generally conceded, and foreigners by custom and treaty usually had a status in private law like that of citizens. They could present their pleas in a permanent court, either in person or through the proxenos. Although they were seldom permitted to become citizens and mixed marriages were usually forbidden, aliens were an important element in nearly all Greek cities.

Political treaties provided for widespread alliances from the seventh century, if not before (Burn, 1960). There were various leagues, such as those dominated by Thebes and Sparta, or the Pan-Ionian League, which united the cities of Asia Minor against Persia. Athens, having emerged as leader in the Persian wars, at one time managed to assert leadership over a substantial part of Greece; as many as 170 allied city-states, mostly of Aegean islands or Asia Minor and consequently apprehensive of Persia, paid tribute to it in the name of the common defense. The Athenian Confederacy had a council formed of a delegate from each member polis, but the union became something like an Athenian empire after the treasury was removed from Delos to Athens, efforts to withdraw were repressed, Athenians were settled on lands of allied states, and garrisons were stationed in them (Botsford, 1939).

Community of feeling was also strengthened by colonization. It provided an outlet for energies and surplus population and was also a token of Greek superiority. Sometimes the founding of a colony, like the building of an important temple, was a joint enterprise of several cities. In 443 B.C. Athens took the lead in a pan-Hellenic movement to replace the destroyed Sybaris in southern Italy. Some cities, as Megara and Miletus, seem to have made a business of organizing colonial parties, for they sent out far more colonists than their whole population (Haywood, 1964). Colonies formed no colonial empire; they went their own ways and freely allied themselves even with the enemy of the mother city.

With the passage of time, mutual acceptance came to rest less upon common origins and more upon acquired understandings and recognized advantages of peace, the ideal of the "Common Peace" guaranteeing individual sovereignty and freedom from oppression (Adcock and Mosley, 1975, p. 150). Trade steadily increased, and it was cosmopolitan in nature (Hasebroek, 1965) rather than identified with particular city-states. It caused some rivalries and conflicts, but the merchants almost always preferred peace. Particularly after the Peloponnesian wars, travel and interchanges of all kinds throve greatly, while loyalty to the obsolescent polis declined. More and more people lived as legal aliens in "foreign" cities, and common feeling and interstate comity tempered the anarchy of independence. Cities freely adopted laws of others, and celebrated men were invited to rule foreign cities (J. Jones, 1956; Haywood, 1964).

The felt unity of Greek culture was strong enough to serve as the basis of an expanded state system after Alexander conquered the East. Throughout the Hellenistic world, small Macedonian-Greek minorities ruled over native masses; joined by language, traditions, and a sense of superiority to the natives, they warred on occasion but had no desire to destroy one another. The elites could hardly afford unrestrained conflict, and patriotic enthusiasm was slight. The general use of mercenaries (soldiering had been a leading profession in Greece since the Peloponnesian wars) also tended to limit warfare. It was not necessary or perhaps even desirable to slaughter the opponent's forces; they could often be hired away or taken over when beaten, and an important part of warfare was to lure mercenary captains from their employers. Owing slight allegiance to any state, the hired warriors felt little hatred and had no interest in killing each other or civilians; consequently, there was much plundering but very few massacres or wholesale enslavements. Prisoners were commonly ransomed and rarely murdered; noncombatants and neutral cities were usually respected. When the code was broken, as when the inhabitants of Mantinea were enslaved after a century free from such practices, the Greeks felt general indignation (Cary, 1959).

Particularly within the Greek homeland but to some extent across the entire Hellenistic world, from Italy nearly to India, there was extensive migration and varied intercourse; and pacific relations became closer and more orderly. Trade greatly increased, encouraged by rulers with an eye to revenues. Customs revenues of Rhodes in 170 B.C. were five times those of Athens in 401 B.C. (Botsford, 1939). Thousands of itinerant merchants filled the highways; and many professionals, as physicians and artists, moved freely from one city or land to another (Rostovtzeff, 1941). Numerous Greeks served in Egypt, Syria, Pontus, and elsewhere without breaking ties to their native polis (Ferguson, 1911). There were pan-Hellenic guilds of artists and performers. In classic times, four great quadrennial games had brought people together from all parts of the Greek world; now scores of international games and festivals did so. Kings would send their entries to the sporting events, while they sent their sons to Athens for schooling.

Among the educated, local dialects were largely replaced by the "koine," or common speech derived from the Attic. Rights of citizenship were granted, by treaty or as an honor, to numerous persons of other cities, unilaterally or reciprocally between allies or among members of a league. Many thus became citizens of several cities at once. Even Athens relaxed, in practice if not in law, the bars to citizenship characteristic of the old polis, and it became fairly easy for metics to be enrolled (Glotz, 1929). Honorary citizenship was given to philosophers (Ferguson, 1911). The institution of proxeny, the naming of outstanding men abroad to represent the city, was much expanded; becoming largely honorary and more social than political, it was sometimes granted to whole classes (Tarn, 1936). Arbitration came to be frequent. As international relations became friendlier and as jury trial became less feasible in the climate of economic agitation, judges from outside were often called in to settle domestic disputes, to the benefit of uniform legal concepts.

International law became stronger; and Rhodesian sea law, which was to serve as the basis of European maritime law fifteen hundred years later, was accepted. Many agreements were made against the enslavement of citizens. States sometimes furnished gratuitous foreign aid to those afflicted by calamity. There was a friendly competition to assist the rebuilding of Thebes after 316 B.C. (destroyed by Alexander twenty years before) and of Rhodes when it was devastated by an earthquake about 225 B.C. (Cary, 1959), and Athens received gifts and loans in 229 B.C. to help pay off a Macedonian garrison (Day, 1942).

The intensity of peaceful intercourse could not have sufficed, however, to sustain respect for independent sovereignty; rather, it might have stimulated drives for unification. But when multiple sovereignties oppose one another within the framework of shared culture, their power relations acquire a limited stability commonly summarized under the concept of balance of power. The idea of counterpoising of power flows unavoidably from the proposition that a plurality of states is to be independent together, none possessing the capability of imposing itself upon the others. Generally speaking, the larger the number of fairly equal independent units and the more widely power within the system is divided, the less improvement one actor can expect by getting the better of another and the more potential resistance will be evoked by efforts toward hegemony. The basis of the balance of power is the fear of loss of independence, hence most members are hostile toward any one that threatens to gain the ascendancy.

This principle prevailed in the Greek state system. Thucydides reported of a Persian leader, "True to his policy to hold the balance evenly between the two contending powers, he sent for the Lacedaemonians" (book 8, chap. 57). Much later, Demosthenes said, "I exhort you . . . not to abandon the Megalopolitans nor indeed any of the weaker states to the stronger" (*For the Megalopolitans,* 32). It was much more observed in practice than explicitly stated. Any city that felt threatened would request help of all possible friends, thus requiring them to decide whether to assist or to risk the rise of a dangerous power. Alliances were easily made and unmade and relations were flexible; on one occasion it was possible for Athens to be on friendly terms with both Argos and Sparta, although these were bitter enemies. The best way to attract allies was to claim to stand for the liberty of all, because of the general esteem for the freedom of the polis. Athens, having led the fight against Persia, was the first to seek general supremacy; but it was distrusted not only because of imperialistic policies but because of its sheer size (V. Martin, 1940). Sparta, imperialistic within its own sphere, stood up as champion of Greek freedom and entered the war that broke Athenian ambitions forever. But Sparta could not rule Greece, and Thebes also failed in a bid for hegemony. In the fourth century, as Greece became defensive, the idea of hegemony passed to larger territorial states. But the balance of power continued to figure prominently in the sophisticated diplomacy of Hellenistic times, as each major state was fearful of the others but unable to conquer its rivals. Because of jealousies within the system, however, they were unable ever to join to repel the Romans.

The international practices of the Indian state system are less well known than the Greek but were perhaps at least as sophisticated. There was a code of diplomatic practice, as given by the *Institutes of Manu,* and ambassadors—sent on occasional missions, not permanent embassies—were held inviolable even in war. According to the *Mahabharata,* "The king who slays an envoy sinks into hell with all his ministers" (Russell, 1936, p. 42). There were confederations; and mutual acceptance was sufficient, in the unity of language and traditions, so that many men traveled freely from state to state, and apparently no disabilities were placed upon aliens (Altekar, 1958). Perhaps largely because of the solidarity of the Brahmin caste, which furnished diplomats and ministers (Modelski, 1964), independence seems to have been remarkably respected. Even as the state of Magadha, maker of the Maurya empire, was rising to supremacy, the victor was adjured to exact only tribute, not to annex the conquered domain. This advice seems to have been usually followed; a deposed king might be replaced by another member of his family, and at worst the beaten state was left as a feudatory with a large degree of autonomy (Altekar, 1958).

The highly developed character of the ancient Indian state system is testified by the rules of war transmitted by less humanitarian following ages. As shown by the *Institutes of Manu*, probaby dating from the Gupta period (4th century A.D.) but based on much earlier sources, the code prohibited various unchivalrous actions: there should be no use of poisoned or barbed arrows; a warrior in armor should not strike one without, or an enemy disabled or down, naked or sleeping, or one whose weapon was broken; warriors should fight only warriors, refrain from surprise, and cease fighting if a Brahmin entered to make peace; prisoners should be treated humanely and might be freed after a term of servitude (Dikshitar, 1948). The initiation of hostilities required elaborate ceremonies and the sanction of the priestly class (Modelski, 1964). A just war, in which the preliminaries were settled by agreement and no artifices or spells were employed, was distinguished from an unjust war, with craft and deceit; the unjust war was permissible only as a desperate defense. The Greek Megasthenes in early Hellenistic times reported that wars did not interfere with agriculture.

In the China of contending states, balance-of-power politics preserved independence for several centuries as interstate maneuverings revolved around the attempt by leading powers to overthrow the equilibrium to their own advantage and by others, mostly the many little principalities, to maintain it for their safety. The balance of power was studied and practiced, each leader suspecting the ambition of others; and many twists and turns were made to adjust relations. Leagues of states, north and south, offset each other. One league, formed in 681 B.C. and led by occasional assemblies of heads of state, lasted more than two hundred years. Other states sought safety by an independent role. For example, Ch'in (which later was to overcome all) long worked as an active balancer between the chief traditional groups. The state of Cheng, lying between two leagues, shifted its allegiance fourteen times in the period 678 B.C. to 549 B.C., usually at the cost of an attack by the spurned ally. It was advantageous to head a coalition, for the leader received tribute and was surrounded by friendly states; however, to maintain this standing it was necessary to keep up expensive forces. Small states sometimes found it expedient to pay tribute (usually slight) to more than one of the greater states (R. Walker, 1953).

Sharing traditions, language, and laws, the states had considerable respect for one another, while they looked down on outsiders as barbarians. Customs of civilized intercourse had existed from ancient times; but international law and practices derived also from practical contacts, expanding commercial relations, and countless embassies and treaties between the states. In a period of two centuries after 700 B.C. the number of missions sent out by the state of Lu multiplied tenfold. In the earlier times diplomacy was an affair of the sovereigns, who would visit frequently among themselves or meet as required by custom; but with the passing of time, diplomatic affairs became the business of ministers. Envoys were protected if they observed protocol (R. Walker, 1953); commonly professionals, they were important participants in the events of the day. There were missions for commercial reasons; but most diplomacy was related to power and security. There were many interstate meetings. In the seventh century Duke Huan of Ch'i invited the states to conferences twenty-six times (Dun, 1965). The states of the Chou League averaged two meetings every three years; these conventions brought many hundreds together, including merchants who went along for business. Leagues adjudicated disputes within their ranks, the leading state serving as arbiter; if the dispute was between the league leader and a lesser power, a third might offer to settle it. Sometimes arbitration gave the verdict to the weaker state.

War was a usual means of settlement, but in the earlier centuries it was restrained. Campaigns were not pressed to a decision, as the conqueror withdrew to enjoy the spoils and honor of victory; chivalry required moderation (Fitzgerald, 1950). A state should not be invaded in the year within which the ruler died, nor when he faced an insurrection, although the temptation to profit from confusion led this rule to be violated. It was also common canon that a ruler should not conquer another of the same surname (R. Walker, 1953). War was made more to exhibit princely valor than to annihilate the opponent (Latourette, 1934). In 598 B.C. the king of Ch'u invaded Ch'en to punish the assassin of its prince and took the opportunity to annex it; being rebuked for his greed, it is said, he restored it to the rightful heir. Although scores of tiny states disappeared, no major state was erased until 479 B.C., when Ch'en was taken by Ch'u. Captives were to be sent to the imperial court for trial. Noncombatants should be spared. In the graceful formalism, condolences were sent to an opponent wounded in battle (Britton, 1935). No assault should be launched without sounding drums and giving the enemy time to prepare the defense. In 638 B.C. the duke of Sung, at war with Ch'u, refused to attack while the enemy was unready. Defeated, he defended his conduct on grounds of teachings of the sages: "The true soldier never strikes a wounded foe and always lets the gray-headed go free; and in ancient times it was forbidden to assail an enemy who was not in a state to resist. I have come near losing my kingdom, but I would scorn to order an attack without first sounding the drums" (W. Martin, 1883).

To establish peace or alliance, treaties were made; more than 140 have been recorded in the principal chronicle. Multilateral or bilateral, they were drawn up with much formality and sworn with a sacred oath. At the signing, an animal was sacrificed, and the document and the lips of the principals were smeared with its blood; the treaty was then deposited in a sacred place. Bond was sometimes given for performance. Often sons of rulers were deposited as hostages; in 571 Cheng yielded a city to Chou as pledge. Treaties of friendship were commonly broken as soon as the interests of the parties diverged, but leaders hesitated to disregard engagements because they needed a good reputation to gain and keep allies.

There was an ambitious attempt to solve the problem of international conflict. In 546 B.C. a middle-ranking power, Sung, proposed a conference to establish disarmament and form a league of peace. Other states agreed or pretended to, lest their peoples be disaffected; and leaders of fourteen states assembled. They haggled long in an atmosphere of distrust; some delegates wore armor to the discussions of permanent peace. When they finally reached an agreement abolishing war and providing for envoys of each alliance to meet for further discussions, there arose a dispute as to who should sign first, and two states refused to subscribe. After the conference, the Sung king, rewarding his minister for the diplomatic success, remarked that arms served to prevent haughtiness of inferiors and consequent discord. Another ruler sliced the antiwar covenant to pieces with his sword (R. Walker, 1953).

International relations among the Sumerian city-states were not dissimilar. Fortified with massive walls, the cities warred frequently for profit and prestige; however, as depicted in the epic poems, conflict consisted of as much taunting and threatening as fighting; submission of one city to another was a blow to pride, more acknowledgment of inferiority than subjection (Kramer, 1963). By one story, when Erech (Uruk) demanded submission of Aratta, the latter city promised to yield in return for a quantity of grain, and Erech countered by asking for lapis lazuli. In another tale, the ruler of Aratta capitulated when the magician he sent against Erech was caught and killed (Kramer, 1952, 1963).

One chapter of the drawn-out contest of the city-states is known in detail from the chronicles of Lagash. About 2600 B.C. this city came into conflict with neighboring Umma, over a border strip and the waters of the Tigris-Euphrates canal on which both were located. Mesilim, king of Kish, to whom both parties looked up, delivered an oracular arbitration and set up engraved steles to mark the border. To consecrate the agreement, the two sides swore to more than half a dozen of the most puissant common deities. But Umma subsequently seized part of the disputed area. Not long afterward Lagash, under a new king, regained strength, defeated Umma, and set aside a fallow strip on the Umma side as a buffer zone. However, Umma was allowed to rent some Lagash lands in the south, and citizens of the two cities were granted mutual freedom of travel and residence. In following decades they came to blows again, fortune and alliances favoring first one and then the other, until generations later the dispute came to a new arbitration and a settlement about the same as that made long before (Gadd, 1962; Kramer, 1956). Although rulers of Lagash engaged in apparently glorious campaigns to the extremes of Mesopotamia, their preserved historical records are filled with this quarrel of neighbors eighteen miles apart, typical of conflicts within a state system.

Downfall

The state system, moved by sovereign self-seeking yet dependent on world order, lives in a state of doubtfully stable equilibrium, resting on a delicate balance of forces; and when special circumstances favoring it wear out, or are destroyed by the actions of the peoples concerned, its life comes to an end. The Greek and Chinese systems lasted about five hundred years; the undatable Indian system may have endured about as long. The earliest known, the Sumerian, held out some centuries longer, perhaps because the pace of change in those times of nascent civilization was slower. Only by enlargement does it seem possible to extend the term much. The two phases of the Western development each lasted about five hundred years, counting the nation-state system as defunct from the time of the world wars. Yet, oddly, state systems have far outlasted great empires, which have hardly gone beyond two hundred fifty years without a major breakdown—oddly because the principal purpose of the ruling apparatus is to preserve the empire, whereas in the state system each rulership looks to its own interests without concern for the system as a whole.

Universal empires are destroyed by their failures, the political, intellectual, and economic degradation that inevitably overtakes them (Wesson, 1967). State systems are undone by their success, by what is commonly called progress; success raises problems the system cannot handle. The component small states are made obsolete by technological change. Alteration of the character of warfare makes them less defensible or probably militarily inviable, a development even more obvious for the modern nation-state than for the Greek polis. Increased de facto internationalism or cosmopolitanism, cultural and economic, deprives them of their moral basis; men of the late fourth or third century B.C. no longer found it fitting and proper to die for Thebes or Argos. The world that has grown together invites unification.

With the fading of local loyalties, the balance of power becomes less effective. Probably many lesser powers lose independence, making less flexible and more precarious the balancing of the remaining leaders, whose fears of extinction rise along with their hopes of supremacy. Moreover, the expansion of the sphere of culture strengthens larger states on the rim of what was the civilized world. Each state system of which we have knowledge has been subdued by a marginal power: the Greek by Macedon, the Hellenistic by Rome, the Indian by Magadha, the Chinese by Ch'in, the Italian by France and Spain; the European has been overtaken by Russia and America. The victorious states are beneficiaries of others' cultural achievements, and turn them to military strength with fewer inhibitions than states of the old heartland of civilization.

Something of this seems to have occurred among the Sumerians. The city-states, originally insulated by tracts of marsh and desert, grew, tamed the waste around them, and came into harsher conflict with their neighbors. It probably also became more feasible to administer larger areas. Warfare became more serious, and armies turned professional; jousts for glory or minor concessions were replaced by fierce contests ending in the sack of cities. Independence became fragile as one city or another came to the fore after the middle of the third millennium, until Lugalzagezzi of Umma, defeating all opponents, made himself high priest in all the cities. Still, he was more leader than master except around his capital. It remained for a semioutsider, the Semitic Sargon of Akkad, to smash all the little states, pull down their walls, and form (about 237 B.C.) the first very big empire of history, reaching far beyond the original Sumerian homeland to Iran, Asia Minor, and the Mediterranean.

The fall of the Chinese state system was similar in outline. The moderating overlordship of the Chou emperor ceased to command even formal loyalty. Respect for established values and the social order dissolved in a ferment of philosophical schools, of which Confucianism represented a conservative current. More and more small states were absorbed by powerful neighbors. Of the nearly two hundred states of the eighth century, thirteen were left by 481 B.C., seven by 403 B.C. The chivalrous understandings broke down, armies grew larger, wars longer, and years of peace fewer (Hsu, 1965).

Those in the center had by then been outstripped by the marginal states with better opportunities of aggrandizement into less civilized territories. Of these, the northwestern state of Ch'in, which had been once held barbaric by the Chinese of the inner circle, was able to push forward because it largely set aside the old feudal relations and had a very militarized regime. In 318 B.C. it defeated a contrary coalition, and its progress toward supreme empire was irresistible. By 221 B.C. its king, having vanquished his last rival, proclaimed himself Shih Huang-ti or First Emperor.

Only in the Greek case is the demise of the state system documented in detail. Decline is ordinarily taken to have begun with the disastrous Peloponnesian wars. The bitter duel between coalitions led by Athens and Sparta involved nearly all Greece and lasted, with breaks, fifty-four years to 404 B.C. The Greek spirit was never quite the same again. However, the state system revived; after the brief Spartan overlordship and some minor wars, the leading cities again became nearly equal, purposes of conquest receded, and international intercourse developed. The wealthy gained by peaceful commerce and disliked the rising costs of increasingly professional warfare, and the masses accepted civic festivals in lieu of military adventures (Pickard-Cambridge, 1914). More and more people lived in alien cities, as travel increased and attachment to the native polis became less important (Glotz, 1929). Philosophers thought less of the freedom of the polis, more of world order. Diplomacy became more flexible, international usages regained respect, warfare was again limited in scope and moderated by understanding, and the great ideal was general peace with independence (Ehrenberg, 1960).

The character of warfare, however, was changing, to the detriment of the city-states. Mercenaries became prominent; professionals abounded while the citizens took ever less interest in fighting. Business and commercial affairs demanded fuller attention as life grew more complicated; campaigns were farther afield and longer (Pickard-Cambridge, 1914). In the developing international community wars came to seem more futile, hence were more demoralizing than invigorating of patriotic sentiment. The new weapons and tactics called for extensive training. The citizen girding on his armor was no longer a match for the experts, and he was less prepared for the rigors of campaign as more urbanized life brought a decline in physical condition. Generals had to be professional to control the professional soldiers and to master the new tactics. So far as citizen contingents were still mustered, they probably found themselves under the leadership of a hired foreigner. Improved naval tactics also required crews trained to precise maneuvers (Kitto, 1951).

But where professional forces held sway, the polis was hopelessly disadvantaged compared to the larger states able to support standing forces always ready for action. Demosthenes, as the fourth century was waning, pleaded in vain for a citizens' army instead of the mercenaries so unsuited for the polis, much as Machiavelli eighteen hundred years later remonstrated against Florentine reliance on hired soldiery. In later days when Athens was resigned to impotence, the training of Athenian recruits changed from rigorous physical exercises to an education in arts and sciences.

Greece was at the same time losing its relative advantages. The land of Hellas is poor; it could prosper outstandingly only by the skills and morale of its people. But other nations learned Greek crafts; in the Balkans, Italy, Asia Minor, and elsewhere native articles largely replaced those of Athens in the second half of the fourth century; cities of the Bosphorus could sell wine and pottery to the Black Sea coast more easily than the Greeks to the south (Mossé, 1962). When larger kingdoms learned to build ships as well as the Greeks, the latter lost power on the seas; as vessels moved farther and more boldly, the islands and ports of the Aegean, so useful when sailors feared to lose sight of land, were no longer of advantage; and channels of trade shifted. Meanwhile, Greek morale decayed with the decline of the polis and its loss of a special role in the world that had outgrown it.

It only remained for states on the fringes to become strong and aggressive enough to overthrow the enfeebled city-states. This was obviously occurring late in the fourth century. In Thessaly, or northern Greece, a strong ruler, Jason, moved toward a monarchic state. In the west, Dionysius gained control of Greek-colonized Sicily, southern Italy, and lands around the Adriatic by skillful use of a professional army. Ending the independence of a host of cities, making citizenship dependent not on participation in the polis but on service to the ruler, he built a small Greek empire (Haywood, 1964). The day of the polis was fading as Isocrates looked to these men, and to Philip of Macedon, to unite the city-states in a crusade against the Persian empire (Pickard-Cambridge, 1914).

Philip used Theban military techniques to make his half-barbarian but ethnically Greek kingdom into an instrument of conquest. With a standing army such as no Greek city-state could afford, he played on the internal divisions of the Greeks and gradually expanded his control, until he ended resistance in 338 B.C. by crushing the combined forces of Athens and Thebes at Chaeronea. However, he left the cities autonomous while forbidding intercity warfare, setting up a league to keep the peace, and requiring contingents to assist in his proposed attack on Persia. On the Macedonian-Greek basis, Alexander conquered the Near East.

After Alexander's death (323 B.C.) his realm broke up into fairly natural divisions under leading generals and their descendants, who gradually settled down to a fairly stable balance of power. It was particularly conducive to stability that Egypt, much of the time the strongest state, sought not hegemony but security. It was, however, a fragile state system. There was little patriotism anywhere. For Asiatic or African masses, the rulership of the Macedonian-Greek elite was only a burden to be passively endured.

In Greece itself, the state came to be regarded less as a joint endeavor and more as a source of benefits, as it increasingly undertook the maintenance of the citizens. The Athenian Theoric Fund, which administered free entertainment and doles, gained greatly in importance; the president of its board became a leading magistrate (Mossé, 1962). The collection of taxes was becoming difficult. The assembly declined, as attendance fell off badly despite the modest payment given; and its lawmaking faculties were increasingly delegated to a special court, the nomothetai (Glotz, 1929). The judicial functions of the assembly were abused, and its checks on administration became a crippling instrument of partisanship (Burn, 1960). Magistracies went largely to semiprofessional or professional politicians, rhetoricians, and demagogues, who raised party passions for their own sake and were increasingly tempted by foreign gold (Glotz, 1929). Generals were professional soldiers instead of leaders of the assembly. Professionalism replaced the amateur spirit; the athletics and music that had been the sport of citizens became in the third century the livelihood of professionals (Ferguson, 1911). The purely private concerns of the New Comedy contrasted with the political commentary of the Old. There were growing private wealth, luxury, and ostentation, finer private houses, at least for the rich, and fewer civic buildings (Botsford, 1939). There was a resurgence of private associations, religious, fraternal, and protective.

One result was the increase of inequality and social tensions. Concentration of landholding was accompanied by agrarian crises. There must have been agitation for the cancellation of debts and the sharing of lands in fourth century Athens, since jurors had to swear not to support these proposals (Glotz, 1929). The aristocrats developed a violent hatred for democracy and became disposed to look to Rome for support.

Softened and divided, Hellenistic society could not stand against the Romans. They took the Illyrian coast in 229 B.C., and shortly after the decisive victory over Carthage at Zama (202 B.C.) they went to war against Macedon in the name of freedom for Greece, where they assumed a right of intervention. In 168 B.C., Macedon was eliminated as a power; interfering here and conquering there, the Romans made the Hellenistic world their own, until the last state, Pergamum, fell to them by testament of the heirless king in 133 B.C.

But the social and moral decay of the Greeks should not be exaggerated. In 195 B.C. Sparta successfully held off the Roman conquerors of Macedonia. In 191 B.C. the Aetolians, whose help had been vital to Rome in the second Macedonian war (200-197 B.C.), refused to surrender to a Roman army and defended their fortifications so ably that the Romans, contrary to their habit, made peace on terms (Boak, 1943). A half century later, after Roman power had long been dominant, the Corinthian democrats refused to bow to the dictates of the Senate and rejected (stoned, it is said) the Roman embassy. Much of central Greece joined the cause, which was at once national and social, for the oligarchies were pro-Roman. The popular forces showed great military capacity, battling for two years until the inevitable end in 146 B.C. (Cary, 1959). Rome then wiped out Corinth as it wiped out Carthage in the same year. The decay of the state system was less inanition than a shift of power relations. The Greek ideal was vigorous long beyond its day, and the relative vitality and respect for law and republican institutions of the Roman Empire may be deemed a tribute to Greek freedom.

2   The Open Society

Republicanism

Power in the universal empire is concentrated and simple; in the state systems it is divided and structured. That power within the international community is stably partitioned and restricted does not imply that it must necessarily be so within each unit. But the state system creates the possibility, although not the necessity, of constitutional, republican, or democratic government. Tyrannies and monarchies in state systems have sometimes, as in the Italian Renaissance or eighteenth-century Europe, been arbitrary and absolutist. But within the sphere of universal empires there have been no republics and few hints of republican or constitutional practices, although the Roman Empire exceptionally retained forms of the republic that had led it to greatness. More broadly, the division of power in the world involves internal limitation of power and a looser kind of society, which has more place for private undertakings of all kinds, private ownership, commerce, and individualism.

The reverse relationship is less clear and apparent; but it can hardly be doubted that republicanism, social pluralism, and the role of commercial interests contribute to the stability of state systems. Republics are not designed for the exaction of tribute from subject nations; it may be assumed that they have been ordinarily less exploitative than absolutist or tyrannical governments and so less avid to take over new lands and peoples. Having to conciliate various opinions, they are less prone to launch adventures; war is expensive and usually poor business. Autocratic rulers are desirous of increasing the number of their subjects, if only that more obey them. Where responsibility is divided, men are less fixed on glory. As Montesquieu observed, "The spirit of monarchy is war and enlargement of dominion: peace and moderation are the spirit of a republic" (*Spirit of the Laws*, book 9, chap. 2). When they conquer, republics are less inclined to confiscate and annex; and the looser state makes a looser empire, like that of Athens or Britain. The obvious example of a successfully aggressive (and noncommercial) republic was that of Rome; but the Roman aristocracy differed from the kingships around more in firmness of determination than in bellicosity. Commercial and republican Carthage put together a makeshift empire, in contravention of republican principles; but it could never compel its subjects to fight for it.

Republics often have more patriotism to resist alien domination, and their armies are apt to fight better; small Greek communities stood up against the flood of Roman power while great kingdoms collapsed. It is harder to overcome and hold in subjection men accustomed to self-rule and less rewarding to attempt it; as Machiavelli noted, free cities must be destroyed or they will be lost (*The Prince*, chap. 5). As a rule, the more equalitarian the society, the more resistant to outside domination. The despotic, hierarchic Inca empire caved in like a house of cards when the ruler was captured by the Spanish; the disunited Mayas and contentious tribal Araucarians of Chile fought bitterly for decades against the conquistadores. If the free were not usually better soldiers than the strongly ruled, there would have been little freedom.

It also ameliorates conflict that commercial interests are strengthened in the loose system. Economic questions can often be settled, unlike political, to the benefit of both sides; calculations of business interest are amenable to compromise and suffer from recourse to violence. Wars mean uncertainty, which is contrary to commercial calculation, and usually they are harmful to trade. As a Florentine statesman of the fourteenth century said, "Let us have peace, and obtain it on behalf of the merchants, that they may transact their business throughout the world and recover their debts" (Brucker, 1962, p. 338). Trade encourages specialization and interdependence of nations, and the needs of merchants for security and mutually respected rights have been basic for the development of international law and customs (Jessup and Deak, 1935). There have been many commercial wars, but they are ordinarily kept within bounds; if they are fought to extermination, it is because political motives have gained ascendancy. They would be even less destructive if the middle classes were better aware how their prosperity and power rest upon the continued freedom of states.

Sumerian Experience

At the beginning of the historical record, the politics of the Sumerian state system made a marked contrast with the absolutism of united pharaonic Egypt. While the Egyptian pharaoh was owner of all land, the Sumerian ruler had only a share of the temple estate; if he wished more, he bought it. In Lagash, temple land was not over a fifth of the total (Kramer, 1963); there was also private (family) ownership of land, and deeds of sale are known from about 2700 B.C. Although some private land was rented or share-cropped, there is no evidence of large estates; even the lower classes had gardens and cattle.

All members of the community were equal in principle, there being no leisure class or native serfs. Some prisoners were kept as slaves and worked for the temples, and indebtedness might lead to servitude; but not many slaves were owned privately, and slaves had considerable legal rights (Kramer, 1969). Slavery became important for the economy only much later under imperial influence (Saggs, 1962). The status of women, as reflected in family law, was much better than in subsequent millennia in the Near East (Hawkes, 1973). The pursuit of wealth was a prominent idea, with no reprobation for the rich (Kramer, 1963). Private merchants handled most foreign trade, which was extensive since the cities required many imports, such as building stone, timber, and metals; they consequently accumulated wealth (increased by loaning at interest) and enjoyed considerable freedom and high status. Organized in guilds, merchants were, as seldom in ancient times, able to deal with the highest authorities on a basis of near equality (Wittfogel, 1957); and merchant interests seem to have been major objects of foreign policy. Rivalry was encouraged in principle. The Sumerians, like the Greeks, were fond of law and litigation (Kramer, 1963). A favorite literary form was the disputation, a dialogue in which each party argued his own superiority. There have been unearthed disputes between summer and winter, bird and fish, cattle and grain, tree and reed, farmer and shepherd, and so on (Kramer, 1960). It was apparently even acceptable to defy celestial powers. The epic hero, Gilgamesh, tore the haunch from the Bull of Heaven and threw it at the city goddess with the taunt, "Could I but get thee, like unto him would I do unto thee" (Adams, 1966, p. 151).

In this milieu, rulership seems to have been much less than absolute. Myths portrayed the gods meeting under the presidency of their senior members, discussing long and freely to reach a consensus. The king of the gods, chosen by his peers, presided over the council and led in battle but was no autocrat (D'iakonov, 1959). Probably early Sumerian government was much like this, with a council of elders and an assembly of citizens, possibly including women (Saggs, 1962), who chose temporary cult officials and military leaders; early texts mention assembly and chief ("tenant farmer" of the god) but not king. The chief or ensi was one of the near equal citizen landholders (Kramer, 1963), with more priestly than military functions. There is no evidence of a royal palace before about 2600 B.C.; the ruler-priest had quarters in the temple (Mallowan, 1961). All free men carried earth for canal construction, the magistrates in the lead (D'iakonov, 1959).

Early inscriptions tell of the works of leaders, canals and temples built, not their victories on the battlefield. But as cities grew and crowded against each other and conflicts became chronic, leadership became more or less hereditary kingship. However, the powers of the lugal or "great man" were limited; he was long theoretically elected and was the representative of the community before the god, not vice versa (D'iakonov, 1959). The assembly and council had such functions as selection and possible removal of the ruler, settling disputes, and advising, especially on the making of war; the ruler could not commit his subjects without their consent. About 3000 B.C., it is reported, when the king of Kish demanded the submission of Erech, its ruler called his council and the assembly of arms-bearing men. The council recommended submission, but the assembly supported the king's desire to resist (Kramer, 1956). In Shuruppak in the twenty-seventh to the twenty-sixth centuries, when Sumer was already old, chronology was not by reigns but by turns of magistrates, chosen by lot perhaps from a governing council composed of representatives of sectors of the city or temple communities. Ashur in the north had a similar institution (D'iakonov, 1959). Even after the Akkadian conquest, the ruler was reportedly sometimes elected, and kings claimed to rule not by right but as elected by the local god from among many thousands (Gadd, 1962). City councils still had important administrative and judicial functions under imperial rulers. Possibly they were elected; in any case, the Sumerians knew the principle of election.

The maturity of this society was well shown by a coup in Lagash, not the most important but the best documented of the cities. About 2400 B.C., a ruler, Lugalanda, was deposed; but he was allowed to continue to live there peacefully. The victor, Urukagina, proclaimed great reforms: temple revenues apparently usurped by previous rulers were restored; taxes were reduced and tax collectors curbed; many fees, as for funerals, divorce, and the shearing of sheep, were reduced or ended; the right of the poor to refuse to sell their house or ass to the rich was upheld; it was implied that no one should be deprived of property without legal process. The social significance of these measures is much disputed (D'iakonov, 1959; Saggs, 1962; Gadd, 1962). But they must have been important, since they have been recovered in four versions. Mentioning "freedom" for the first time in history, they may, like Magna Carta, have restricted the power of the sovereign.

Chinese Monarchy

In China, even more than in the Near East, the prevalent tradition has been imperial monarchy; and the record of the competitive states has been transmitted by a series of despotic empires. It is evident, however, in the Chinese as in the Sumerian case, that the state system was basically of the pluralistic genus. There was not much slavery, while the commercial class was important; some even speak of "merchant capitalism" of the period (Fan, 1958, pp. 222-23). Most trade was in the hands of private merchants, who passed without great hindrance from state to state. Transportable wealth greatly increased by the sixth century B.C. (R. Walker, 1953), including rhinoceros skins from the south and dogs from Siberia. There must have been a high degree of specialization; tens of thousands of molds have been excavated from a single bronze factory (Hsu,

1965). All capitals of states were commercial centers. The ruler of one state abolished tariffs to stimulate business; another made an agreement with the merchants not to injure their interests, in return for which they promised not to move elsewhere. In the sixth century B.C., Lu had a special department to protect trade. War between Chin and Chou was said to have been restrained by fear of hurting trade. Some magnates acquired wealth comparable to that of kings. In Chou, the central state, it was reported, "No one wanted to be an official, all wanted to be craftsmen or traders" (Fan, 1958, pp. 221-22).

Some political power inevitably fell to the rich merchants. As early as the seventh century, merchant organizations were strong enough to negotiate with princes. By an old story, a merchant and the prince of one state made a compact to respect mutual rights (Granet, 1952). Excluded from the aristocracy in the early part of the period, the merchants made their way increasingly to the top as society developed. Titles were sold after 500 B.C.; the new rich to a considerable extent replaced the old aristocracy in administration, to the subsequent indignation of Chinese historians. Over half of persons mentioned in the chronicles of the later centuries were of obscure origin (Hsu, 1965). Various merchants became ministers; one of them rose to the acme of power, becoming for some years the real ruler of Ch'in when that state was already the strongest of all.

The extensive histories related a few instances in which the exigencies of international conflict put power, even if briefly, in the hands of the people or a council of some sort. In 582 B.C., while the ruler of Cheng was prisoner elsewhere, the people besieged the small state of Hsü to show that they could carry on without him (Fan, 1958; R. Walker, 1953); how the people were organized and led is not related. The king of Chou was defeated in 505 and he was thereupon deposed by a council that proceeded to overcome the enemy; this council seems to have been composed of elected community elders (Perelomov, 1962).

There is evidence that in the eighth and seventh centuries authority had largely passed to oligarchies of leading families, and the prince was often only nominally in charge. After the ruler of Chin had tried to reduce the power of the aristocrats (514 B.C.), they turned him out and split the land into three new states. It is related that the people of Chin, somehow organized, once refused to accept as sovereign the son of a consort from the unfriendly state of Ch'in but picked another even at the risk of war (R. Walker, 1953). At least one ruler won his throne by generosity to the people (Hsu, 1965). Reportedly, some rulers staged public debates on policies, and on occasion the people might be called upon to decide the removal of a capital or the enthronement of a king. There was some local self-government; at least a few states had responsible and respected city councilors or elders with independent status (Liang, 1930). There was a theory that the king should make nominations and promotions in council and with the agreement of leading nobles, that punishments of death or banishment should be proclaimed in the public square and approved by the people, that authority required equally the sanction of the superior and the consent of subjects (Granet, 1930). It was felt that the ruler was responsible to the people, who could depose him if he was unworthy. This idea continued attenuated into imperial times, but then it meant little more than that rebellion was legitimate if successful.

As states grew larger and the rewards of power increased, there were tendencies toward bureaucratic absolutism, wherein officials were entirely at the service of the ruler (Hsu, 1965). But there was a contrary tendency of thought exemplified by the democratic sentiment of Mencius: "The people are the most important element in the nation . . . and the sovereign is least important of all." There was no divine right, and not everyone stood in awe of kings. In the fourth century B.C., Chuang Tzu urged that there be no rank of birth but only of age and merits.

The accounts that have been preserved assume that the Chinese never knew other government than monarchy. But the celebrated burning of the books under the First Emperor was merely the worst of many intellectual purges. Historiography was the more sensitive as it was made the support of the imperial ideology, and the Chinese were and are very prone to draw often subtle moral-political lessons from the past. The accounts we have of times before 221 B.C. were drawn up or at least edited under governments often as power oriented as modern totalitarianisms. After a few centuries of absolutism, it doubtless became very difficult for scholars, especially of an isolated realm like China, to understand anything like republicanism even if it had not been antipathetic. The literati studied primarily to enter the imperial civil service, shared the interests of the ruling powers, and could only draw a picture suitable to the imperial-bureaucratic order, in which monarchical authority was taken for granted. Modern less-than-universal empires, such as Stalinist Russia, have well demonstrated the potentialities of rewriting history.

It is consequently fair to suspect that the political life of China's great period was more pregnant and varied than appears from the endless chronicles of kings and dukes and their ministers. Sometimes, it is told, the people acted independently of their sovereign or against him. For such action there must have been suitable political institutions, but of these next to nothing is related; indeed, the detailed recital of events tells virtually nothing of political institutions of any kind. Hence, while the record could not be entirely falsified, it is fair to assume that the reality was richer than what filtered through many centuries of the world's most refined and sophisticated absolutism.

Republican India

In Buddhist times the larger part of Aryan India may have been covered by aristocratic republics, although the largest and strongest powers were apparently always monarchies (Masani, 1938). Republics were very stable; some were possibly in existence in Vedic times, about 1000 B.C., yet a few even survived the Maurya empire, which ended the state system (Altekar, 1958).

The Vedic songs portrayed kingship with an advisory council and assembly of warriors, as in Homeric Greece. It seems that in some places this gave rise to simple monarchy, as occurred in Macedonia; elsewhere, especially among the smaller states of the more advanced regions, the assembly was able to reduce or entirely displace the king. By Buddhist times, in some lands, "the whole community was consecrated to rulership," (Sarkar, 1918, pp. 581-606), and there were numerous city-states run by merchant guilds (Nehru, 1946). When Alexander was pushing into the western edge of India, he met several fairly large republics and many small ones, some aristocratic and some more democratic with elected generals; he is supposed to have transferred to a king fifteen republics with five thousand cities (Mookerji, 1952).

The Indian republics were by no means weak, although deprecated by later tradition. Buddha favored them, saying that so long as they met in council and harkened to the words of their elders they should prosper. They are credited with popular leaders, just and efficient administration, and full treasuries (Mahajan, 1970). Despite factionalism, they were known for patriotism and valor; in the *Mahabharata* they are called "invincible": "Neither power nor cleverness can overthrow them; they can be overthrown only through division and subsidy" (Sarkar, 1918, p. 589). The *Arthasastra* gave such advice for dealing, or double-dealing, with republics; they were to be conquered only from within. Fighting, according to Arrian, to uphold "the liberty which for so many ages they had preserved inviolate," they are said to have mobilized their whole manpower and offered stiffer resistance to Alexander than the monarchies (Altekar, 1958, pp. 133-36). It is a token of their prestige that, as the story goes, the patricians of a republic considered a neighboring king insufficiently dignified to marry one of their daughters.

The republics were evidently for the most part aristocratic, at least in the later times for which there is most information, government being by the ruling clans of the Kshatriya (warrior) caste. The ruling body was the assembly, perhaps including all the aristocracy, as many as some thousands of members. This might be divided into parties that sat as groups, as in a modern parliament. The assembly elected executive and military leaders; like the Greek assembly, it might receive ambassadors and decide questions of peace and war. In Buddhist times the Sakyia Republic carried out its business in a public assembly, in which old and young alike participated; the president of the assembly was head of the state (Altekar, 1958; Sarkar, 1918). The "Raja" of republics held office temporarily and might be a simple citizen. Of one clan republic it was written: "Amongst them, the rule of having respect for the high, the middle ones, the oldest, the elders, is not observed; everyone considers himself to be the Raja; no one becomes the follower of another" (Prasad, 1928, p. 159). Some of the republics were relatively extensive, perhaps the largest of ancient times until the rise of republican Rome.

Other states were monarchical; but the kings were long somewhat limited in power, restricted by an aristocratic council after the assembly had disappeared (Sarkar, 1918). The largest kingdom was decentralized, with a good deal of local autonomy (Courtillier, 1945). Another in the time of Alexander had dual kings in Spartan style with a council of elders. At one time kings were elected, and traces of this practice lingered into imperial times. The law was regarded as sacred and not lightly to be changed by the will of the monarch; it is recorded that one had to abdicate because he violated the law. The king ought to follow the opinion of his council, which should be strong enough to control him; if it could not, the people should. Some writers advised the people to emigrate en masse if he were evil; this drastic remedy, possible only if states are small and loosely ruled, is said to have brought some rulers to their senses (Altekar, 1958). Kings were also judged by their ability to attract immigrants (Modelski, 1964). Shookra, early in our era, spoke like Mencius of kings as servants of the people, held them liable for violation of the law, and treated them with little reverence: "Does not even a dog look like a king when it has ascended a royal chariot?" (Sarkar, 1918, p. 584).

It is part of the same picture that the economy was fairly free. Before the Maurya conquest, there were no state monopolies or royal ownership of mines, which became the rule under the empire; land was freely bought, sold, and rented; there was no evidence of regulation of prices, later a common practice (Bandyopadhyaya, 1941). Slaves were not numerous and had considerable rights. Peasants owned their land (Courtillier, 1945). Commerce was esteemed; the *Mahabharata* commented that the exchequer might fail if trade were excessively taxed, and warned that tradesmen from abroad should not be burdened; rather, merchants and craftsmen should be subsidized for the prosperity of the land. An early king boasted, "Merchants coming from many a realm prosper here, and I look to their welfare and protection" (Bose, 1945, pp. 319-21). Import duties were 5 percent, higher than the Greek but moderate by common standards. The laws protected commerce: lenders were supported, defaulters were imprisoned or enslaved, and the debtor's heirs were bound by his debts; business contracts were held sacred and were enforced by the state. Merchants, the chief support of Buddhism in its early years, were probably richer than landowners. It was no disgrace for a prince to turn trader; kings leaned on wealthy capitalists for support and advice. The presidents of industrial and banking organizations were often advisors of the king and members of the royal council (Bandyopadhyaya, 1941; Davids, 1903). The merchant community was served by a system of commercial education, covering correspondence, accounting, and money (Das, 1925). Preimperial India of many competing states thus seems to have had a bourgeois, pluralistic society.

Greek Pluralism

COMMERCIAL SOCIETY

In the open society of the innumerable city-states of classic Greece, trade was sufficiently free and secure that it became the lifeblood of many of them, especially after the invention of coined money made wealth easily transferable. To what extent major poleis were dedicated to commerce in the way the Renaissance Venice was is debated by historians. (A contrary view, for example, is given by Hasebroek, 1965, and Starr, 1961.) It may well be that the largest single fraction were farmers. Commerce and industry were certainly vital, however. The towns were not administrative centers nor could they fatten on taxation of agriculture; they could exist and prosper only by production and exchange. Ships were so many that one town, Phocaea, loaded the whole population on board and sailed to Corsica to escape the Persians. According to Xenophon, the majority of the rather important city of Megara lived by making vests, a degree of specialization indicating dependence on a broad market. Athens brought large supplies of grain from the Black Sea region in exchange for olive oil and wine; the ability of the city to withdraw within its walls during the Peloponnesian wars and supply itself entirely by sea shows how commercial it had become.

Since each city had its own coinage and only a few, as the Athenian, were widely negotiable, there was much business for money exchangers. Holding deposits, loaning money on real estate or on shipping ventures, they in effect became bankers and came to possess such liquid wealth as to become indispensable to state finances. Business was private; the Greeks, unlike ancient empires, had practically no state monopolies of trade or production (Botsford, 1939). Tariffs were only 1 or 2 percent (Haywood, 1964; Botsford, 1939). Taxation was farmed out to individuals or joint stock companies, and the silver mines vital for Athens were exploited by lease. Marketplaces and shops were provided for traders. Athens had special legal forms for recovery of loans; and expeditious courts, which had to give judgment within thirty days, were set up for civil actions, primarily to protect and encourage the employment of capital (Calhoun, 1926). Traders were even protected by law from derogatory comments and ensuing losses (Hasebroek, 1965). The right of contract was recognized from the earliest codification of law (Botsford, 1939). Ownership of property was an essential freedom; each year the archon in Athens formally proclaimed, "What each possesses, he shall remain possessor and absolute master thereof" (Glotz, 1926, p. 158).

In the freedom to make money, there was inequality between rich and poor. At the beginning of the fourth century B.C., when daily wages of a building worker were a drachma (Zimmern, 1931), and the average wealth per citizen was perhaps 3,000 drachmas, there were fortunes equal to at least 500,000 drachmas. But large land ownership was reduced from early times, and Attica in the fifth century was a land of small holders (Flacelière, 1959). In the face of equalitarian sentiments, there was a little display of wealth (Robinson, 1959). The wealthy and well born, according to the *Old Oligarch*, came out badly in satire (Alexander, 1963). The inequality of commercial fortunes was mitigated by mobility. An ex-slave, Pasion, rose by industry and acumen to become one of the richest men of Athens; many of the leading bankers of that city began as slaves or foreigners and won prestige and citizenship along with opulence.

Despite the presence of slaves and the hauteur of such writers as Plato, productive labor was usually respectable. A smith, Hephaestus, was one of the major gods to have fair Aphrodite as wife. Odysseus sowed and reaped along with his men. One of the earliest writers, Hesiod, said that man should enrich himself not by war and conquest but by his honest labors, the fruits of which no prince had the right to rob. In Athens, work was fairly well regarded at least up to the time of Pericles (Mossé, 1962), who invited men of finance and industry as well as artists and writers to make Athens their home. Athenians recorded their manual occupations on their tombs, and craftsmen of statues were remembered along with the sculptor-designers. Laws penalized idle citizens and required fathers to teach their sons a trade (Glotz, 1926). Athenian aristocrats came to look down on physical labor and trade, but when Demosthenes orated in his own defense, he thought it politic to emphasize his business background, and other fourth-century orators showed high respect for traders and manufacturers (Calhoun, 1926).

Except in Sparta, where citizens were far outnumbered by the semienslaved helots, slaves were not so numerous as to make their control a major concern. Unlike those of Rome, Greek slaves never rose in class revolt until late in Hellenistic times when Greece had become part of the Roman system. A seventh-century tyrant of Corinth forbad the purchase of slaves (Haywood, 1964), a measure that would have been impossible had they been essential to the economy. At Athens, most labor was probably free during classical times, and there were no complaints that free men suffered from slave competition (Rostovtzeff, 1941). Farmers were usually citizens, often with slave helpers; although numerous slaves were employed in shops, industry, and mines, perhaps half of them were domestic servants. Slaves could hardly have been more than a third of the total population of 250,000 to 275,000 at its height (Agard, 1942; Botsford, 1939), and perhaps, only a sixth. A reasonable estimate for Periclean times is 150,000 citizens, 35,000 metics, or resident aliens, and 80,000 slaves (Robinson, 1950). Slaves do not seem to have been essential to the economy (Littman, 1974). Less wealthy and militarily less potent towns probably had relatively few slaves (Haywood, 1964).

Slaves in Athens, aside from some who worked in the mines and industrial enterprises, were rather persons in bondage than chattels. They had certain legal rights, even against state officials, and their owners could not kill them with impunity (Glotz, 1926). Some lived and worked independently, paying a tribute to their owners, or managed a farm or shop, the profits of which were to be given to the owner. A few held responsible positions in business. Slaves owned by the state were practically wage laborers; some were clerks in government offices or policemen. According to Demosthenes, Athenian slaves had more freedom of speech than citizens of less tolerant states (Agard, 1942). In the building of the Erechtheum in Athens, as in constructions at Eleusis in the fourth century B.C., citizens, aliens, and slaves worked together for the same pay, and slaves were foremen over free workers (Zimmern, 1931).

Antiphon in the fifth century said, "We are all and in all respects of the same birth," and quoted from a contemporary comedy, "Though a man be a slave, my master, he is nonetheless a human being as thou art; he is made of the same flesh. No one is a slave by nature; it is destiny which enslaves men's bodies" (Glotz, 1929, pp. 259-60). The *Old Oligarch* said in effect that needs of commerce required that slaves be treated with dignity, deploring that "a slave will not step aside to let you pass him in the street," and that "the Athenians are not better clothed than slaves or aliens, nor in personal appearance is there any superiority" (Kagan, 1965, p. 101). A successful drama, Euripides' *Trojan Women*, showed deep sympathy for enemy captives going into slavery. In several crises it was moved, usually unsuccessfully, to free able-bodied slaves (A. Jones, 1957).

Between citizens and slaves stood metics, or resident aliens, a class less than half as numerous as that of citizens. Not permitted to own land, not distracted by political occupations and benefits, although subject to service in the fleet and army, they concentrated in and apparently dominated manufacturing and commerce in Athens, whereas many citizens were small farmers (Littman, 1974). Despite the fact that many of them were non-Greek—Lydians, Syrians, and the like—they seem to have been justly treated; commercial laws were the same for slaves, metics, and citizens (Glover, 1926; Mossé, 1962).

GREEK DEMOCRACY

The democratic order that the Greeks evolved was marred by slavery. Equality was for male adult citizens only, and citizenship was held the more exclusively as it was much cherished. But with this limitation, the Greeks were extraordinarily inventive of political institutions giving a voice to ordinary people, permitting citizens, as Aristotle required, to rule and be ruled in turn.

The political form of the polis grew up with the city-state. As the Greeks were emerging into history, the Greek king stood only a step above his nobles and had to listen to the assembled warriors. Agamemnon is presented by Homer as sovereign, directly or through vassals, of much of Greece; but when he called first a council of princes and then a general meeting of the troops to debate an assault on Troy, he had difficulty in dissuading them from sailing home. Achilles berated his nominal superior, "You winesack with a dog's eyes, a deer's heart"; and a commoner, Thersites, railed against them both, that Agamemnon grabbed all the loot and Achilles was a slacker (*Iliad*, book 2). Servility was unworthy. "Yea, for I shall be called coward and man of naught, if I yield to thee in every matter howsoever thou bid" (*Illiad*, book 1). The lesser kings, too numerous and too poor to command great respect, were only primus inter pares in their councils. In the *Odyssey*, the nobles of Ithaca made sport of the king's son, although afraid that he might summon an assembly to put them in their places (*Iliad*, book 16); and the hero had to assert his rights by craft and strength. As

Sophocles had it, the seer stood up firmly to King Oedipus: "Though thou art a king, an equal right I claim to give thee word for word" (*Oedipus Tyrannus*, 408-409).

From Homeric times, kingship declined. The Ionian cities were probably without kings by 800 B.C. (Haywood, 1964), and most of the rest of Greece followed in a century or two. Kings were not cast out by violence, so far as is known, but reduced by degrees until they had only a religious or ceremonial role like modern constitutional monarchs. Kingship was made elective, then reduced in duration, and finally made an annual ceremonial office, perhaps open to all citizens (Freeman, 1950; Dunham, 1915).

The gathering of people into small independent cities was an obvious reason for this decline, and kingship is less appropriate for a commercial than for a military-agricultural society. The more advanced and commercial the city, the sooner the kingship fell; and when this occurred in one place, others followed. Miletus was one of the first to become republican about 900 B.C. Agricultural and imperialistic Sparta kept dual kings, much reduced in power, to the end of its history. In larger and more backward Macedonia and Thrace, kings ruled as long as independence lasted.

After the kings, the aristocracy took power, and there was a period when only mounted knights were first-class citizens (Burn, 1960). But they did not remain unchallenged. Not long after Homer had Achilles defying the king, Hesiod, as a man of the people, was bitterly rebuking the injustice of the nobles. New men were coming up; as Theognis lamented, "Those who were base are now noble" (Kagan, 1965, p. 40). The style of fighting changed; knights and aristocratic champions gave way to the solid phalanx of foot soldiers, wherein each man had to protect his neighbors in perfect cooperation (Littman, 1974). At the same time, commercial wealth was in most places gaining the ascendancy over landed wealth.

For security and regularity of government, the growing commercial classes wanted the laws to be fixed; this was in the seventh century the first demand of the rising democratic party (Glotz, 1929). Written codes came first in the colonies where conflicting traditions of a mixed population required formal agreement as to what law was accepted (Burn, 1960); by 600 B.C. they were generally introduced and carved in public places. But defining powers tends to restrict them and makes possible republican government; and laws, made effective through regularized courts, give rights. As Euripides said, "With written laws, people of few resources and the rich have the same recourse to justice" (Kagan, 1965, p. 132). The formulation of codes, with the concomitant abolition of collective guilt, also meant the assertion of the new state over the ancient clans and a turn from semireligious custom to manmade and rationalized legislation. There grew up a strong sense of law. The word of Leonidas at Thermopylae was, "Passerby, go and tell Sparta that here three hundred Greeks died to obey her laws." To esteem the law was to guard freedom, said Demosthenes (J. Jones, 1936, p. 70). The Greeks abhorred illegal government, or tyranny, as unbecoming to human dignity. According to an Attic orator of classic times, the Greeks of old "deemed that it was the way of wild beasts to be held subject to one another by force, but the duty of men to delimit justice by law, to convince by reason, and to serve these two in act by submitting to the sovereignty of law and the instruction of reason" (Kagan, 1965, p. 134). The Greek state, oligarchic or democratic, was uniformly constitutional. In 403 B.C. it was enacted in Athens that no one should be tried except by written law and that no law should prevail against an individual but against all alike (Gomme, 1962). The oath taken by Athenian youths upon admission to citizenship included, "I will submit to the existing laws and those that the people shall unanimously make: if anyone shall attempt to overthrow these laws or disobey them, I will not suffer it, but I will fight for them, whether singlehanded or with my fellows (Glotz, 1929, p. 133).

Aristocratic rule was broken, however, not by popular risings but by strong men, called tyrants or illegitimate rulers, from the merchant or industrial classes. Most Greek states passed through a stage of tyranny in the seventh and sixth centuries; but the tyrants almost always maintained constitutional forms and by opening power to new classes broadened the state. As Aristotle wrote, the tyrants rose by flattering the people and slandering the notables (*Politics*, 1310b); they made concessions to the middle or lower classes, often confiscating wealth of nobles for distribution to the poor. They usually encouraged trade; and they were pacific, aware that any defeat could be fatal (Haywood, 1964; Glotz, 1929). Tyrannies usually lasted only a single lifetime, and they raised no monuments to themselves. Becoming outmoded by 500 B.C., they subsequently recurred chiefly through foreign intervention or with the support of foreign soldiers. Miletus, for example, became a tyranny under Persia late in the sixth century but reverted to democracy in rebellion against foreign domination. According to Herodotus, when the Persian ruler was in peril an Ionian tyrant favored helping him: "It is through Darius that we enjoy our thrones in our several states... there is not one of them which will not prefer democracy to kingly rule" (book 3, chap. 137).

Having discarded monarchy and usually having passed through tyranny, the polis came to have nearly everywhere the same basic institutions, the originally aristocratic council, and the more or less democratic assembly. They always somewhat balanced each other, and the council was usually elected by the assembly. In some places the council remained oligarchic; in many others it came to represent the whole body of citizens. In some the assembly would meet only as called by the council and could not initiate or debate but only accept or reject what was proposed to it; in others it gained powers to choose magistrates, judge offenders, and decide policy. In oligarchic states, magistrates were usually elected; in the democratic, they were selected by lot (Andrewes, 1956). Full citizenship was sometimes only for those able to provide themselves with hoplite armor (Haywood, 1964); participation was limited formally or informally, the poor man knowing that state affairs were not for him to decide (Andrewes,

1956). In the democratic states, all descendants of the original community shared power, that "no one is compelled to obey unless he may in turn command: thus liberty and equality are combined" (Glotz, 1929, p. 205).

Everywhere democratic and oligarchic tendencies contested. Usually the maritime and commercial towns, as in Ionia, were more democratic than the more agricultural areas. There were violent shifts: Miletus moved between oligarchic tyranny under Persian influence and extreme democracy with magistrates changed monthly. Little or nothing is known of the form of government of the large majority of the numerous poleis, unless it is inferred from lack of records of eminent individuals that the people ruled. But the Greeks were proud of their form of government. Sophocles, enumerating the achievements of man, noted along with the building of ships, the domestication of animals, and the learning of language, the "aptitude of civic life" (*Antigone*, 332-35).

CONSTITUTION OF ATHENS

The only democratic Greek constitution known in detail, as well as the most important, was the Athenian. Athens was exceptional in uniting a relatively large area; it is likely, however, that it was typical of many, although direct democracy presumably functioned better in many smaller centers.

The kings of Athens were displaced by nobles in the eighth century, but wealth soon came to prevail over birth. By 682 B.C. the main offices are said to have become annual; and the executive office, or archonship, was pluralized to seven. Solon, at the beginning of the sixth century, did much to free the economy, to attach the individual to the state instead of to older ancestral and religious associations, and to democratize Athens. Son of a wealthy merchant, he canceled outstanding debts, ended debt slavery, limited landholding, based classes on wealth instead of birth, opened up the assembly to all classes and gave it major power, reorganized the council, and established democratic courts, although high office was still reserved for the rich. Before Solon, Athens had been rather insignificant; whether cause or effect, democratization coincided with its rise.

Tyranny was brief and rather mild. Peisistratus, who came to power as much by commercial as political or military means, permitted his political opponents to remain in the city. Cleisthenes at the end of the sixth century redivided the population into ten tribes to reduce aristocratic influence, admitted the industrial classes to full citizenship, and strengthened the assembly and popular courts. He also checked military influence by placing command in a board of ten generals. He gave the citizens an opportunity once a year to ostracize or exile anyone whom they distrusted by writing his name on a potsherd; although subsequently misused, this was an essentially democratic measure to lop off ambitions. In the middle of the fifth century the last important aristocratic institutions were stripped of power and democracy was made virtually complete by substituting sortition for election to most offices. Thereupon, citizens had an equal chance to become councilors, high magistrates, or jurors; and these offices were modestly paid to enable all to serve. Under the leadership of Pericles, who believed the state should use its resources for the benefit of all the citizens, Athens became something of a welfare state. Measures were taken to ensure cheap bread. First, war orphans and incapacitated veterans were supported at public expense, then disabled workers were given pensions (Glotz, 1929), and budgetary surpluses were used to finance festivals or occasional handouts to all citizens. Schemes for socialization of property were mooted—and mocked by Aristophanes in his *Ecclesiazusae* and *Plutus*. A result of these benefits and the fruits of the Athenian empire was that the sovereign citizens became the more interested in barring aliens from citizenship.

The basis of the constitution was local self-government of the ten "tribes," each divided into several "demes." Demes and tribes alike had their own functions, religious observances, assemblies, registry and officials (Haywood, 1964). Civic education and loyalties began here, and these groups, synthetic as they were, competed spiritedly among themselves. Each tribe shared in the management of the city; each had its own general, and its men fought together as a company; the bones of its heroes were buried together (Glotz, 1929).

The sovereign assembly included all male citizens of twenty or over, country as well as townsfolk. Beginning at dawn and lasting the better part of a day, it met at least monthly and as many as forty times yearly. To make it possible for all to attend, Pericles introduced payment, at least for the first-arriving quorum. The chairman, chosen by lot, was the acting chief of state; he held office only for a single day. There was usually also an unofficial leader, who lent coherence to the assembly's actions; and informal parties gathered. Committees were sometimes established to report on proposals (Bonner, 1933). The agenda was drawn up by the council, but the citizens could treat it as they liked. Much of the business of the assembly was routine checking on government, but it decided policy and made or ratified all laws, voting by show of hands or secretly with pebbles when serious personal matters were at stake (Glotz, 1929). It even assumed such responsibilities as fixing the composition of fleets and armies. At times it acted as a high court of justice.

Older men were heard first, and the assembly preferred to listen to informed and skillful speakers; the incapable or ignorant were likely to be hooted down. The powers of comprehension of the assembly are indicated by the involvedness, even obscurity, of reported speeches (Glover, 1926). Summoned to the tribunal, the orator put on the myrtle crown of inviolability; but he had reason to be careful. All motions had to be in writing and were checked for illegality; even so, the mover was subject for a year to accusation of improper procedure, under severe penalties. If his proposal turned out badly, he might be charged with "deceiving the people"—a grave charge to which the influential were especially vulnerable. Even thus, the assembly refrained from exercising the fullness of its powers. Laws had to be formally drawn up by the council and duly affirmed before they became effective, while the courts might reject decrees as illegal ("unconstitutional"). Law in the strict sense was to be altered only at a yearly review by the council with a set procedure for thorough consideration (A. Jones, 1957).

The council was as democratic as could be devised. Fifty men selected by lot from each of the ten tribes (these being apportioned to the smaller divisions, the demes, according to numbers) made up the body commonly called the Five Hundred. The fifty corresponding to each tribe had active duty for a tenth of the year, during which time they lived in the council hall to devote full attention to business (Haywood, 1964). The term, as in Greek democracies generally, was never more than a year, and a man could be councilor only twice and not consecutively.

Normally holding public sessions, at which citizens could speak and make proposals, the fifty would meet every day except holidays. They supervised administration, treated with ambassadors, carried out decisions of the assembly, and drew up proposals for submission to it. The prerogatives of the council were such that power might well have gravitated to it from the unwieldy assembly; it seems, however, to have preferred to pass all important matters to the assembled people. Anyone could prosecute the council before a court for illegal actions (Glotz, 1929).

The courts were also instruments of popular rule. All jury and no judge, they were panels of not less than 201, chosen by lot from volunteering citizens over thirty. One selected by lot presided. In political cases juries often numbered some thousands. Pericles introduced pay for jurors as for the assembly, one third drachma, the conventional subsistence amount, plus free places at the drama. This amounted to welfare for senior citizens (Robinson, 1950) and encouraged a class of semiprofessionals, for there was always a demand for a great many. Appeals to juries were hence on a lower level than assembly speeches, with demagoguery and emotional pleas (Pickard-Cambridge, 1914). However, in part because their size made bribery difficult, they do not seem to have been corrupt.

There were no official prosecutors, as it was assumed that all citizens should be interested in observance of the law. Denunciation was encouraged by giving the accuser a portion of fines. This led to abuses and perhaps blackmail, but the denouncer who did not receive at least one fifth of the votes was fined or whipped. An expression of community feeling more than an organ of state power, the court left it up to the plaintiff to collect any damages awarded, aided only by public opinion (Bonner, 1933). Plaintiff and defendant had to conduct their own pleas. Any politically prominent person was likely to have to defend himself against a charge of irregularity, which was in effect a denunciation of his policies, and the juries drove many capable leaders into exile at some time during their careers. But their shafts were directed against the powerful, and they were effective guardians of the democracy. Law and litigation were part of the spice of a contentious existence. But there were sensible measures to resolve disputes, such as petty courts for minor cases and boards of arbitrators (Aristotle, *Athenian Constitution*, chap. 53).

Still more deviant from modern practice was the administrative system, designed to engage as many as possible in the business of the state. Nearly all of the approximately seven hundred offices were filled by election or sortition. Each official served a particular function with no superior but the assembly or council; for staff, there might be a few technically competent helpers, usually aliens or slaves, employed for only a year to avoid giving them advantages of long experience over the magistrates. Religious ceremonies were also performed by such impermanent lay officials, except for some hereditary priesthoods. Terms of office were one year, and no one was permitted to hold the same position twice, except that indefinite reelection was allowed to the critical position of general. It was difficult to occupy even different magistracies consecutively, since the outgoing official had to give an accounting before he was eligible for another post (Glotz, 1929). In less democratic states, office-holding was for those with leisure to serve gratuitously, but Athens paid small salaries. A few officials, chiefly military officers and ambassadors, were elected in the assembly by show of hands. But most, to avoid influence and electoral contests, were picked by drawing lots. As a result, citizens could expect to spend a year or so in important public office. Thousands could look forward to having their single day as chairman of the council and head of state.

The Greeks felt that sortition, rationalized as evidencing the divine will, was fairer than election, since the vote gave advantages to family and reputation. (On the mechanics of sortition, see Brumbaugh, 1966.) Only those over thirty in good civic standing and supposedly of good character were eligible (Aristotle, *Athenian Constitution*, chap. 55); and public opinion and fear of examination inhibited the incapable from presenting themselves. Moreover, there was little opportunity for abuses. Officials, including council members, could be denounced and deposed at any time by the assembly, were subject to monthly audit, and at the end of their term had to pass severe scrutiny. Important duties were entrusted not to single individuals but to boards, decreasing the likelihood of corruption and virtually assuring that there would be some capable men on any board. In such a loose amateur state, one might suppose that the elected generals would wield great influence, but they remained executive officers implementing the policies of the assembly.

Officeholding was no object of campaigning, no source of wealth or power. Elected officers might exercise leadership; Pericles was a general. But he was legally no more than nine others, and his power rested only upon his influence with his fellow citizens. Leadership depended not upon officeholding but upon ability to carry the assembly.

Finances were conducted in the same spirit. The state tried to keep expenditures to a minimum and avoided direct taxation, which was considered an injustice (Bullock, 1939). Most revenues came from the light duties on imports and exports, from a few state enterprises such as the leased silver mines, and from tribute while the empire lasted. If the treasury had a surplus, it was shared out to the citizen-owners of the state; Athens distributed part of the silver mined at Laurium. As much as possible was done at private expense; even military equipment was largely furnished by the citizens. For many functions, as the mounting of spectacles and the outfitting of triremes, the wealthy were called upon. They took turns in these undertakings, called "liturgies," wherein civic pride mixed with a spirit of potlatch; many rich Athenians subscribed more liturgies than required. The taxpayer had at least the pleasure of supervising the spending of his money instead of turning it over to the government. He also sailed into battle on the ship he had provided (Glover, 1926). The navy provided by private enterprise gave Athens dominion of the seas for many generations. In the decline of the polis, however, civic spirit weakened and the liturgies became onerous, in effect a heavy tax upon wealth.

Self-government was far more extensive than our age would dare. But in calling upon the capacities of the common man, the polis educated civic spirit and political intelligence. The awareness of each that he would probably come to high position increased interest; and the law was more compelling and decisions were more deserving of support as they were made and carried out by all alike. Ordinary citizens were expected to know much law and parliamentary procedure; the chairman of the assembly, although picked by lot, was subject to penalty if he admitted an illegal motion. As seldom in history, the ruled were rulers and the interests of individuals corresponded with the interests of whole community. Despite all measures to spread power, there was some tendency for cliques of semiprofessional politicians to take charge (A. Jones, 1957); but far less than in modern societies was there a political elite. When Athens had elections, corruption entered as in other democracies (Glotz, 1929); but in the absence of political place-seeking and contest for spoils, party strife was centered on policies.

The Athenian democracy suffered the frailties of popular government, instability, nasty politics, and the urge for glory without reckoning costs. It committed many errors, including the martyrdom of Socrates. Errors sometimes arose from an excess of democratic feeling, as in the banishment of able leaders. The democracy was unskilled in foreign relations and war. But it managed long and competently the affairs of a community of well over a hundred thousand citizens, men, women, and children, at its largest in the fifth century B.C.; the huge assembly actually functioned as a fairly adequate organ of government. Such men as Pericles and Thucydides were elected leaders; in few other states would Sophocles have been made a general because of esteem for his *Antigone* (Glover, 1926).

Freedom of association, political action, and speech were as nearly unlimited as in any society. Euripides called it a slave's lot to be unable to speak freely. Leaders and public policies could be pilloried in public festivals, attacked even in wartime with impunity. The paean to democracy that Thucydides put into Pericles' mouth is well remembered: we invite the world into our house; we scorn those who take no part in public affairs; baring our actions in free discussion, we have the clearest sense both of pain and pleasure; yet, living well, we do not shirk danger.

The government of Athens presupposed a civic spirit in which nobles took the lead in democratizing the constitution and the masses usually preferred to vote for aristocrats (Botsford, 1939). There was a law that anyone subverting the democracy should be regarded as an enemy of the people and be liable to death. But democracy could endure only so long as the people really wanted it; and they upheld it through all the generations of their brilliance. Even though it broke down briefly during the Peloponnesian wars and led them to defeat at the hands of Sparta, they restored it in fullest form after a few months of oligarchy under Spartan tutelage—which was less effective because Spartans who came into contact with the democratic society were likely to be politically subverted (Adcock and Mosley, 1975). The system did not suit everyone; but immigrants flocked to Athens, although citizenship was difficult to achieve and aliens lacked political rights. The constitution was kept unimpaired until Macedonian rule forced restrictions.

The Athenian constitution, systematic and well devised, must have been the fruit of now lost cogitation and analysis. It was an extraordinary invention made possible by the extreme splitting of power in the Greek world. It was the polar opposite of the autocratic empire, a government in which power was checked, divided, and made available to ordinary people to a degree incomprehensible to the world of nation-states.

HELLENISTIC AFTERMATH

As the polis lost importance after the Peloponnesian wars and especially under the shadow of Macedonian domination, traditional forms were retained; but democracy decayed along with the sentiments that had made it possible. In Athens, after suppression of the anti-Macedonian rising of 322 B.C., the franchise was limited to possessors of two thousand drachmas and the citizen body was thereby reduced to less than half (Ferguson, 1911); the powers of the popular courts were diminished; payment for state service was decreased or eliminated. Subsequently, seapower being lost and commerce having flowed to newer centers, there was some return to land-based aristocracy as in days before Solon. Macedonian overlords were freely deified; the Athenians addressed one, "Other gods are far away; Thee we see face to face" (Grant, 1963, p. xxiv). But when the Macedonian garrison was expelled by the turns of international fortune, freedom and democracy or at least democratic forms were several times restored (Ferguson, 1911). Under Roman domination, in 105 B.C., there was an oligarchic revolution; but the democratic element continued strong enough to rise futilely in 88 B.C. against Rome.

Most other Hellenistic Greek cities had laws similar to those of Athens (Glotz, 1929), with government by assembly, council, and courts, the council and magistrates being chosen by lot. All towns of the Achaean League, for example, were democratic. When it was too late to save the Greek world, there were remarkable experiments in federalism; nearly all of continental Greece, except Athens and Sparta, was gathered into half a dozen federal leagues, which tried to combine unity for defense and joint policy making with representative government and internal freedom (Larsen, 1955; Tarn, 1936).

Experiences of tyranny imposed by Macedonian kings confirmed hatred of it; no polis strayed long from republicanism. Government tended, however, toward plutocracy as popularity and position were largely bought; and the chief magistracies often formed effectively governing cabinets. High position was rather burdensome than remunerative because of the obligations increasingly laid upon it; and it came to be that only the rich, mostly merchants who could finance public shows and buildings, could aspire to high office.

The larger and middle-sized states of the Hellenistic world were inevitably monarchies, and in the areas of ancient despotism they adopted much of the style of Eastern autocracy. Monarchy was rationalized on various religious-philosophical grounds, from the kingship of Zeus among the gods to the ideal of the shepherd caring for his flock (Bengtson, 1950). Kings were often accorded divine honors; this was the easier as the Olympian gods were neither very admirable nor much revered. But Hellenistic monarchs were more like strong European rulers than Asiatic despots, retaining something of the ways of Macedonia, where the king was legally primus inter pares. They called themselves simply "king," unlike Alexander himself, and were relatively unpretentious. The army assembly, which once chose the king in Macedon, in the other Hellenistic monarchies became part of the government, with functions of recognizing accessions, choosing regents, sometimes making or at least ratifying great decisions (Bengtson, 1950). The kingdoms stood between the democratic polis of the classical age and the imperial despotism to come in the unified Roman world.

3 Creativity

Sumeria

It is axiomatic that the pluralistic society, like the pluralistic international community, is wasteful because of its contentions and quarrels, the expenditure of energy by individuals, groups, or states in rivalry and conflict with one another, the anarchy of undirected industry and of internecine conflict. Yet times of pluralistic anarchy and conflict have often been times of what is commonly called material progress, of technological development and growing prosperity. It may stand to reason, prima facie, that the planned economy is more productive than the unplanned; but the reverse may be the case, at least if the unplanned is based on a healthy society. The Athenian economy was more rationally ordered in its uncontrol than the Persian, which was severely regulated, just as the Athenian polis was a highly ordered structure in contrast to the essential anarchy of power at the summit of imperial autocracies. It is likewise self-evident that the peace of the empire should open an era of prosperity, since trade is protected and the costs of warfare are no more. But if this may seem briefly to be the case, it does not last long; hosts of extortionate officials and insatiable tax gatherers are more dangerous than embattled armies to industry and commerce. Great empire invariably signifies in the long run not only intellectual torpor, but impoverishment and material degradation.

It seems to be broadly true that the state systems have been the outstanding arenas of creativity, for reasons partly obvious and partly less so; they have been primarily responsible for innovation, artistic originality, and scientific thought, philosophic as well as geographical exploration. The historical record, however, is less clear then it might be; and the difference of productivity of states and empires is not always obvious. One reason is that the empires are impressive. They strive to impress and succeed through magnificence and self-congratulation. In modern times, totalitarian states have often inspired visitors with admiration and awe unjustified by reality; and historians are somewhat like three-day visitors to empires of the past, viewing mostly records that the rulership desired to leave behind. The empires produce the grandiose palaces and monuments; no free city-state could or would aspire to erect the Pyramids. The Parthenon was modest in comparison with the palaces of Darius, and the best works of Greece were invisible to the tourist eye.

The empires also have a strong psychological advantage in the human penchant for unity and order. It is naturally expected that a great empire should do great things, and it receives the benefit of the doubt. Further, there are deficiencies of the record. Until rather recently, nothing was known of the Sumerians, and Babylonia received credit for the Near Eastern civilization that it received but did little to advance. Egyptian civilization seems practically to spring up full blown in the First Dynasty; it remains unclear how much the work was of the preceding period of disunity, which left no monuments. The Greek state system is fairly well known and consequently appreciated, and it is common knowledge that the Greeks were considerably more creative than the Romans who enslaved them. But only a minute fraction of the products of Hellenistic times has survived, and it is not commonly known that much or most of the literature that ornamented the early Roman Empire was only imitation of Hellenistic works.

It is hence a reasonable assumption that state systems deserve more credit than they have ordinarily received; and, while the creativity of various periods cannot be readily measured, it appears that the major periods of civilization building have been those of state systems. In particular, it is clear that the Sumerians deserve prime credit for the techniques and institutions of civilized life. Theirs were a host of inventions or innovations, including sailing ships, potters' wheels, wheeled carts and chariots, pottery vessels, dried and then baked bricks, temples with dimensions in hundreds of feet with arches and domes, cylinder seals (presumably to protect property), water clocks, fresco painting, and excellent sculpture. Their metalsmiths learned to weld and rivet as well as to cast, and made greatly improved tools as well as ornaments. They invented the plow, to which they harnessed oxen or asses (Clark, 1962; Parrot, 1961); their agriculture was perhaps superior to that of modern Iraq. They paid regular taxes and had formal armies. Their system of sexagesimal notation became the basis of Babylonian mathematics and the forerunner of Hindu-Arabic numerals (Kramer, 1963). Mathematical curiosity led them to tackle many problems beyond material needs (Hawkes, 1973). They had a sensible system of weights and measures, using simple multiples of a basic unit. Little is known of many aspects of their life, as of their medicine; but a text of 2500 B.C., giving a series of prescriptions without spells, rituals, or mention of gods or demons, indicates that it was much less magical in spirit than that of following ages (Hawkes, 1973; Taton, 1964).

Before 3000 B.C. the Sumerians devised, originally on a pictographic basis, a system of writing with wedge-shaped marks in clay, which evolved from pictographic to largely phonetic, with some five hundred to six hundred signs. Many schools were established, separate from the temples, to teach this system of writing. Although the cuneiform seems clumsy, it was adapted to many and totally different languages and endured nearly until the beginning of our era; and all other systems of writing of the Old World may well owe their inspiration to it. Sumerian scribes made word lists for study; and to judge from exercise tablets from 2500 B.C., and probably long before, there were regular schools and school compositions. These tablets show much knowledge of plants, animals, geography, and so on, and grammar was treated with considerable sophistication (Kramer, 1963). About a thousand proverbs have been recovered, such as "Marry a wife according to your choice," "Don't pick it now; it will bear fruit later," and "Tell a lie; then if you tell the truth it will be deemed a lie" (Kramer, 1963, pp. 225-226, 255).

Catalogs listed over two hundred literary works; some were love poems of flirtation and courtship. There were also at least nine long tales, which might be called epics. The favorite was that of Gilgamesh, repeated, adapted, and extended throughout the Near East for millennia, eventually to become the prototype for the tales of Hercules. It is filled with the yearning to escape death: "Man perishes, heavy is the spirit. I looked over the wall and saw corpses floating in the river. I, too, will end thus, that is certain" (Moscati, 1960, p. 39). The gods give the hero adventures and power and advise him to cherish the little one who holds his hand and the wife he presses to his bosom; but he must lie down to rise no more. Compared with the Greek epic, the Sumerian is burdened with much more superstition and unrealism; but it has a poignant theme that the ringing narrative of Homer lacks.

The Sumerian was also a materially productive society. By 2500 B.C. the region seems to have reached a zenith of prosperity that it has not known again in the subsequent forty-five hundred years (Gadd, 1962). After Sumeria was overcome, its civilization was taken over by successive conquerors and became, unlike the Egyptian, the heritage of many peoples. It had an enduring hold over the minds of those who came into contact with it. The language was used as a written and ritual tongue for fifteen centuries after it had ceased to be a vernacular. A series of empires used Sumerian art, technology, religion, and law for two thousand years after 2500 B.C., but they hardly improved the ancient sculpture, jewelry, pottery, and agricultural techniques. As Moscati wrote of Sumeria, "Its literary works, its laws and its artistic creations form the basis for all the succeeding civilizations of Western Asia, in which we shall find them copied, adapted and worked over, often being marred rather than improved in the process" (Moscati, 1960, p. 56).

China of the Hundred Schools

The centuries of division, during which the bases of the Chinese literature, philosophy, and science were laid, were a time of exceptional intellectual aliveness; later ages, despite considerable accomplishments, suffer by comparison. Above all, it was the time when radically different schools of thought competed, in contrast to the single official outlook of following millennia.

Great advances had been made long before, in the bronze age around 1600 B.C. The ideographic system of writing was in full use by the beginning of the time of division. But with the decline of Chou power, progress accelerated. Early in the period there were such practical developments as the use of iron and ox-drawn plows. Subsequently, irrigation was expanded; agriculture improved in many ways; steel came into use for tools; the economy became monetary and commercial. The best time was about 500 to 250 B.C., the age of the Hundred Schools and wandering scholars. The magnitude of material progress during this period is shown by the great geographic expansion of the Chinese states, despite their continual struggle against one another. In the earlier time of the western Chou empire, when there was a fairly strong central authority, the barbarians were active and aggressive; afterward, improvement of military capability more than compensated for loss of unity, with China expanding at the expense of the nomads (Lattimore, 1962).

An extraordinary new scholar class arose; literally thousands lived by their wits or learning, scholars or politicians, going freely from court to court, offering advice or embellishing the capital with their learning or arts. Princes would invite savants with humble language and rich presents; the king of Ch'i is said to have hosted more than a thousand well paid intellectuals without specific duties (Creel, 1953). Mencius traveled escorted by tens of chariots and hundreds of traveling students. The result of the sellers' market for learning was a tangled growth of ideas.

Perhaps because princes perceived that knowledge is power, savants not only graced the court but gained a high place in their councils, and rulers preferred them to native aristocrats (R. Walker, 1953). When the duke of Hsiao employed many foreigners, protests were raised, but the practice was upheld as traditional. The somewhat backward state of Ch'in, with no outstanding scholars of its own, raised itself by the recruitment of foreign experts from the more advanced states to the east. Among these was Li Ssu, who, after training in Legalistic philosophy, went to Ch'in as the state most appropriate for the application of his theories. At one time there was jealous pressure for his expulsion, but he argued that Ch'in had reaped great gains in the past from the employment of aliens; talent and ideas should be borrowed for the greater glory of the state, just as beautiful women receive jewels from abroad (Bodde, 1936).

The princes founded many academies, the most famous of which was established in Ch'i in 318 B.C. Books were abundant; and literacy, no easy accomplishment in Chinese script, was expected of all in the upper class (Creel, 1953). Although lacking the breadth and variety of the Greek, art and literature showed vitality and originality. One of the earlier classics, the *Book of Odes*, dated to the seventh or eighth century, is notable for its highly personalized laments, songs of courtship, and errant loves.

Philosophy especially throve. During this time of no orthodoxy or even any predominant trend of thinking (although attention to the problem of conduct seems one-sided), there were many important schools. Only a part of the philosophy of that age has been transmitted; in particular, no works of the sophists and dialecticians of the latter fourth and third centuries have survived. Yet the thought of that day so dominated following ages that it has been considered possible to write histories of Chinese philosophy without going beyond the founding of the Ch'in empire, 221 B.C. Subsequent thinkers have not offered much more than refinements and commentaries upon the Confucian school.

Confucius, born in the middle of the sixth century, wandered through and taught in six other states; like Plato, he wanted a prince to introduce a reign of wisdom on earth, and his wisdom, more than Plato's, stressed harmony. Schools multiplied in the century or two after Confucius. Lao Tse, prophet of Tao or the Path, instead of reforming the world would withdraw from it. Taoism became, like Buddhism, a corpus of magic and superstition, but it had elements of an intellectual philosophy like existentialism. A stronger attempt to break out of old patterns was that of Yang Chu. Skeptical and nihilistic, he questioned the superiority of kings and held to atheistic fatalism (Hirth, 1911). Very partially preserved in a compilation of some centuries later, he may have been more forceful in the original. Mo Tzu opposed war on moral grounds and proclaimed universal love as the remedy for the evils of this world. His school, which lasted into the first century B.C., also sketched a theory of scientific method, systematically treating evidence, perception, and causality (Needham, 1960), and using experiments to investigate optics and mechanics. In contrast to what later became the accepted Chinese approach, Hsün Tzu attacked superstition and argued for a naturalistic approach, viewing the universe as essentially mechanical rather than moral. He reinterpreted rites as being merely forms to express the sentiments of those who perform them, opposed excessive idealization of the past, and was essentially pragmatic.

Such non-Confucian doctrines gained wide popularity. In the words of Mencius, ablest interpreter of Confucius: "Unemployed scholars indulge in unreasonable discussions, the words of Yang Chu and Mo Tzu fill the empire. ... Now, Yang's principle is,—'each one for himself'—which does not acknowledge the claims of the sovereign. Mo's principle is—'to love all equally'—which does not acknowledge the peculiar affection due fathers" (Thomas, 1927, p. 209). It would be interesting to know whether these or such philosophies were ever as dominant as Mencius suggests. But Mencius himself, who wandered like the Sage from state to state to present his theories, was something of a skeptic. "It would be better," he wrote, "to have no books at all than to believe all that they relate."

The intellectual achievement of the five centuries preceding unification may be summarized by noting that at the beginning of the period China was several centuries behind the leading centers of civilization; at the end, it had fairly well caught up with Greece, which had meanwhile come forward rapidly. A recent Chinese scholar could say, "All the great thinkers of China lived during the three hundred years between 530 and 230 B.C." (Liang, 1930, p. 28). This is an exaggeration; subsequent centuries, in particular the time of division following the fall of the Han dynasty, were by no means barren. But when the anarchy ceased, free discussion ended. Chinese philosophic history is divided into the period of the philosophers, up to the imperial canonization of Confucianism, and the period of classical study (Fung, 1952). A statesman of the seventeenth century, Huang Tsung-hsi, concluded regretfully that Chinese society had been evil since the Ch'in unification and that the only salvation was to turn back the clock two thousand years (Bary, de, 1957). There was never another time faintly comparable to the great days that later Chinese students called "intellectual and political anarchy."

Indian Enlightenment

The India of independent states, like the contemporary Chinese system, was an open society, with political conflict, unsettling dissensions, economic growth, and social fluidity. It gave rise to a brilliant civilization that is not to be less esteemed as succeeding ages preserved little of it. Through subsequent centuries of turmoil, only what suited the Brahmin priestly class survived. But it is clear from the meager, reworked heritage that there was, particularly in the sixth and fifth centuries B.C., a remarkable search for answers to the riddle of existence, an intellectual inquiry as never afterward in Indian history.

Like other highly productive eras, it was a time of mixed trends, of sorcery and science, of pleasure-seeking license and passionate asceticism, of opinion against opinion, of doubt and self-assertion. A university at Taxila, near modern Peshawar, was noted for its science and medicine. Learned men traveled freely over the whole region, which was united by a common language and culture. Probably literacy was high; the later carved edicts of Asoka seem to assume that the ordinary people could read.

Although the Vedic poems are very ancient, the time of Buddha was the golden age of Indian literature, with virility and vigor, a combination of humor, earnestness, and depth. The classic epics, the *Mahabharata* and the *Ramayana*, are roughly attributed to pre-Buddhist or Buddhist times; although hardly appealing to Western tastes, these interminable poems have become virtually part of the Hindu canon. The *Upanishads* also became a gospel, and there were many other less remembered works. As stated by Davids, "The learned, ornate poetry of later times is to the literature of this period what the systematization and learned commentaries of Buddhaghora and Sankara are to the daring speculations and vivid life of the early Upanishads and of the Four Nikayas" (Davids, 1903, p. 187).

The progress of scholarship may be seen in the work of the grammarian Panini, dated from the sixth to the fourth century. He laid the basis for systematic study so well that he is still used as a basic authority on the grammar of Sanskrit. A theory of psychological evolution is traditionally attributed to a thinker of the seventh century B.C., and a theory of wave propagation of sound was probably evolved. How much should be attributed to this period remains obscure, however, because of Hindu indifference to chronology. Scientific achievements between about 500 B.C. and 500 A.D. are almost undatable, even to a century or so; it is clear only that by the first Christian centuries there was great development in chemistry, physiology, mechanics, and many other fields (Seal, 1958).

From the preserved writings it would appear, quite likely wrongly, that the chief interest was philosophical and religious. Many wandering teachers, mostly neither Brahmins nor ascetics, went around tolerantly discussing ethics and metaphysics, nature and mysticism. They were sufficiently respected that lecture halls were built for them (Davids, 1903). Philosophers were in the lead of the resistance to Alexander. Questioned after being taken prisoner, they impressed the Greeks with the acuteness of their answers, as related by Plutarch (*Life of Alexander*, chap. 64). Subtlety in logic was their forte; Hindu discourse and philosophy, as transmitted to our day, delight in refinement of concepts and intricacy of thought.

In times shortly preceding Buddha, new intellectual currents entered the old Hindu religion. Then there seem to have grown up the main ideas that became the heart of dogma thereafter: the world soul, metempsychosis or reincarnation, Karma or the accounting of merit from the past, Dharma or moral law, and Yoga, the means of overcoming evil Karma. Ritual and sacrifice became less important in the Upanishads, giving place to concern for knowledge and soul: "The fools who delight in this sacrificial ritual as the highest spiritual good go again and again through the cycle of old age and death" (Bary, de, 1958, p. 28).

Stronger reactions against priestly obscurantism were Buddhism and Jainism. Founded by teachers wandering from state to state like countless others, these religions grew up and found support in the clan republics. Buddhism, later encrusted with a thousand superstitions, began as a philosophy without a god, a scheme of the fixed order of things in which man by meditation could discern his way or from which he could find release, not by ritual but by illumination (Courtillier, 1945). It held that the personality is an aggregate of qualities, in which the Karma that survives death is determined by deeds and may eventually be extinguished by righteousness. Jainism was rather similar in philosophy, equally insistent upon deathless Karma, but more inclined to asceticism and renunciation of worldly pleasures. It was not really theistic, finding not divine will but natural law to guide the universe; its god was only the highest manifestation of powers latent in the human spirit (Courtillier, 1945).

Buddhism and Jainism were only the most successful of many teachings or the most appealing to later days. There were at least eight schools of importance, some of them very bold. One fatalist doctrine held that man has no power over his destiny, efforts being unavailing either for good or evil. There were skeptics who rejected all knowledge of self and sought only immediate peace; others denied sin, moral distinctions, and causation (Radhakrishnan, 1958).

Most radical was a critical-materialistic doctrine. There are hints of such ideas in the epics and pre-Buddhist writings, but they were fully developed only in the intellectual riot of Buddhist times. Teachings of materialism survive only in the writings of opponents who used them as a foil for rebuttal; however, they seem to have been more sophisticated than comparable Greek doctrines. There were several tendencies with different interpretations of the relation of mind and body and the qualities or basic elements of matter. It was taught that there was no universal truth, only learning from perception; inferences drawn from perception might be true or false, with only a probable value dependent upon induction. Some contended that the world was composed of four basic elements, earth, water, fire, and air (an idea strikingly like that of the Ionian philosophers of about the same date), with qualities of goodness, passion, and darkness, and that these elements gave birth to all things, including consciousness, an emergent function of matter, like color. Others believed that there was no soul or immortality, heaven and hell being inventions of impostors, and gods arising from misinterpretation of natural phenomena; that there was no good or evil in nature, morals being conventions only, and that no one had a natural right to command another; that the good of man was pleasure, to be sought in self-assertion and in disregard of authority (Radhakrishnan, 1958; Gupta, 1938). In sum, as reported by a Buddhist source, "There is no merit in almsgiving, sacrifice or offerings. . . . There is no afterlife. . . . Man is formed of the four elements; when he dies, earth returns to the aggregate of earth, water to water, fire to fire and air to air, while the senses vanish into space." Denying any form of spiritual liberation, the materialists ridiculed priests and all infallibility. Despite the attacks upon it, the skeptical-materialist philosophy was long influential. Centuries later, a morality drama satirized it as a widespread vice (Radhakrishnan and Moore, 1957). Post-Buddhist India, alternating between empire and disorder, counted substantial technical and scientific achievements, for example, in astronomy; but there was never another time of comparable intellectual openness.

Greek Success

After about 2400 B.C. the Near East became as sterile as it had been fertile in the preceding millennium. The Assyrians of 800 B.C. were little more advanced than their Sumerian predecessors, except in the arts of war and rule.

Those who created a new and potent civilization, laying the foundations of modernity, were the Greeks—not the agriculturalists of the plains and valleys but the traders of the islands and peninsulas, especially the Ionians on the fringes of

Asia. They were, above all, individualists. Already the Homeric heroes, standing alone in hardship, speak with more self-assertion than those of the ancient stories; for example, in the *Iliad*, "Though fates of death stand over us, ten thousand of them, let us go forward, whether we shall give glory to some other man, or another yield it to us" (Burn, 1960, pp. 8-9). The poet looks to human spirit, not to divine help (Cook, 1962).

Lyrics appeared along with the polis. About 650 B.C., the first individualistic poet, Archilocus, more impressed by the misery than the glory of war, sang about having dropped his shield to run away in battle, with insolence inconceivable in more solemn societies: "Never mind, I will get me another as good." He was not impressed by appearances: let the general "be a man, even bowlegged, as long as he stands firm on his feet, full of heart" (Snell, 1953, pp. 48-51). His successors rejected the pompous and showy for the personal and tender, and there was a new awareness of lonely human destiny. Alcaeus sang of politics, love, and wine; the ship of state, he lamented, was overcome by tempests: "But for me, dear companions, I would forget these things and make merry here with you and Bacchus." The waning of youth became a frequent theme, as in Anacreon: "My temples are turned gray and my crown is white, of sweet life not much time is left." The first of the great dramatists, Aeschylus, has his characters, more than those of Homer, act on independent judgment; those of Sophocles stand still lonelier against the world, and Euripides went on to plumb individual psychology as none before (Snell, 1953, pp. 64, 103-110).

The imperial Near East has left hardly any names except those of rulers, but thousands of Greeks excelling in all fields are known as individuals. Many makers of Attic wares, potters as well as painters of the designs, inscribed their names upon their works. They enjoyed being inventive and different; the potteries never turned out the same design twice (Glotz, 1926). In the same spirit, from the seventh century the Greeks shook off the prudery and restrictive sexual mores of the Near East; they found the body not shameful but beautiful.

The polis, unlike the old empires, did not require magic and superstition for its government. There was no orthodoxy; a civic function, not a compulsory belief, the Greek religion of near human gods left men free to make their own way and think their thoughts as long as they did not seem to injure civic institutions. There was no idea of a divine power making the individual insignificant (Cook, 1936). Men usually performed their own ceremonies, or took turns in religious offices, as they did in the offices of state and in the choruses; there was no priestly caste with a vested interest in mysticism or traditional obscurantism. Virtue was primarily valor, good sense, and temperance. Very early, from the seventh century, the Greeks showed clarity of thought in a world wrapped in obscurantism, rising above the ancient morass much more strongly than the men of the Renaissance freed themselves from the grip of the Middle Ages (Burn, 1960). They wandered widely, observed, compared, and questioned. The first geographer, Hecataeus of Miletus, detesting not only the mythology of the Asiatics but that of his own people, said, "The stories of the Greeks are in my opinion no less absurd than numerous" (Singer, 1959, p. 18). His contemporary, Anaximander, first to make a map of the world, postulated an evolutionary theory whereby land animals derived from slimy sea creatures, an idea perhaps suggested by insect metamorphosis. Thales, a philosopher-merchant who visited Mesopotamia and Egypt and is credited with a keen business sense, went beyond the empirical geometric formulas of the ancients to generalization and proof (Bell, 1940). He is also perhaps the first in the Western tradition to have sought a natural explanation for the world, the primal element of which he believed to be water.

Thales and his fellows speculated wildly and with little basis in fact, but they sought ideas in analogies of the real world, not in myths or pious lore. They preferred commercial analogies to magic or divine command as explanations, and stressed quantitative terms (Mason, 1962). Some saw man as having risen from savagery, a belief implying an ideal of progress and contrary to the notion of an ordained social order (J. Cook, 1962). Heraclitus of Ephesus (540-475 B.C.), a skeptic and prophet of change, was essentially scientific in his emphasis on change in opposition to the emphasis of mythology on the changeless. In his words, "The things of which there is sight, hearing, and knowledge: these are the things I prize." Xenophanes, another Ionian, concluded from the examination of fossils that the world must have gone through a process of development. He also ridiculed conventional ideas, declared that men discover by hard seeking (Snell, 1953, pp. 139, 145), rejected the anthropomorphic gods, and even derided the athletic prizes for mere physical skill. Critias, at the end of the fifth century B.C., theorized that men had invented gods to discourage secret evil-doing (Botsford and Shiles, 1915). About this time, the Sophists were teaching that truth must appeal to individual reason (Willoughby, 1903). Anaxagoras taught that the sun was not a god but an incandescent mass that illuminated the moon. His beliefs brought the first recorded official persecution of scientific thought; accused in Athens, he withdrew to his native Asia Minor. For him, the worth of life was "viewing the heavens and the whole order of the universe." Democritus, developer of an atomic theory, said that it was better to learn a truth of origins than to be king of Persia (Edelstein, 1963, pp. 15, 16).

An Egyptian priest told Solon loftily, "You Greeks are always children." But for Herodotus, who toured the Near East for enlightenment, the chief distinction of the Greeks was freedom from silly notions of the barbarians. Although he collected myths as well as facts, he looked to natural causes; he tried to explain the rise of the Nile in physical, albeit naive terms, and gave a rational estimate of the time required to form the delta. The Near East had much learning, and the Chaldeans made more accurate observations and calculations of sidereal movements than did the Greeks. But the Chaldeans viewed heavenly bodies as deities and observed them mostly for astrological purposes. The Greeks scoffed at this prestigious degradation of intelligence. Not until the Roman world state did astrology return to its full power.

Greek speculation outran testing and application; but Plato, whose supposed preference for the inner vision was in large part the attribution of later ages

(Brumbaugh, 1966), spoke for only a part, perhaps a small part, of the Greek mind. Aeschylus and Sophocles, who exalted the practical inventiveness of man, were probably more representative. The common idea that the Greeks were satisfied with abstract speculation, while inferiors did the work, probably owes much to selective transmission by the Byzantine empire, for which this was roughly true. In fact, they were rather gadget-minded. There was probably extensive (although entirely lost) writing on economic problems (Salin, 1944). In the Ionia of the sixth and fifth centuries B.C., so fruitful in ideas, there was also great improvement of crafts; and "sophia," which later meant wisdom, then signified knowhow or technical skill (Mason, 1962). From the sixth through the third centuries B.C., Greece was the "workshop of the ancient world" (Clough, 1953, p. 82). Up to the Peloponnesian wars, the arts and sciences were inseparable, and practical men were creative thinkers (Farrington, 1953). In architecture, for example, they perfectly combined theory and practice. An example of their mechanical engineering is the tunnel that the small state of Samos bored near the end of the sixth century—thirty-four hundred feet long, 6 feet square, straight through a mountain, with a channel below for water. Although there is no point on the mountain from which both ends are visible, measurements were so accurate that the tunnel borings met neatly in the middle (Goodfield, 1964). Sorokin (1957) found Greece of the fifth and the first part of the fourth century as technically minded as his own day.

Solon exulted, "There is no limit set to human wealth" (Salin, 1944, p. 9), and the Greeks were relatively wealthy in a world that, then as now, lived mostly near the level of subsistence. Already in the seventh century B.C. there was a great increase of civic building. In the sixth century, Xenophanes was castigating his Ionian compatriots for effeminate luxury. Although material wealth was very modest by modern standards, Athenian prosperity drew many Orientals, much as Mexicans might emigrate to New York to improve themselves despite the handicaps of living in a strange land. There are numerous accounts of affluence; for example, it is said that in a small town of Asia Minor a thousand citizens assembled wearing golden diadems and purple mangles worth their weight in silver (Glotz, 1929). In a hardly notable Greek town, Acragas in Sicily, fine mansions had hundreds of thousands of gallons in the wine cellar and could sumptuously sleep hundreds of guests (Freeman, 1950). Clearchus said of the Sybarites that they were so fond of sleep that they forbad the mechanical professions and the keeping of cocks; for comfort, they covered the streets with awnings. But this city, the population of which may have reached one hundred thousand, grew rich by trade and production in a region that has since become the poorhouse of Italy (Burn, 1960). It founded no less than twenty-five daughter colonies.

The wealth of the Greeks, like that of Sybaris, a merchant colony among alien peoples, was based on their aptitude in manufacturing and agriculture as well as commerce. Farmers in Greece lived fairly comfortably and even accumulated property although nature was niggardly. The poverty of the soil hindered instead of inviting invaders; as Aeschylus said, "For Grecian soil is their own ally. . . . It starves to death excessive numbers" (*Persians*, 792-794). Greece was stony, semiarid, and less than a quarter arable, yet the Greeks were well fed and rich while the dwellers on fertile plains of the Near East lived on the edge of starvation. Nor was Greek prosperity to any great extent the work of slaves. The largest number of these, being servants, figured more in consumption than production and were very likely more of an economic burden than an asset.

Nor was wealth the fruit of conquest, extracted from beaten peoples. To live and prosper on their rocky shores, the Greeks had to produce goods for foreign trade. Athens imported at least twice as much grain as was grown in Attica and all its timber, iron, and bronze; imports were paid for partly by mining silver but mostly from export of wine, olive oil, and sundry manufactures and the profits of commerce. Greek pottery was in wide demand for utility and beauty, and many metalwares no less so. Miletus was famed for woolen goods, Chios for fine wine, and so on (Haywood, 1964). The mastery of shipbuilding supported a large and profitable carrying trade. For several centuries there was steady progress in speed and safety of marine transportation; maps were in use by the fourth century, and ships might be of three hundred tons burden (Cloché, 1931).

Against peoples to the north and west, Greece stood out somewhat as the Europe of the sixteenth century stood over the peoples of Asia. The Greeks planted colonies around much of the Mediterranean and Black seas in already occupied territories at distances overseas comparable, in terms of travel time, to those the first British colonists to Virginia had to overcome. Frequently the natives were friendly and welcomed the trader-farmers; there is a story, for example, that settlers were welcomed at Marsilia (Marseilles) because the king's daughter chose their leader as suitor (Freeman, 1950). But others, as peoples of Sicily, tried unsuccessfully to drive the colonists away. When the diffusion of technology deprived the Greeks of their special advantages after the fourth century, colonization came to an end.

Industrial advance made possible a new style of fighting with metal corselets, greaves, and a shield, and with thrusting spear as the main weapon. But the hoplite formation was superior over chariots, cavalry, and archers primarily because of discipline and spirit (Andrewes, 1956), much as the Swiss pikemen of the Middle Ages, standing firmly together, threw back the mounted knights. As a result of well-made armor, good physique, morale, and cohesion, the city-states were able not only to defend themselves but to send men to fight far afield. The Greeks were much in demand as mercenaries, worth many times their number of Asiatics; for centuries this was a major business as it was of the medieval Swiss. At the beginning of the sixth century, Greek soldiers were fighting in the south of Egypt and regarding things Egyptian with great irreverence (Burn, 1960). In 525 B.C. when the builder of the Persian empire, Cambyses, conquered Egypt, there were Greeks on both sides. In a foray of 459 B.C., the Athenians alone undertook the liberation of Egypt from the Persians; they were frustrated largely by the Phoenicians. In the epic of the Ten Thousand, related by Xenophon,

Greek mercenaries found themselves trapped in the heart of the Persian empire. When their leaders were treacherously killed, they elected others; when their tactics proved wanting, they devised new ones and trained horsemen and slingers to stand off the Persians (Spaulding, 1937), eventually to fight their way to freedom. When Alexander led a force of Macedonians and Greeks against Persia, he encountered his strongest opposition from Greeks hired by Darius III.

The Greeks became aware of their superiority. In Homer, Greeks and Trojans were the same sort and had the same gods; but pride was raised by victory over Persia, by far the greatest empire the world had known, and grew thereafter as Greece advanced and the Near East continued to decay. To the Greeks, foreigners or barbarians were dirty, slavish, cruel, ignorant, greedy, and superstitious (Hadas, 1959). It was an expression of deep pride that Pericles said (according to Thucydides), "We throw open our city to the world, and never by alien acts exclude foreigners from any opportunity of learning or observing." In Euripides' *Medea*, Jason informs his much abused and rejected wife what a blessing it was for her to be brought to a civilized country, where "thou hast learnt what justice means and how to live by law, not the dictates of brute force (*Medea*, 537-538)." Isocrates less arrogantly praised Athens and Hellenic culture as the marvel of mankind. Unhappily, the awareness of superiority helped to justify the enslavement of non-Greeks, which was made possible not by Greek imperial power but by technical superiority; and slavery gave satisfactions of social status, lowered the prestige of manual labor, discouraged the invention of labor-saving machines, and contributed to the failure of experimental science to keep pace with theory. It may be that the lesser use of slaves in commerce than in manufacturing contributed to greater progressiveness of the former. It is a tribute to the vitality of Greek society that it was not more poisoned by this institution.

Although superiority gave a moral basis for slavery, it also favored political freedom. Ability to settle overseas helped to relieve pressures as population grew from the eighth century or earlier. Those defeated in civil strife often departed, leaving better civic harmony behind; and rulers knew their people might sail away if excessively discontented. In the hoplite system, whereby the citizens furnished their own heavy weapons, they gained equality as warriors, from which flowed equal rights. Furthermore, a high cultural level, possible only in conditions of considerable wealth, was necessary for the functioning of democracy. By the time of Socrates, probably almost all citizens were literate (J. Jones, 1956). The law of ostracism assumed that any citizen could scratch a name on a potsherd. The lower-class characters of Aristophanes are literate (Flacelière, 1959). Hippodamus of Miletus wanted all jurors to write on their ballots the qualifications of their verdicts. Selection of high officials by lot presumed a standard of culture not widely to be found today. People had to have leisure to participate actively in the affairs of the polis and train themselves for responsibility. Prosperity also gave confidence and élan to Greek society, pride that fortified patriotism and a high opinion of the human worth.

If the strength and attainments of the Greeks thus made possible their free political life, Pericles justly spoke of greatness springing from the form of government. The community of free and equal citizens, wherein justice and law were respected and all could rise according to their deserts, made good relations and banished rancor (Thucydides, book 2, vi, 37). The Greeks were better soldiers because self-respect forbad deserting comrades. Trade could thrive because men learned, in the clublike polis, to be reliable in their dealings. In common understanding and purpose, government was easy and effective and there was little crime despite the lack of police controls (Botsford, 1939). As Aeschylus blessed the Athenians, "May they return joy for joy in a spirit of common love, and may they hate of one accord; for therein lieth the cure of many an evil in the world" (*Eumenides*, 984-987).

Hellenistic Civilization

The cultural empire of Greece spread as political eminence fell. In a demonstration of intellectual power unmatched in history except by Sumeria and by Western civilization, Greek ways and civilization imposed themselves on myriad peoples and states, and lands of venerable and refined civilization took on at least a Greek veneer. Alexander did most to carry Greek learning and ways over the whole Near East; but long before him, Greek culture had been flooding out. By the middle of the fourth century, non-Greek rulers in Asia Minor widely worshipped adopted Greek gods, patronized Greek culture, and wrote inscriptions in Greek; the Greek language was penetrating the Persian empire. Alexander passed in a flash, but Greek culture remained, as Hellenistic monarchies with overwhelmingly Oriental populations kept a remarkably Greek character, finding in the superiority of Greek culture support for their rule of non-Greek lands (Ferguson, 1911). The Seleucids established Greek poleis, with the classic forms but a largely Asiatic citizenry, in far Iran (Frye, 1962). Distant outposts of Hellenism, such as Bactria, showed an amazing tenacity in the maintenance of Greek culture (Rostovtzeff, 1941). The literature and law of Parthia in Roman times were largely Greek in language and inspiration (Sykes, 1951). Centuries later Sassanid Persia patronized Greek philosophers and savants. Greek documents are found in the ruins of Kurdistan, and Asoka used Greek to communicate with his subjects in northwest India.

Hellenistic writers do not enjoy the reputation of their classic predecessors; they seem to suffer from lack of originality and from elegant shallowness. Much of their surviving work is formal, filled with classical allusions, witty and *précieux*, somewhat in the spirit of European baroque. The Middle and New Comedy, little of which remains, dealt not with civic affairs, as did the Old Comedy of Aristophanes, but with gilded youth and private amours. The plots of Menander are ingenious and smooth, with mistaken identities and intriguing slaves, rather trite or trivial, like those of some of Shakespeare's early comedies. But if Hellenistic talents were weaker in some ways, in others they were more fertile. Supported by official patrons, literature expanded tremendously. Names of some eleven hundred Hellenistic writers have come down. Prose fiction grew up; love romances and the popular new genre of biography showed talent and originality. Rhetoric was fashionable, and writers of history multiplied. Epistolary writing and tales of adventure flourished. Public readings became common. Poetry abounded, from the lyric to the didactic, pastorals, satirical verse, parodies, and long epics glorifying cities of bygone greatness. Treatises in prose and verse dealt with almost every imaginable subject; literary criticism flowered. Drama was very important, as was music, now entirely lost (Botsford, 1939).

Every sizable city tried to hold dramatic festivals. Drama was so important to the Athenians that from the fourth century it was legally prohibited to transfer money from the theater fund to defense. A multitude of tragedies were performed by professional actors. Greek theaters sprang up across the Near East, and works for the first time were translated to and from Greek. Babylonian and Egyptian priests wrote long histories of their own lands in Greek, and a Greek historian accompanied Hannibal on a campaign (Bengtson, 1950). Learning throve on an unprecedented scale; the library at Alexandria, rivaled by that of Pergamum, was said to contain seven hundred thousand scrolls (Bonnard, 1961).

If the Athenians of the early second century B.C. preferred contemporary to classic drama (Ferguson, 1911), they may not have been grossly in error. We do not know Hellenistic literature. In the half century before 261 B.C. Athens produced sixty-four notable comic writers whose work has entirely perished, except perhaps as transmitted by Roman imitators. Few writers are represented by more than a few quotations; no belles-lettrist has been even fairly well preserved. Later ages, with an increasingly traditional outlook, copied and transmitted older classics, cherished for the purity of their language, and works most esteemed as school texts (Cary, 1959; White, 1927). The formalistic Byzantine empire seems to have chosen, among later productions, those distinguished by conceits and style, not by original thinking and fresh approaches.

Hellenistic sculpture is much better preserved. In the early part of the fourth century sculpture was liberating itself from the classic tradition and moving toward fuller realism, turning from religion to ornament and portraiture, just as literature came to concern itself more with private life. Leaving behind idealization and the traditional sobriety, Hellenistic sculptors strove for originality and variety (Botsford, 1939). Sometimes they overwhelmed by sheer size; there were innumerable statues fifty feet or so in height, none of which remain. They also depicted strikingly personal features and emotions, not shrinking from the painful, such as death in battle. The poor were for the first time held worthy subjects of art, as in the statue of an old market woman. The famous group of Laokoon and his sons being strangled by snakes was typical of the quite unclassic work of later Hellenistic times. Sculpture even more than literature became an industry. Under Rome, Athens made a living largely by the export of statues to the Roman market. Yet sculpture was overshadowed by painting; in the art market, famous paintings sold for prices equivalent to many thousands of dollars (Glotz, 1929).

Education, which had been private and informal in classic times, likewise expanded and became a leading concern of the state. In some places, it was sought to make education—mostly athletic and moral, but including grammar, poetry, and rhetoric—general for all free boys. Some schools, called gymnasia from their origin as places of physical training, had libraries; and the gymnasiarch who supervised them became an important city official (Tarn, 1936). For higher learning, students gathered around a recognized teacher, as in the days of Plato.

In science, the Hellenistic age far outshone the classical. Compared with that of earlier times, brave in speculation but weaker in observation, Hellenistic science represents virtually a new growth. It became independent of the philosophy with which it had been wrapped; and, with material support for schools and investigators, it outgrew the amateurism of the city-state. Theophrastus, succeeding Aristotle at the Lyceum in Athens, criticized his master's teleological approach and took a more scientific view of biology (Farrington, 1953). His successor, Strato, held knowledge to originate in sensory data perceived by the brain; instead of speculation, he resorted to physical experiments with apparatus constructed for the purpose, as in the making of a vacuum and compressing air. Another post-Aristotelian, in the methodical spirit of the age, developed a science of music; and a Hellenistic physicist, probably Strato, attributed sound to the elastic vibration of air.

After Strato, there was little science at Athens. The philosophers stayed there for freedom of thought, but scientists drifted to other centers, chiefly Alexandria, where, at the original Museum, over a hundred savants devoted themselves to learning at the expense of the state. All major branches of science throve, but progress was outstanding in medicine. The physicians, much in demand for the health of rulers, developed excellent instruments and operative techniques (Bengtson, 1950). Dissection taught such things as the relation of nerves to the brain and distinguished sensory and motor nerves; a form of anesthesia was developed, only to lost until modern time. Herophilus of Alexandria was practically the founder of anatomy; among his many achievements was the measurement of the pulse by waterclock (Bonnard, 1961).

Mathematics progressed at the hands of such as Euclid and Apollonius, analyst of conic sections; Archimedes was apparently held back from a breakthrough to modern analysis only by lack of suitable symbolism. Poseidonus measured the circumference of the earth as 24,000 miles, a value that in Roman times was miscopied as 18,000 and as such went down to the Middle Ages (Rothrock, 1966). Precision astronomy began about 300 B.C. and advanced about as far as was possible without telescopes; astronomers were not afraid to postulate the sun as the center for revolving earth and planets. The greatest astronomer of ancient times, Aristarchus of Samos, concluded that the sun was approximately three hundred times larger than the earth, and hence that earth and planets must revolve around it, while the stars formed a distant background. This idea was rejected on grounds that no displacement or parallax of the stars could be observed, as was impossible without modern instruments. Aristarchus explained that their distance must be too great, but his age was unwilling to accept the implied vastness of the universe (Santillana, 1949). His work helped to inspire Copernicus. Hipparchus subsequently chalked up such achievements as making the first known comprehensive star chart and figuring the sun's mass at 1,880 times that of the earth and its distance at 1,245 earth diameters; he calculated the lunar month with an accuracy of one second and the solar year to within less than seven minutes, gave a close estimate of the distance of the moon, and probably discovered the precession of the equinoxes and the eccentricity of the earth's orbit. Ptolemy (fl. 127-141 B.C.), who wished to adopt the simplest hypothesis consistent with the facts (Dampier, 1943), returned to the geocentric system, but he gave an ingenious rationalization of it that was accepted until after Copernicus. With such advances in various branches, the two centuries from Alexander into the Roman period were by far the best for natural science until modern times; as transmitted but not improved by Rome and the Arab world, they provided the starting point for the Western development.

The Ptolemies and other rulers supported science not only from pride in cultural achievements but because engineers, geographers, and the like were useful. Greek skills were applied to larger resources to make many enormous monuments, and shipbuilding so progressed that a vessel of 3,300 gross tons was built at Syracuse (although it was not successful). Many exploratory expeditions went as far afield as the North Sea and the Baltic (Woodhead, 1962), and to India via the Red Sea. Military technology, especially siegecraft, made great progress (Bengtson, 1950). Philo of Byzantium made an extensive study of ballistics. Archimedes not only devised various machines for the defense of his native Syracuse, such as a catapult capable of hurling stones of 1,800 pounds, but also the compound pulley and the screw pump. Nor do we fully know the mechanical abilities of the postclassic Greeks. A few years ago there were found in the Aegean the remains of a bronze computer with a complex gear system, probably dating from about 82 B.C. Designed to calculate the times of astronomical events, phases of the moon, eclipses of the sun, and movements of the planets, it was comparable to a seventeenth-century clock and was far ahead of comparable Islamic devices made in the fourteenth century. Yet nothing like it, or nearly so advanced in mechanism, is known from ancient texts (Price, 1959). The Hellenistic world was prepared to proceed to industrialization (Brumbaugh, 1966).

In this new world, free thought flourished as it was not to do again until modern times (Dampier, 1943). Philosophy was cultivated as never before; hundreds of students came every year to sit at the feet of the masters in Athens, where freedom of teaching was guaranteed by law (Ferguson, 1911). But abstract metaphysics declined, yielding place to ethics, for men were no longer so interested in understanding the world as in finding their way in society. Values changed; whereas the classical philosophers prepared men for participation in the state, the new thinkers looked mostly to the individual pursuit of tranquility or private fulfillment. For the Epicureans, vigorous and essentially rationalistic thinkers, political participation was insignificant or probably foolish and withdrawal was virtuous. For Diogenes, neither the city-state nor Greek versus barbarian mattered; he and his Cynics believed only in individual moral and intellectual integrity. Zeno and the Stoics taught individual self-sufficiency in the brotherhood of humanity, directly opposite to the old emphasis on the close-knit community at odds with its neighbors. They also adapted themselves to the new political conditions by supporting monarchy, exalting the wisdom and virtue of the great man, and teaching the duties of the monarch to his state. Attention shifted from achievement and knowledge to character and relations to authority, from self-fulfillment to self-conquest. Social philosophers addressed themselves to the rising antagonisms; some propounded communistoid utopias (Sabine, 1961). Iambulus preached a utopia of no classes and no government, wherein all men should be equal and possess all things in common. Strong currents of skepticism questioned not only myths but values and knowledge, in the old tradition on a higher level of sophistication. Euhemerus postulated that the old gods were glorified heroes.

Religion evolved away from the ethically indifferent polytheism of the polis. People loosened from the little state with its narrow and near human divinities wanted a broader faith; the Olympians became less relevant as the cities over which they presided lost authority. Gods from many lands were amalgamated, Greek deities being identified with those of Egypt or Italy (Grant, 1963). Men who felt themselves at the mercy of great forces elevated Fate to a supreme deity (Ferguson, 1911), and the philosophers spoke vaguely of a Supreme Being. The stronger state supported religiosity, as men looked up to deified or near deified monarchs as masters of their lives. The lower classes particularly, but increasingly all strata, turned to magic, astrology, and mystic cults served by growing priesthoods. Asiatic creeds, to which classic Greece had been indifferent, were welcomed for reassurance and salvation in a less satisfying world. Multitudes adored the Great Mother of Isis, some of whose statues later found use as images of the Madonna.

In sum, the Hellenistic state system, with its several fair-sized states united by Greek culture, was more than any other like that of Europe from the sixteenth through the nineteenth centuries. Rationalistic and unprejudiced in outlook, given to sundry mystic and philosophic creeds, fond of money making, with free and easy intercourse over an area from Marseilles to India, it was strikingly modern, a world in ferment, reaching out for improvement and novelty. It had labor troubles and socialistic or communistic theories. Its state-supported science surpassed that of all other premodern civilizations. But under the Roman shadow scientific interest disappeared from philosophy, the chief concern of which became to teach civilized conduct and to instruct in the arts of persuasion. Slavery greatly increased, and local democracy was stifled.

After a last challenge to Roman dominion in 88 B.C. and the massacre of a large part of the Athenians by Sulla's legions, the Greeks could only seek to please their masters. The stony hills, which had been poor and sparsely populated before the rise of Greece, reverted permanently to poverty, their chief asset being monuments to draw Roman tourists. There were better days and worse. Nero, fond of things Greek, favored the land; the Flavian emperors withdrew privileges; Hadrian gave cultural autonomy but did not restore the pretense of freedom that Nero had allowed. Some sparks lingered. Greek intellectuals could lead a mild opposition to a tyrant like Domitian and help to blacken his image in retrospect. Despite efforts to spread Latin, the Greek language stood its ground and spread to cultured circles of the Western empire. Greek culture dominated Roman civilization not merely by the works of the past but also by the skills and talents of the living; Roman contempt for Greek cleverness was a compliment.

4 Effects of Pluralism

Size

Culture being accumulated learned behavior, one would suppose, prima facie, that civilization should have grown rather simply, through a process of accretion. By peculiar genius or accident, from time to time people have made discoveries and inventions, which have been retained because of their utility and spread, while true and useful ideas and techniques serve in turn as stepping stones to further advances. But only in the Western world in the past millennium has there been a fairly steady and continued growth of civilization. Nearly all of history shows a very different picture of occasional and local episodes of material and cultural development, surrounded spatially and temporally by stagnation, often decadence.

Western civilization itself was an isolated upsurge until it became so powerful as virtually to swamp the earth, although the Asian, African, and other peoples left behind were not evidently less gifted. And prior to the ninth century, Europe itself was slumbering. For centuries after the consolidation of the Roman Empire, intellectual and material standards, arts, science, and wealth declined; it was not until the thirteenth or fourteenth century that levels of the second century B.C. were reattained.

This setback was not unusual. All great upswings preceding the one presently under way have come to a halt; and the areas of all major civilizations have seen stagnation. The progressive societies of history have been few among the many unprogressive, although so far as we know, the native endowment of peoples is fairly equal; and the progressive periods have been relatively brief. Civilization has been nearly as much or nearly as often self-limiting as self-compounding, although technology promises wealth and power. For centuries men sink into lethargy and forget much of what their ancestors learned. With some reason, Sir Henry Maine wrote, "Nothing is more remarkable than the extreme fewness of progressive societies. The difference between them and the stationary races is one of the greatest secrets enquiry has yet to penetrate" (*Ancient Law,* 1905, p. 22).

This book has suggested a general answer in the state system. Mankind has usually and in the vast majority lived under oppressive social and political rigidity, if not despotism, with small scope for criticism, invention, and innovation. Only under exceptional conditions, where independent sovereignties have formed a reasonably stable system of interacting units of suitable size for their technological level, has political power been sufficiently limited to release a larger part of the human potential. Other conditions may be assumed to be necessary, of course, such as good agricultural land, possibilities for irrigation (for the earliest cultures), suitable climate, and the like. But it seems clear that a suitable political environment, the international freedom of competing sovereignties, which permits internal political and intellectual freedom, is commonly, if not invariably, associated with progressiveness.

Whatever the importance of nonsocial factors in the growth of culture, the organization of the world in such a way as to combine freedom and conflict with an adequate degree of order is of special importance because it is manmade. That climate has been correlated with achievement (Huntington, 1945) is of ample interest, but it is more helpful in human terms to consider such a variable condition as the allocation or partitioning of power in the monistic or pluralistic universe.

In addition to the historical experience reviewed above, there are several deductive reasons that international pluralism should be conducive to a relative degree of intellectual and political movement, social tensions, and an output that may be roughly summarized as cultural achievement and material progress. The first is the simple fact, implicit in the definition of a state system, that the units of political control are small in comparison with the sphere of interaction and awareness.

Apart from the common admiration of grandeur and bigness, and awe before the potency of overwhelming dimensions, it is harder for Americans to appreciate the advantages of smaller units if they forget that their huge but creative and productive country is governed under a federal constitution originally drawn up for a set of very small states and, despite substantial centralization, has very many subdivisions with some de jure and de facto autonomy. (Dahl and Tufte, 1973, suggest that size of subunits is more important for sense of participation in a democratic society than size of the nation.) But expansion has ordinarily been by conquest, which places victors over vanquished. (As among the Greeks, aristocracy was usually the result of the subjection of an earlier population—Whilbey, 1896/1971.) It is axiomatic that the larger state (primarily in population, secondarily in territorial extent) will have a more complex and specialized governing apparatus relatively exempt from popular control. The larger and more heterogeneous community will probably be more class-divided, with something like a ruling aristocracy. The government assumes more responsibility for adjustment of differences and probably control of the economy, and its structure is more hierarchic. It looms more powerfully over the citizen and exercises greater coercive powers; political position is relatively important (in regard to African politics, see Schapera, 1956).

The expanded or imperial state is more inner-directed, self-righteous, and self-regarding, hence inimical to criticism or deviation. With less natural cohesion and sense of common interest in opposition to its neighbors, it has greater need of symbols of unity, political myths, and artificial bonds. The indispensable keystone of a huge structure lacking the cement of common purpose is an exalted monarch; the power of the autocrat is propped up by fears that if he were deposed the edifice might fall apart. If there is no better reason for loyalty, the people need a father image at the summit to keep the world in order. But despotism probably comes much less because people want or need it than because they do not know how to prevent it. A large state provides the better platform for exalted leadership, in the prestige that surrounds the ruler of immeasurable lands and countless cities, and in the resources for glorification, the palaces and splendid displays that overawe criticism, smite doubting souls, and lift men into seeming gods. There is a sense of helplessness before unreachable authority. For ordinary folk, rulership in a vast land is essentially mysterious and borders on the sacred; how, but for some holy immanence, could a single person have millions at his beck? It is easier to stay atop an empire than atop a city-state. Expansion has countless times led in the direction of despotism, from the Sumerian cities that became more monarchic as they grew, to the Hittite state, in which authority shifted from the council to the king as the empire expanded (Hicks, 1974), through the Roman empire that sought to remain republican, to the Russian, crushing the people, as Kliuchevsky noted, in proportion to the weight of empire: "On the contrary, in proportion as Russian territory expanded with the growth of the strength of the nation, the nation's internal freedom became restricted" (Kliuchevsky, 1913, p. 4).

The smaller sovereign state has corresponding advantages from the point of view of limited government. Montesquieu assumed that a democratic state had to be small while very large ones were invariably despotic, and writers from Rousseau to Robert Dahl (Dahl and Tufte, 1973) have pointed out how much more effective popular participation should be in the smaller unit. The leaders of the small states cannot rule absolutely unless they can seal their borders; this is by definition an impossibility in the state system. They must face the people and deal directly with them, while an emperor learns of their wants and needs only what his officials report. A contemporary of Confucius observed that great states cared only for prestige, but lesser ones were concerned with the welfare of the people (R. Walker, 1953). The more life is international, that is, free from the control of any state, the opener the society and culture.

Autocracy comes hard where the citizens know each other and the tyrant cannot raise himself out of the sight of ordinary men; at best, he can tyrannize only to the extent that his character is strong. The leader of a modest state cannot enjoy the absolute power that corrodes the character of imperial rulers. Tyrants of Greek and Italian city-states rose and maintained themselves by personal strength and craft; they were likely to be overthrown as soon as they made a serious mistake or lost their flair, much as primitive tribes disposed of the petty god-king when his magic failed. Where the people know each other and their sovereigns, political myth and consecrated despotism fail. Rulers of small states have to be more aware of their subjects' needs and open to consultation; people correspondingly have less veneration for the authorities. Respect is less, though love may be greater, close at hand; proverbially, a man is no hero to his valet. Contrariwise, the provinces are likely to hold sacrosanct the monarch whom they know only as a distant, awesome principle of power. Roman provincials were much readier to exalt the divinity of Caesar than were the inhabitants of the capital. They were the first to erect statues to Augustus; and they insisted on regarding Tiberius as a god upon his death, although the Senate refused deification (White, 1927).

In a small state the armed forces, unless hired from abroad, are less suitable as an instrument of repression; the ruler of a huge domain, controlling the center, can mobilize the imperial forces against any local dissent. The expansion of Rome converted the army from a body of armed citizens to the maker first of dictators, then of caesars. It has been a regular practice of great empires to station troops outside their native areas; the Cossacks were the standby of the tsars. The larger the empire, the more foreign the military forces to the people, and the smaller the proportion of the population needed to be kept under arms to intimidate the rest.

The intimacy and informality of the smaller state also tend to curtail arbitrary powers. Its society will be more homogeneous and probably better able to settle differences informally. Everything in it can be less structured and formal. Amateurs can manage a city-state, but the citizens who were at home in the polis assembly would have had to admit ignorance of the affairs of a large and necessarily bureaucratic polity. In any very big organization, control tends to gravitate into the hands of those who manage lines of authority, and the greater differentiation of rulers and ruled also means greater divergence of purposes and less responsibility. The larger the structure, the harder for the individual to understand its workings, to reject its verdicts, or to organize an opposition; the control of the few is proportional to the incapacity of the many. People identify more closely with the smaller group; in the more intimate society, they feel less need of the psychological security of the strong hand. A smaller group can discuss and perhaps reach a consensus or make their own law; a large mass requires direction and leadership, the many at best consenting, more likely tolerating, what the few decide. Smaller government means less government.

Size is mostly a matter of numbers of people, making government more complex and less manageable, much as a large mob is less rational than a small assemblage. It is also a matter of territorial extent. When rulers are farther away, they are less controllable, and scattered people are less able to get together against the rulership. In closer contact, as in a town, people can assert themselves collectively, as agriculturists cannot. The effects of size, moreover, are conditioned by technology. Ease of movement, the ability of people to spread information and learn about the affairs of the state, and the awareness of events in the broader sphere all serve, in the well-worn phrase, to shrink the world or to make more of civilization international with a given size of political unit. The ordinary African kingdom of some hundreds of thousands—such as that of Dahomey, the Ganda, or the Bantu empire—has been thoroughly despotic. On the other hand, it is possible today for states of many millions to be administered with considerable responsibility to popular feelings.

Interaction and Variety

Even if the ruler of a small state in the state system could be formally absolute at home, his power is limited by the fact that he rules only a corner of his world. Part of the affairs of the people must be beyond his power; and this proportion increases with the division of the world more than geometry of itself would indicate; there are more borders and the borders become more permeable. Not only is the alternative world farther away physically from the people of the empire; it is easier to build a wall around the great state to enclose and more thoroughly subdue it. There is less border for the given territory, and there is less need and less incentive for anyone to look abroad for material or intellectual needs.

The division of authority in the world, moreover, implies variety; and the coexistence of independent states not only favors the autonomy of people but stimulates creativity. Conflicting powers and interests make room for individual ideas and innovative concepts. If the division of Greece gave freedom to think, variety gave materials. Among the large number of affined states, each a neighbor of the others by sea, there was no single accepted right but a multiplicity of constitutions. Aristotle, having migrated from polis to polis, drew on the institutions of 158 for his treatise on *Politics;* and he shaped his ideal, a middle-class compromise, by mixing the elements of various types. In Greece, nothing was or could be fixed and settled; improvement always seemed possible; no master could impose his fiat or dogma. Doubt and inquiry were mixed with hope and ambition; quarrelsomeness went with creativity. New ideas are born of the anarchy of disorder and the confrontation of differences. As the Roman world was settling down to somnolence, near the beginning of the second century A.D., Pliny wondered that there had been so many scholars in the contentious Greek world, so few in the peaceful empire (*Natural History,* II, pp. 17-18).

The logic is the same as that of biological evolution: a number of partly separated environments with partial or intermittent communication offer favorable conditions for the emergence of new forms. In a divided area there are more possibilities of divergent trends than within a single population, and mutations and new combinations have better chances of becoming established. When barriers are after a time removed, as when an island group becomes a single land, the best adapted of the variants can impose itself; cross-fertilization may also offer favorable possibilities of forward leaps. Variation, separate development, and recombination yield new order (Shull, 1951; Merrell, 1962). In this manner, the variety of life on earth has gone up and down with the splitting and fusing of continents (Valentine and Moorer, 1974).

The evolution of ideas comes about through something of a random input like mutations, with competition and selection by the sieve of utility or suitability, subject to recombinations, with each advance providing a basis for further advances. And in this process, as in biological evolution, there needs to be both separation and communication, with groups large enough for stability or order but small enough for variation or freedom, set apart but not isolated, intermingling without uniformity.

Movement

The multiplicity of sovereignties offers not only variety but choice, that is, freedom, through the ability of men to move from one jurisdiction to another. Not only are men aware of different ways and institutions, able to demand for themselves rights that their neighbors have or seem to have; they can remove themselves from a tyranny, and the mere knowledge that this is possible undermines coercive power. If dissenters can go abroad, it is difficult to repress dissent. Unpopular regimes are insecure if neighbors are prepared to shelter and encourage nonconformists. Hence, rulers must act with restraint and govern for the benefit of the community; they may, as often related of ancient kings, offer incentives for men, especially merchants, to come to their realm.

Movement has been especially facilitated by sea. It is easy to carry passengers and goods by ship, difficult to launch an amphibious invasion; the waters serve as highway, moat, and territorial demarcation. The breadth of the sea invites the broadest contacts. On land a nation touches only a few, but each seaport is in contact with an indefinite number of others. When sailors feared to get out of sight of land, no area was so made for a maritime civilization as the interpenetrating land and sea of Greece, where each polis dealt with scores of others whom it could not hope to conquer. With reason, Plato spoke in his *Laws* (705) of the sea as "begetting in the souls of men uncertain and unfaithful ways." While philosopher-scientists of eastern, maritime Greece, such as Heraclitus and Democritus, forwarded empirical truth-seeking, those of the less exposed western lands, as Pythagoras, Parmenides, and Empedocles, rather hindered it by mysticism and absolutism (Farrington, 1953). For them, conduct was more important than knowledge (Cook, 1962).

The importance of the division of sovereignty in encouraging independent thinking and weakening the hold of tyrannies is evident enough; less obvious but perhaps ultimately more important is the effect of the movement of goods and wealth among political jurisdictions. When merchants can travel and trade internationally, they have some power; they are desired because they bring wealth, and they must be treated with consideration. Unlike those of the empire, they cannot be so readily hounded by extortionate officials or subjected to heavy taxes and cramping regulations. Hence the well-functioning state system comprises more or less mercantile societies; and it is given to private ownership, which functions better than the state-owned enterprises of imperial rulers. And the merchant class stands for lawful, reliable government responsive to private, or individual, interests.

This entrains many consequences. State systems have more or less of a middle class based on production and trade, alongside peasant farmers and landed aristocrats, perhaps displacing them. Commerce implies achievement by work and corresponding values. Politics deals in myth as freely as in fact, but commerce is based on facts and requires rationality. The competitive marketplace stimulates productivity and technology. Traders are also bearers of ideas across boundaries, and in marketplaces not only goods but ideas are exchanged.

Commerce is, moreover, vital to the existence of the state systems, since it creates an interest in peace and international understanding. It requires and rewards civil behavior. Treaties are for trade, and this is the first and prime reason to tame the international anarchy. It is true that there may be quarrels over trade and disputes leading to war, but this is rather exceptional; wars among the Greeks, for the best example, came over power, prestige, and territory, seldom over commercial questions that were privately handled, and to a large extent by foreigners at that. If there should be a war for commercial advantage, it can hardly be so bitter as one born of fear and ambition, and it should be capable of settlement without the destruction of the loser.

The best illustration of these relations for antiquity is provided by the trade-based Greek state system. The importance of seaborne commerce in the making of Greece is clear in the contrast between the island-peninsular region that constituted classic Greece and inland Greece of Thessaly and Macedonia, which contributed practically nothing except military power (V. Martin, 1940). Conquest-based aristocracies of birth were relatively backward (Whilbey, 1971). Agricultural Sparta, too, made its task the enserfing of earlier inhabitants of the Peloponnesus and was inventive only in discipline and arts of domination. Its cultural creativity came to an end after 600 B.C.; thereafter, the Spartan way had no place for skepticism or critical reason, but rested upon tradition and supernatural sanction given by oracles. To maintain their order, the Spartans devoted themselves to military strength, banished foreigners, severely limited foreign trade, and used immobile iron for money. For the sake of rule, they renounced the essence of being Greek.

Contention

The obvious traits ordinarily associated with the open or pluralistic society include limited instead of arbitrary government, broad loadership with participation of many citizens instead of narrow elitism and professional-bureaucratic power, legalistic instead of personal-political procedures, decentralization and local autonomy instead of concentrated authority, preference for voluntary-persuasive over coercive means, private instead of state-controlled economy, social mobility instead of class hierarchy, equalitarianism rather than elitism, authority based upon common need instead of supernatural or ideological sanction, a rationalistic approach open to innovation instead of the traditional approach; a future instead of a past orientation. All of these are enhanced by the fact that the state in the state system finds itself in earnest, perhaps deadly competition with neighbors, compelled to struggle continually for its position and right to sovereign existence. The independencies are doomed to uncertain and often destructive contention, but contention is an essential part of their life and maker of their qualities. They must be competent in order to survive.

The strife of contending states makes people valuable, both as fighters and producers, and gives a shared cause and vital interest to high and low. In a static and unthreatened society, the elite may find the relative poverty and ignorance of the masses positively desirable, enhancing their own status; if all together struggle for honor if not survival, there must be mutual respect. In the secure society the elite may with justice suspect that the poor would despoil them if they could; in the common fight, the masses readily accept and support the authority of the leadership if this appears competent. The common cause gives ordinary men, otherwise indifferent, an interest in affairs of state. It generates an overarching unity within which autonomy and variety can be tolerated. It makes mobilization by myth unnecessary; the truth of the need of the community is enough. This makes feasible a democratic government, wherein aristocrats and plebeians trust one another sufficiently to decide jointly state policy.

In ancient times the need to secure the consent of the warriors was a prime reason for assemblies. The wars of Athens broadened democracy because it was necessary to reward the valor of the foot soldiers (Glotz, 1929), and the rowers in the fleet, who were among the poorer strata (Robinson, 1959). When the Ionian cities revolted against Persia in 499 B.C., the aristocrats secured the cooperation of the people by promising equality of rights (Haywood, 1964). Participation in the war with Persia caused pressure on the authoritarian Spartan system, and the oligarchs withdrew in order to save their position. The commoners of republican Rome gained many rights because they were needed as soldiers;

for example, in the middle of the fifth century B.C. by refusing to enlist in the army they secured access to consular office, the highest in the republic (Cowell, 1962).

In a still cruder way, too, the international contest has made people valuable. War is an age-old remedy for overpopulation. In a pacified empire, humans may exhaust the social surplus by multiplication; and overpopulation makes people worthless, increases to an abyss the gap between those of elevated status and the masses on the margin of subsistence, demoralizes and corrupts. In the state systems, the cruelty of war has kept population moderate in relation to resources and permitted relative abundance and leisure, thereby making possible the development of arts and sciences.

In war, performance reigns. The more capable have a better chance of rising to positions of authority; there is a general expectation of honesty and exertion for the cause of the community. Work and effort are essential, and they thereby become important; life is uncertain but people can do something about their fate. The contest also promotes productivity by the forging of a productive temper and morale. Aldous Huxley (1969), found it necessary, in his peaceful antiutopia, to give regular injections of "Violent Passion Surrogate." As Hesiod put it in early Greek days, "She [strife of the better kind] stirreth even the helpless to labour. For when he that hath no business looks upon him that is rich, he hasteth to plow and plant and to array his house: and neighbour vieth with neighbour hasting to be rich: good is this Strife for men. So potter with potter contendeth; the hewer of wood with the hewer of wood: the beggar is jealous of the beggar, the minstrel jealous of the minstrel" (cited in Mair, 1908, pp. 1-2).

Competition generates cooperation. Virtues associated primarily with the commercial or middle class—thrift, honesty, calculation for the morrow—are the basis of prosperity. Neither civic endeavors nor business, trade nor manufacture can prosper when many or most people consider it proper to cut corners, to cheat as much and to work as little as possible, when personal too regularly overrides social interest. People need to be able to trust each other, leaders and directors of enterprises have to rely on their subordinates. It is especially vital that technicians and managers, whom no one can properly oversee, and inventors and improvers, whom no one can coerce, should feel their responsibility. In no sphere can rules be drawn to meet all possibilities of deceit and cheating, and attempts to regulate too much lead to disrespect for the law. With good teamwork plus individual effort, where people are at once thrifty and charitable, they grow rich in relative poverty of natural resources. For Athens, literary excellence was not so important as the honesty of the bankers, whose records were acceptable as legal proof (Glotz, 1926). In Hellenistic times Rhodes gained commercial preeminence, it is said, for no other reason than moral qualities (King, 1914).

The relative prosperity of state systems also serves to set them apart from their outer worlds and gives a sense of superiority and confidence; this, in opposition to the fatalistic resignation of the poor, has undoubtedly contributed enormously to their creativity. People who feel sure of themselves question, experiment, and invent; those with no basis of self-assurance do as their ancestors did or as the authorities decree.

But it is not enough that the independent states are relatively productive. If they were merely rich, they would be all too easily overcome and looted by larger powers. They have to compensate for their smallness by superior fighting capacity through superior morale. In the battles of antiquity, the biggest asset was order and coherence. A huge army in disorder was helpless, and the basic aim in battle was ordinarily to break the enemy's ranks. Victory required above all determination and discipline, and these were best achieved by the states wherein men grew up with the idea that theirs was a community in perennial and potentially dangerous competition. It was by this virtue (together with superior weapons) that the Greeks could defeat the Persians who vastly outnumbered them, although the Persian empire in its earlier and more vigorous times made exceptional efforts to enlist the loyalty of its subjects. It is by no means necessary that peoples belong to a state system as here defined in order to make excellent or superb soldiers; but the conquering nations, from Hittites and Assyrians to central Asian horsemen, have uniformly learned their martial capacities in the school of contest and danger, probably engaged, as in the case of Mongols and Turks, in chronic internecine strife. In each case, after military capacities reaped an empire, they radically diminished until the great domain was less potent than the marauding tribesmen had once been.

The most fractionated of state systems, the Greek was the most competitive, as the many states vied for standing or improvement in the world of which they were jointly masters. According to Heraclitus, conflict made the world and ruled it (Chamoux, 1963); the atmosphere was of rivalry and emulation, both collective and individual. Through the fifth century, the prime function of art was the glorification of the polis. No other people, so far as is known, has been so imbued with the passion for victory, so given to races and sporting competitions, in which skill and intelligence were more esteemed than brawn. Prizes, usually only symbolic, were adjudged for the best ode or play; actors rivaled with actors (Kitto, 1951), like the athletes in the games; there were honors for outfitting the best ship or making the best statue. There was an award for the tribe adjudged best in its month's service as executive committee of the council (Glotz, 1926). There were crowns for civic service. Isocrates looked back upon the days of Athenian greatness as the time when men rivaled most of all to do service for the state (Glover, 1926).

The sometimes friendly, often bitter and dangerous interaction of the city-states made interesting all community endeavor. Everyone could feel that his part was vital. The polis gave maximum opportunities and expected maximum return; in it man could be Aristotle's "political animal," whose fruition was civic life. An individual's world was intimate, integrated, and important; in it, competition and individualism concorded with cooperation and duty, and the one could be loyal to himself and to the community. Nowhere else was it so easy to be a rounded citizen, as was the Greek ideal. Thus, despite bitter factional struggles arising from the intense political life and feverish ambitions, like those of the Italian cities of the Renaissance, the Greeks were strong as individuals and as communities and excelled in art, philosophy, production, and soldiering alike.

Generality

ANCIENT CIVILIZATIONS

If the principles here outlined are valid, they should be valid universally. This means in particular that the form-universe of all great civilizations must have been created in a competitive-pluralistic world of divided sovereignties within a cultural unity. It also implies that groups of sovereign or near sovereign entities that do not form effective state systems may be expected to show some of the same characteristics, the state systems and universal empires-being only extremes of a continuum. Moreover, the same basic patterns should be applicable, with due appreciation of differences of technology, to prehistory and to the present world.

Evidence does not, however, permit a categoric affirmation that all civilizations have had their origin in something recognizably like a state system. This was clearly the case with the Sumerian-Babylonian, Indian, Chinese, Greco-Roman, and Western. The formative period of the Indus Valley civilization, centered on Harappa and Mohendjo-Daro, is still buried if not obliterated. The best that can be said is that this culture, flourishing about 2300 to 1750 B.C., was apparently unified and singularly static.

In the case of Peruvian culture, however, if rulership may be inferred from pottery, it seems that the time of creative development was one of multiple sovereignties; these were followed by big and less creative empires, the last of which was the Inca. Especially during several centuries after 250 A.D., there were numerous regional centers, supposedly corresponding to states; this was a time of rapid change and new techniques, different styles and freshness and freedom in design contrasting with the stylization and uniformity of later days (Bushnell, 1957; Brundage, 1963). Art and technology, apparently spread by voluntary borrowing (Service, 1975), reached levels not later surpassed. Toward the end of this period, as pottery came to special elegance, there were wars of conquest leading to imperial unification (Lanning, 1967). Whether there was such a sequence or sequences in Meso-American antiquity remains unclear in the sketchiness of the record (Sanders and Price, 1968).

Egypt is closest to being a counterexample. It appears unified at the beginning of the historical record. But at least foundations were laid in predynastic times, which had invented a decimal system of numeration and an accurate calendar, developed funeral customs, and set the religious styles of their distant descendants (Fairservis, 1962; Aldred, 1961). Prior to unification under Menes (c. 3000 B.C.), towns carried on an extensive commerce with each other and with Nubia up the Nile and Syria by sea (Cottrell, 1963). Their territories, separated by branches and arms of the Nile, more or less corresponded to the historic nomes, of which there were about twenty in the small territory of lower Egypt. Although close together, they differed culturally; and each was presumably independent, economically and religiously, of its neighbors (Hayes, 1953). There were leagues and partial hegemonies, as some of the little units were able to dominate others, while commerce led to mutual recognition of divinities and juridical relations. The spreading cult of Osiris may have been associated with a rising merchant class, and there seems to have been arbitration by the oracle at Heliopolis, a recognized shrine city. It has been inferred that autonomous towns were ruled by councils, "ten men," without divine sanction (Pirenne, 1961).

Conquest came, in the classic manner, from poorer and cruder upper Egypt; and in the First Dynasty, Egyptian culture was not far from completion. There were fine metalwork and jewelry, excellent architecture, and a mature, rather naturalistic art. Conventions had been established that prevailed for millennia thereafter, such as the curious Egyptian style of presenting the human figure. Sculpture had reached an excellence hardly surpassed later, except in size (Murray, 1963). The art of writing had all the essential features it ever attained; syllabic and with signs for single sounds, it was on the verge of an alphabet, as anything could potentially be spelled out.

Nonetheless, Egyptian culture continued to advance, especially in arts of building, through the first four dynasties, a period of perhaps five hundred years. Unless the Egyptian empire was somehow quite exceptional, this would imply that there must have been only slack or intermittently strong central rulership; and there is evidence that this was the case. Not until the Fourth Dynasty was centralization completed, and only in the Fifth did deification of the monarch reach its culmination (Childe, 1951). Consolidation then meant the near cessation of cultural progress. The early period of Egyptian history, through the Third Dynasty, gives an impression of chaos by contrast with the nearly changeless Egypt of later days (Fairservis, 1962). The art of the first dynasties was never excelled (Breasted, 1937). The script developed no further, remaining a complicated mixture of ideographs and phonetic signs and indicators. The techniques of monumental building, an art appropriate for the empire, also reached a climax early, as pharaohs gloried in resources and in the capacity to mobilize labor. The Third Dynasty began the construction of pyramids; the Great Pyramid, one of the grandest monuments ever conceived, was built early in the Fourth. Thereafter the construction declined, as the Egyptian became among the most static of cultures.

PHOENICIA

In some cases, small states have formed a group somewhat like a state system, but too much overshadowed by bigger powers to develop fully and autonomously. The best example is the villages on the islands and bays of the sheltered coast of present-day Lebanon, which about 1150 B.C. gained independence of Egypt. Scores of little ports, each free and sovereign in a total area a tenth the size of Belgium or Switzerland, rose to extraordinary prosperity as the chief carriers of the Mediterranean, intermediaries between the Near East and the slowly rising lands to the west. Led by the cities of Tyre and Sidon, they were soon founding colonies, at first and primarily trading posts, in Cyprus, Sicily, North Africa (especially Carthage, near present Tunis), southern France, and Spain. In the ninth century the Assyrians established their dominance and exacted tribute; but the Phoenicians were fairly autonomous as tributaries, while Tyre, located on an offshore island, managed to remain independent for another three hundred years. Later the Phoenicians came under Persian sway, but they were rather vassals than subjects, and the Phoenician fleet was one of the greatest assets of Darius and Xerxes in the wars against the Greeks (Harden, 1962).

The cities naturally competed with each other, for commerce if not hegemony; and like the Greeks, they were unable ever to unite. But they were too business-minded and too much subject to foreign powers to fight much among themselves. Of their internal political life, little is known. The merchant class was strong, and probably all the cities evolved a degree of republican government at some time. Tyre early had government by king and council, the royal powers being much restricted by the wealthy families; Isaiah speaks of Tyre, "whose merchants are princes" (23:8). In the sixth century, the council became supreme and established a republic with one or two executive officers called suffetes holding office for short, probably annual, terms (Moscati, 1968). Under Persian influence kingship was restored, but it is possible that the Phoenicians were as devoted to freedom as the Greeks, since slavery had no place in their society. Carthage had a government by two elected officers, an aristocratic senate, and the general assembly of citizens. Its republican constitution was sufficiently well ordered to win the praise of Aristotle, who generally held non-Greeks to be natural slaves.

The Phoenicians are best remembered for the alphabet, which they at least improved and passed on to the Greeks and many other peoples. Despite the minuteness of their land, they were so prominent in Egypt that their language greatly influenced Egyptian for about five hundred years after 1300 B.C. The Homeric poems pay tribute to their crafts; their textiles, metalwares, and glass were outstanding, although they made cheap copies of Egyptian or Assyrian wares for export (Harden, 1962). Phoenician artisans were much in demand in Egypt and elsewhere; they built Solomon's temple. As traders, the Phoenicians were equals of the Greeks; at one time they had posts at Thebes, Corinth, and other Greek towns. In the making and handling of ships, they were long without a peer. They were the greatest explorers of antiquity; sailing boldly beyond the Pillars of Hercules, they brought tin from Britain and gold and ivory from equatorial Africa; they probably circumnavigated that continent nearly two thousand years before the feat of Vasco da Gama. In naval development, the Phoenicians competed with and usually surpassed the Greeks, whose vessels were inferior in equipment and speed. The mere rumor of the approach of a Phoenician fleet was sufficient excuse for the Athenians to remove the treasury of the Delian League from the island of Delos to safer Athens.

But the Phoenicians appear more as transmitters of arts and crafts from East to West than as inventors, just as their trade was more in foreign than in their own wares. Their art was strongly influenced by foreign styles; their architectural styles were mostly borrowed from Egypt, the Near East, or Greece (Rawlinson, 1889). It is a significant detail that they almost totally refrained from depicting themselves. Their statelets were too small and weak to make their own world in the manner of the Greeks, and they were barred by language and religion from fusing with the ampler Greek state system.

ARABY

The Islamic powers of the Middle Ages, on the other hand, failed to become a fully functioning state system because, apparently, of insufficient interaction. Coming from the southern margins of Near Eastern civilization, Arabs mobilized in the seventh century by a new religion marched to victory over many diverse and often more civilized peoples. Within a century the Islamic empire was larger than that of Rome at its zenith, stretching from southern France across northern Africa and into central Asia and India.

But there were too few Arabs and distances were too great to hold together the dominions so quickly gathered. Almost as soon as the empire had reached its maximum extent, the ruling dynasty was overthrown (750 A.D.) and disintegration began. Spain was split away immediately, and not long afterward Morocco, Tunisia, Persia, and Egypt followed; there came to be a dozen and more dynasties on the territory of the former empire (Spuler, 1960). Yet the whole was tied together by a common religion (despite the divisions into sects that accompanied some dynastic splits), culture, and language; Arabic went with the Koran and became the speech of the educated and usually of the masses. The mandatory pilgrimage to Mecca gave awareness of the whole Islamic world. The educated Moslem was everywhere at home. Scholars traveled freely and in large numbers among the courts, seeking favor for their teachings, battling over grammatical technicalities, or courting applause for their poetry. A Mongol vizier of central Asia, to reward those who had composed in his praise, sent money to six writers in Spain and four in North Africa.

Political breakdown was accompanied by intellectual upsurge. Measured by the number of great names, cultural creativity increased sevenfold in the first fifty years after the empire began to split up, and threefold again in the following fifty years that saw the completion of the breakup, to remain near that high level for the following several centuries until the middle of the thirteenth century (Sorokin and Merton, 1935). From about 750 to 850 was an age mostly of fruitful and stimulating translation from the Greek, not unlike the later Renaissance of the West. Emphasis on religion, the written scriptures, and the need for teaching Arabic turned attention first to lexicology and grammar. Later there was more originality, especially in medicine, astronomy, and mathematics; the arithmetic notation called Arabic in the West was taken over and applied. Literary production was enormous, especially of florid amatory verse and prose tales, some of which came into the Western heritage as the *Thousand and One Nights,* compiled in the tenth century. The great capitals of the Arab world, such as Bagdad, Cairo, and Córdoba, adorned with innumerable magnificent buildings, throbbed with a life graced by a highly ornamental if notably aristocratic culture, elegant and luxurious. Outwardly Arabic, this civilization was the work of many peoples, from Persians to Spaniards, and of different creeds—Moslems, Jews, and Christians—who were, so to speak, given new life when brought together by the Islamic conquest and then made independent by political fission.

This civilization came to its height in Moorish Spain. Teachers from Persia and Iraq frequented the University of Córdoba; and its Spanish-Muslim savants journeyed to Egypt, Syria, Iraq, Persia, and beyond in quest of learning. The calif is said to have had a library of over 400,000 volumes, and the city produced seventy to eighty thousand yearly. According to a Dutch writer of the time, "Nearly everyone could read and write," while in northern Europe few but churchmen did (Hitti, 1953, p. 531). Philosophy throve as never before or after in Spain.

However, this wealthy and thriving civilization has earned more credit for the revival of Greek accomplishments and their transmission to Europe than for its own creations. The immense prestige of religion, in the name of which the conquests had been made, and which seemed to provide much of the basis of society, meant that energies were predominantly given to it; and tradition was exalted to the detriment of innovation. There was not much questioning of fundamentals. Exceptionally, in tenth-century Spain, as commercial wealth was growing, there were numerous free thinkers and schismatics; but they stood outside the mainstream. Averroës, who taught that Aristotle was superior in wisdom to the Koran, that intellect was supreme, and that science and religion should be harmonized, was more influential in Jewish than in Moslem thought.

Politically, the Arab world hardly moved from personal rule. Possibly Islam ("submission"), with its emphasis on utter obedience to the will of a Supreme Being, has been propitious for autocracy; the great Islamic empires of Turkey and India have been among the most blatantly despotic and exploitative. When the Umayyad conquerors of the empire lost power, the eastern part of the Arab sphere was gripped by despotism in Persian style and traditions, which degenerated into irresponsible tyranny of the Turkish slave bodyguard as the lands acknowledging the puppet calif dwindled. In Spain, also, the calif bore himself more like a Persian monarch than like an Arab chief of preimperial times. He was master of life and property, supreme judge and source of all authority, a splendid figure in a ceremonious and rank-conscious court. There was no notion of anything like a constitution or fixed distribution of power; everyone simply assumed the full sovereignty of the ruler (Levi-Provençal, 1953).

With expanding commerce, however, there grew up a wealthy middle class of merchants and small industrialists. The califate, dependent on import and export dues, became respectful of property rights. The judges of Córdoba were reputedly impartial and incorruptible, often disregarding the wishes of ministers or even defying the calif in the defense of law and private rights. Local autonomy gained strength, and the calif became subject to an oligarchy. Once the leading men of Córdoba declared the califate abolished and set up a government of a council or senate. Seville followed the example of Córdoba, electing a leading citizen as governor and agreeing to recognize the sovereignty of the calif only if he would refrain from entering the city. Moslem Spain was then an aggregation of petty states and kingdoms; the two chief cities were republics; the would-be calif was head of a loose coalition (Dozy, 1913). But after a few decades incipient republicanism was destroyed by violent politics.

The effects of division of sovereignty in the Arabic world were thus rather superficial, presumably because interaction among the units was largely literary-intellectual, with only a limited volume of trade and with only local political competition. It is fairly understandable that Arabic civilization was more brilliant than deep.

PARTIAL DIVISION: JAPAN AND CHINA

Sovereignty is of all degrees, from the self-will of an imperial or dominant state through the formal freedom of weak states to protectorates and semi-autonomous feudatories. Feudal Japan furnishes an example wherein the small units never claimed full sovereignty. The Japanese imperial government, largely modeled after the Chinese empire, lost strength through the tenth century, with growing lawlessness and disorder and falling revenues. The emperorship was reduced largely to a ritual position. Centuries of more or less division, disorder, and civil conflict followed, as local powers asserted autonomy with their own armed forces. In a complex of feudal and legal relationships, authority came to rest with the great landowners, an aristocracy of ornately armored and mounted warriors. By the fifteenth century, there were a score or so factually independent lords with well defined territories, the daimyo, and several hundred semi-independent magnates, in a feudal system reminiscent of that of medieval Europe.

Although warfare was almost continuous, few civilians and not very many warriors were killed; travel increased and the economy expanded. Agriculture doubled in some areas, in part because of more intensive cultivation of divided holdings (Reischauer and Fairbank, 1960). The peasantry acquired nearly complete freedom (Sansom, 1961). A new artisan class grew up. With the shift to a money economy, merchants acquired stature. Some large dealers, as rice wholesalers, traders in livestock and fish, and moneylenders, were strong enough, in their control of necessities, to stand on occasion against the nobles (Sansom, 1961). Monopolies broke down, and markets were free and untaxed (Takekoshi, 1930). Commercial cities rose alongside the older religious and political centers. Some, left to themselves among competing daimyo, secured self-defense and autonomy (Kitagawa, 1966). The Japanese became prominent as seafarers, traders, adventurers, and pirates; and they were mercenaries for Spanish and Portuguese (Reischauer, 1961).

This was a period of literary and artistic excellence. Japan, ceasing to be so fascinated by China (Kitagawa, 1966), saw its first important independent culture and styles. Landscape and other painting, artistic gardening, the philosophy of Zen Buddhism, and the *No* drama all came forward in this best time of Japanese creativity. Japan entered the feudal period weak and emerged from it advanced in economy and the arts (Reischauer, 1961).

At the end of the sixteenth century, Japan was reunified by conquest, somewhat in the manner of empire overtaking a state system. The new rulers, the Tokugawa shoguns, brought peace, stability, and centralization. To prevent disturbances, the realm was isolated; foreign trade was severely limited and it was forbidden to build ships. An efficient police system was established; and many measures were taken to control the daimyo, such as keeping their families at the capital. Farmers were reduced to serfs. The merchant class was placed at the bottom of the social scale (Reischauer, 1961). A neo-Confucianist ideology was set in place. There was substantial literary and artistic production, and literacy increased remarkably, but there was very little innovative movement until foreign pressures became irresistible in the nineteenth century.

Weakness or breakdown of the Chinese empire similarly permitted divergent, less authoritarian tendencies to develop from time to time; the earlier discussed period of Contending States, one of the best examples of a state system, was merely the longest of many lapses of imperial power, favored by the fact that the Chou emperor, like the Japanese Son of Heaven, continued to serve as a symbolic center and so helped to stabilize the condition of division. Again, after the later Han dynasty, from the beginning of the third to the end of the sixth century, there was something like an unstable state system in China. In this condition, individualism came to the fore, bureaucratic status lost importance, merchants prospered, and more inventions appeared. There was intellectual controversy as had not been known since unification in 221 B.C. Buddhism entered and flourished (Balazs, 1964; Goodrich, 1951). Imperial unity was reestablished under the Sui and T'ang dynasties. Upon the end of the T'angs, 907 A.D., another half century of fragmentation brought a relaxation of orthodoxies, a more pragmatic politics, and a wave of invention and innovation (Eberhard, 1952; Shafer, 1954), before China was again solidified in the imperial mold of the Sung dynasty.

As the experience of China and the world shows, the conditions propitious for a well ordered state system are rare and unrepeatable. A given territory, such as China or the Near East, may see an indefinite series of empires, but there has never been a new state system in the domain of an earlier one. For various reasons, even though no universal empire covers the ground, states in contact may fail to realize the potentialities of a state system. They may be too few or too big; when China was divided among two or three empires, liberalization was not great. The states may be too small to make their own way with confidence, as were the Phoenician city-states. They may be too large in terms of their means of transportation, and interaction may be too slight, as presumably was the case with the states that came out of the Arabian empire. The political units may lack stable independence, as did the Japanese daimyo.

Yet power of the governing political apparatus is proportional to centralization and unity. Any fractioning of the ruling power implies its enfeeblement. Whereas political power inherently tends to conservatism and is interested in possession, hierarchy, and order, its weakening opens larger spaces for the nonpolitical powers, for unofficial, especially commercial classes, for private wealth and power, for changes of social structure and institutional and intellectual innovation—for the chaos that is probably painful but may be creative. These principles, with due attention to qualifying circumstances, apply equally to the more complex Western experience.

Part Two

The West

5 International System of the West

Independence

THE TWO SWORDS

The greatest fact of world history in the past two thousand years is that the Roman empire could not be reestablished in the West. Thereby was made possible the rise of the Western state system and of a powerful culture, modern science, and industrial civilization. In China, India, the Near East, and so on, as well as in the eastern part of the Roman domain, the imperial tradition, once thoroughly fixed, was never long or fully broken; and the respective civilizations remained essentially static. But in the western Roman realm and lands to the north, no single hegemony could be reimposed, except for brief conquests soon overturned. This made possible a state system unique not only for its ultimate prowess but for its longevity, for its complexity, and for the continental extent it achieved. It is also unique for the metamorphoses it has undergone. Its early phase was as a system or system of systems of feudalities and autonomous towns; this attained its acme in the fourteenth and early fifteenth century. Thereafter, it became a system of nation-states, which attained its best functioning from the end of the Thirty Years' War (Peace of Westphalia, 1648) to the French Revolution or the industrial revolution. During more than five hundred years the major nation-states of Europe were virtually immortal through all vagaries of war and politics, and they held the stage of history. Now the European system has become, or through the twentieth century has been becoming, a total world system. But whatever the changes, the principle of multiple sovereignty has prevailed for over a millennium in the West.

There has been no lack of would-be unifiers prepared to take up the burden of ruling the West—from Charlemagne, who briefly half succeeded, through Gregory the Great, Charles V, Louis XIV, Napoleon, and Hitler. But for historic and geographic reasons, Western Europe proved refractory to solidification. With relatively primitive technology, the Romans managed to subdue and unite a huge area of the Western and Mediterranean world, although it had never known unity and, except for a slight nostalgia for Alexander's empire in the East, took local independence for granted. Rome made its world into a coherent autocratic-bureaucratic empire, evolved effective instruments of rule, and replaced the ideal of local independence by that of the universal sway of Caesar, seconded after Constantine by the Church Universal. Yet for all succeeding time no one managed to reforge the unity of a Europe haunted by the Roman tradition and the ideal of universal authority.

This anomaly is explicable partly by the fact that the Roman empire was a circum-Mediterranean world, the important parts of which were in easy reach of the water. By defeating the naval power of Carthage and planting its forces on both sides of the Mediterranean, Rome established its mastery. It was by sea that the legions went to Greece, Egypt, and Syria; the spoils and revenues of empire, the grain to feed Italy, came by ship, immensely cheaper than movement by cart. Nearly all of the empire was fairly accessible to the uniting waters. As distances from them lengthened, in Central Europe or Persia, the legions came to a halt.

Yet after the fall of Rome, mastery of the Mediterranean could not be recovered. Vandals and other invaders swept over North Africa in the first chaotic centuries. Then the Arabs, bursting out of the desert and dashing triumphantly to Spain, established Moslem rule of the Mediterranean. The Italian city-states restored European control in large part; but the Italians, contending among themselves, were no candidates for the imperial diadem. Since then, none of the would-be masters of Europe, from Charles V to Napoleon and after, has ruled the seas, a fatal handicap for governance of the peninsula of peninsulas. In recent centuries, the strongest seapowers, the Netherlands and England, have sought not to conquer but to prevent others from conquering.

A power controlling the inland sea could govern the classical civilized world, which was practically the islands and shores of the Mediterranean. But the Romans, although not advancing civilization, spread it, bringing the interior to the level of the coast. Then invasions and migrations erased the old line between Roman civilization and the ruder north. When Charlemagne attempted to revive the empire, nearly half of his realm had never belonged to Rome. The new wave of Viking incursions further broadened Europe, now including not only Germany but Scandinavia. This northward shift was more significant because new agricultural techniques, particularly better plows and harnesses, now made more fruitful the moister and cooler lands of northern Europe, giving them wealth

Part Two

The West

equal or superior to that of the southlands. Rome, shut off from the more productive parts of Europe by the Alps, was no longer a practicable center from which to rule Europe. Indeed, the unsuitability of Rome had become evident much earlier; by the time of Diocletian, the Eternal City had ceased to be even one of the four administrative capitals of the empire. The center of power was thus divorced from the center of universalist aspirations.

Sooner or later it should have been possible to dominate Europe from some center north of the Alps and so rebuild the empire. That it was not may be laid partly to historical accidents. The Roman empire was harder to restore in the West because it did not break down in the East. Caesars continued to rule at Byzantium, and their suzerainty was acknowledged by the Western rulers over whom they had no power. Until the Holy Roman emperors, kings in the West did not think of themselves as aspiring to the imperial title; this gave local powers some centuries in which to solidify their standing. Even when the Holy Roman Empire had been accepted, its claim to universality was clouded by the existence of the Byzantine claimants to universal authority, who were more direct successors of Augustus and were surrounded by more of an aura of ancient civilization.

More fateful for later times was the separation of church and empire, of ecclesiastical and secular powers. The Roman Church, gathering strength as the chief institution of stability in times of turmoil, acquiring considerable temporal power, and carrying on much of the Roman tradition, had a strong claim to be recognized as a universal power (Coulton, 1930). As early as Gregory I (590-604), the papacy claimed rulership of all Christians. But the pope, successor of Peter, was tied to the city by sacred traditions and by the authority pertaining to the bishop of Rome. If a strong temporal ruler had made Rome his seat, he would doubtless have subordinated the bishop and made the Church auxiliary to the state, as the rulers of Byzantium made themselves masters of the patriarchs, and so reimposed the empire.

But temporal and spiritual power were separated geographically and so could be independent and opposed. The barbarians, who for many generations had looked up to the empire and its institutions, stood too much in awe of Rome to appropriate it and make it their capital, although they were prepared to sack it. The pope called in Charlemagne, a Frankish ruler, and dubbed him caesar to save Rome from the more pressing Lombards; and the pope did well, for Charlemagne and succeeding Holy Roman emperors could not settle down in Rome. They were German kings, whose power basis rested to the north.

Separation, however, could not bring harmony between two powers claiming universal jurisdiction. There ensued the clangorous centuries-long clash of the two swords, each representing an aspect of the Roman heritage that dominated the Middle Ages, a ceaseless tension that kept Western society always at least a little unsettled. The claims of the pope gave legitimacy to opposition to the would-be universal emperor, and to some extent vice versa. The pretensions of both combatants were called into question, and around their quarrel grew up much of the political thinking of the Middle Ages. Neutralizing each other, they permitted towns and nations to claim freedom.

Charlemagne and early emperors regarded themselves as clearly superior to the popes. Anointed defenders of the faith, they shared in the papal election. They recalled that Christ had suffered under Augustus and regarded themselves as heirs of Constantine and Justinian; some of them had their decrees inserted in the corpus juris. In the twelfth century, the emperor was seen as the sole source of true law even in England (Haskins, 1927). Although his power never came near his pretensions, the emperor represented an overwhelming ideal. Being temporal head of the Church, he enjoyed catholic authority. All Europe recognized the councils that he called. He was peacemaker, if not ruler, of the universe; and to resist him was to oppose a divinely ordained power. Christian lands acknowledged his precedence, though not his power. Only he had the power of creating kings (Bryce, 1905). Down to the end of the empire, the coronation included a brandishing of swords to the four quarters in token of world rule.

But the popes held larger advantages. They had the power to condemn or absolve immortal souls; and they vaunted the manifest superiority of the heavenly power, which delegated authority to the emperor. The popes could absolve vassals and subjects of their vows of fealty, the key cement of the feudal hierarchy. They had the material advantage that their legions were everywhere in Europe, and they could draw support from a much wider area than the emperor; it is said that in 1240 papal agents took half the cash of England for the anti-imperial struggle (Thompson, 1932). Clerics everywhere, as the learned men, were ministers and advisors of kings. Within the emperor's domain, most of the army was furnished not by feudal lords but by the abbeys and bishoprics (Barraclough, 1963). The pope could call for disobedience to an emperor much better than the emperor could call for disobedience to the pope. The pope also had a better organization beneath him. Charlemagne's empire was a tour de force based largely on Frankish tribal loyalties and personal revenues, and the Holy Roman emperors were able to develop only the creakiest of administrations. The emperors also had only a feeble power of taxation; secular rulers could compete financially with the Church only after nation-states were consolidated.

It was also a fundamental weakness of the emperors that they had to seek dominion of Italy; chasing the phantom of Roman sovereignty, they lost power in Germany. It was difficult to get an army together to cross the Alps, and many concessions had to be given in payment for vassals' support. Passes were open only in summer, disease decimated the northerners, and Italian expeditions were regularly grievous. Yet only in Rome could the emperor be properly crowned. There were always parties in Italy inviting his intervention, although they usually turned against him later; and the wealth of Italy perennially tempted the would-be caesar. Eventually exhausted by these struggles, the emperor had become so ineffective by 1346 that he had to promise to enter Rome only for his coronation, and to leave the same day. The pope, pressing his advantage in alliance with discontented German nobles and the French, was able to turn the empire into a loose federation. By the Golden Bull of 1356, the empire was virtually surrendered to the semisovereign electors who had acquired the privilege of choosing the emperor; and they, selling their support dearly, took care lest he find means of recouping power. The emperorship, lacking revenues and forces, became an expensive honor.

The papacy, as wielded by such men as Gregory VII (the Great), regarded itself as the supreme power of Europe, the judge over all kings, whose titles it sanctioned, practically a would-be theocratic empire. But popes had in their spiritual powers a means of pressure, not of governing; they could better summon resources for their defense than exercise the extensive secular authority that Christian theory denied them (Sabine, 1961). The popes were elected monarchs, probably elderly at accession; reigns were usually brief, and each succession was at least potentially a time of weakness. Moreover, so far as the popes became secular rulers, they sacrificed the spiritual prestige upon which their broader power rested. Europe, with two would-be masters, had no master.

FEUDAL EUROPE AND FREE TOWNS

The absence of strong administrative structures and the splitting of the highest power permitted a fractioning of medieval Europe, especially the areas more or less subject to the Holy Roman Empire, into thousands of sovereign or semisovereign units—kingdoms, principalities, dukedoms, abbeys and bishoprics, and a vast medley of miscellaneous territories, mostly fitted into tangled feudal hierarchies, but many only nominally subject or quite free. Like the Holy Roman emperor, kings hardly ruled, exercising more suzerainty than sovereignty—a key charcteristic of the feudal order is supreme authority more respected in theory than in practice. With the chief exception of slightly isolated England after the Norman conquest, lines of authority were rather loose and often alterable, as vassals acquired legitimacy through attachment to higher lords in return for limited services. In effect, government was decentralized and largely private, the work of individuals of restricted competence (Cantor, 1963).

The situation of feudal Europe was thus like that of feudal Japan with its powerless divine emperor and contending warlords, but much more complicated and diverse. It was a loose and competitive order wherein men at all levels of the ladder gained some freedom because of their ability often to choose which master they would obey, and the inability of the lords to coerce strongly. Even peasants might escape bondage by fleeing to another jurisdiction or to a town. Everyone was beneficiary of some fixed rights, and no authority was arbitrary. Schools under different auspices could take somewhat different approaches; criticism of orthodoxy began as soon as learning seriously revived in the eleventh century and never ceased. Petty lords competed for power and prestige; if this meant continual bickering and frequent fighting, it also meant that little courts took pride in architecture and poets. Many rapacious barons preyed on commerce, but when commercial dues became important, the more far-seeing tried to encourage merchants.

Consequently, as soon as the turbulence of the breakup of the Roman Empire, the Germanic incursions and migrations had settled down, there began a gradual resurgence of trade. Towns also reappeared; the Roman cities had become almost deserted in the turmoil, when it was hardly possible to live except on the land. As early as the tenth century, towns began reviving, especially in Italy, mostly situated on natural trade routes, rivers or harbors, or where merchants could find some kind of protection. By the twelfth century, they were an important leaven in the formerly wholly agricultural population, and they may have multiplied tenfold from the beginning of the twelfth to the beginning of the fourteenth century (Barnes, 1937). They sprang up like mushrooms, dotting Europe from Spain to England, Germany, the Baltic, Bohemia, and as far as northwestern Russia.

Wherever they could, the townsfolk began shaking themselves loose from the feudal order. In the twelfth century, a wave of municipal freedom, following the example of the Italians and borrowing their institutions, swept over Europe. As though in a conspiracy, which it often was, the burghers would swear an oath to their brotherhood and form a self-governing voluntary community or commune to protect the trade upon which they depended. The commune undertook housekeeping functions, as the management of the port and marketplace; it also assumed governmental powers, so far as it could, of settling disputes, taxation, and defense. The formation of a commune thereby became a revolutionary act against the established order and was so regarded by Church and feudal state (Mundy and Riesenberg, 1958).

The communes had to struggle for recognition and charters of their rights, liberation from both the order of nobles and serfs and the tutelage of the Church, which at first held trade sinful. Through endless political maneuvering, many risings, little wars, defeats and victories, the contest between municipal and feudal powers went on for many generations. One town would send for copies of the charter of another as a basis for its own demands (Kropotkin, 1903), but the self-willed communities seldom drew together effectively against the larger powers. Hence towns had to rely on oppositions of traditional powers, as of counts versus bishops, king against barons, or emperor against papacy (Barnes, 1937). Kings frequently favored them, both as an offset to unruly nobles and as a source of revenues.

In southern France, where territorial lords were much divided, and as long as many of the nobility were drawn away to the Crusades, a constellation of towns rose to brilliance. Some called themselves republics, as the men of Marseilles wrote to their ally, Nice, in 1219: "God is our support; with his help we have gained the freedom of our city and made our Republic great and assured its lasting peace. God on high alone governs our city, Marseilles" (Kiener, 1900). Towns made little wars, alliances, and treaties of peace (Limouzin-Lamothe,

1932). Rivalry of the king of France and the count of Flanders, and the Hundred Years' War between England and France permitted the towns of Flanders to gain autonomy in the twelfth and thirteenth centuries and independence in the fourteenth. The ineffectiveness of the Holy Roman Empire enabled the cities of the Hanseatic League, on the Baltic, to acquire much power and autonomy, although they never sought formal independence. And in Italy, the power of the pope offsetting his secular rival made the most favorable conditions for independence.

It was in the towns that the life of the Middle Ages hummed, in the weaving of cloth or the erection of cathedrals. To them is owed the art, literature, and science of the Middle Ages and the Renaissance, the intellectual quickening of Europe that was by no means accelerated when large states took command and kings turned to absolutism. While the kings had political glory, the towns generated most of the political energy. It was the merchant communities much more than the monarchs who reached out abroad; not only the chief Italian republics but Marseilles, Montpellier, and Narbonne of France, Ancona and Barcelona of Spain, and Ragusa of Dalmatia had colonies in Constantinople in the fourteenth century. While Italian cities were acting as lords of the eastern Mediterranean, their German brothers made the Baltic their own and went colonizing in its eastern parts.

The cities formed, so far as they were free, something like small state systems; and they contributed much more than their share to the emergent Western culture. But they were seldom nearly so unshadowed as the Greek poleis and never so assured. They had no ideology to oppose to the doctrines of the universal authorities; they developed little in the way of political or economic theory. Few of them were ever able to legitimate their independence and escape the paramountcy of a feudal overlord; at best they became de facto republics. They formed many leagues, but only in Holland and Switzerland could they join effectively, laying the basis for small nation-states.

The Italian towns enjoyed fuller and longer-lasting freedom than any others until overtaken by the rising nation-states, overrun by the French at the end of the fifteenth century and brought under Spanish domination early in the sixteenth. Forming virtually a small state system, Italy for three centuries or so was almost a civilization to itself, with its own international manners, political institutions, and cultural creativity comparable to that of the Greeks.

The authority of the Church was decisive for Italian independence. Because of veneration for the ancient capital and its bishop, barbarian conquerors never set up their rule in Rome, which remained the pope's city. While lacking military force to establish a temporal empire of its own, the papacy succeeded in frustrating for many centuries all attempts at control of Italy, by the emperor or anyone else. In the latter part of the twelfth century, an ambitious emperor, Frederick Barbarossa, razed Milan and scattered its inhabitants, and imposed his officers on many cities. But with the moral and material support of the pope, the Lombard city-states joined in a league and compelled him to recognize their freedom to form associations, to fortify themselves, to choose their own consuls, and to enjoy all their time-honored privileges; soon they were assuming the sovereign prerogative of issuing their own coins. Thereafter, the emperor was usually too busy elsewhere to give much thought to Italy. He seldom crossed the Alps to receive the imperial diadem at Rome; and when he returned north again, his shadowy authority disappeared.

Many cities thus acquired substantial although usually insecure independence. There were seventy to eighty practically sovereign entities in Italy at the beginning of the fourteenth century. During the next two centuries, in the course of innumerable little wars, most of the weaker ones were swallowed. City-states tended to expand; and as they did so and became more active, conflicts grew more intense. One would usually be the enemy of its neighbors and would seek an alliance with their neighbors, as in the ancient Indian scheme of Kautilya. At times the pattern of cities favoring the papacy, against the background of those friendly to the emperor, formed a veritable checkerboard. However, the jealous attachment of city-states to independence, the natural division of the country, the localism of the city-states, which never extended citizenship beyond the city wall, and the anxiety of the papacy to prevent the emergence of a master kept Italy in a delicate state of equipoise. Countless alliances were made and unmade, mostly in the interests of the balance of power, an Italian specialty; it was from Italy of the fifteenth century that the idea of the balance of power entered European history. In the latter part of the fifteenth century there remained ten states of importance, five of which were accounted major powers: Milan, Venice, Florence, the Papal States, and Naples, relations among which were stabilized by the Peace of Lodi (1454). By that time the larger Italian states had become territorial holdings much like the nation-states emerging elsewhere in Europe. But they were still small enough that bigger powers looked greedily at their riches.

THE NATION-STATES

The Middle Ages were dominated by the universal powers, papacy and Holy Roman Empire, at the top level, and by local lords and towns at the bottom. But the territorial kings, from around the thirteenth century or earlier, began to build up their power over nobles and burghers and to assert their claims to independence of the universal powers. With cultural progress, centralized states became more capable of governing larger territories; and the revival of Roman law gave monarchs a better opinion of their own powers. The nobles could not compete with professional standing armies, and the introduction of gunpowder in the fourteenth century made castles vulnerable. With ever growing trade and improving communications, local tolls and duties were whittled down or gradually abolished. The kings subdued the towns by force when necessary, more often by interfering in local quarrels, demanding payments, and extending protection. Municipal autonomy in France was largely destroyed in the thirteenth century, in Flanders in the fourteenth. Charles VIII of France invaded Italy in 1494 and overcame with little difficulty the disunited forces of the peninsula. In 1530 Florence, the last important Italian republic (except Venice), was taken over by the Spanish.

England, conquered by Normans bent on profiting by their victory, became the first well integrated nation-state. Nationalism, a sentiment sometimes held to date from the wars of the French Revolution, was evident in the Hundred Years' War, which engaged England and France from 1337 to 1453. France, too, found itself as a nation in this long contest, although Pierre Dubois (c. 1250–c. 1320) had earlier looked to the French king as leader of Europe (T. Cook, 1936). France became the touchstone and model for the development of European states. Poland, Hungary, and others began sensing their national identities about this same time (Cheyney, 1936). The union of Aragon and Castile in 1479 brought a Spanish state into existence. Machiavelli's passion, early in the sixteenth century, was for the welding of Italy into a nation-state. Germany lagged. Weakened by the struggle for Italy, the Holy Roman Empire never recovered the power to rule Germany; and in 1437, at the same time that nation-states were taking shape, the emperorship became hereditary in the Austrian house of Hapsburg. The empire had nonetheless sufficient strength to stand in the way of German unification, which could not finally be sealed until Bismarck's triumph of 1871.

The new rulerships whittled away the powers not only of barons and towns but of the clergy and the Church Universal, insisting on control of appointments and rights over the enormous properties of the Church. Pope Boniface sought to secure his overlordship in 1296 by forbidding kings to tax church properties, but power had shifted markedly to the kings. Both Edward I of England and Philip IV of France defied the papal edict. Philip, supported by his clergy, warred against the pope, defeated him, and transferred the papacy to Avignon as a French ward. About the same time, Wyclif was precursing the Reformation in England, and the English king obtained considerable control over ecclesiastical finances and nominations. Thereafter, the Church lost cohesion, and interdict and excommunication weakened. The ideal of unity was waning; and in the worldliness, rationalism, and skepticism of the Renaissance, the papacy itself became much like a monarchy among monarchies (Figgis, 1907) at the sacrifice of moral authority. In the middle of the fourteenth century Florence justified its fight against Milan as a fight for the rights of the Church; fifty years later it evoked republican liberty (Baron, 1955). The political power of the papacy was virtually ended by the sack of Rome, in 1527, by troops of Charles V.

Faith became national. In the fifteenth century Wyclif and Huss exalted national values, but they could not succeed because the secular rulers did not yet feel strong enough to stand alone. In the sixteenth century national power gave permanence to heresy and made the Reformation. Luther's indignation was first aroused by the sale of indulgences, which drained money from Germany to

Rome; and Lutheranism rested on the support of the princes, to whom it ascribed many of the prerogatives and transferred the material assets of the Church (Dunning, 1905). Luther rejected not only the papacy but all universalism. He held, contrary to the medieval assumption, that the normal order was independence of kingdoms. In *Of Earthly Government* (1523), he made obedience to the lawful prince a religious duty. The Anglican schism came because Henry VIII saw no need to submit to any outside earthly power and insisted the clergy should obey only himself; he succeeded, thanks to English national feeling. Calvinism, too, promoted national self-awareness by integrating communities of laymen with their teachers. The Reformation, made possible by the growth of secular powers, prevailed where and only where supported by rulers whose interests overrode those of the Church. In countries that stayed within the Catholic fold, also, the state found itself much stronger; the pope was in no position to coerce those who remained faithful.

The Church Universal being broken, the principal states of Europe stood forth, from Portugal to Scandinavia, in something like their modern shape, with well-organized, strong governments, distinctive languages, and peoples known by their modern names—French, Spanish, Italians, and so on (Huizinga, 1959). A unique set of sizable polities, fortunate in its cultural level and resources, formed a new state system, the main outlines of which remained stable for the next four centuries.

That Europe maintained itself in a stable state of division for so many centuries of unexampled progress is historically miraculous; sovereign states seemed immortal through innumerable wars. Amalgamation that swallowed up the towns and city-states halted, permitting a system of relatively large interacting powers such as has proved viable nowhere else. The nation-state is a halfway house between two natural and common types: the city-state of intimate acquaintance, whose territory is no wider than the ordinary experience of man, a palpable entity composed of people who know each other fairly well and have common ancestors and common interests; and the universal state that represents an ideal of harmony and a supreme law knowing no bounds, the state whose all-embracing grandeur and inescapableness constitute its legitimacy. The nation-state lacks immediacy yet is not complete and perfect; it transcends the familiar yet is limited by arbitrary boundaries. It is unnatural and essentially unstable. Middle-sized states, in the Near East, Central Asia, or China between imperial dynasties, have not usually lasted very long, being easily broken up or amalgamated. Yet European nation-states have outlasted the grandest empire.

There is no visible reason in the European character that consolidation proceeded to the level of middle-sized states and halted there, no lack of arrogance or servility. The West has been heir of the Roman-universalist tradition, and from time to time enterprising rulers have been more than willing to overcome the anarchy and establish a single order. Several times it seemed that Europe had found its master, from the days of Charlemagne to those of Hitler. And even when no prospect of total rule allured, the lords of Europe have ever been pushing against their neighbors and seeking indefinite aggrandizement in the ebb and flow of scores of wars. It would seem inevitable that one, by luck or skill, should have emerged paramount.

The primary cause seems to be geography. In a Greece dissected into hundreds of islands and peninsulas, these cut by rugged mountains, with few plains, a world of city-states could endure uniquely; the division of Europe by water and mountains on a larger scale made possible the permanence of nation-states. As Montesquieu noted, "In Asia they have always had great empires; in Europe these could never subsist. Asia has larger plains; it is cut into much more extensive divisions by mountains and seas... in Europe, the natural division forms many nations of a moderate extent, in which the ruling by laws is not incompatible with the maintenance of the state.... It is this which has formed a genius for liberty; that renders every part extremely difficult to be subdued and subjected by a foreign power... there reigns in Asia a servile spirit" (*Spirit of the Laws*, book 17, chap. 6).

Italy is cut off by the Alps; Spain by the Pyrenees, readily passable only at the extremities. Boggy Holland could become independent because access from landward was difficult; the more accessible parts of the Low Countries remained under Hapsburg dominion. Denmark, half islands, is narrowly connected to the mainland; Sweden and Norway effectively form an island and are themselves separated by mountains. The nations with good natural borders—such as Spain, France, and England—have generally been more stable than those without—such as Germany, Austria, and Poland. In Central and Eastern Europe, with fewer natural divisions, nations there have been less coherent, less libertarian, and less inventive. Yet even there crisscrossing highlands have furnished some protection; Bohemia, particularly, is sheltered by a semicircle. There has been very little strife over the mountainous boundaries between France and Spain or France and Italy, but recurrent war over the open boundary between France and Germany. Most important of all has been the position of England, secure as long as it ruled the sea, yet not isolated culturally or hindered in active engagement in the politics of the continent. Without conquering England, no would-be ruler of Europe could be secure; yet England has defied all imperialists since William the Conqueror.

The ocean has been of paramount importance both as political divider and commercial highway, facilitating trade and travel while discouraging conquest. By helping to set off nations, it has made the balance of power possible. It is difficult to invade a well organized state by water. But the sea made possible the growth of commerce; until the coming of the railroads, the only reasonably cheap transportation was by water. Caravans were for silks and spices. The sea invites to broadest contacts; each seaport is a potential trading partner of all others. Western Europe lies within two hundred miles of the sea, and it is the maritime states that have led in the Western state system; the distinction between maritime and continental powers has seemed equivalent to that between open-commercial and closed-imperial powers.

DEFEAT OF EMPIRE

The dividedness of Europe took political shape in the balance of power—a principle that potentially works in any field of international contention but that is often inefficacious because of fears, greed, and ignorance or the blindness of leaders. In Europe there have been efforts, at least once per century from the beginnings of the nation-states, to reassume the vocation of the caesars. They have been frustrated, in the conditions of European division, by the tendency of threatened states to combine against whichever became too strong.

The French invasion of Italy, in 1494, began the period of European alliances and counteralliances, whereby it was unfortunate to seem too strong. The Holy League of 1495, joining Venice, Milan, Aragon, and Austria against France, was the first of many balance-of-power coalitions; and alliances were freely made and unmade in subsequent decades according to the needs of the balance. Charles V, elected Holy Roman emperor in 1519, was the most promising candidate for universal monarchy since Charlemagne. Heir of the Hapsburg realm of Central Europe, the Low Countries, much of Italy, and Spain with its overseas empire, and holder of the sacred medieval title, he regarded himself as the leader of all Christendom and expressed the hope of restoring the ancient splendor of Roman rule to make an end to wars (Merriman, 1925-36).

Charles failed because he could not force his scattered and particularistic domains with growing national feelings into an effective administrative structure. He also failed because his chief antagonist, France, could form alliances with small Italian powers afraid of Charles' successes, and with Scotland, Denmark, Sweden, German princes, and the Turks, without whose intervention (in 1529 Suleiman besieged Vienna) Charles might conceivably have become master of Europe. Charles could not crush German Protestantism when its fortunes were low because he needed German support against the Turkish invaders. The pope, pressed by Spanish power in Italy, also reverted in some measure to the ancient policy of trying to check an emperor grown too strong. Politics overriding religion, he negotiated with Suleiman and called upon German Protestants for help (Symonds, 1894). When Charles abdicated in disgust, Lutheranism was given official recognition, a double admission of failure of the imperial ideal (Merriman, 1925-36). Moreover, a revolt of German princes, resentful of Spanish influences in Germany and aided by France, prevented Charles from passing the Holy Roman Empire to his son, Philip. Spain was separated from the empire, itself paralyzed by religious disunity.

Despite this setback, Philip II of Spain had prospects for general hegemony. Although the Hapsburg Austrian possessions and the title of emperor went to his uncle Ferdinand, Philip was much richer than his father by virtue of treasure flowing to Spain from Peru and Mexico; and he ruled a land infused with a sense of imperial destiny (Merriman, 1925-36). France was weakened by internal religious conflict; and England was for a time under Philip's wife, Mary Tudor. Consequently, Philip could reasonably hope to promote the Catholic cause and his own ascendancy in France and England, and also in Poland and even

Scandinavia. But he reaped only disappointments. In the face of English feeling, Mary Tudor could give her husband no authority before she died. The French throne went not to his candidate but to his enemy. Philip's most prosperous territory, the Netherlands, rose against foreign rule, taxation, and religious persecutions, with the assistance of the Protestants of Europe. Apprehensive of Spanish power and desirous of freedom to trade with the Spanish possessions in the New World, England lent direct assistance to the rebels of the Low Countries and indirectly helped them by preying on Spanish commerce. Exasperated, Philip made his bid to add dominion of the sea to that of the best lands of earth, and in 1588 met crushing defeat in the loss of his Armada.

Thereafter, Spain was unable to hope for supremacy. In the Thirty Years' War (1618–1648), however, it seemed possible that the Hapsburgs might consolidate rule of Central Europe, in addition to Spain, the Spanish Netherlands, and Italy, and so overthrow the balance of power. In this conflict of confused purposes, religion ceased after a few years to be the dominant issue. As much as anything, at stake was the attempt to revive imperial power against the particularism of hundreds of princelings; and at one time it seemed near success. But France, representing the national state against the imperial ideal, intervened against its coreligionists. Subsidized by Richelieu, Gustavus Adolphus of Sweden brilliantly entered the fray and in effect saved two closely allied causes, the Reformation and the principle of national independence.

As a result, religious division reinforced the division of nationality; Lutheranism became dominant in Germany and Scandinavia, Calvinism in Holland, and Anglicanism in England. Protestantism also transferred to the independent states functions formerly of the universal Church, such as charity and education. Moreover, the Holy Roman Empire, or Germany, was prevented from being welded into what should have been the dominant nation of Europe. The Peace of Westphalia, sanctioning the religious split and giving autonomy to the multiple components of the old empire, made it into an inert mass, capable of resistance to conquest but incapable of aggression. If Germany, representing the largest bloc of peoples in Europe and the best foundation for European empire, had not remained immobilized, the European equilibrium would have been very difficult to sustain. When it became solidified after 1870, the European order became unstable.

The Peace of Westphalia, ending the last pretenses of European unity and consecrating the principle of the balance of power, ushered in the new age of self-conscious national independence and purely political rivalries. It also led to an era of French ascendancy. The beneficiary of French power, Louis XIV, looking to a renewal of the empire of Charlemagne, waged war frivolously and ruthlessly for glory, or, as he said, "to give peace to Europe" (Clark, 1950, p. xiii). To bring France to its "natural boundaries," fairly well attained in the south but alluringly open to the north and northeast, Louis laid claim to the Spanish Netherlands. It seemed easy to secure the noninterference of Holland and England, which were at war; however, they perceived their greater interest and joined forces, along with Sweden and the empire. Louis had to content himself with minor gains. To free himself to punish the Dutch, he purchased the neutrality of England by a pension to Charles II, and he also bought off Sweden. He had some success against Holland while this country was alone, but soon the Holy Roman Empire, Brandenburg, Spain, and some minor states came to its assistance; the English Parliament forced Charles to join the anti-French alliance; and Louis again had to settle for limited acquisitions.

Next Louis tried to expand on the eastern frontiers and again evoked a contrary coalition, led by William of Orange, his Dutch opponent, who became king of England by the revolution of 1688. Louis gained nothing from eleven years of fighting and had to make concessions to the allies. But a finer opportunity came in 1700 when his grandson became heir to the throne of Spain. The rest of Europe was terrified that, as the word went, the Pyrenees had ceased to exist and Louis would control Spain and the Spanish empire. England, Holland, Austria, several German states, and Portugal joined to make this the biggest and least successful of Louis' wars. England, for the first time since the fifteenth century, threw an army onto the Continent. Louis was lucky to be able to make peace without major losses of territory. Worn out and somewhat chastened, Louis at the end of his life admitted, "I have been too fond of war," and urged his successor, "Do not copy me, but be a peaceful prince" (Nef, 1950, p. 261).

Various nations of Europe thus joined repeatedly to forestall excessive aggrandizement of France—that is, to preserve the balance of power. Most effective were the great maritime powers, England and Holland. The pro-Catholic Stuart kings preferred alliance with Louis; but after the overthrow of James II in 1688, England returned actively to the traditional policy of supporting the balance of power and preventing potential enemies from controlling the Low Countries. This policy was the more effective because England did not covet continental empire and had two mobile and flexible instruments, navy and money, the result of rising commerce. The Netherlands also played an important part in the maintenance of the balance of power for similar reasons.

France again became a threat when the revitalizing Revolution released its energies. The French republic at first renounced annexation; but in 1792, the assembly, swept by revolutionary zeal and intoxicated by a few victories, practically declared war on the other powers as enemies of freedom. Under the leadership of Napoleon, France won spectacular victories over opposing coalitions until in 1812 its emperor directly or indirectly ruled the greater part of Europe, a huge realm simply called "The Empire." Napoleon wanted to impose uniform laws and institutions on all his subjects, and created an "Order of Reunion" to symbolize the fusion of the nations (Tulard, 1974, p. 51).

The empire was too large, but not large enough. The French soldiers were willing to conquer the world (Madelin, 1948), and Napoleon saw Paris as political and cultural center of the universe; but it was an unsound state. The only ideal that Napoleon could write on his banners was liberation from feudal bonds, but liberation meant freedom from French rule as well. One had to be a partisan of freedom or of the traditional order. There was a corresponding contradiction in Napoleon's desire to be accepted as a regular European monarch, which meant acceptance of the balance of power; he would have only vassals (Markham, 1965). Napoleon based his power primarily on French nationalism and favored France in all ways; but French nationalism, which stimulated other nationalisms, was no basis for a universal empire. Attempts to spread the French language, which was less widespread in 1812 than in 1750, only lent vigor to other vernaculars (Godechot, 1965). The hollowness of the regime was clearly shown when Napoleon's government, as defeat neared, called for freedom.

This disharmony might have been transcended if the empire could have been made all-embracing. To achieve legitimacy, Napoleon had to seek universality. But he could not match English seapower, and as long as England did not bend, a new coalition could always be formed against him. Napoleon attempted to exclude English trade, but the industrial strength of England made this a hardship. He tried to subject Spain and became engaged in a campaign he could not win as long as the British helped Spanish guerrillas. Worse, he had to force Russian compliance with his system. For the invasion of Russia, Napoleon gathered his greatest imperial force, a host reminiscent of the army of many nations that Xerxes once led against the Greeks. Germans, Austrians, Italians, Poles, and others joined with French to die for imperial glory on the plains of Russia.

Far from seeking vengeance after the defeat of Napoleon, the victorious powers sought above all to restore the European balance of power. They left France with the boundaries of 1792, and the indemnity collected was less than a tenth of Napoleon's extortions; the Louvre was even allowed to keep masterpieces looted across Europe. The main controversy of the Congress of Vienna revolved not around France but Poland, as Britain, Austria, and smaller powers sought to prevent Russia from becoming too strong. Even after Napoleon's sortie, which ended at Waterloo, France was left with favorable boundaries and kept its place as one of the five great powers.

Thereafter, except for several short wars during the period from 1854 to 1871, Europe had a century of peace during which the permanence of nations seemed assured. But the rise of united and industrialized Germany raised new fears, brought about a polarization between two alliances, and led to the world wars that would have overthrown the balance of power in Europe but for the intervention of a marginal power, the United States.

Community of the West

SHARED HERITAGE

A state system is like a family, whose members quarrel but have much in common. The states engage in close and fruitful competitive and cooperative interaction for a long period without destroying one another, feeling themselves apart from exterior heathen or barbarian peoples even while engaging in sharp but not wholly desperate wars.

This has been the condition of Europe for a millennium. It has always been felt that wars between European powers were in some degree civil wars; and there has been a community of culture, no less in the Middle Ages than in recent times. Medieval traditions, lore, and legends of chivalry were international, and students and scholars traveled freely everywhere in large numbers. Thousands of pilgrims from many lands flocked to shrines or to the Eternal City. Even artisans traveled widely; a French saltworks foreman early in the fifteenth century studied the industry in Burgundy, Lorraine, Provence, Poitou, Germany, Italy, and Spain (Russell, 1969). Maritime law and the law merchant were almost uniform across Europe in the thirteenth century. Political ideas were much the same, as were gild and municipal institutions, from Italy to Scandinavia (Cheyney, 1936).

There could be a family of nations in Europe because they were children of the Roman empire. Rome stood for civilization, faith, and authority. The summit institutions that it bequeathed, the Catholic Church and the Holy Roman Empire, represented the legitimation of order and rulership, ideals to be revered, however disobeyed. As the empire was falling, barbarian kings had their subjects baptized to make them more orderly; and ever since, the Church, faith, and legal ideas of the Romans have been a large part of the framework of the West. Eternal and omnipotent Rome, remembered as empire, not republic, loomed over the Middle Ages, to the complete neglect of Greece (Haskins, 1929). Its spirit helped authority on all levels, encouraging kings to rule and subjects to obey. Its sense of natural and sacred law, universal and transcendent, served as the basis of the international law of the West and gave order and relative stability (Sabine, 1961).

The Roman and Christian ideal integrated the universe, which for medieval and early modern men was not simply a sum of parts but a whole that gave meaning to the parts (Heydte, von der, 1952). As late as the sixteenth century, kings hardly felt capable of renouncing the universal sacred "Roman" authority that stood vaguely behind them, and the theoretical claims of the Holy Roman Empire were practically unchallenged (T. Walker, 1899). In theory, wars were still rebellions (Figgis, 1967). To claim full independence, Henry VIII thought it necessary to designate England an "empire" (Dickens, 1965). Late in that century, it was difficult for the Dutch to bring themselves to admit that they were warring against a legitimate sovereign, while the Spaniards maintained that oppressed subjects could rightfully appeal only to the pope (Butler and Maccoby, 1928).

The Roman heritage was mostly carried by the Church, with its encompassing organization, single head for believers, uniform law, supreme ethics, and universal language. The West grew up as a collectivity united above all by the Church, which represented the order and structure of society and stood almost like a superstate over the whole (Mattingly, 1955). Those outside it belonged to another world, and the sense of the specialness of Western Christendom increased with the Moslem incursions in the East and the decline of Byzantine Orthodoxy—a feeling that did not disappear even after the Reformation. The Church prohibited treaties with the heathen and patronized alliances of Christian powers against them, while it tried to regulate and moderate conflict among Christians. Wars against the infidels were held just, those between Christians unjust (Bozeman, 1960). The medieval Truce of God barred fighting on weekends and on the numerous holidays and protected noncombatants, theoretically under pain of excommunication (that is, exclusion from the company of believers). Popes claimed the right of mediation in all quarrels of princes, and canon law provided a basis for international relations. Medieval powers could not appeal to Staatsraison but justified actions in terms of the divine law, of which the Church was custodian (Ritter, 1964).

The Church also made an intellectual community of Europe by the schools, philosophy, and intellectual traditions that it patronized as the chief, long the only, repository of learning. Schools and universities, controlled or at least guided by ecclesiastical authorities, were virtually the same in system and content across Catholic Europe; the intellectual life of the Continent was as homogeneous as within a modern nation-state (A. Hall, 1954).

The Church also kept up and spread the use of a common language, Latin. The Western state system is unique in linguistic diversity; all others, so far as known, had a single language, albeit with dialects. But the West was for many centuries a Latin-writing civilization, culturally united by the language patronized by the Church and weighted with the prestige of the one-time universal empire. It was the written language of Western Christendom, the language not only of religion but of scholarship, law, and administration, used not only in the former area of Roman rule but taken up by such nations as Sweden, Poland, and Hungary. It was strongly revived but made artificial by the humanists of the Renaissance, and in the fifteenth and sixteenth centuries there was produced a voluminous literature in that language. Afterward, although nation-states mostly favored their vernaculars, the erudite continued to use Latin as the means of making their work known to the world; Newton and many even after him published in Latin. It was still an international diplomatic language in the sixteenth century and through the seventeenth century the possession of the educated, even of England, as Lord Shaftesbury said, "absolutely necessary to any considerable station" (Gray, 1966, p. 41). Until the beginning of the eighteenth century, more Latin than German books were published in Germany (Bruford, 1952), and lecturing in Latin continued into the nineteenth century. Latin was also kept in official use in some places; in Hungary, it was an administrative language until 1848. Classical studies continued to be the heart of the European gentleman's education until quite recent times.

As Latin, a difficult tongue, receded from general use, it was partly replaced by Italian and more strongly in the seventeenth century by French as the medium of cultivated society and of diplomacy. In the eighteenth century negotiations were almost always in French (Butler and Maccoby, 1928), the language of Frederick the Great of Prussia and Catherine the Great of Russia. The upper classes of such countries as Germany and Russia spoke more French than German or Russian until well into the nineteenth century; French was almost a national language of Poland. It was a sign of the growing difficulties of the state system in the nineteenth century that men began exalting national language as symbolic of their freedom and title to statehood. They even resurrected nearly forgotten tongues as a basis for separatism, especially in eastern Europe and the Balkans, with rueful results for the peace.

The intellectual, cultural, and spiritual unity of Europe was shown in the pan-European enterprise of the Crusades, beginning in 1095 and continuing with decreasing enthusiasm for two centuries. In the fifteenth and sixteenth centuries, European learning was still cosmopolitan. Erasmus, for example, could live and write indifferently in a dozen cities scattered over Europe. The nation-states, ever more dominant over the lives of their subjects, raised a stronger claim to loyalties; but there remained a sense of cosmopolitanism, especially among the learned and the aristocrats. The eighteenth-century Enlightenment was one, from Edinburgh to Naples to Berlin; and the philosophers saw themselves as a sort of club (Gray, 1966). Writers such as Rousseau and Voltaire regarded themselves as citizens rather of the world than of their own country and spent a large part of their lives abroad. One traveled practically without hindrance or formalities around Europe west of Russia. National armies had international officer corps; the king of Prussia, in the style of the day, preferred foreign nobles to Prussian burghers. Rulers were joined by ties of blood, a common way of life, and ideas of correct conduct; the royalty of Europe thought of itself as a single great family. As Burke said, Europe had come to possess "a system of manners and education that was nearly similar in this quarter of the globe, and which softened, blended and harmonized the color of the whole" (Nef, 1950, p. 268). Many writers called Europe a great republic, so close together seemed its states and so set off from less enlightened humanity without. As Vattel put it, "Modern Europe is like a republic whose members, themselves independent but all joined by a common interest, unite for the maintenance of order and the preservation of liberty" (Gershoy, 1944, p. 149).

Conversely, relations between Western Christendom and those who did not share its heritage were difficult and harsh. In wars between German princes, defeat was hardly perceptible to the common people; in wars between Germans and pagan Slavs, defeat meant practically death, loss of lands, or enserfment. It has been hard for Europeans to learn from the Moslem world despite large-scale trade and close contacts since the beginnings of Western civilization; Europeans wanted the silks and spices of the East but did not want much of its thought. Similarly, as Europe forged ahead, the Arab world remained extremely loath to take up ideas even of the most obvious utility; with all facilities for learning, with technology thrust upon it by Western imperialism, Araby preferred to seal its mind in its religion-centered ways. Although books were printed in Arabic in Italy early in the sixteenth century, the printing press was not utilized for Arabic writing in Arabic countries until 1720, and then in mostly Christian Lebanon (Hitti, 1957). The dramatic impact of science and industry in the twentieth century partially awakened the Arabic peoples, or their leaders; but the spiritual barrier has been such that in the 1960s the most celebrated university of the Arab world, Al Azhar of Cairo, was teaching classical subjects on the basis of thirteenth- and fourteenth-century commentaries (Kraemer, 1965); not until 1964 did it introduce courses in medicine and engineering.

Moslem Turkey has likewise remained outside the European system until our day, although contacts—largely hostile—have been continuous since the Turks appeared on the European horizon in the fourteenth century. Geographically, and in terms of ease of communication and transportation, Turkey was for centuries more accessible to Western Europe than was Russia, yet Russia came fairly well to participate in European affairs and was recognized as a European power from the time of Peter the Great. Russia sought to import Western ideas and inventions, at least so far as they seemed useful; Turkey sought, rather, to exclude subversive influences. The Turks failed to acquire even the arts of war but used Christian renegades for military technicians and artillerists. Only after crushing defeats and loss of the remainder of the empire could Turkey really begin westernization in the 1920s. It has been hard to take seriously peoples of different race, millennial cultural background, alien political ideas and religion, either to learn from them or to keep with them a peace of mutual respect.

INTERNATIONAL PRACTICES

The unity of the state system has not deepened with passing centuries but has changed character; the secondary and material unity of the eighteenth or nineteenth centuries was quite different from the pristine spiritual unity of the eleventh. As occurred with the Greeks, much of the common heritage was lost and much new was gained from the practice of states dealing with one another.

The universal powers receded, and with them their law and legitimacy; but diplomacy was institutionalized and an articulated international law developed. Latin was replaced by national languages, but French became the speech of aristocrats and the medium of diplomats. The community of scholars basically broke up, but it became larger and acquired more means of communication. Europe ceased to feel itself so superior by virtue of its faith, but more so by virtue of its technology. Commerce increased hugely in volume while becoming more national. Community turned into interdependent civilization. The conscious amelioration of relations among the competitive entities was evident in Italy by the twelfth century, as provisions for the protection of commerce were included in political agreements. By the thirteenth century the communes were adopting commercial treaties banning reprisals. Courts were set up to deal with native and foreign claims, the commune in its solidarity often accepting responsibility for the foreign debts of any trader. There was also occasional use of arbitration, usually by the pope (Russell, 1936). The development of rudimentary international law was facilitated by the common legal system—revived Roman law. There were agreements for mutual protection against piracy and for the safeguarding of shipwrecks (Nussbaum, 1947). In the thirteenth century, Venice adopted the Consolato del Mar, based upon ancient sea law; it contained rules regarding shipwrecks, responsibility for losses, and the protection of neutral goods and ships. Common legal understanding and better relations were also forwarded by the practice of hiring high officials, *podestàs* and captains of the people, from foreign cities, in order to have impartial magistrates over the violent domestic factions. Employed mostly as judges for one-year terms, these officers are reminiscent of the foreign judges used by Greek cities in Hellenistic times.

Led by Venice, "the school and touchstone of ambassadors," the Italian cities were the first to have regular and permanent envoys. In the thirteenth century, ambassadors usually stayed only two or three months, but they gradually lengthened residence at the host court. The first known permanent ambassador was that of Venice at Genoa in 1455 (C. Hayes, 1922), as the world of towns was yielding to that of nation-states. The Italians also developed consular institutions. Having domestic officials called consuls, the city-states adopted the practice of naming consuls over merchant colonies abroad, especially in the Near East. These became defenders of the city's interests with the local authorities.

France, Spain, and other countries began keeping regular missions in the sixteenth century, although the resident ambassador was still regarded with some suspicion and hostility (Butler and Maccoby, 1928). From the seventeenth century all important states felt compelled to send ambassadors to all other important nations to keep informed regarding their intentions, to seek assistance, to urge their neutrality, or to forestall their actions. As trade increased, the ambassadors also looked to commercial interests, and the consular office became prominent. Diplomatic representation bespoke mutual acceptance and hence was restricted to the European community except for occasional embassies to Turkey, which remained outside the sphere of European intercourse until the middle of the nineteenth century.

The diplomatic profession was internationally minded; an ambassador had much more in common with his foreign colleagues than with the middle classes of his own country. Men often served without distinction of nation. Grotius, a prominent Dutch statesman, represented the king of France in Sweden; the king of Prussia employed a Scotsman as ambassador to Spain, where an Irishman was foreign minister. In 1815 Alexander I of Russia had as advisors on foreign policy two Germans, a Greek, a Corsican, a Swiss, a Pole, and one Russian. As late as 1862, it was not unnatural that Bismarck, having served as Prussian ambassador at St. Petersburg, should be invited to enter the service of the tsar. As men freely worked for foreign sovereigns, statesmen likewise saw little amiss in receiving payment from foreign governments; it was quite ordinary in the eighteenth century to offer statesmen large gratuities in return for an alliance or the favorable conclusion of negotiations (Morgenthau, 1960). Under these conditions, statecraft was dispassionate; and the diplomatic profession, a powerful section of the narrow elite, was an important force for peace. The work of the diplomats was the settlement of disputes, and peace was their success; war represented failure and the cessation of diplomacy.

The practice of international relations advanced as trade and shipping grew and diplomatic relations became general; but international law, a mixture of custom, ethics, legal doctrine, and rules of convenience, was not explicitly formulated until after the twilight of universal authorities made it more necessary to define the rights of the sovereign states, especially in conflict. The first great publicist of international law was Gentili, a Protestant Italian who found refuge at Oxford. His *De jure belli* (1585) stressed with documentation from history the main features of international law subsequently elaborated: the inviolability of envoys, the distinction between civilians and combatants, the limitation of the inhumanity of war, and the independent sovereignty of states. During the seventeenth century the Dutch, preferring legal to political decisions, took the lead in international law; in particular, they looked to protection of trade and shipping in wartime and favored arbitration of differences. One of the few Dutch statesmen ever exiled for political reasons, Hugo Grotius (1589-1645), became almost the father of international law. Writing during the Thirty Years' War, he held that international law was based not on divine sanction but on human needs, since its violation threatened the stability of the international system. He strongly advocated freedom of the high seas to promote the needs of commerce, countering the claims of many nations to rule large areas. He also introduced the idea of extraterritoriality of embassies and made proposals for the humanizing of warfare (Wilson, 1968).

Among the successors of Grotius were Pufendorf and Vattel, both sons of Protestant ministers. Pufendorf, a German who lived long in Sweden and published in Holland, maintained that peace was the natural condition of mankind. Vattel, a Swiss, stressed the laws of neutrality. Neutral rights were slow to gain recognition because they implied abandonment of the old distinction between just and unjust war, which was still the basis of Vitoria's writing early in the sixteenth century. But in the eighteenth century they achieved more respect than before or usually since. At the same time, the idea of formal equality of states was finally accepted (Butler and Maccoby, 1928).

The heart of international law is the regularization or mitigation of conflict, a necessary condition for viability of the state system. This was attempted by the Church from very early times, as previously noted. Among the Italian city-states in the twelfth century, war was usually somewhat stylized. The angry citizens would gather, send a herald to announce themselves, and march gaily to the attack. There was seldom much interference with commerce. As the towns grew larger and wealthier, the business of fighting was gradually turned over to mercenaries, who were disposed to make wars chronic but, as with the Hellenistic Greeks, not very dangerous. In the fifteenth century, war had degenerated almost to a sport. Battles required agreement; when one side accepted the gage of the other, the battlefield would be selected and leveled for comfortable jousting. One or the other side usually had reasons to postpone the encounter; and when battles occurred, they were frequently more positional maneuver and charade than bloodletting. It was more desirable to take prisoners than to kill, for prisoners meant ransom. Generals were most of all interested in conserving the forces that were their capital.

Among the emergent nation-states, war was at first more barbarous, and was so regarded by the more civilized Italians. Differences of religion intensified passions after the Reformation, and the savagery of the Thirty Years' War (1618-1648) is notorious. After it, however, the idea grew that it was foolish to kill for doctrinal questions (Ogg, 1925). Wars were dynastic rather than ideological, and material purposes require less slaughter than moral ones. In the seventeenth and eighteenth centuries, usually not more than .3 percent of the population of belligerent countries was mobilized; in the aggressive France of Louis XIV, battle losses were statistically trivial compared with deaths from disease and hunger. In 1704, a decisive year of the War of the Spanish Succession, England won three glorious battles but lost not over two thousand soldiers and sailors. Armies spent the campaign season maneuvering, in effect dodging each other, seldom came to blows, and retired promptly to winter quarters. It was again more important to preserve armies than to win actions (Robson, 1957). Armies were, in any case, as much for ornament, with precise drills and colorful uniforms, as for fighting.

Armies fought more to possess the field than to destroy the foe; it came to be considered improper to pursue a routed enemy. There were more sieges than battles, and sieges were not desperate. In 1705 Louis XIV authorized the surrender of fortresses once a small breach had been made and a single assault repulsed; these rules remained in effect until the French Revolution. When a fortress surrendered opportunely, the victor was not entitled to plunder (Robson, 1957). The cultural values of Europe were more highly prized than in ruder ages, and the vanquishing of the enemy less so; James Wolfe in 1759 avowed that he would rather have written Gray's elegy than taken Quebec. Perhaps because of lack of experience with mass war, there were no political murders in Europe during the century preceding the French Revolution (Ford, 1976).

Moderation did not apply to warfare against the Turks and Moslems, which continued barbarous, just as the chivalrous crusaders had massacred quite mercilessly in Palestine. But within the European sphere, it was not unusual that the French and allied armies cheered each other in 1745 before the battle of Fontenoy. Infantrymen, marching toward each other in parade-like formations and gaily bright uniforms (unmilitarily conspicuous but preferred until World

War I), would challenge the other side to fire first. Truces were readily granted, and a truce might become a carnival of mutual entertainments of the official enemies (Nef, 1950). Civilians were largely exempt from the hardships of war. One could usually travel freely, even in an enemy country; passports were invented as a safe-conduct. Laurence Sterne in *Sentimental Journey* tells of going to France without remembering that England had declared war; far from being prosecuted, he was given a friendly reception. Montesquieu found it barbarous that Spain forbad commerce with England during wartime (*Spirit of the Laws,* book 20, chap. 14). Nor did war much hinder cultural borrowing; during the wars of Louis XIV against England and Germany, French influence was spreading strongly in those countries.

Conflict was ameliorated in part by a growth of humanitarianism; concurrently, war was less cruel and men were more revolted by its cruelty. For the Enlightenment and the philosophers of the eighteenth century, human nature was essentially good, civilization should be improved by reason, and war was barbarism. Leaders were influenced to mitigate sufferings and spare civilians; Louis XV refused a new kind of gunpowder as too destructive. Increasing commerce also assisted the idea that war was disorderly and wasteful. All-out commercial war was recognized as self-defeating, and territorial gains in Europe were not necessary to prosperity; the Dutch were most convinced of this and most moderate of all in their conduct of war. At the same time, expansive energies of the leading nations were taken up in enterprises overseas.

A concrete reason for limited war was the use of mercenaries. The armies of great powers were international; two thirds of Frederick the Great's Prussian army was hired and foreign; Louis XIV had troops of half a dozen nationalities. Most hirelings were furnished by German princelings, who derived a large part of their incomes by selling their subjects. Those taken for military service, either as mercenaries or under the banner of their own sovereign, were often bludgeoned or tricked into uniform; taken from the lowest social orders and treated accordingly, they had little interest in the outcome of battles. Captains had to take great care to avoid giving them an opportunity to desert, and leaders were consequently restricted in their movements. Wide use of mercenaries made war more like an expensive sport. For the princes, they represented an investment, while the captains were concerned to keep their troops alive and had a positive interest in the continued existence of the enemy. On the other hand, mercenaries like wars as long as they are not dangerous; and while wars were light during the eighteenth century, they were continual.

War was also moderated by the nature of the state. The ability to tax was limited; armies and navies being costly, they were to be husbanded. Hence defense was emphasized and sieges were preferred to battles. The powers were repeatedly brought to peace by empty treasuries. Moreover, passions were not really aroused because not much was at stake. The permanence of the major states was assured; hence, princes usually strove for limited goals to be pursued by limited means, the honor of victory or a frontier province. Wars were rarely carried to the exhaustion of the loser, and peace treaties were not imposed but negotiated.

The powers were prepared to resign themselves to small gains in large part because, in the balance of power, the aggrandizement of any one was likely to be regarded as menacing by a predominant number of others (Toynbee, 1934). The balance of power, the natural tendency of states to join against any one that threatens to endanger the security of the rest, does not keep the peace; but it prevents the tyranny of a single rule, so that a bickering family of free states may continue to exist for many generations. It is analogous to the theoretical free market economy in that the self-interest of numerous independent units should lead to the optimum result, security for all.

It does not always function well because of human foibles, the prevalence of greed and ambition over prudence, and simple miscalculation; states may try to save themselves by being on the winning side, hoping for the benevolence of the victor. But so far as it functions, animosities are more diffuse and impermanent, all powers being potential allies or antagonists of all others. Power politics loses some of its desperate passion and becomes a game to be played for limited stakes with limited commitments on the basis of cold, even cynical reckoning. Big powers are protected, although small ones may be sacrificed to diplomatic maneuvering. Wars are not too serious and can be made lightly, if not frivolously. They can also be called to a halt when no longer purposeful, without need for total victory. Each power, jealous of the gains of any other, feels entitled to compensation for any shift of the balance; this can be a source of much friction, but it is an essential means of maintaining equilibrium.

The balance is more stable and less precariously dependent on statesmanship if there are numerous powers offsetting each other and able to join for the general safety. Many powers generate numerous cross-cutting antagonisms, causing opposition to be qualified and shaded. If there are only a few, perhaps three or four main contenders, events are likely to give preeminence to one or another, and the dangers and the lures of competition are greatly increased. But the traditions of the balance of power sustain the beleaguered. Hopes for help from Venice or the papacy gave Florence courage to resist Milan at the beginning of the fifteenth century (Baron, 1955). England never lost confidence that Napoleon and Hitler could be overthrown.

The balance of power was espoused in something like modern form in Italy of the fifteenth century, as each of the five major states felt that its security depended upon preventing accretions of power for any other. Subsequently, Venice, fearing both France and Spain, tried to hold the balance between them. England with increasing consistency tried to act as balancer of Europe; and coalitions arose, as previously noted, to frustrate would-be masters of the world. The balance of power was already idealized; an allegorical painting of the time of the accession of Charles (1519) portrayed it as a golden scale over which the

Madonna watched (reproduced in Williams, 1970). After Louis XVI, there were no hegemonial prospects until the French Revolution released new forces.

In the eighteenth century, the high season of the European nation-state system, the idea of the balance of power prospered as never before or since. It was made a conscious theory and accepted goal of statecraft, a synonym for international justice, the "liberty of Europe" being taken, with good reason, as equivalent to the independence of nations. Vattel did much to propound the theory, which appealed to the rationalistic and optimistic temper of the age. Aspiration to general hegemony, the ideal of an earlier day, came to be held a monstrous evil (Butler and Maccoby, 1928). Equilibrium became the goal of the diplomatic profession, the existence of which depended on maintenance of the system. The Peace of Utrecht, signed by the major powers in 1713, explicitly affirmed the balance of power; and it was consecrated in many subsequent treaties. The record was marred by the aggression of Frederick the Great, who expanded Prussia by the acquisition of Silesia. But this aggrandizement was so difficult that the uninhibited monarch was afterward disposed to keep the peace. He acknowledged that, as armaments were similar throughout Europe and the sides were balanced by alliances, little was to be expected from war (Robson, 1957).

The balance of power was praised as a means to peace, since it should discourage aggression. Yet it used war as an instrument; its aim was less peace than the preservation of independence or, more truly, at the preservation of the international system, since weak states as Poland might be sacrificed. Small countries, however, were most interested in it, because the division of the great was the chief guarantee, however imperfect, of their existence. Britain and Holland, having only defensive interests in Europe, were most diligent in defense of the balance; but others whose ambitions subsided, such as Austria, sought on occasion to hold a position of balancer. The idea of the balance of power was sometimes used as a cover for aggression, one state claiming compensation for an alleged gain of another. But its acceptance, along with international law, helped the stability of the European system, just as the contrary ideals of authority and universal dominion worked against it.

The storm of the French Revolution and the ensuing decades of war shook the European structure to its foundations. Emotions of conflict rose to intensities unknown since the wars of religion, the place of which was taken by ideology. Conscript armies, drilled in patriotism and summoned to die for the cause and the fatherland, replaced mercenary forces; nationalism acquired violent force. International law was torn to shreds, and both sides dealt as they pleased with neutrals. The English in 1807 even destroyed the fleet of neutral Denmark as a precautionary measure.

Yet, after the defeat of Napoleon, the European system was restored and functioned more systematically than ever before. The conservative victors stressed stability over justice. The Congress of Vienna, in 1815, stifled demands for vengeance and went to great lengths to apply the balance of power, weighing in detail the potential of territories shuffled, as measured by extent, productivity, and population, using the statistics lacked by earlier ages to apply the ideas of balance carefully if not scientifically. There were no major changes on the map; but the five great powers—England, France, Prussia, Austria, and Russia—offset each other well enough that each felt it had to respect the majority.

Perhaps, as a result, the following century was the most pacific that Europe has ever known; and the conflicts breaking it, the Crimean War and Bismarck's three wars for German unification, were somewhat in the style of the eighteenth century. International trade and contacts of all kinds expanded enormously. Although the international aristocracy had to share power increasingly with less cultivated classes, the general level of enlightenment rose steadily, and war came to seem a barbarism that, by 1914, many thought humanity had outgrown. International law resumed its progress. By the Crimean War, in 1854, the British were inclined to regard capture at sea as barbaric (Butler and Maccoby, 1928). Belligerents allowed enemy ships caught in their ports upon the outbreak of hostilities several days in which to load and sail away; and similar concessions to enemy shipping prevailed in wars through the Russo-Japanese. Further rules to protect shipping were incorporated in a treaty of 1856, to which nearly all important maritime nations adhered. The International Red Cross was established in 1864 and agreements were reached to improve the treatment of wounded and prisoners. Shortly afterward, attempts were made to prohibit some weapons considered inhumane, and the laws of war were codified by The Hague conventions of 1899 and 1907. Arbitration, common in ancient Greece but rather little used in Europe, gained some importance; an international tribunal was established at The Hague in 1907.

The balance of power was also supplemented by informal mechanisms of peacekeeping. From the middle of the fifteenth century, when a Bohemian king proposed a union of Christian princes with a European parliament (Krofta, 1936), there were many schemes for joining the nations in some kind of organization. The first concrete step was the all-European diplomatic assembly called to end the Thirty Years' War. Subsequently, such assemblies were held from time to time to agree on conditions of peace. After Napoleon, it was sought to use them as a sort of supergovernment of Europe to adjust differences and prevent wars. The Concert of Europe, embodied in the diplomatic gatherings, had no organization and no charter except the understanding that the great powers were responsible for keeping the peace. But there were seven pan-European congresses (attended by sovereigns or foreign ministers) and twenty-five conferences of ambassadors during the nineteenth century; they could solve many problems by consultation and negotiation, because it was usually possible to weigh the forces on each side and reach an acceptable decision. For example, the Congress of Berlin in 1878 redrew the map of the Balkans after the Russo-Turkish war. One of their failures, the Crimean War, might have been forestalled but for a delay in communications (Hinsley, 1963). Practical necessity also brought the sovereign nations to many forms of cooperation; following the Universal Telegraphic Union of 1865 and General Postal Union of 1874, such international organizations proliferated to scores and hundreds.

But the rise of German industrial and military power after 1870, like the release of French energies by the Revolution, overstrained the traditional European system. The attempt to maintain stability through the Concert of Europe gave way to the attempt to assert or prevent hegemony through rigid opposing alliances. The brutality and severity of the resulting general wars were perhaps worse than any since Roman days, and international law was again treated like a scrap of paper. The very idea of the balance of power was discredited as hopelessly inadequate and largely replaced by the aspiration to collective security, a new and more strongly organized concert of nations to keep peace, or by the hopes of some for revolution to alter the bases of society.

Yet the independence of European nation-states, if not the old balance, was saved because extra-European powers came to the rescue; unification was defeated by the expansion of the system. When the medieval city-states were superseded by the nation-states, these were prevented from falling under a single master not only by the divisiveness of European geography but also by states outside the original sphere. The Turks played a vital role in checking the unbounded ambitions of Charles V. As the Turkish empire decayed to passivity, Russia, more assimilable to the European system, gathered strength; and the existence of that huge state to the east, too large to be conquered but too backward seriously to threaten Western Europe, has been as frustrating to would-be unifiers of Europe as England standing offshore on the other side. In World War I, even these two proved incapable of resisting the might of Germany, but America entered the lists. George Canning's famous phrase, "I called the New World into being to redress the balance of the Old," referred not to the United States but to Spanish America. But a New World was needed to preserve the independent states of the Old.

6 The Western Political Achievement

Medieval Freedoms and the Towns

In the loose-jointed medieval world wherein the papacy could hardly aspire to secular imperium and the pretenses of the Holy Roman Empire to universal earthly rulership became ridiculously ineffective, decentralization and vested rights everywhere checked political power. Authority of kings was regarded as conditional upon their observance of traditional law. Their powers of legislation, conscription, and taxation were very limited; seldom could they impose new obligations without consent. Those who were affected by a measure and would have to cooperate in its execution were entitled to share in the decision. It was a time of parliaments or estates, usually representing the three leading interests, church, nobility, and towns; especially in the second half of the thirteenth century parliaments became prominent in Spain, Germany, England, and France, all enjoying indefeasible legal rights, especially concerning taxation (Cheyney, 1936). The nobles, loosely bound to obedience to a feudal superior, could maltreat their inferiors only at the risk of their defection to rivals (Lodge, 1943). Everyone had rights. In theory, feudal law guaranteed a trial by one's peers according to the law of the land (Sabine, 1961).

Slavery had disappeared, and the serfs had at least more freedom and a more bearable existence than their predecessors of the Roman Empire (Bark, 1958). From the ninth to the thirteenth century, their status improved, until serfdom widely faded away in the face of the monetary economy (Thompson, 1932). Villages, imitating the trading towns, sometimes established communes, the better to deal with the lords. In the thirteenth and fourteenth centuries numerous jacqueries and popular risings attested to the strength of equalitarian feelings (Cheyney, 1936; Mollat and Wolff, 1973). Extreme ideas of equality, like those that found expression in the French Revolution, were circulating in Flanders, England, France, and elsewhere in the late Middle Ages (Sabine, 1961).

Many writings of the age showed more respect for law and the community than for either ecclesiastical or royal authority. In medieval political theory, the kingly office, conferred by popular will, was to be exercised for the common good in cooperation with representative assemblies (Taylor, 1938). Thomas Aquinas wanted limited or elective monarchy with leading posts filled by popular choice. John of Salisbury believed that kings were little more than judges, entitled to apply law, not to change it; and if the king were bad, his subjects had the right to execute him (Burns, 1954). In the thirteenth century William of Occam conceded absolute authority to no one but implied the democratic right of judgment of the mass of the faithful (T. Cook, 1936). Marsiglio of Padua, whose writings of the early fourteenth century inspired thinkers four centuries later, held the people sovereign: "Human law is a command of the whole body of citizens, or of its prevailing part . . . commanding or deciding by its own choice or will in a general assembly" (Sabine, 1961, p. 296). It was widely felt that monarchy was vaguely elective, although the king's son should have preference; Marsiglio held that it should also be revocable by the decision of men of worth and substance. The Church he considered to consist of the whole body of believers, which should be governed by a council of clergy and laity (Laski, 1936). In the next century, similar sentiments were expressed in the controversy over the place of the papacy and councils in church government. Nicholas of Cusa, for example, held that government without consent was unrighteous.

Such theories were not merely idle speculation; free political institutions grew up in the independent or semi-independent towns. Outside the feudal order, they were centers of individualism; all who could establish residence became free and, in principle or if they owned property, equal citizens. The degree of democracy varied widely; but even if the constitution gave power to a narrow group, this was usually not oppressive. The town government in most places did little beyond managing external affairs, defending and protecting trade; these functions the ordinary man was fairly satisfied to leave to his betters. Most of life was regulated by self-governing professional groups, sectors, or neighborhoods, themselves constituted as small communes. Differences were softened by community spirit, as youths and sometimes all citizens would swear or renew their oaths to the commune, and elections and other political events were made civic celebrations.

Political institutions were fairly similar over a very wide area, somewhat as the Greek polis had considerable uniformity around the Mediterranean world. Typically, there was a small governing council elected for short terms, ordinarily representing various groups, especially guilds; large councils, more or less restricted to the upper classes, guided and checked the administrators. Assemblies of all citizens, to judge major issues, were summoned by the great bell that was the symbol of communal liberty from Italy to Russia. Political power commonly rested primarily with the merchants, whom the commune was built to serve.

As towns grew larger and richer, wealth and political power tended to become concentrated in aristocracies. But the lower classes hardly ceased to demand a share in town government, and democratic movements were always shaking oligarchies. They were sometimes successful; in Toulouse, for example, a radical-democratic party ruled for some years in the thirteenth century (Mundy, 1954). In 1378 a popular uprising in Florence turned into something like a social revolution when the proletarians took over from the lesser guilds. A wool carder became the master of Florence. Three workers' guilds, headed by the wooldressers (the "Ciompi," who gave their name to the rising), were formed and took three priorships in the Signoria. But they were not satisfied and went on to demand a virtual proletarian state as they suspended payment of debts to employers, called themselves "children of God," and claimed to scrutinize candidates for office (Sismondi, 1906, p. 438). Such pretensions repelled the lower middle classes, however; and the extremist movement was beaten back after six weeks.

In Flanders of the fourteenth century, the organized weavers and workers, having defeated the French king, gained control of several cities. In sovereign or semisovereign polities that were at once small, with about ten to twenty thousand inhabitants, and industrial (textiles were the base of the economy), something like workers' governments could be established as perhaps never elsewhere before or since. An insurrection of 1326–1328 had the spirit of the French Revolution, antiaristocratic, antiproperty, and anticlerical (Pirenne, 1900). Subsequently, democratic forces, led by the weavers of Ghent, were practically masters of Flanders for several decades. But the curse of freedom, as usual, was disunity; and when towns went to war with one another the feudal powers crushed independence.

Even on the far fringe of the Western European development, a few Russian towns that escaped Tatar conquest were firmly republican. Chief of these was Novgorod. In the thirteenth and fourteenth centuries its elected prince was a figurehead; there was an elected mayor and council, but supreme power resided in the popular assembly. The several quarters of the city had their own assemblies, militia companies, and administrations; so likewise did subdivisions of the quarters, and divisions of these, in a repeated fracturing of local government reminiscent of that of Athens (Porfidirov, 1947). Churches were dedicated not to nobles but to unions of artisans. It is indicative of the basis of Novgorod's republicanism that princes sought to check foreign trade in order to strengthen their own position.

Italian Republics

The most important of the free cities, those that came nearest to forming an independent state system, were the Italian; and they were best able to develop politically. The Italian cities were at one time uniformly republics with elaborate mechanisms to control the exercise of power. They were more or less aristocratic, with franchise and officeholding restricted to the wealthier or to those qualified by occupation, although some tended to democracy. They were susceptible to tyranny; but this was generally exercised, as in Greece, with a facade of constitutional form. Until late in the day, tyranny was insecure and dependent upon personal leadership and cunning. Various mechanisms of Italian cities, such as short terms of office, rule by amateur committees, and sortition of magistrates, resembled Greek counterparts. The Italians resembled the Greeks in their zestful interest in politics (which degenerated into extreme factionalism), free movement of men and parties, rationalistic and individualistic irreverence, and pride in citizenship in the native city.

Republicanism was as old as the independence of the cities. The Normans made the south monarchical, and it remained so, but the burghers of central and northern Italy brought the nobles under control or expelled them. A government was first formed under the resident bishop, who was advised by a council taken from the enfranchised burghers and by consuls representing divisions of the town, the title chosen to recall Roman dignity (Previté-Orton, 1926). There was also an assembly, or *parlamento*, of citizens and a number, sometimes a multiplicity, of small and large councils and representatives of sundry groups. There were few or no legally hereditary privileges, distinctions being of wealth or occupation. Society was based on occupational guilds, and consuls of the guilds found a place alongside the consuls of the commune. All citizens were subject to military duty. The nobility were expected to serve as cavalry, but they were commonly excluded from the government; sometimes burghers found guilty of disorders were placed on the register of nobility as punishment (Sismondi, 1906). Especially in the earlier centuries, there was a substantial measure of democracy, with minimal class distinctions and maximum participation of citizens in civic affairs, not only in the assemblies and central regime but also in the guilds that managed much of ordinary life, in the democratically organized militia companies, and in the autonomous sectors or boroughs (Mundy and Riesenberg, 1958).

Even more than that of the polis, this communal government arose from the strength and influence of merchants and bankers; it served the needs of the trading bodies, the guilds, which were the primary organizations within the state, always able to reconstitute it in case of trouble. The merchants wanted freedom to do business, orderly justice, and security for persons and property; for this they made, so far as they were able, a government that they could check and control.

The result was competent government, for the merchants had sound ideas of economics and they usually pursued fairly intelligent foreign and domestic policies. But since power was nontraditional, those excluded always clamored for a greater share. The lower orders pressed their claims for a larger voice in the state, and it was not easy to deny them. More insistently and more dangerously, the higher orders, old nobility or new magnates, reached for more power. The nobles built fortress palaces and remained a largely alien and unsettling element, ready to use their military capacity. Hence, and because the Italian commune was less an organic unit and more a bundle of organizations than the Greek polis, there arose bitter and persistent factional strife. The cities were torn by bloody quarrels, especially those between Guelfs and Ghibellines, parties theoretically loyal to pope or emperor, respectively, the one more popular and the other more aristocratic—a feud reflected in the story of Romeo and Juliet.

To maintain a modicum of harmony, some sort of arbiter was needed, and it became customary from the thirteenth century to hire manager-judges. These officials, *podestàs*, were drawn from abroad and often from smaller towns for impartiality. They were given the rank of highest executive officer, subject to the council; as foreigners without familial relations, hired for a year only and under the guidance of one or more councils, they should not be dangerous.

The equalitarian republicanism of the early small cities soon began to give way to oligarchy. The *parlamento* of Milan, once composed of all self-supporting citizens, in the thirteenth century had been limited to eight hundred aristocrats. Venice, a pure democracy in its beginnings, as early as the twelfth century yielded most power to a coopting Grand Council, which chose the Doge; the circle of full citizens became ever narrower. The democratic republic set up in Rome by an insurrection in 1141 became oligarchic within less than half a century. In the thirteenth and fourteenth centuries cities were falling under one-man rule; in the fifteenth, free popular institutions survived, in the face of much strife, chiefly in Genoa and Siena; Florence was republican only in form under the Medicis. It was calculated that 1.8 million Italians were voting citizens in the thirteenth century; in the larger population of the fifteenth century, only about 18,000 still held the franchise in the remaining republics (Symonds, 1888).

But the Italian despots generally maintained the full apparatus of republican communal government, with elections and councils (P. Jones, 1960), and vassal towns retained their institutions and autonomy (Ady, 1936). The dictator-bosses needed much political dexterity to achieve and maintain power; dictatorship in the West has almost always been something to excuse and apologize for, in theory accepted only as temporary. Many lasted only a few years, to be cast down by an uprising, often in the name of liberty, that brought no liberty but refurbishment of tyranny. If there was a dynasty, it was usually short. Many despots rose by commanding mercenary troops. Having little claim to power, they were unscrupulous. However, although they filled their purses, they were likely to refrain from increasing civic burdens. The better of them sought to magnify themselves in their cities, erecting fine buildings and patronizing the arts. Many looked to glory and distraction in foreign conquest. Withal, a certain bourgeois spirit survived. The rule of towns came to be quoted on the market, as they were purchased for revenue, like other investments (Symonds, 1888). Gradually, however, as the land came under foreign domination, it became accepted that sons of rulers should succeed their fathers and that men had not to govern themselves but should look to a supreme lord. The city-states became hereditary domains like the rest of Europe.

The republics did not fall quickly or easily. Although more or less narrowed or corrupted, they continued to play a substantial part in Italian affairs through the fifteenth century, making Italy Europe's chief center of free institutions. After the Medicis became bosses of Florence in 1434, the republic still came back, fought for its existence, and was restored again despite nearly hopeless conditions. The republics resisted the conquerors of the sixteenth century longer and better than did the tyrannies; Sienna stood until 1555, Lucca and Genoa held out much longer in partial freedom, and Venice never fell under Spanish hegemony. When the Genoese recovered their liberty in 1528, they were so eager to erase inherited distinctions that all citizens were required to take one of twenty approved surnames; the others, with their possibly aristocratic connotations, were abolished in the name of democracy (Symonds, 1888).

But in comparison with the Greek, Italian republicanism was relatively unsuccessful. Attachment to rule of law and resistance to tyranny were less profound. The Greeks, having experienced tyranny, abhorred it; the Italians became resigned. Even less than the Greeks were the Italians able to expand their institutions beyond the narrow confines of the town. Internally, more or less democratic communes would exclude and oppress the peasants of country districts under their control. It was exceptional that Bologna, one of the most democratically minded, in 1257 granted citizenship to its peasants. Likewise, the Italians were even less inclined than the Greeks to form leagues or federations of towns. Smaller or weaker communities were never brought into any sort of overall republican structure but were more or less ruled and exploited, and the republics were as bad in this regard as the despotisms.

Factionalism was unbearable and incurable; the commune was practically structured for division. The aristocrats wanted liberty for themselves but were unwilling to concede much of it to the lower classes, whose attempts to invade privilege set off repeated disturbances. Internal politics were always inflamed by broader issues, one party or another being encouraged by pope or emperor. Republicanism, with its devices for restraining power, became unable to cope with externally stimulated violence. The multiple mutually restraining councils and short-term magistrates found it difficult to cope with growing intercity conflict. Armies were professionalized, and the mercenary forces that came into use everywhere around the beginning of the fifteenth century were an instrument of personal power.

At first, commerce was equalitarian, permitting the rise of new classes and elevating commoners to dignity and power. Later, as wealth became more concentrated, the wealthy came less to desire divided, limited government and equality than a firm rule to protect them from the lower classes. Social conscience declined, giving way to intense individualism that stimulated men to be ambitious for themselves only. Moreover, autocracy was in the atmosphere. The traditional greatness to which Italians looked back was that of Caesarian

Rome. The legal system was based on the code of the Roman Empire, as transmitted by the Digest of the despotic Justinian. Standing over the city-states, both pope and emperor claimed to represent divinely appointed power. Around, there were strong governments except only Switzerland: the Byzantine empire in the East; southern Italy and Sicily, monarchical since Norman days and much influenced by Arab-Near Eastern despotic styles; the feudal monarchies of France and Spain, turning absolutist as these countries were unified. It is remarkable that some republicanism lasted as long, functioned as well, and aroused as much loyalty as it did.

Nation-states: The Authoritarian Tide

From the ebbing of the Middle Ages until the latter part of the seventeenth century, during and following the consolidation of nation-states, the political climate of Europe was turning more authoritarian-absolutist. Feudalism, which meant decentralization of authority, was declining after the twelfth century; thereafter, especially after the fourteenth century, a tide toward concentration set in. Despite sporadic, often violent resistance, kings and their servants elevated themselves, lowering all others (Tilly, 1975). Towns in most places lost more or less of their autonomy to royal officers. Progress toward the emancipation of serfs ceased, and serfdom continued in some parts into the nineteenth century. The old equality of craftsmen diminished, it became more difficult for apprentices to qualify as masters, and mastership sometimes was made hereditary. Guild masters became capitalistic aristocrats. Artists were divorced from craftsmen, and there was a general deepening of social distinctions (Renard and Weulersee, 1926; Cheyney, 1936). Parliaments lost more or less of their authority in the fifteenth and sixteenth centuries. After the British nobility was weakened in the War of the Roses, Henry VII was able to reduce Parliament to a shadow of its former authority. About the same time, French monarchy was much strengthened, administration was centralized, and the king gained the right to make law by his sole fiat; the Estates General was practically obsolete after the fifteenth century. By the sixteenth century the old feudalism was nearly dead, and with it most of the contractual autonomy of the barons (Burns, 1954). The authority of the Church, which had done much to offset that of secular powers, suffered during and after the captivity of the papacy at Avignon. The Church itself, after relatively democratic councils at Constance and Basel in the first half of the fifteenth century, became autocratic, giving unqualified authority to the pope (Coulton, 1930).

Most marked was the erosion of local autonomy. The towns, divided among themselves and divided internally, were unable to call upon forces comparable to those at the beck of the kings; losing economic self-reliance in the expanding world, they surrendered to the tax collectors and judges of the centralized national administration, usually without much resistance or even loud protest. Kingship consequently came to be nearly unchecked. The Middle Ages thought kings had to be good; the Renaissance, while recognizing absolutism as an innovation, saw kingship only as power.

This seems to have been a result of the material progress of Europe. The lesser powers of the Middle Ages, especially the towns, made a world that they could no longer control, much as the Greek poleis long before them. Among material changes contributing to the centralization of power, the most conspicuous is the professionalization of warfare, whereby citizens' militias lost value and power fell to mercenaries and standing armies. Cannon became important at the end of the fifteenth century, and neither walled cities nor nobles' castles were secure, while hardly anyone but a king could afford an artillery force. As techniques developed, it became difficult for small states to maintain good forces in all branches: cavalry, artillery, arquebusiers, and pikemen (Laffan, 1964). This required money, and the kings could gather it as never before, partly because of the growing monopoly of means of force. There was also more extensive trade to be charged, in one way or another, while royal officers were gaining control of towns; and it was easier to increase exactions on the new bourgeoisie than on ground rents. The capitalistic development of towns and differences between owners and workers, as guilds changed character, also made them more subject to control, while expanded education made it easier to build a bureaucratic apparatus independent of clerics (Ogg, 1925).

The revival of classical learning contributed to the regrowth of caesarism, Roman law being useful to rulers claiming new jurisdiction. An impressive and sophisticated structure, it treated the state not as an association of corporations and functions, in the way of the Middle Ages, but as an organic whole subject to a single rule (Previté-Orton, 1926), and it rested on written codes made by the sovereign will instead of less readily alterable customary law. Roman law and lawyers served the consolidation of monarchy, not only in justifying the overriding of old rights, but also in providing indoctrinated cadres to execute the royal will. In lands never under the Roman Empire, and in England where Roman culture was obliterated, it seemed more difficult for sovereigns to set aside the traditional rights; but how much of the greater apparent tameness of the lands formerly subject to Rome may have been due to ancient traditions can hardly be conjectured. The revival of Roman law, in any case, was as much effect as cause. It had never been lost to sight, having always been useful both for commerce and for rulers; the growth of central authority created a favorable mentality for its study and an enlarged demand for its practitioners.

The hardening was general. Society took on hierarchic stiffness. There was new stress on ceremony and precedence; any aristocrat had to have all manner of servants, carriages, and palaces (Ogg, 1925). Hand labor was held degrading as never since the Roman Empire. Differences between workers and proprietors deepened (Renard and Weulersee, 1926). Slavery returned to Western life through overseas conquests. Serfdom in some places worsened; in Austria many freedmen were reenserfed.

The powers of the state were practically boundless. After the Reformation, and partly because of it, rulers, Catholic or Protestant, claimed authority over the Church and over the beliefs of their subjects; religious intolerance was at least as much a matter of politics as of faith (Acton, 1930). The economy was also more regulated; mercantilism, the economic theory of the age, proposed the subjection of all economic interests to the needs of state or kingly power, especially to acquire gold with which to buy military forces (Heckscher, 1955). Akin to fascist doctrines of economic control, mercantilism represented the victory of political over economic forces. An antithesis to medieval economic policy, by which imports were unhindered, its vogue was in the period of absolutism, and its most thorough application was in the France of Louis XIV.

Theory kept up with practice. Roman law was interpreted to mean that the people had totally and irrevocably surrendered sovereignty to a ruler to whom all was permitted (Ogg, 1925). Monists such as Bodin and Hobbes exalted sovereignty beyond measure. By the theory of Divine Right, kings arrogated the emperor's claim to sovereignty by choice of God, translating the universal-imperial into the national right (Figgis, 1934). Kings also assumed the right of the pope to interpret the will of God. Monarchy was changed from an institution into a religion, which it was blasphemy to criticize. Ruling families were held sacred; there was something godlike about even nobles (Ogg, 1925), near the king and far above ordinary men, although they had lost their erstwhile independent standing.

Some European states went farther than others. A few, Switzerland and the Netherlands in particular, always remained attached to their liberties. Some brought monarchic powers earlier to their zenith, while others lagged. But the evolution was general; with rather minor deviations, European states west of Russia and north of the Balkans coming out of the Middle Ages moved on roughly parallel curves of rising authoritarianism.

The way in which each developed depended upon specific historical conditions. In Spain, for example, the shift was complete. In the fourteenth and fifteenth centuries, prior to unification and during the struggle against the Arabs, Spain was among the freest nations of medieval Europe (Merriman, 1925-36). Especially in the federation of Aragon-Catalonia, the kings were much restricted, the towns were autonomous and rather democratic, the parliament was willful, and the constitution was held semisacred.

The old institutions showed signs of decay from the early part of the fifteenth century; and after the union of Aragon with Castile, in 1479, by the marriage of Ferdinand and Isabella, liberties were severely cut down. The parliaments fell into disuse or became rubber stamps; the formerly unruly nobles were domesticated; the towns were put under royal governors. Religious toleration gave way to the Inquisition, and Jews and Moslems were expelled.

The consolidation of the Spanish state was perhaps reason enough for loss of liberties, especially when in 1519 Charles V joined the vast Hapsburg holdings to the Spanish crown. But aristocratic tendencies were fortified by the acquisition of immense and profitable empire. Exploration and conquest followed rapidly upon Columbus' discovery, and the stream of precious metals began to pour in during the first part of the sixteenth century, became very large after 1535, and reached a maximum about the end of the century. Colonial revenues made the king inordinately rich without having to secure consent for taxation. Possession of the New World also placed an infinity of privileges in the hands of the king to bestow or withhold positions, monopolies, and estates. Governing the vast area and immense indigenous populations called for strong authority, and its administration and exploitation required a huge apparatus; bureaucratization spread from the Indies to Spain. Monarchs who ruled all that was valuable of the New World and much of Europe could even dream of universal empire. A project of Philip II was to deport all Danes to Spain or Spanish America (Lauring, 1960). As a court poet put it, all the earth should be under "one monarch, one empire and one sword" (Elliott, 1964, p. 242).

Domestically, the result was centralization, exaltation of the ruler, degradation of independent classes and institutions, the statization of religion, a swollen bureaucracy, and regulation and eventual ruin of the economy. Charles V brought in foreign troops against the nobles and replaced these in high circles by lawyers and servants raised from the middle classes. Introducing the pomp and ceremony of the Holy Roman imperial court (Altamira, 1946), he magnified the center of the government; expenses of the court rose to four times those of the reign of Ferdinand and Isabella (Hume, 1931).

Charles's son, Philip II, convinced he was the instrument of God and entitled to rule the world, declared his power to annul laws as he pleased, raised taxes on his own authority, and expanded the bureaucracy beyond measure. To house the government and symbolize his power, Philip made a virtually new capital of Madrid, hitherto a village. For seclusive dignity, he built a huge and appropriately somber palace, the Escorial, thirty miles out of the capital (Merriman, 1925-36). Supremely devoted to his faith, he raised the Holy Office to its zenith as a sword against not only heresy but against any deviation. For Philip, the church and the monarchy were inseparable, two phases of an absolute truth united in his own person; but monarchy came first. As a literatus-statesman wrote at the end of the seventeenth century, "In our Spanish masses there is no opinion more deeply set than this: the king is the absolute master of the lives, the possessions, and the honor of all of us" (Crow, 1963, p. 226).

After Philip the Spanish monarchy decayed in corruption and perversion, and the realm sank into stagnant impoverishment. But there was no release. Spain continued to be possessed by its empire until the nineteenth century.

France followed a similar course but was never so burdened. Early medieval French kings were only elected overlords among equals, ruling a domain around Paris smaller than those of several vassals. In the fourteenth century, Italian-educated Roman lawyers were beginning to teach that the state was a superior entity to which the people owed obedience as to God, and that law was the will of the prince; and the foundations of bureaucracy were laid. But there were many turns of political fortune, and only after victory over the English in the Hundred Years' War and the gathering of nearly all France into his control could Charles VII (reigned 1422-1461) set the monarchy on a firm basis. He gained the right to impose taxes by sovereign will, brought the nobles into his service, and restricted papal authority. His successor, Louis XI, virtually completed the unification of France by acquiring Burgundy and Provence; he also established a standing army. From the first part of the sixteenth century the administration was strongly centralized, and law was enacted by the fiat of the king, who called himself "emperor" for dignity.

Religious conflict filled most of the second half of the sixteenth century and gravely reduced the powers of the crown. But Henry IV (reigned 1589-1610) brought France together again and restored the royal authority. Kingship thereafter suffered from accidents of succession, but the trend was toward absolutism. The Estates General had once seemed to be evolving toward parliamentary power, as when in 1484 they gave a subsidy for only two years and on condition that meetings be summoned regularly (Aubry, 1947); in 1614 they were ingloriously dismissed, not to assemble again until 1789. Richelieu, becoming advisor to Louis XIII in 1624, sought to make his master absolute for the sake of national power. He destroyed nobles' castles, proscribed private war, set inspector generals (intendants) over the provinces, and punished conspiracies by death.

A reaction flared up in the rising of the Fronde, from 1648 to 1653, five years of near civil war stimulated by the successful opposition of the British Parliament to the Stuarts at this time. It was led at first by the Parlement of Paris, which drew up bold political demands: that intendants be abolished, that the Parlement be allowed to examine all aspects of policy, that a national assembly be convoked, and so on—in effect, that France become a constitutional monarchy, if not a republic. There was heady talk of freedoms and natural law, and Parisian mobs stormed into the palace; but the movement failed for lack of unity.

Louis XIV as a boy lived through these troubled times and so was the more determined to make his power unassailable; but most important for his prestige was the preeminence of France in Europe. Under Richelieu, France had defeated Spain and the Holy Roman Empire; with the Peace of Westphalia, the former receded and the latter was paralyzed, while France rounded out its territories with Alsace and emerged nearly master of Europe. An able finance minister, Colbert, provided Louis with the greatest resources in Europe; Colbert also made the navy the largest in the world. Another outstanding minister reorganized the army. Louis consequently had a regular force of over a hundred thousand men, and he was ruler of much the most populous of European nations. It was self-evident to Louis that France should be master of Europe and the world, as he was master of France (Hassall, 1902). In 1661 he compelled Spain always to give precedence to French diplomats, and the following year he forced diplomatic humiliation on the pope. The French monarchy was, as he desired, a model for the world.

The greatness of the king of France was thus not unlike that of an emperor of China or a Roman caesar; and Louis endeavored to rule as they did, surrounding himself with an aura of divine majesty. He was the Sun King, radiating blessings on his subjects as the sun over earth; in court pageants he took the role of the sun and sang praises of himself. The silver-tongued prelate Bossuet informed him in 1662, *"Vous êtes Dieu"* (Prestwick, 1957, pp. 110-111). Previously, the style of the French court had been fairly free and easy; but Louis delighted in the most elaborate ritual. Fifty pages of the official manual were required to describe the rising and the retiring of the Sun King. A dozen servants were needed to bring a dish at dinner (Bailly, 1946), as he sat alone while a multitude clustered around. He kept some ten thousand domestics, including about three thousand huntsmen and grooms. Thirty-thousand horses were needed to transport his household for a weekend (Nicolson, 1962). Majesty also called for a grand setting. Versailles was turned into one of the greatest of palaces, an unreal semi-Oriental world, whose principal contact with Paris was through household servants spreading gossip (Duby and Mandrou, 1948), a debilitating gilded cage for the nobility, domesticated to permanent docility.

Power was completely concentrated in the royal person. After the death of Mazarin in 1661, Louis unprecedentedly abolished the prime ministership and made himself dictator by divine right at the age of twenty-three. He assumed command of the army and had officers report directly to him; high titles, as Grand Admiral and High Constable, lapsed as incompatible with the royal dignity. Relatives of the king were excluded from important positions in order that, as Louis said, they should have no security except in his heart (Lough, 1954). The most prominent nobles and prelates were likewise barred from high councils, which were filled with men of humbler birth. No council had any statutory rights; the king might hear opinions, but the decisions were his, and ministers had to attribute all ideas to him (Ogg, 1925). There was in theory no fundamental law that he could not set aside. He claimed ownership of all property; although he did not press the point, there was some idea of taking over the land in order to rent it out. The Lieutenant General of Police became a high figure in the government, while police power through the land was brought entirely into the hands of the central government. A *lettre de cachet* sufficed to imprison anyone indefinitely; even the intendants could sentence men to the galleys at their discretion.

The middle classes, who had prospered early in the century, were no more independent than the nobility and had much less prestige. The guilds were state-controlled, manufacturing was minutely regulated, and permits were required for any enterprise. Church office was in the royal gift, and many of the upper clergy were courtiers. Louis revoked the Edict of Nantes, which guaranteed toleration to Protestants, causing the emigration of hundreds of thousands. The grand monarchy took on the appearance of Oriental despotism.

The example was contagious. German rulers whittled down their parliaments, which had been very influential in the fifteenth century, and practically did away with them in the seventeenth and eighteenth centuries. Sweden had a long libertarian tradition and a powerful parliament (*Riksdag*), but the edifice of constitutionalism was rather easily overthrown in 1680 and after by Charles XI. His son, Charles XII, a powerful personality and outstanding conqueror, made himself a virtually absolute monarch; but parliamentary government came back after his death in battle (1718) and the loss of the Baltic empire that Sweden had garnered. Poland, with a federal structure going back to the Polish-Lithuanian union of 1386, was in the fifteenth and sixteenth centuries exceptionally free and liberal for the Eastern European milieu; in the seventeenth century the constitutional order disintegrated, religious toleration was ended, the social structure stiffened, and the country became subject to the foreign intervention that led to partition in the period from 1772 to 1795.

England, for all its attachment to Magna Carta (1215) and traditional liberties, drifted toward absolutism during this period. From the thirteenth century until the accession of the Tudors in 1485, the authority of Parliament fluctuated with the fortunes of kings. A peasant revolt of 1381 even looked to democracy without lords or lawyers. But the first Tudor ruler, Henry VII (reigned 1485-1509), was able to subdue the decimated nobility as had no king since William the Conqueror; and his son, Henry VIII, became perhaps the strongest of British rulers. Having made himself head of the Church of England, he converted Parliament into a tool of his sovereign will. He gained broad lawmaking powers and could send opponents to the block with little difficulty. The royal power was not much weakened by two female reigns—of Mary and Elizabeth. When James I came to the throne (1603), he was encouraged to believe that subjects had not rights but duties. If some questioned this, James was led only to assert more strongly that kings were properly called gods and enjoyed godlike powers. He commanded his first Parliament that "none therein shall presume henceforth to meddle with anything concerning our government or deep matters of state" (G. Smith, 1966, p. 299). James and his successor Charles I tried to carry on as much as possible like absolute monarchs in the grand style. But theirs was a difficult and ultimately losing struggle against Parliament and newer forces, because commercial England was ahead of the Continent in its development.

Switzerland and the Netherlands stood, then, practically alone in adherence to libertarian principles during the age of absolutism. Even here there was backsliding. The fiercely democratic Swiss Confederation of the fifteenth century became rigidly oligarchic in the seventeenth. Towns were run by coopting councils, and a large part of the population was reduced to something near serfdom (Oechsli, 1922). The Netherlands had become a model democracy in the war of independence against Spain, from 1568 to 1648. But during the second half of the seventeenth century the Netherlands acquired a colonial empire, mostly in the East Indies. The burghers were raised up to rulers and exploiters; and their free society became increasingly oligarchic and immobile.

Thus throughout Europe, around the middle of the seventeenth century, republicanism, democracy, ideas of freedom and of personal rights, and whatever was contrary to the divine right of the masters of the triumphant nation-states were at a low ebb. The fashion was respect for power, which made itself sacred, as is its wont, by the weakness of competition. But centralization—the gathering of powers previously disbursed to local authorities, nobles, ecclesiasts, municipalities, or vassals, and the liberation of the states from the universal powers and restraints of medieval times—had been completed. Newer forces were beginning to erode the golden thrones.

Nation-states: The Libertarian Drift

The victory of absolutism in Europe was never so total as pretended. The skeleton of medieval rights and institutions remained in existence even where kings deprived them of power, and flesh could be put on the bones again when circumstances permitted. Thus the French parlements and the English Parliament remained in being, ready to reassert traditional powers and more when the weakness of monarchs encouraged them to regard themselves as proper representatives of the nation. The philosophy of absolutism, likewise, was never absolute but increasingly qualified by the idea of contract, derivative from the medieval idea of mutuality of rights. Thus the leading British apologist for royal powers, Thomas Hobbes, stressed social contract as the basis for royal authority, leaving open the question of what might be done if the king failed in his part of the bargain or the nation desired to revise the contract of government.

Even as absolutism was moving to its apogee, the Reformation had fundamentally strengthened the idea of popular sovereignty; lacking a pope, Protestantism implied that authority should derive somehow or to some degree from the community of believers. It emphasized more the liberal-libertarian aspect of Christianity, the value and equality of all human souls as children of God. The Reformation also gave for the first time a choice of religions in the Christian and European community, a choice that could not be limited to any two or three but multiplied endlessly (Randall, 1954). Although Luther exalted the state, he held that citizens had a right to disobey if it acted contrary to the dictates of conscience; at one time he called for a priesthood of all qualified believers. But whereas Luther accepted the religious supremacy of the state, Calvinism denied it and authorized citizens to check the ruler while the congregation participated in the government of the church. Calvinists and other sects, without hope of official support, were driven to theses of limited monarchy. The religious struggles of the sixteenth century produced the first considerable antimonarchic writings of the West. The German serfs were ahead of their day in taking Luther's teachings to mean freedom for themselves, and the Anabaptists horrified most Protestants, but they correctly grasped the implications of the rejection of papal authority. The split of the Church pointed the way toward toleration, equality, and democracy. It was not pure caprice that led Louis XIV to revoke the Edict of Nantes and the Stuarts to court unpopularity by moving back toward the universal Church.

However, the determining factor in the trend toward liberalization was clearly the progress of science and technology. The printed word became more and more important; pamphleteering became a major means of communication, leading to regular papers in the latter eighteenth century and to modern journalism in the nineteenth. Not only did the press inform; it became a powerful interest in favor of freedom. Travel and communications continued to improve, educated publics grew up, and a torrent of revolutionary scientific discoveries encouraged skepticism and questioning of all authority. As long as the process of consolidation of nation-states was continuing, the dominant political units were becoming larger and more authoritarian, much as in medieval and Renaissance Italy expansion of city-states led to the decline of republicanism. But when expansion came to a halt, continuing and accelerating cultural development in effect began shrinking the nation-states and making their world more international and hence less authoritarian.

The model monarchy of Louis XIV decayed in its last decades, and some began calling for security of property and an end to religious persecution and arbitrary government (Mayer, 1939). In the eighteenth century, climatic change became apparent. Personal monarchy decayed into bureaucratic as government became professionalized. Roads, communications, and postal services that governments fostered for ease of administration and improvement of national economies, made for greater political awareness. New middle classes deriving wealth from nonofficial sources acquired more importance (Lindsay, 1957), and there was a revolutionary increase of foreign trade, which expanded fivefold from 1717 to 1750 (McManners, 1967). Growing knowledge of faroff lands broadened horizons and assisted criticism of domestic foibles. The idea that the wealth of the people made the greatness of the sovereign, spreading from England to the Continent at the beginning of the eighteenth century, grew into the thesis of "benevolent despotism," by which it became fashionable to think of princes ruling not by divine mandate, which lost intellectual respectability, but because enlightened, therefore benevolent despots were responsible for the progress and happiness of their peoples—a doctrine dangerous for monarchy. Although the philosophers saw no alternative to monarchy, recollection of medieval natural law gave a basis for new ideas of rights; and several thinkers derived sovereignty ultimately from the people. Power became a trust rather than a God-given privilege, a mandate to be exercised by reason. Contract theories of the state, a reflection of the importance of commercial relations, gained in importance. Men felt freer to inquire into institutions. Political thinking acquired new sophistication and significance with Montesquieu and his followers; and Gibbon and others undertook the rationalistic interpretation of history, which invited rationalistic criticism of the present (Wilson, 1957).

In the optimism of the age—and optimism favors freedom as pessimism inclines to resignation—the belief grew that humans were naturally good and worthy of care. There were more efforts to ameliorate the conditions of the poor, and in the latter part of the century harsh criminal codes began to soften (Gershoy, 1944). Jews, still suffering medieval impositions, saw more toleration. Most countries reformed education. The pleasure motif became philosophically acceptable in utilitarianism (Cobban, 1963), an individualistic idea contradictory to the authoritarian ideal of duty.

Economic theory moved away from mercantilism. Emphasis shifted from precious metals to useful commodities, from the treasures of the state to the benefit of the population, from political management to the workings of the marketplace. The key idea of the Physiocrats as of Adam Smith was freedom—to use capital, to choose employment, to trade internally and externally. Even Spanish writers saw controls as a cause of poverty (Habakkuk, 1968). In the same vein, Malthus rejected the absolutist notion of numbers of people as desirable for the power of the state.

As the eighteenth century ripened, the liberalization of society continued. Trade grew, especially foreign trade, which was less fettered by regulations and official control than domestic trade. Commerce and the power of money gave a new fluidity and material support for legality of relations and emancipation from feudal restrictions. The old order was outworn well before it broke down in the French Revolution.

England and Parliament

The English, a century ahead of the Continent, led the way toward the new liberalism in the seventeenth century even as the Sun King was near the zenith of his brilliance. There was a parliamentary tradition from the fourteenth and fifteenth centuries from which precedents were easily drawn to counter kingly claims of authority when the country became ready to support such challenges; and for a century industry and commerce had been expanding and breaking out of traditional controls. The chief interest of the mercantile community was freedom to make money, and the prosperity of the Dutch created a demand for freer government in England.

The Stuarts lacked the tools of despotism. They had no effective tax-gathering service and no real bureaucratic apparatus. If they had great difficulty raising revenues—on the eve of the civil war taxes were only about a quarter as heavy as in France (Nef, 1950)—it was not because they respected law but because they lacked means of exaction. There was hardly any police force—indeed, England had none until the nineteenth century—only a few watchmen in the towns and constables in the villages. Law enforcement was mostly in the hands of unpaid justices of the peace, men of substance who cooperated in accordance with their conscience; laws would remain dead letters if these magistrates did not like them. There was no standing army to assure against rebellion; and, unlike continental rulers, British kings could only with difficulty hire foreign mercenaries to subdue their subjects. There were only local militias ready to spring to arms; if any shire rebelled, it could be repressed only if the others were willing (Hassal, 1895). Hence Charles, to manhandle Parliament, had only his personal guard. A mob forced him to sign the death warrant of his best servant in 1640 (Ashley, 1961).

The centers of resistance were the towns. Although in England these never gained the near independence of French or Flemish counterparts, since the overall authority of the king was established before they rose to strength, they had self-rule with ancient charters and respected liberties, which were secure because they, not the king, had militias. Most important was London, chief port as well as the capital, holding close to a tenth of the population of the whole kingdom and a much larger share of its wealth. The city was a state within the state, governed by neither monarchy nor aristocracy but by its merchants, who directed the militia and kept order. In 1629 the merchants of London suspended trade for several months, accepting great losses rather than pay the royal imposts. In the ferment of 1640, even before the fall of Strafford, the king's right-hand man, London became like a free republic intoxicated with liberty, somewhat like the Paris of 1789. A little later, when members of the Commons were pursued by the king's men, London gave them refuge. It was the men and money of the metropolis that enabled the Parliament quickly to raise a military force.

In defense of the rising middle-class interest, Commons at times equated political rights with the sanctity of private property; and the Puritans, holding work equivalent to prayer, found a sacredness in wealth. A mixture of self-interest with faith and moving principles was necessary to lead men to side with Parliament, an unknown and unreliable master, against the king whom they had always known, revered as the symbol of English greatness, and learned faithfully to obey. This faith was mobilized by a flood of printing, which the government was quite unable to control. Political theory was wrapped in religious garb; and economic, political, and religious issues were inextricably confounded. If the king could tax freely he could do without Parliament and manage the Church as he fancied; if unrestrained by Parliament, he could tax as he pleased; if he could make the Church what he wished, he could set up a despotic power and do away with Parliament. The three aspects were discussed in a single breath, and the more sharply Parliament came to oppose new taxes, the more unorthodox became its religious leanings.

It had been the error of Henry VIII to seek to keep an authoritarian church in his own hands while abolishing the sacred authority of Rome and to uphold Catholic hierarchic doctrines while putting the Bible in the hands of the people. Under the stimulus of growing contacts with Protestant Europe, conflict with the political Catholicism of Spain, the expansion of commerce, and the rising self-confidence of the people, sentiment grew for carrying further the logic of the break with the papacy, for simplification (or purification) of ceremonies and government of the church by its members. Feeding the interest in religion, religious books of diverse tendencies appeared in large numbers. Many were smuggled in; one young man boasted of having brought some twelve thousand volumes into the country, and a Puritan tract was published in English in Holland in ten thousand copies (Cahen and Braure, 1960). In Elizabeth's time, a Puritan party had grown up especially among the commercial classes and in the ports; seamen and privateers were mostly strong anti-Catholics. The Puritans were essentially antiauthoritarian, looking to individual inspiration and regarding sacraments as unimportant beside the illumination of the soul. James, who was raised in a Calvinist atmosphere, viewed them with horror, not for religious but for strictly political reasons. He stated sharply, "If you aim at a Scottish presbytery, it agreeth as well with monarchy as God with the Devil," and, "No bishop, no king" (G. Smith, 1966, p. 289). King and nation drifted apart in religion as the ruler and Parliament grew more extreme in their opposition; as more people favored a simple and democratic church stressing faith, the Stuarts, for the plenitude of royalty, felt the more driven to make the official Church sacramental, priestly, and authoritarian, while churchmen looked to the royal absolutism to protect them from lay powers. By the same token, while Charles called for Sunday merrymaking and the court was becoming more corrupt and immoral, the nation was growing more idealistic, or at least more puritanical.

Despite such contradictions, the royal power seemed secure but for foreign contingencies. The would-be absolute monarchs were drawn toward the absolutist powers of Europe, especially Spain, which was regarded by most Englishmen as a natural enemy. Whereas the Tudors had identified themselves with national aspirations, the Stuarts did the opposite; and while the Tudors could use foreign needs to rally support, the Stuarts resented popular or parliamentary interest in foreign affairs as an infringement on their prerogative; James rebuked ministers who ventured to speak of them publicly (Davies, 1959). Commons was thus indisposed to grant funds for doubtful purposes.

War and defeats that tarnished the royal prerogative forced the calling of Parliament in 1628. Meeting in an atmosphere of hostility caused by forced loans, the quartering of soldiers on civilians, and other oppressive acts, it used Charles's difficulties to attack his favorite Buckingham and to compel acceptance of the Petition of Right, sharply limiting the prerogatives of the crown. Chastened by this experience, Charles managed for eleven years to do without Parliament by strict pacifism, a policy only a little less galling for the king than bowing to the commoners assembled in Parliament and almost as damaging to his prestige. Managing for so long, Charles imagined he might avoid parliaments indefinitely (Davies, 1959).

His downfall came out of a foolish determination to order the Scottish church like the English. The Scots, even more Protestant and freedom-minded than the English, rebelled against the royal dictates and went to war. Led by veterans who had served with the Swedes in the Thirty Years' War, they strode easily to victory and invaded England. They demanded money and an agreement ratified by the Parliament. Charles had to call Parliament in 1640; and the Scottish army, encamped near London, guaranteed its power (Ashley, 1961).

Parliament thereupon took command, ousted the king's chief advisors, sent his favorite, Strafford, to the scaffold, and released a flood of political writing by ending censorship—between 1640 and 1662, twenty-two thousand pamphlets and papers were published (Stone, 1970). Parliament dissolved the council courts, removed the king's power of dissolution, and provided for regular meetings regardless of the royal wishes. Opinion evolved so rapidly that by 1642 Parliament demanded control of the government and army and claimed the right to legislate without the royal assent. It also sought to reform the Church. The moderates reacted by turning to the king, who set up the banner of civil war in the north.

The strongest supporters of the crown were the great landowners of north and west and the rural areas; the bastions of the parliamentary cause were London and other ports and the newer manufacturing regions. The royalist cause appealed most in the areas least touched by the economic progress of the preceding century. The Parliament had much more financial strength; men were more willing to pay taxes imposed by Parliament alone than by the king alone. The navy also helped decisively, as the seamen adhered strongly to the parliamentary side; trade flowed to it, while the royalists were blockaded.

The victorious parliamentary army came out of the wars more radical than the Parliament it was supposed to defend. Many demanded full political equality to restore, they claimed, rights of Englishmen lost since the Norman conquest. For one of the leaders, Ireton, the only basis of right was "that we should keep covenant with one another" (Davies, 1959, p. 144). Some even went to communism, believing with Winstanley that "all the men and women in England are the children of the Land, and the earth is the Lord's." Contending that the land had been stolen by the squires, they sought to conquer by love and example; from their plowing the commons in community, they were called "Diggers" (Bernstein, 1963; Brailsford, 1961).

In the divided nation, the commanding general, Oliver Cromwell, resorted to military dictatorship and virtual restoration of monarchy with himself as Lord Protector. After Cromwell died in 1658, the Presbyterian leaders decided to end the anarchy by calling to power the only man with a legitimate title, Charles II, son of the beheaded king.

Thus the Puritan Revolution seemed largely to have failed when Charles II was called home from exile and raised without conditions to kingship. But the cause of Parliament had made permanent gains. The prerogative courts were not revived, and the nation was aware of the potential power of the Commons; the measures to which Charles I had agreed remained valid, and no subsequent king sought to raise money extralegally (Clark, 1934). But political freedom in England, unlike Holland and Switzerland, was not associated with a struggle for national freedom, but with disorder and failure. Fears of a new civil war hindered resistance to autocracy and justified the burning of incense to the king, guarantor of order.

Reared at the court of Louis XIV, Charles II and his brother, James II, were as fond of absolutism, in theory and practice, as their father and grandfather. They had no little success, cowing Dissenters, undermining or removing by legal means the autonomy of the towns, using the courts against the opposition, and raising the new standing army to thirty thousand men. But when the threat of a Catholic succession arose, James II was toppled with astounding ease by a force from Holland led by his son-in-law, William of Orange. William and Mary then became sovereigns by the grace not of God, but of Parliament and the nation.

Thereafter England was a parliamentary monarchy. The freedom of the press was virtually complete, religious toleration was established, the power of the monarch to veto an act of Parliament became obsolete, and Parliament gradually gained power not only to check the king's ministers but to name them. In the heyday of imperial expansion during the second half of the eighteenth century, George III made some effort to restore kingly authority, not by attacking Parliament but by trying to manage it; but the success of the American colonies in breaking away was ruinous for him. In 1832 Parliament was reformed and the franchise—already the most extensive in the world outside America (Hawgood, 1964)—was broadened. In 1867 Britain introduced near manhood suffrage. In the latter part of the century, there was a revival of empire building; and pride and economic interests in the colonies doubtless contributed to aristocratic and traditionalist biases. But the British empire, like the Dutch, was a product more of commercialism than of militarism, born less of ambition to rule than of technical and economic superiority. British institutions did not lend themselves to effective exploitation of subject peoples, and the more productive areas were given self-rule.

Thanks at least in part to nonrestrictive and responsive government, England led the world into the industrial revolution, and during the first part of the nineteenth century enjoyed industrial and commercial preeminence like that of the United States in the middle of the twentieth. England was at the same time the principal champion of economic and political freedom—a paradoxical position for the holder of the world's most glorious empire, a situation understandable only as part of the history of a creative and therefore powerful state system.

France, Revolution, and the Rights of Man

The Sun King was never so absolute as he pretended, never wholly the master of the lives, minds, and possessions of his subjects. He pretended to divinity; but compared to a Chinese emperor of a great dynasty, he was a weak and semiconstitutional ruler. Louis built Versailles to overshadow the palace that his finance minister, Fouquet, built with peculation; an Asiatic despot would have severed his favorite's head and assumed his estate. The rich speculators, contractors, and tax farmers enjoyed considerable security and were real powers in the land. Although he clipped their wings, Louis left alive the provincial estates and parlements and sometimes even listened to their objections. He never swept away traditional exemptions and privileges. Louis never came near being the ruler of Europe; and in the latter part of his reign, his authority was undermined by defeat. At home also his prestige sank with his finances. Toward the end of his reign, he had to cajole bankers for money (Bailly, 1946). At times he sacrificed his gold plate for the treasury.

Louis XIV left the government to a regency, which was followed by the lazy, incapable, and careless Louis XV. Louis XVI, coming to the throne in 1774, was still weaker. The cultural and intellectual leadership of the court shrank, and skepticism toward authority and faith in science replaced admiration for monarchy. Even the intendants, special and direct agents of the king, were becoming entrenched and independent (Mathiez, 1962).

The nemesis of the regime and direct cause of its eventual downfall was the perennial deficit. Taxes were very high, but waste and graft were higher, and the attempt to secure revenue by selling monopolies, positions, and tax exemptions only worsened the situation. Resistance to the demands of the corrupt and arbitrary regime centered around the parlements, especially the Parlement of Paris, highest court in the land, which represented a section of the hereditary and ennobled bureaucracy. However oligarchic and often venal the Parlement was, no other body had a better claim to represent the nation; consequently it felt entitled to discuss policy, so far as the weakness of the king allowed. Although quite different in composition from the British Parliament, the French was encouraged by the similarity of name to emulate the other body and even to borrow its slogans; and the Parlement was regarded as a substitute for an elected body although composed of a generally selfish nobility (Furet and Richet, 1970). The king would have been glad to replace the judges, but he could not easily do so because they held office by right of purchase and he lacked funds to compensate them; they also had status by virtue of wealth and professional solidarity. He could exile them, but he always had to call them back to help administer justice. The king legally had the power, but the Parlement won the points.

It was possible for the Parlement, supine in the seventeenth century, to defy the king in the eighteenth because French society had matured. The power of money, slight at Louis XIV's height but rising thereafter, released France from the Old Regime. Agriculture became capitalistic, with money rents replacing payments in kind. There was much movement to the towns, partly to escape feudal restrictions (Renard and Weulersee, 1926). A mass of restrictions impeded the penetration of the industrial revolution into France; but there was considerable development, especially in those branches to which the government paid least attention, such as iron, coal, and glass, and those producing for export (Wilson, 1957). Trade grew immensely, especially foreign trade less fettered by regulation and barriers, which expanded four times over in the seventy-five years before the Revolution (Gershoy, 1944). With better roads and coaches, travel times were halved in the generation after 1760 (Palmer, 1968). The merchant marine increased enormously. The bourgeoisie, accustomed to passivity, was slow to assert itself politically; but the importance of commerce made inherited privilege unrealistic and the monarchy an obstacle to progress. It lent fluidity to society: it patronized learning and gave a new support for men and ideas of legality and freedom from old trammels (Palmer, 1968).

Popular opinion gained force also because of the changed position of France and influences from abroad. Exhausted by the wars of Louis XIV, France needed many years to recover. When wars were resumed in 1740, the results were mediocre to poor. It was clear that France, though still the most populous and potentially strongest of the nations, could no longer pretend hegemony. Nearly all the extensive colonial empire was lost in 1763.

As early as the first part of Louis XIV's reign, slogans of the English revolution made their way into France; and an Englishman translated the Cromwellian constitution, prefixing to it a declaration of the rights of man. After the inglorious outcome of Louis XIV's reign, even the regent admired the example of England, where there were no *lettres de cachet* or arbitrary imprisonment; and the English example became all-powerful as the century advanced, more and more books were smuggled in to defeat the censorship, and England became more powerful and prosperous than France. The French upper classes envied the active role in political life of British aristocrats, whose power and dignity contrasted with the empty life of the French nobility. Voltaire, who lived three years in London, implicitly criticized French servitude by praise for British freedom. Montesquieu and many others popularized British institutions, while men like Horace Walpole, Gibbon, and Hume were the lions of French salons. The *Encyclopedia*, which so encouraged critical thought, was originally a reedition of an English work. A nobleman of Louis XV's court wrote, "England has conquered us," and "A philosophical wind of revolution is blowing to us from England" (Seignobos, 1932, pp. 249, 258).

More important than specific ideas was the encouragement of independent attitudes and new ways of thinking. Already, as Louis XIV had passed his zenith, science was eroding the divine right, and some protested the classic canons in literature. Under the carefree Regency and the indolent Louis XV, intellectual criticism erupted and impiety became the fashion. Science, which had belonged to a very few in the seventeenth century, became popular; a tide of material inventions began to change life, raising the prestige of reason and nourishing hopes for improvement, in effect undermining traditional authority. Important works of criticism were appearing; Montesquieu's *Spirit of the Laws*, Buffon's *Natural History*, and Rousseau's and Voltaire's attacks on the old society laid the groundwork for revolution. The Seven Years' War, ending in 1763, further discredited and impoverished the government and raised the idea of people and nation as something beyond kingship. Talk of popular sovereignty and rights of resistance became current in the latter years of Louis XV; under Louis XVI, they became so thoroughly accepted among the upper classes that the king was pleased to talk often of natural laws and the rights of man (Tocqueville, de, 1876).

The chief effect of foreign ideas was skepticism. The *Encyclopedia* of Denis Diderot and Jean d'Alembert presented not a philosophy but diversity of views, sense of inquiry, and critique of accepted ideas (Duby and Mandrou, 1958). Deistic and rationalistic ideas circulating in England around the beginning of the eighteenth century caused little excitement; imported to France, they were infused with hostility toward everything old and sacred (Cobban, 1952). Dislike for the monarchy was easily and safely expressed against the official Church, which was at once traditional, antirational, political, and unspiritual. Scientism and faith in material progress plus opposition to the government and hatred for religious compulsion (the absence of which in England was admired) made the upper classes highly irreligious; it became the universal fashion of the salons to scoff at faith from about the middle of the eighteenth century. Even priests and bishops lost piety; many left monastic orders; unbelieving churchmen were commonplace. Louis XVI himself had little respect for his church (Mathiez, 1962; Duby and Mandrou, 1958).

As ideas of political freedom and natural religion or atheism penetrated the highest spheres, the state was powerless to suppress them. Almost all works of the *philosophes* were condemned by clergy and Parlement, but they were smuggled in or printed clandestinely. Many French books were published in Holland, Switzerland, Germany, and England, partly for sale in those countries, where French was widely known, partly for export to France (Lough, 1960); Montesquieu, for example, published his attack on absolute monarchy in Germany. Louis XV, who established an official newspaper to enlighten the people, tried to prohibit the *Encyclopedia*, but it was too useful and too many people liked it. The government in 1757 passed a law condemning to death the writers, printers, and sellers of works attacking religion or the state (Tocqueville, de, 1876); but although some writers, like Voltaire, were harried or imprisoned, censorship was intermittent and more of an annoyance than a terror. Reducing respect for the regime, it was more effective in stimulating interest in works than in preventing their circulation (Perkins, 1897). Sharp attacks on the existing order were passed around on handwritten sheets or in epigrams that everyone repeated in the salons.

The littérateurs found enough to criticize in the inherited privileges, wastrel court, decadent and parasitic nobility, discredited Church, restricted bourgeoisie, and oppressed peasantry. But the event that broke the government was the American Revolution. Ill-advised as it would seem for the absolutist monarchy to help American republicans, this was an opportunity to damage England. And the French upper classes genuinely sympathized with the struggle for independence; not a few of the nobility volunteered to fight for revolution and republicanism, were struck by the freedom and prosperity of the American colonies, and came back inspired and eager for reform at home. Republics, ancient and modern, became the mode (Fay, 1966). The constitution of the American colonies gave the idea of a written document that declared the rights of the citizens. There was a party, known at times as the Americans or

Anglomaniacs, who wanted to turn France into a constitutional monarchy (Mathiez, 1962).

The war also saddled the monarchy with unbearable debt. The parlements, ardently supported by conservatives who wanted to maintain all old rights and by radicals who wanted reform, resisted all new taxes. The call for a meeting of the Estates General, heard from time to time in the past, became irresistible. Tax collection became difficult and the court had to suspend payments. Censorship broke down and critical publications blossomed. When Louis agreed to call the Estates General, the monarchy was a shambles.

The nobility thought that now, as in previous centuries, they could use the weakness of the monarchy to reassert themselves. The king, equally prisoner of the past, thought he had only the nobility to fear and so might safely seek support of the middle classes. For this reason, the Third Estate was given the same representation as the other two orders together in the Estates General. Ideals of equality were such that in this assembly all nobles, high and low, had equal voice, as did all clergy; in the Third Estate, all taxpayers, including artisans and peasants, were given the franchise. Having thus made the assembly representative of the nation, Louis first opposed its claim and then, lacking support, yielded to it. It declared itself sovereign; and the nobility, frightened at the wave of rural disorders and infected by libertarian propaganda, renounced feudal privileges. The constitution drawn up by 1791 was an attempt, however, to copy the British system. Elections were to be indirect with limited suffrage, and the king was given a suspensive veto and the right to name his ministers.

This settlement might have prevailed but for the assembly's attempt to establish its control over the clergy, the resultant papal condemnation, the attempted flight of the king, foreign intrigues, and wars with foreign monarchies. Defeats brought a rising in 1792 of the radicals of Paris, who were continually trying to propel the Revolution forward; the Revolution was primarily an urban and Parisian movement. The king was deposed, and France then sought to turn absolutely away from the past. To inaugurate the new era, years were numbered from the birth not of Christ, but of the Republic. A new calendar gave poetic names to the months. The day was to be of ten hours of one hundred minutes of one hundred seconds. Old weights and measures were replaced by the logical metric system. All titles were abolished, and everyone was to be addressed simply as "citizen"; the common folk were exalted in a passion for equality while noble origin was a black mark. Priests were harried and churches were closed, as one faction pressed for atheism while another worshipped the Goddess of Reason. But revolutionary freedom was alloyed with harsh new authority. In the latter years of the Old Regime, imprisonment of a seditious writer was scandalous; the summary justice of the Revolution guillotined suspects by the thousands. Carrying out aspirations of autocracy, the Revolution abolished the troublesome parlements, the provinces with their separatism and ancient rights, and internal barriers to trade.

Economic troubles, however, along with controversy over religion, revulsion from bloodshed, and improvement of the military situation led to a reaction, the overthrow of Robespierre and the Jacobins in the movement of Thermidor (July 1794). Radical Paris was subjected to the more conservative central government. A new, less democratic constitution represented the victory of private property, but after a few more years of incompetent and corrupt government, the country was defenseless against the most competent and ambitious of the generals. Elevating himself as his realm expanded, Napoleon gave himself the old Roman title of First Consul, and then, when a beaten Europe lay at his feet, he became hereditary emperor. The pope himself came to Paris for the coronation in 1804 and poured on the holy oil; but the new emperor of the West seized the crown with his own hands.

Having erected his empire over the wreckage of the state system, Napoleon, who swore to defend liberty and equality, established an imperial regime. He governed by personal decree, crushed local autonomy more thoroughly than any Bourbon, made himself master of the Church, built up a political police, severely censored writing, overlaid education with indoctrination, set up an elaborate and ceremonious court, and glorified himself to the edge of deification. But the empire rose too swiftly to give itself an ideological basis and did not last long enough to become ingrained in the French, much less the European, mind.

The collapse of Napoleon's empire and restoration of the state system brought back a king to France and permitted the partial reerection of the old order across Europe. But much that the Revolution achieved—including religious toleration, written constitutions, legal equality for all, and suffrage for at least a fraction of the citizenry—proved permanent. Mingling with the ideas and example of British government by law and civil liberty, it set the tone for the political evolution of the nineteenth century, especially after the French-centered revolutionary wave of 1848 broke the reactionary powers of Central Europe. Urbanization, industrialization, and the spread of literacy to the general public gradually swung Europe toward more liberal forms; by the eve of World War I, all European governments had some representative element. Where stiff authority remained, as in Prussia, it seemed clearly to be softening; and it was assumed that parliamentary rule was the inevitable way of the future.

7 The Western Creativity

Rise of Europe

In mechanical devices and scientific theories, in volume, originality, variety, and sophistication of literature and the arts, in every realm of activity distinguishing the civilized from the primitive, the Western state system has so far outdistanced its predecessors that it has come to stand virtually alone, equivalent in the common view to modern civilization. Only recently has Western power and culture quite overwhelmed the leftovers of other major civilizations, such as the Chinese and Indian, through modern science and industry; but the Western superiority has been strong for a very long time. In the seventeenth century cultivated Europe looked down upon Turks and Arabs as marked inferiors; in the fifteenth century European enterprise was beginning to encircle the globe; from the time of the Crusades (eleventh and twelfth centuries) the tide of invasion from the Asian periphery, which repeatedly swept into Europe, was reversed; and the heathen seldom thereafter posed a threat to Europe.

There are several apparent reasons for the exceptional Western accomplishment. The West began, early in the Dark Ages, at a much higher level than had the Greeks. Despite losses in the decadence of the Roman Empire, most of the classic heritage was preserved or could be recovered as medieval man became capable of appreciating it. It was also possible to take advantage of some of the learning and crafts of Araby. Second, the West profited by its size; there have been many more opportunities for mutually fertilizing inventiveness in the continent-sized state system than in Greece and vicinity, or in the section of the Yellow River valley occupied by the Chinese Contending States. Perhaps most important, the West has had a continuous history of accumulated invention about twice as long as the better known rivals. This has been made possible by the evolution of the West and its ability to absorb the expansion of its polities from feudal fiefdoms and autonomous towns to nation-states without these succumbing to a general unification, such as overtook the Hellenistic or the Chinese states when they approached the same order of magnitude as ordinary European nation-states. Happily, too, for the West, its progress has never been seriously interrupted and has suffered only one important deceleration, around the fifteenth century when the world of city-states was giving way to the new world of nations.

The beginnings go back into the obscure times of invasions and disorders, when Europe became turbulent and divided after the collapse of the Roman Empire. The Germanic intruders, who had been making useful innovations on the outside while the empire stagnated (Hodges, 1970), brought many things, from butter to barrels, including new crops and sundry practical devices (Bark, 1958). Invention and adoption of borrowed ideas, especially from peoples of the steppes, became easier in the looser social structure. Devices neglected by the Romans began to find widespread application. Thus, the waterwheel, known from the early days of the empire, was put into use and much improved, until by the end of the tenth century thousands were employed for fulling, the operation of forges, grinding, and so on (L. White, 1962). As towns reappeared, trades became specialized and technical manuals were copied. There were treatises on chemistry, chiefly the preparation of dyestuffs, from the eighth century. In the ninth century and afterward, several inventions made horses more useful: the stirrup, perhaps borrowed from the Arabs, nailed horseshoes, and the horse collar. Previously, horses had pulled against a harness around the neck; with a collar set lower against the shoulder, they could pull three times as much (Klemm, 1959). Hitched to the new wheeled plow, horses could cultivate heavier and richer soils of northern Europe. From the eighth century, better crop rotations, with three fields instead of two and with spring sowing, raised agricultural output (Bark, 1958). From the ninth to the twelfth century yields rose at least 25 percent (Russell, 1969).

As early as the eighth century, the West was gaining an ascendancy in weaponry with better armor, mounted lancers, and the crossbow (L. White, 1963). There were no important invasions of Western Europe after the tenth century. In the eleventh century, Europe was pushing outward. The Italians were penetrating the Levant, the Teutonic Knights pressed into pagan and Slavic northeastern Europe and the Baltic, the English were beating back the Welsh and Irish, Spanish Christians turned the tables on the Moslems and began the Reconquest. In the same century the Arabs were expelled from southern Italy and Sicily, and Venice had outstripped Byzantium in shipbuilding (Clapham, 1929). The Crusades, preached in 1095, showed a rising confidence in confrontation with the Arab world. Disunited and operating at a great distance from home, the crusaders were able to occupy parts of Palestine for a century against an enormously more numerous native population. The third Lateran Council of 1179 issued stern decrees against the sale of arms to the infidels (Nussbaum, 1947). The East still had more luxury and polish, and the West owed it much;

but Western Europe, thanks to numberless unrecorded craftsmen, had surged ahead in practical ways. About the same time, the voyages of the Vikings to Iceland and North America showed not only a restless spirit but seafaring skill not seen since Phoenician days.

The stream of inventions became a torrent. In the eleventh century alcohol was distilled; and in the twelfth, such useful reagents as nitric and sulfuric acids and saltpeter were discovered. In the twelfth and thirteenth centuries, scores of towns were vying in the erection of cathedrals; the great Gothic masterpieces required the townsfolk to solve architectural problems much beyond the capacity of the Romans, as stone roofs were set on high, thin walls with the aid of vaulted arches and flying buttresses. Lofty, elaborate, and light filled, they represented the triumph of a new spirit. By the twelfth century, waterwheels were supplemented by windmills for grain mills, sawmills, for the working of bellows for metallurgy, and so on; and their numbers multiplied in the thirteenth century. In the twelfth century there appeared larger ships moved by sails without oarsmen and steered by another simple invention that antiquity overlooked—the hinged rudder. In the thirteenth, the compass with a suspended magnetic needle made the open seas less fearsome, and maps were being drawn in unprecedented numbers. The wheelbarrow was invented in the same century, as were spectacles, inaccurate mechanical clocks, and various machines for the manufacture of textiles (Klemm, 1959). The idea was taking hold that better devices should be used to make better use of resources with less labor (A. Hall, 1954). Material improvements had brought considerable wealth; eighty cathedrals built in France in the twelfth century by voluntary endeavor of a scanty population cost the equivalent of about a billion dollars (Mason, 1962). Through the twelfth and thirteenth centuries, material prosperity rolled forward (Blum, Cameron, and Barnes, 1970); by the fourteenth century, numerous merchants of Italy, Germany, and France had fortunes equivalent to many millions of modern dollars.

Mining was becoming important; in 1307 an ordinance was issued to control coal smoke in London. By the beginning of the fourteenth century public dissections were regularly used for teaching at Bologna. Mechanical clocks with all manner of complicated gadgetry became a fad, the pride of countless towns. The fourteenth century also saw such inventions as artillery and lockgates on canals; it brought Europe well ahead of the Byzantine Roman Empire in technology. The Turks, although excellent warriors, required Christian renegades to handle their artillery and military engineering.

The twelfth and thirteenth centuries saw an intellectual renaissance as notable as that of the fifteenth and sixteenth centuries. The earlier upsurge was less literary but more original, more philosophic and scientific (Randall, 1954). Much natural science was brought from the Arabs, and through them from the Greeks. Many universities were started which, though later turning conservative, perhaps obscurantist, were at first centers of inquiry. The larger, such as Oxford, Paris, and Bologna, had tens of thousands of students (Walsh, 1970). Toward the end of the Middle Ages, probably as large a proportion of the population was receiving a higher education of sorts as in Europe of the 1920s (Rashdall, 1926). Mathematics reached a height above which it was not to climb for hundreds of years afterward. Historical writing rose rapidly as Europe came into new self-awaremess (Haskins, 1927). In the thirteenth century, Roger Bacon thought in terms of experiment, measure, and power over nature through sciennce. The thirteenth-century encyclopedias of Roger Bacon, Albertus Magnus, and others contained much accurate information regarding chemistry and such practical matters.

There was a new freedom of the mind. People were no longer convinced that the world was a mere waystation and that human nature was entirely evil; there was more frankness and joy in human feelings (Randall, 1954), as attested by the wide popularity of Ovid's amatory poetry. Although teachers at official institutions could not openly contravene orthodoxy, there was an undercurrent of free, or at least questioning, thought, and a burgeoning of heresies in the towns (Coulton, 1930). Then, in contrast with following centuries, few thought that Aristotle had said the last word; and speculation led to radical criticism even of doctrines held essential to religion. Roger Bacon (1214–1292) held, as did various contemporaries, that nature should be described quantitatively and mathematically; he went on to dream of such things as airplanes and telescopes. Pierre de Maricourt experimented with magnetism about 1269. William of Occam attacked the Aristotelian categories, made experience the only test of physical truth, and enunciated his famous principle against the spinning of hypotheses. In the fourteenth century, Nicholas Oresmus, who speculated that the earth revolved around the sun, envisaged the world as a clockwork set in motion by God; and Nicholas of Autrecourt pushed philosophic empiricism to a depth not surpassed until David Hume in the eighteenth century (Crombie, 1953). Europe had thus gone far toward the mastery of nature, both in practice and theory, by the thirteenth and fourteenth centuries.

Florescence of Italy

Universities and monasteries, capitals, provinces, and little courts shared in the cultural upsurge of medieval Europe. But most original thinking and creativity was the work of the free or semifree towns, which especially produced practical learning against the elegance of the courts and the scholasticism of the convents. There were many humming and productive towns, especially in Germany, France, and Italy. Among the earliest to raise themselves from the dark ages were those of southern France, which formed almost a diminutive state system in the twelfth century. Outwardly, the land was prey to disorder and almost continual fighting. Yet commerce, which was almost free of taxes and restrictions, throve (Emery, 1941). Merchants of southern France, rivaling those of Italy, were widely installed across the Mediterranean. Although northern France excelled in architecture and education, cities of the south were even more prosperous and brilliant; Toulouse outshone Paris (Oldenbourg, 1959). Class lines were blurred, as men could rise from a lowly condition with relative ease. Jews could sometimes occupy municipal office. Learning was substantial, but the outstanding art was literary; the songs of the troubadours formed the first developed literature of post-Roman Europe, which influenced such poets as Dante, Petrarch, and Chaucer; their language was briefly the politest of Europe, cultivated by men like Richard the Lion-Heart of England (Trueta, 1946).

The most important group of towns, however, was the Italian; and theirs was the major contribution to the rise of the West and the Renaissance. Until into the thirteenth century Italy was hardly ahead of France; but the Italian communes, gradually amalgamated into larger city-states, carried on after the French towns were submerged and became the leaders of Europe during some three centuries.

Intellectual interests in Italy quickened with the revival of commerce, and even in the tenth century there were a number of schools and libraries. Bologna was famous for a school of logic and grammar from the eleventh century and, from the beginning of the twelfth, for a school of Roman law, which made that city the leading European center for legal studies. About 1200, it had ten thousand students, mostly mature, studying law, medicine, grammar, logic, rhetoric, arithmetic, astronomy, geometry, and music. Half a dozen other towns followed with comparable, though smaller, centers. The Crusades and closer contact with the Byzantine heirs of Greece further stimulated the thirst for knowledge. Enthusiasm for collecting, translating, and commenting on classical texts became a passion of private persons and merchant princes alike. Classical learning became necessary garb for a gentleman, as a fervor of emulation spread. Bloody tyrants called upon poets and scholars to keep them company, ruthless intriguers and mercenary generals delighted in stately and ornate poesy. Savonarola, hater of paganism, went away to monkhood not with a psalm but with a verse of Virgil on his lips.

Enthusiasm for learning embraced all classes and permeated the population to a degree hardly surpassed in history. According to Villari, Florence, with a population of 90,000, in the fourteenth century had 8,000 to 10,000 children in schools of reading; there were also 1,000 to 1,200 in six schools of arithmetic and 600 in schools of Latin grammar and logic (Schevill, 1936). In the fifteenth century, Cosimo de' Medici, generous patron of the arts and humanities, created probably the first serviceable public library. In the Tuscany of the eighteenth century, illiteracy was almost total; yet it appears that three centuries earlier most people were literate, and to be considered educated a man should be able to write passable poetry.

Yet the Italian achievement was not merely or chiefly artistic and scholarly but broad and practical. Italy was rich less because of the genius of artists than because good methods of production and high quality made Italian goods preferred. Fourteenth-century Florence introduced many types of advanced textile machinery and developed factory production in near modern style, with specialized workers performing a single task; by 1339 there were two hundred textile factories with approximately fifteen thousand workers (Beard, 1938). Italians developed instruments of finance, as letters of credit, bills of exchange, double-entry bookkeeping, and insurance. There were joint stock companies as early as 1000 A.D.; by the end of the fourteenth century they were comparable to the modern organization, with directors, audited accounts, and branches throughout Europe (Caggese, 1949).

Early in the fourteenth century there were schools of commercial arithmetic in Genoa, Florence, and Lucca, while mathematics at Paris dealt mostly with the calendar and astrology. The Italians were the first in the West to make practical use of Arabic (or Hindu) numbers, introduced by Leonardo of Pisa (Fibonacci) in 1202. In the first fifty years of printing, Italy produced about two hundred books on mathematics and over fifteen hundred in the next century (Bell, 1940). In science likewise, Italians contributed more through the sixteenth century than any other people. Modino, father of modern anatomy, was dissecting at Bologna early in the fourteenth century. There were practical and technical improvements also. For example, in the twelfth century Italy began to excel in the revived art of glass making, especially stained windows. Even farming, stepchild of the trading towns, rose under care and science; by the thirteenth century Italian agriculture had become the model for the world, and it so remained through the fifteenth.

War-wracked Italy was the richest spot on earth. The streets of Florence were reported paved early in the thirteenth century. Italian towns, with buildings ten to fifteen stories high, were models of elegance and splendor in comparison to Paris and London; French officers entering Florence in 1494 stood agape at the sight of the fine buildings. Although Florence was at war more often than not in the fourteenth century and the countryside was often ravaged, its revenues were surpassed only by those of the king of France. It has been claimed that the cities of north and central Italy alone possessed more wealth than the rest of the Continent together. Italian bankers, by giving or withholding loans, could determine whether kings should go to war; the French and Spanish invasions were largely financed by Italian houses. Most of the banks of France were long Italian owned. Italian bankers were prominent in England from the thirteenth and fourteenth centuries; the Sienese were followed by the Florentines, who financed church transactions, the wool trade, and wars. Florentines were called upon to manage the London mint (Clapham, 1929). Most of the estate of Edward I of England went to Italian creditors (Einstein, 1902). The carrying trade of England was largely in Italian hands in the fifteenth century. Even in the sixteenth century, when Genoa was a satellite of Spain, Genoese merchants had a large part of Spanish commerce (Hume, 1931).

The traders were seafarers and seafighters as well, and they wrested the Mediterranean from Saracen-Turkish domination. Early in the thirteenth century, Venice, with a population of less than two hundred thousand, was able thoroughly to best the Byzantine Empire and assert virtual mastery of the Mediterranean, hardly challenged except by the Genoese. In the thirteenth and fourteenth centuries Venice gained and colonized Corfu, Crete, most islands of the Aegean, and part of mainland Greece, while Genoa held other Aegean islands, built a naval station to control the Bosphorus, and in 1300 proposed to station a squadron in the Red Sea at Aden (Mundy and Riesenberg, 1958). Genoa had half a dozen colonies in the Crimea in the fourteenth century, managed the Persian navy, and competed with Pisa and Venice for the trade of the Golden Horde (Spuler, 1943). Somewhat as Portuguese, Dutch, French, and British contended over the carcass of the Indian empire a few centuries later, the fleets of Venice and Genoa once battled in the very harbor of Constantinople (Diehl, 1957), in a demonstration of superiority doubtless more striking to contemporaries than *The Last Supper* of Leonardo or Michelangelo's *Pietà*. In the fifteenth century, Venice had some three thousand ships and was one of the great powers of Europe, the chief bulwark of Europe against the Turkish empire in the Mediterranean. Venice was still powerful enough in 1508 to fight fairly successfully against a league of the pope, the emperor, France, Spain, and some minor powers.

Only by qualitative superiority in weapons production and the arts of war could the disunited Italian cities defend themselves against the Holy Roman emperor. From the twelfth century, Milan, then rapidly growing in commerce, was renowned for quality of arms; production for the armies of all Europe became big business. Disunity kept the Italians, like the Greeks, from conquering their neighbors, but their military influence spread far and wide. In the fifteenth century hardly an army of Europe lacked Italian soldiers and officers; rulers bid for Italian mercenaries, although as footsoldiers they were inferior to the Swiss; Ivan the Terrible used Italian artillerymen. Italian works on military science and engineering, fortification, gunnery, and so on were the handbooks of generals everywhere (Einstein, 1902). As late as the middle of the sixteenth century, Genoa, conceded autonomy by Charles V of Spain, was a main reliance of Spanish power and the furnisher of the Spanish navy.

In more pacific activities, the Florentines, who shone for what some considered an excess of intellectual mobility, were engaged as ambassadors by many nations. The political thinkers of the Middle Ages were almost entirely Italians (Dawson, 1958). The most famous jurist of the Middle Ages was Bartolus of Perugia. Many prelates in England and elsewhere over Europe up to the Reformation were Italians. Until into the seventeenth century the phases of European art were phases of Italian art spreading over the Continent (Artz, 1958). Italian architects worked on the Moscow Kremlin, and Italian scholars trooped to Oxford in the fifteenth century. Wherever they went, they met men versed in Italian, the elegant language of Europe during two hundred years, spoken by Henry VIII and Elizabeth. Numerous books in Italian were published in England in the sixteenth century. Shakespeare's comedies use many a plot from Italian sources, and Milton wrote a quantity of verse in Italian. As an English humanist said, "For me, who is really learned is an Italian, even though born among savages" (Einstein, 1902, p. 44).

Courts and polite society aped the Italians, who were held to surpass all others as writers, artists, physicians, diplomats, astrologers, and savants. Through the fifteenth and sixteenth centuries, all manner of polite customs and articles of fashion, clothes, ornaments, musical styles, and instruments were imported from Italy. The northern countries perused Italian manuals of polite behavior, although the dominance of Italian ways led to a reaction against slavish imitation. The feeling grew that the Italians were too subtle and cunning, their elegance a front for immorality.

The Italians regarded themselves as the first gentlemen of the world. Until the sixteenth century, when the Renaissance was progressing in England, Italians resident in that country felt themselves as exiles among barbarians. Machiavelli wrote, "Look how in duels and contests of a few the Italians are superior in strength, dexterity and intelligence. But when it comes to armies they make a poor show." He looked upon the French and Spanish invaders much as the Greeks regarded the Persians: "This barbarian domination stinks in the nostrils of everyone" (*The Prince*, chap. 26).

The Italians sought to merit their reputation for special mental agility by the broadest cultivation of faculties, and many made all learning and arts their domain. Michelangelo, a supreme painter, sculptor, and architect, at the same time a poet of merit, was also a capable engineer who worked on the fortifications of Florence. Leonardo, author of the world's most esteemed painting, was also architect and sculptor; he studied mathematics, became an engineer, and worked on draining swamps and on town planning. Delving into botany, geology, and mechanics, he made many mostly premature inventions and notable scientific suggestions. A keen businessman and ruler, Lorenzo de' Medici, wrote a quantity of verse that his contemporaries esteemed above that of Petrarch.

Such men could flourish only in an atmosphere of the most intense stimulation, where actions were judged by success and gentlemen were recognized by appearance and worth, not pedigree. Men were not born noble or made noble by a sovereign but ennobled themselves by industry, intelligence, and skill. All were invited to do for themselves; for the Florentines, he who failed to achieve honor had only himself to blame. "Thou, o God," said Leonardo, "dost sell us all good things at the price of labor" (Jacob, 1960, p. 47). Many careers were only a little less spectacular than that of Cola de Rienzo, a man of the humblest birth who conceived the daring notion of reviving Rome from its degradation amid classical ruins. By will and personality, he made himself tribune of the people and drove out the nobles, only to fall from excess of ambition.

Rediscovering himself as an individual, man felt newly free to try his hand at anything and to make his own way. Scholars helped merchants convince themselves that wealth was respectable and virtuous. "The whole glory of man," it was said, "lies in activity" (Hay, 1961, pp. 126-127). In the fifteenth century men felt themselves to be modern, regarded their ancestors as benighted, and believed a glorious new age had arrived. The established and formally recognized was to be turned to sport. Typically, the Venetians mocked the Byzantine emperor by costuming a Negro slave in imperial robes and parading him in a ship bedecked like the royal galley; later they set a prostitute on the throne of the patriarch. Men sought worldly rather than spiritual immortality, and official dogmas rested lightly. The celebrated Latinist, Lorenzo Valla, criticized the pope, denounced various pious forgeries such as the *Donation of Constantine*, and even denied the Apostles' Creed; yet, without recantation, he was engaged as private secretary of the pope. Many turned for a time to new faiths. In the tenth and eleventh centuries, Lombardy, like southern France, was honeycombed with sects; and in the eleventh and twelfth in Florence and other cities, the Cathari and Paterini condemned the wealth and depravity of the Church. Doctrines ranging from free love to vegetarianism found followers, and Catholic mystics such as St. Francis mingled with free thinkers. Since each town wanted its own, there was an extraordinary output of saints; in the two centuries after 1350, Italy produced eighty-two saints, about twice as many as the rest of Europe combined (Hay, 1961).

But the tone was of individualism and skepticism rather than religious fervor, heretic or orthodox, as men turned away from faith. Leonardo even argued that ghosts were a physical impossibility (Mayer, 1939). Italy was reputed a great center of atheism, but atheism appeared mostly as rejection of moral and religious restraints; the intellectuals did not attack the Church but ignored it (Martin, von, 1966). When Florence for a few years came under the sway of Savonarola's fervent eloquence, he excited indignation at vices in the Church but did not lead toward any reconsideration of religious values or novel faith. Nor were the Florentines really religious even when swept by a revivalist mode; they were more concerned with civic freedom than with salvation and were most impressed by Savonarola when he orated on politics (Villari, 1888).

Disrespect for authority also meant loosening of the restraints of morals. An English traveler of the sixteenth century said that he found more freedom to sin in nine days in Venice than in nine years in pleasure-loving London. Unbridled lust was cultivated with great refinement and elegance. Aside from some fondness for treachery, the Italians usually had more respect for life than the French or Swiss, not to speak of the Spanish. Machiavelli held Italian amorality merely the counterpart of northern brutality. Violent vices were shaded by virtues; Lucrezia Borgia devoted herself with equal earnestness to murder and works of charity. Despite the intrigue and faithlessness recommended by Machiavelli and practiced by countless tyrants, the practical Italians were commercially reliable, as the bankers of Europe had to be.

The creative society of the Italian city-states was thus loose and given to extremes, as individualism rejected the fetters of authority. It brought forth unscrupulous popes and fervent reformers like St. Francis. Emotions were violent and mercurial; it is told of the factions in Florence that "they would fight one day and eat and drink together the next, recounting to one another their various deeds and prowess" (Villari, 1901, p. 142). Men who were indifferent to religion and principles, who scorned any ideals as vulgar and exalted the delights of the flesh, spent years and fortunes on ancient manuscripts. At the behest of Savonarola, the sensuous people of Florence made a bonfire of their vanities and young men briefly renounced the orgies of carnival to collect alms. They went on to mingle songs of ribaldry with mystical devotions.

In the competitive rivalry of the cities, civic pride was high. For a long time, luxury was more public than private, as the wealthy dressed modestly but spent lavishly on public buildings. Each town was proud of its appearance; different centers consequently developed original styles. Siena built a splendid cathedral to match that of Florence. Padua, Naples, Vicenza, and various others emulated the University of Bologna.

Scholars, profiting by the existence of many small states, usually preferred not to fix their abode for long, but migrated from town to town and from patron to patron. Even a whole university could benefit. In the fourteenth century the University of Bologna quarreled with the municipality. Students and professors decamped to Siena; they were lured back by promises of full freedom and increased pay. Others moved under compulsion. As with the Greeks, exile was a common punishment for political crimes; and exile often increased productivity (Symonds, 1894). Enforced idleness abroad led Machiavelli, a man of action like Thucydides, to compose his immortal works. Dante fled Florence under death sentence and composed his major works as a wanderer abroad.

With a loose class structure, men could aspire to rise to any position. Many of the greatest artists were born in cottages or educated in workshops. That large numbers of citizens shared in the government of the city enlivened minds and nourished idealism; the more creative cities were the more democratic. In commerce, the Lombard towns remained in the lead as long as they were republican but were displaced after they became tyrannies, yielding primacy to Venice and Tuscany, which retained their liberties longer. In the latter part of the fifteenth century the rule of the Medicis was splendid but Florence lost its technical lead; and exports and prosperity declined (Ady, 1936).

The advent of tyranny by no means ended progress, so long as the city-states themselves remained free; if the art of the tyrannies was less vibrant, it was luxuriant. The shifting political struggles kept the courts in perpetual agitation and heightened the sense of particularity and individualism. According to Sismondi, "All the despots, dependent upon diplomacy for safety in the midst of so many ambitious little states and conflicting interests, caught the spirit of intellectual liberation and surrounded themselves by men of letters and artists, who gave distinction to their courts" (1906, p. 661). Magnates and small dictators bid competitively for the services of artists, architects, sculptors, and poets, in the zeal of many to equal the most magnificent. For prestige and popularity they sheltered learned men, and they adorned the city to reconcile the burghers to loss of liberties; and as some did this, others feared to appear meaner than their rivals. The Medicis were particularly lavish patrons, gathering a swarm of gifted men. If painting tended under them to lose feeling, technique advanced and volume of production grew; they were also glorified by a whole troop of first-rate but now forgotten students of ancient learning. Somewhat differently, the papacy supported a large staff of scholars and writers for its defense in the controversies of the age. So long as the rulers remained insecure and their subjects were free to leave one city for another, they were driven in some ways to foster rather than stifle intellectual activity.

It should be remarked, however, that the Italian achievement failed to come up to the Greek. Despite the social ferment, intense individualism, and considerable indifference to dogma, the Italians produced no significant original philosophy; the height of philosophic discussion was between Platonists and Aristotelians. Thomas Aquinas of Naples (1225-1274), who mostly taught in Paris and was hardly a participant of the central development, was essentially conformist, his achievement being the reconciliation of Aristotle and Catholicism. Among the humanists, many spoke against church doctrines and were reputed atheists; but the result was indifference to religion rather than search for new truth. Although heresies sprouted for a time, the Italians never really questioned fundamentals. Political thinking also fell short. The republican constitutions were not well fashioned; that of Florence, for example, with new institutions piled atop a jumble of old ones (Brucker, 1962), was much less systematic and consistent than that of Athens. The assemblies in which citizens voted but could not debate were not so educational as those of Greece. The commune remained an improvisation and failed to establish fully its legitimacy.

The Italians lived too much in the shadow of greater powers and sacrosanct glory for deeper originality. For most of the four good centuries, Latin was the obligatory vehicle for serious work, and humanism was the study of the classics. Nominal allegiance to that phantom of bygone glory, the Holy Roman Empire, was universal, although its authority was rejected; and the values of the empire always weighed on the commercial society. Aristocratic pretensions perennially intruded into political life and stirred factionalism. The Roman Church, conservative and authoritarian, also loomed inescapably over the city-republics, reducing possibilities of intellectual independence. No national feeling called for independent attitudes or philosophical self-assertion, as in France or Germany. Italians took pride in the papacy, whatever its spiritual condition, and in the religious primacy of Italy; the practical-minded esteemed the revenues and trade it brought. Florence, as banker for the Vatican, was especially restrained from moving contrary to the wishes of the pope. When it did, there was the likelihood of an interdict, which included holy license to rob Florentine merchants anywhere. Within the city, the Church represented a powerful independent corporation, uncontrollable and opposed to all that the commune stood for. Florence was unable to make clerics subject to commune courts or to control church courts (Brucker, 1962). Opponents of church policies could not basically oppose its spiritual claims, even when these clashed with the demands of the age. Hypocrisy resulted; without denying the authority of the Church to prohibit the taking of interest, merchants ignored it and squared consciences by crediting their earnings to God (Hay, 1961). Deep inquiry being heretical and unacceptable, the urge to intellectual freedom was diverted to licentiousness (Symonds, 1894).

Eclipse of the Towns

After the upsurge of learning and science from the eleventh into the fourteenth centuries, progress slackened. Architecture of the sixteenth century represented no improvement in engineering over the Gothic. Natural science was neglected. In the fifteenth century the study of anatomy decayed, as dissections were left to menials while the demonstrator merely pointed out facts supporting ancient texts (Crombie, 1953). The fourteenth-century anatomist Mondino was a standard authority until supplanted by Vesalius in the mid-sixteenth century. The universities lost vitality (Baron, 1957). An exposition of the inductive approach written about 1290 was often reprinted more than two centuries afterward. The sixteenth century took its inspiration not only from antiquity but also from the "classics" of the thirteenth and fourteenth centuries (A. Hall, 1958). Grosseteste and others, seeking a mathematical analysis of nature, introduced the experimental method in the thirteenth century; Galileo built on their work over three hundred years after. By 1375, observers had come close to the laws of motion that he proved early in the seventeenth century.

If natural science achieved relatively little for about two centuries, from the middle of the fourteenth until well into the sixteenth century, blame is sometimes laid on the Renaissance, which drew attention from the present world to the ancient, from practical problems to scholarly-literary pursuits, from the external world to the humanities, from immediate nature to a poorly understood past (Randall, 1954). Some humanists, such as Erasmus, viewed natural science as a distraction from humane and moral studies. The classics, although a weapon against dogmas of the Middle Ages, substituted a new authority and a new scholasticism for the old. But the revived classics included not only literary works but Hellenistic science, the mechanics of Alexandria, and especially the works of Archimedes; Lucretius, with his atomism and rationalistic world view, was rediscovered in 1417 (A. Hall, 1958). Copernicus was inspired by Aristarchus. The Renaissance, marked by eager curiosity and questioning, introduced nonchurch education and sanctioned individualism against the ideal of monastic submission. Moreover, not only abstract theorizing but also practical invention suffered. Although the fifteenth century saw important inventions, such as printing and mobile artillery, mechanics progressed little from the fourteenth to the seventeenth century. The clocks of the fourteenth century were not substantially improved until the pendulum clock in the seventeenth. Roger Bacon's thirteenth-century work on lenses remained authoritative for several centuries (Burns, 1954). The European economy as a whole grew little if at all from about 1325 to 1460 (Nef, 1950; Crombie, 1963); but Italy, where the Renaissance took hold first and most strongly, showed most material progress.

The plagues that took a large part of the population during this period may have had something to do with the trough that centered around the century from 1350 to 1450, since they disturbed the economy and reduced the volume of trade. However, Flanders and northern Italy, although they were struck by plague, were not much affected except as their foreign trade was hurt (Green, 1964). Political tensions, cultural depression, and economic stagnation come rather from overpopulation. The plagues, reducing crowding on the land, raised wages and increased per capita amounts of capital, in effect making people more valuable. This must have raised incentives to technical, that is, labor-saving innovation.

These were also times of consolidation of political power and loss of liberties. The fabric of medieval society was tightened, as the Church ceased effectively to offset secular powers, local authorities of all kinds lost more or less autonomy, and the state hardened its rule—a change that contributed to the wave of peasant revolts sweeping over Europe in the fourteenth and fifteenth centuries (Mollat and Wolff, 1973). In most of Europe the trend was from natural science to more authoritarian pursuits, the study of law and scholastic letters, both useful for administration. Interest in mathematics and astronomy continued best in Italy and Germany, where centralization was less marked (Randall, 1954). By the fifteenth century art styles were largely dictated by the ducal or royal courts (Hay, 1957).

This was one of the great "Ages of Conflict" of Western history (Quigley, 1966, p. 9). Through Europe, territorial lords expanded their domains and gained new powers to tax and to command. Municipal freedom and vitality suffered in some places sooner and in others later, in some quietly and hardly perceptibly, in others dramatically. The Hansa cities faded out over several centuries; but the downfall of the towns of southern France was quick, brutal, and total. The latter were struck down in part because of their intellectual virtues, bourgeois mentality, and consequent proclivity to heresy. Less attached to the Catholic Church than the Italians, for whom the papacy was a support and almost a national cause, they became infected by religious ideas related to Manichaeism brought by traders from the Near East. To destroy the dissidence of the Albigenses, the pope called a crusade, which nobles of northern France gladly undertook for the sake of loot and glory as well as their souls' salvation. Fighting and slaughter went on through most of the thirteenth century; and the stricken region, made into a dependent province, never recovered.

Eastern Spain, which shared the culture of Provence, was degraded later and more gradually. The culture of Catalonia has been nearly forgotten, but from the thirteenth through the fifteenth centuries Catalan was a leading language of Europe after Italian. Reinforced by troubadours driven from France by the persecutions of the Albigenses, Catalan letters were original and brilliant. Barcelona gave a magnificent prize for the best poem of the year (Merriman, 1936). Painting and other arts were also notable, although nowadays little remarked. Education flourished, most schools being under the patronage of the municipalities. From the end of the thirteenth to the end of the fifteenth century, six universities were founded in Catalonia. Religious toleration was the rule. Francesc Eixemenes, a great thinker of the fourteenth century, held the feudal order to be outworn. "By nature, everyone is free," he wrote; therefore, the proper government was representative democracy (Trueta, 1946, p. 71).

In 1295 a versatile Catalan writer, Ramon Lull, produced the best handbook for mariners until after Columbus. Barcelona had probably the first public bank in the world. Catalonia rivaled the great Italian cities for the Eastern trade and dominated that of northwest Africa; from the middle of the thirteenth to the middle of the fifteenth century, Catalonia claimed the greatest navy of the West; yet Barcelona, its only large center, had a population of not over thirty-five thousand. In the fifteenth century, Catalonia had fifty-five consuls to protect its interests abroad, whereas united Spain in the middle of the eighteenth century had only twenty-two. Sardinia, Mallorca, Sicily, and sundry Near Eastern areas came under Catalan domination for some generations. Catalan mercenaries, who used little or no defensive armor but relied on spirit and skill, were much in demand; they adventured as far afield as Armenia and Persia, and late in the fourteenth century, Catalans were fighting Navarrans for the control of Athens. The dashing Roger de Flor went to Constantinople in the hire of the Byzantine emperor with fifteen hundred horsemen and four thousand troopers and became virtual master of the realm. Like Xenophon's generals, Roger was murdered by the Orientals who hoped thus to paralyze his forces; instead of yielding, the company chose new leaders, crushed Byzantine armies, and briefly erected a Catalan empire of the Near East.

But in the fifteenth century, the kings began pressing against local liberties; and after the union of 1479 Catalonia suffered from neglect and oppression and withered to poverty and obscurity. It is enough to remark that Barcelona early in the fifteenth century had received more than a thousand ships yearly; in 1505 only five came; and the shipyards were closed (Trueta, 1946).

In Italy, most of the smaller republics were annexed to larger by the fifteenth century, and the larger had nearly all become tyrannies. Moreover, well before independence was lost, trade suffered as merchants abroad were robbed or taxed by the strengthened kings (Brucker, 1962). The really bad times, however, began with the French invasion of 1494; thereafter, Italians could hope at best to expel one foreign power by calling in another. After 1530 and the fall of the last Florentine republic, Spanish power was almost unchallenged. The king of Spain ruled Naples and Milan directly, the lesser rulers paid homage to him, and Spanish soldiers garrisoned many cities. In a few decades, Italy received an Inquisition modeled on the Spanish (Pontieri, 1957), and it held full powers through the peninsula. All Italy became a Spanish sphere of influence, nearly closed from foreign currents (Ogg, 1925); and there was not much difference between lands directly and indirectly ruled, between monarchies and oligarchic republics (Roberts, 1968).

Reduction of independence and importance brought a spirit of immobility, indolence, and conformism; and in the lack of self-confidence the sense of reality faded. Old forms were maintained in the title-ridden, stiff, and hierarchic society, but the aristocrat families found themselves reduced to the status of courtiers (Ogg, 1925). Although Genoese bankers and merchants profited in their relations with Spain, commerce and manufacturing slowly sank in an atmosphere of sloth and lethargy, as Italy became a supplier of raw materials for more progressive lands. Princes and viceroys, standing over a society of narrow privilege, established multifarious controls of trade and burdened the economy with monopolies and excessive taxes; they discouraged manufacturing and commerce in favor of landholding, which better suited their ways and values. Yet once-productive fields were deserted, as magnates surrounded themselves with hired rascalry, and banditry took over large areas of the countryside (Symonds, 1894).

The inspiration of past generations was strong enough that genius still appeared, but creativity ebbed after 1550. Music, least political of the arts, rose strikingly. Galileo, who had his troubles with the Inquisition, made formidable contributions to science in the first decades of the seventeenth century. But by his time ignorance, hypocrisy, and intolerance had largely replaced the zest for inquiry and learning. Painting and sculpture, called upon to serve the state, became superficial and purely ornamental; its expression was Mannerism, with its elegant virtuosity, and Baroque (Nussbaum, 1953). All over Europe, however, there were Italian artists and teachers, whose homeland was no longer suitable for intellectual endeavor, much as the learned men of a subjected Greece once became tutors for the Roman Empire; and cultural pilgrims continued for generations to trek for education and inspiration to a somnolent Italy.

Nation-states and Science

The repression of the liberties of the towns and consequent loss of their creativity was, of course, only part of the centuries-long, Europe-wide trend toward the consolidation of political power. This should not be regarded as the sole cause of the hiatus in the European development; but it seems clear that the first effects of the affirmation of stronger territorial authority were negative. Invention, however, was only slowed and did not halt entirely; and many, mostly unrecorded improvements, set Europe again and more strongly on the path to discovery. Thus, from 1460 to 1530 the output of European copper and silver mines increased approximately fivefold (Nef, 1950). But the second rebirth of Europe rested mostly on better means of transportation and on printing, which gave freedom and power to ideas. In the view of Francis Bacon, at the beginning of the seventeenth century, the world was remade by gunpowder, the compass, and printing, all fifteenth-century applications.

By the fourteenth century, long sea voyages, as from Italy to England, were an everyday occurrence (Clapham, 1929). Overseas explorations, patronized by newly powerful, affluent, and ambitious monarchs, began exciting the imagination in the fifteenth century. The voyages of exploration were dangerous; a large part of the participants never came home. They were also usually a bad investment. But they appealed to the sense of adventure and curiosity. At the beginning of the fifteenth century, Chinese of the youthful and vigorous Ming dynasty made remarkable voyages of discovery as far as Africa; but they went home and shut the imperial door. The Europeans creeping outward were only aroused to go farther. Distant commerce, made possible by numerous improvements of technology, in turn demanded better organization of trade and a new study of geography. It brought a revival of astronomy and called for better means of navigation, new instruments, and mathematics. Revealing indefinite new vistas, enticing curiosity, and making evident the deficiencies of classic texts, knowledge of new worlds stimulated the study of nature in all aspects.

Even more pregnant was the invention or practical application of printing. This was not a difficult innovation once the requisites—paper (introduced from the Orient to Spain in the twelfth century), ink, efficient presses (as for wine making), and facilities for casting metal—were at hand; and there was a large and growing demand for books. Printing with movable type was invented in Europe largely independently of much older block printing in Asia. The first books were printed in Germany near the middle of the fifteenth century; the advantages over hand copying were so enormous and so evident that by 1500 the art had spread over a receptive Europe (Turkey and Russia excepted), and more than 1,700 presses were working in 300 towns. In the time of Luther there were about a thousand printers in Germany alone. In the first half century, almost 40,000 editions were published in 15 to 20 million volumes (Hay, 1958). Most of these were religious in content, but science had its share. By 1500 there had been published about 1,050 scientific titles in 3,000 editions (A. Hall, 1958); in Italy alone, some 200 books on mathematics were published during this time (Bell, 1940). Books poured out ever faster; in England, for example, the number published increased fourfold in the half century after 1500 (Hay, 1958). (On the coming and impact of printing see McLean, 1972.)

Printing not only made knowledge inexpensive as never before. It gave navigation cheap, accurate maps and tables. It helped science even more than literature, since it facilitated the exact reproduction of drawings and diagrams for medicine, natural history, engineering, and the like—a necessity for scientific texts but impossible for scribes. With printing, science could graduate from dilettantism, as of Leonardo, to professionalism (Boas, 1962). Eventually it made possible the journals so essential for the dissemination of scientific discovery and the newspapers that, spreading from Holland early in the seventeenth century, kept people informed politically. It encouraged authorship and intellectual effort by giving writers rapid and wide circulation and fame, although at first, in the absence of copyright, it gave little immediate monetary reward. By the sixteenth century, a large number of writers were producing for the presses. Less commonly emphasized is the fact that it helped production by facilitating the spread of information about business developments, markets, and processes.

Printing also counteracted effects of political centralization. It made censorship more difficult as so many more works were profitably published at low cost. Printing establishments, which could carry all necessary equipment in a cart, easily escaped surveillance. It became much more necessary for the Church to censor writings, and harder to do so; the Church became dependent on frequently uncooperative civilian authorities to repress dissent (Hay, 1962). Too late to halt it, authorities realized that printing was a deadly threat to religious and political orthodoxy (Morley, 1974). Books being transportable and advantageously produced in large series, printers from the beginning distributed them far and wide over Europe; a very large part of the books sold in England, for example, were printed in Germany or Italy as long as Latin continued in common use. In sum, informational capacities were multiplied manyfold; in the favorable environment of Europe an explosion of knowledge was almost inevitable.

In the sequel came the end of religious universalism. This no longer corresponded to the political realities of Europe, and the Reformation came with the rise of nation-states. Practically speaking, the Reformation was successful where and only where it was favored by the political authority. But the Reformation would have been difficult without printing. Luther's Ninety-five Theses could spark a religious conflagration because they were immediately printed and distributed across Germany; the monk's doctrinal challenge was made a public issue. A prime demand of those opposed to the Catholic Church, from Wyclif on, was to place the Bible in the vernacular in the hands of the people; without Scriptures at hand, the authority of the pope would hardly have been challengeable. Luther's German Bible sold nearly one hundred thousand copies in the years after its appearance in 1522.

The Reformation, in turn, loosened intellectual bonds. The religious rebels had no idea of freedom of thought—Luther thundered against reason, and Calvin had no notion of tolerance; they wished a new orthodoxy for the old. But they broke the dam and could not stem the tide. The spiritual monopoly and traditional authority of Rome could never really be replaced. Dissenters could with difficulty justify the persecution of dissent. If Luther could reject Rome, others could reject Luther; if there were no vicar of Christ on earth, no bishops could be certified holy. The national church could hardly claim to be the sole way to salvation. What certitude remained but the Word and the souls of men? But the more people read the Bible for themselves, the more interpretations, until there were on every side schismatics and sectarians, all demanding freedom at least for their own opinions. Before Luther, the Hussite movement in Bohemia brought a substantial measure of toleration (Krofta, 1936). Pleas for toleration were heard almost from the beginning of the Reformation (Dickens, 1964). Absolutes being rejected, not even the Bible seemed a final word, but men looked to the continuing revelation of the conscience. To many, the rites that sanctified traditional authority came to appear merely superstitious and misleading; in the view of English Puritans, "The more ceremony the less truth" (C. Hill, 1961, p. 24). The rejection of authority and formalism opened the way to science.

The new teachings, turning from ritual to preaching and doctrine, were intellectually more demanding (Ogg, 1925) and called for education. Calvinism particularly wanted educated laymen to stand with an educated clergy in the church. The Reformation, placing men on their own, also encouraged enrichment, that is, production, as argued by Max Weber (1958). Medieval businessmen felt guilty in garnering wealth, particularly in defying the old prohibition on usury; Protestants regarded worldly success as a testimony of virtue and saw in their religion the message that they could and should raise themselves. It became one's duty to use his talents; and hard work, benefiting the community, seemed a better form of charity than almsgiving. The Reformation had a more direct effect on the economy, also, as the wealth and income of the Church were much reduced in Protestant lands. Far fewer persons went into religious vocations, and men turned from the glorification of God to mastery over creation. In Catholic Europe of the sixteenth and seventeenth centuries, the numerous priesthood and nobility enjoyed privileges and mostly escaped taxation, while the middle classes and peasantry were heavily charged (Nef, 1950). The situation was the contrary in the Protestant countries after the Reformation, and these were generally much more prosperous.

In the immediate aftermath of the Reformation, however, violent religious controversies made an atmosphere of intolerance and turned people to theology. The sixteenth century was not a time of great theoretical advance, but it saw much practical invention in response to the needs of mining, navigation, gunnery, and the like. Men turned to observation; chemistry progressed less from the theoretical work of the alchemists than from the experience of industrial arts, such as dyeing and metal refining. Science was becoming practical, and scientists began helping artisans by writing printed manuals (Boas, 1962). Vesalius corrected Galen's anatomy by observation, although he did not challenge the classic ideas. Before Copernicus' theory was accepted, his approach was used as a better way to calculate astronomical tables. Tycho Brahe, while keeping the Ptolemaic scheme of the spheres, made observations of planetary positions over a hundred times more accurate than those of Ptolemy. Toward the end of the century, Europe was becoming statistics-minded, as governments tallied people and commerce.

The seventeenth century saw the breakthrough to modern science. Galileo, hearing of the Dutch invention, made a telescope, opened new universes to view, and exploded the geocentric cosmos. Experimenting and calculating, he put mechanics on a sound empirical basis; Newton gave it a finished formulation that was in many ways the last word until Einstein. Kepler formulated the mathematical laws of planetary motion toward the end of the century, and Newton's law of gravitation brought order to heavenly movements. There was enormous progress in means of measurement and communication. The thermometer, barometer, pendulum clocks, and balance-wheel watches came one after another. By 1620 there were tables of logarithms and of trigonometric functions. Descartes followed with analytic geometry and Newton and Leibnitz with calculus, the basic tools of physical science. Boyle made chemistry scientific. Studying the hearts of animals as well as humans, Harvey learned of the circulation of the blood. The microscope revealed new worlds as marvelous as the rings of Saturn and mountains of the moon. In every field, from biology to acoustics, investigators grew from dozens to hundreds or thousands, and knowledge mushroomed.

In the seventeenth century science became a part of Western life, in the spirit of power in measured motion. England and the Netherlands contributed most. In the Italy of Galileo, cultivated opinion was turning away from scientific observation; the professors could not be persuaded to peer through the telescope. But in most countries, especially of the north of Europe, the prestige of science was surging. There was a great deal of curiosity about the new marvels, and patronage of science became fashionable with aristocrats and kings. They especially liked to toy with telescopes and microscopes. Academies, museums, botanic gardens, and collections of plants and animals multiplied; and scientific societies began carrying out and encouraging experiments, at first in amateurish curiosity, then more systematically. In 1665 scientific journals were started, a weekly in France and a monthly in England. Others followed in short order, and scientists came to form an international community (Nussbaum, 1953). The age grew proud of its new learning, far surpassing the best of the ancients, and began dreaming of boundless progress. Most of all, the Newtonian laws of nature, universal and majestic, caught the world's imagination; and many forgot to grieve that the universe had been changed from a thing of will and purpose to a mechanical system.

It was difficult, withal, to assimilate so much; the new scientific approach was slow to percolate from the laboratories and learned discussions to the popular mind and all realms of life and thought. The seventeenth century was very respectful of authority, and there was a lingering feeling that scientific knowledge was dangerous for the people. There were still much mysticism and obscurantism in the most enlightened countries. Many scientists devoted much of their best efforts to theology; Newton, greatest genius of the age, spent more time on cabalistic speculation than on physics. The political ordering of the world remained backward. Fontenelle, around the beginning of the eighteenth century, foresaw endless material progress but had no hope of improvement in government (Ogg, 1925).

Barring a political catastrophe, however, continued growth must have been inevitable. The eighteenth century, confident in reason, education, and Enlightenment, saw less amazing innovation than its predecessor; but science was becoming more systematic, spreading to wider circles, gathering much more data and making more experiments. With the beginnings of large-scale application of technology to production in the industrial revolution, the way was ready for the nineteenth century to transform civilization and man's view of himself.

Prosperity of the Netherlands

It is the essence of the state system that its influences are pervasive. Men and ideas travel from state to state, and discoveries may be made or great books written almost anywhere. But certain areas, specially favored by history and circumstance, have been most invigorated and have risen accordingly out of proportion to their natural and human resources. Such was the fortune of the Greeks of the Ionian sphere. The towns of northern Italy grew rich even by modern standards; an ordinary middle-class dowry in Florence toward the end of the fifteenth century was 2,500 to 3,000 florins, calculated to be equivalent to 15,000 to 20,000 modern dollars (Lucas-Dubreton, 1961). Such, too, were the Netherlanders who, pressed to secure their independence of Spain, worked so well as to become, practically without natural resources, by far the most prosperous people of the seventeenth century.

A commercial and seagoing folk, much divided among themselves, the Netherlanders successfully stood off the strongest power of Europe, the Spain of Philip II, in decades (1568–1648) of desperate warfare, and grew prosperous while fighting; before the war was ended, the republic of about a million souls had become the leading trading nation of the world, with more sizable towns than England, France, or Germany (Wilson, 1968). Toward the end of the sixteenth century the Dutch were carrying goods to the Italians, rather than vice versa; Dutch ships trading illegally with Portuguese colonies outnumbered legal Portuguese ships; the Dutch had triumphed over the Hansa cities and a majority of ships entering the Baltic were Dutch. Britain was largely dependent on Dutch shipping. While at war with Spain, the Dutch carried the bulk of Spanish commerce, and Spain would have gone hungry but for grain brought by enemy ships (Vlekke, 1945). Without timber or natural advantages for shipbuilding, the Dutch built the world's best and most economical ships. They had more than half the shipping and carrying trade of Europe. Their navy was twice that of England and France together, and other nations depended upon them to supply naval vessels. Angry at Dutch molestation of English trade, James I said, "You are masters of the sea wide and large and can do what you want" (Vlekke, 1945, p. 184).

As masters of the sea, the Dutch built up a global empire (Wilson, 1968). Netherlanders at one time held parts of the American seaboard (New York and Delaware), Brazil, the West Indies, the southern tip of Africa, posts in India, and the East Indies. They also had explored in many lands, as New Zealand, and held a monopoly of Japanese foreign trade. It was as purely commercial an empire as any that has existed, a network of trading posts acquired for the most part by private action. In contrast to the Spanish empire, there was little state control and less evangelical drive. Dutch wealth was based on good business, not imperial positions (Riemens, 1944).

As Pirenne observed, the Dutch had a weak government and a strong national will; their brothers south of the border had strong government and weak will. Every man was master, but the Dutch house was kept in admirable order. Reliable and efficient banking, with payments easily made by draft, helped make Amsterdam the financial capital of the world, not only for tradesmen but for foreign governments. There was free trade even in precious metals, a rare liberty for mercantilistic days. Capital was abundant and interest rates very low (Coleman, 1961). Dutch capital and skills were widely exported to the then less developed countries of Europe. Trading companies of Sweden, Denmark, and Brandenburg were managed by Dutchmen competing with Netherlands companies. Dutch money and credit were sound while the English were struggling with debts, the French were floundering in the financial morass that ultimately brought down the Old Regime, and the Spanish were repudiating their obligations (Clark, 1950). The Dutch were the leading foreign investors, exporting capital and skills, somewhat as did the United States after World War II; and poorer states regarded them as exploiters (Wilson, 1968).

The Dutch liked to consider their material prosperity as proof of their virtue. Perhaps it was, for the Dutch were credited with such traits as cleanliness, stolidity, patriotism, modesty, and straightforwardness (Barnouw, 1940). They seemed practically immune to bribery. Honesty was one secret of their commercial success. Incidentally, no other people provided so amply for their poor as the mercantile Dutch (Wilson, 1968).

Foreigners recognized that the Dutch were energetic, quick witted, and inventive beyond other peoples. The commercial Dutch led the world in experimenting with new crops and techniques to raise soil fertility. Dutch workmen were brought to England to teach tricks of iron-working (Dietz, 1942); Colbert, despite his aversion for their ways, imported Dutch artisans (Coleman, 1961). Queen Elizabeth of England said that monarchs should take lessons from the Dutch republic (Wilson, 1968).

Education throve as each municipality took pride in its school, and after Leyden acquired its university all the other provinces had to have their own. In the sixteenth century, when illiteracy was the rule in most of Europe, practically everyone in Holland could read and write, many in more than one language. Few tracts were banned for heresy, and publishing was freer than anywhere else; hence the Netherlands became the greatest center of book production, especially for forbidden works. Many foreign students came, of whom the most famous was Peter the Great, determined to learn Western secrets for the strength of Russia. The least militaristic of the nations of Europe, the Dutch were pioneers of military engineering, the arts of fortification and siegecraft; the military men of Europe looked to Holland for their lessons.

The Netherlands became the leading land of science. For two centuries the University of Leyden was considered the greatest scientific center in the world (Randall, 1954). The numerous investigators included the many-sided Huygens, who formulated the wave theory of light and invented both pendulum and balance-wheel clocks, the first accurate timekeeping devices; a thoroughly rationalistic spirit, he looked for evidence of everything. Leeuwenhoek explored a new world through the microscope. Swammerdam was the first systematic observer of insect life. The leading scientists were not connected with official institutions of learning, but, like many of their compatriots, were moved by intellectual curiosity. Descartes found street crowds discussing mathematical problems. Anatomical studies became very popular; the public flocked to dissections in Holland as to heretic roasting in Spain (Barnouw, 1952).

The Dutch were less inclined to metaphysics although they can take some credit for Descartes, who spent most of his creative life there, and for Spinoza, born to Portuguese Jews in Amsterdam. John Locke lived six years in Holland, while England was politically inhospitable, and there completed his greatest work, *On Human Understanding*. In what was then a branch of philosophy, Grotius fathered modern international law. Atypically imprisoned for political activities, he escaped to write his treatise in the service of foreign princes. Various of his compatriots carried on his work. Bynkershoek (1673-1743) moved from the natural law tradition to base international law entirely on observed reality: the ordinances, treaties, and deeds of states.

Literature of various genres prospered at the same time, but the Dutch specialty was painting, brought to high perfection by Rembrandt, Frans Hals, Vermeer, Ruysdael, and many others, the best of Europe at the time. Nourished not by the vanity of a few great patrons but by widespread love of art, more pictorial of life and nature than purely decorative, Dutch painting was an essentially popular art.

In the latter part of the seventeenth century, decline was setting in; such a small country could hardly maintain its extraordinary preeminence very long. Larger countries applied themselves to sea power, and geography was no longer advantageous for the Netherlands. When other countries became protectionist, Dutch manufacturing suffered from lack of domestic materials. The burdens of defense required heavy taxes on the small nation (Wilson, 1968). Political decay was also a cause and symptom of decline. Oligarchies became more covetous of their advantages; corruption entered, and ambition turned partly away from commerce to official careers. Such tendencies may be attributed in part to the psychology of success, complacency, and ripening of wealth, as the elite prefer to enjoy their estates instead of exerting themselves like their grandfathers. But in part they must be laid to the growth of territorial empire and dominion over native peoples, especially in the East Indies, where trading posts gradually turned into colonial domains during the second half of the seventeenth century.

Attention shifted from competitive European trade to the exploitation of monopolistic positions in the empire.

Even in decline, however, little Holland continued to be a leading power in the world of the eighteenth century, almost the economic peer of rising England. Wages were still higher in the Netherlands than in England and France—a fact that hurt its competitive position. While commerce weakened, the financial dominance of Amsterdam remained; the Netherlands capital was important in the financing of England's eighteenth-century wars. The Netherlands, a model for the modernization of the English economy in the seventeenth century, was still an example of successful economic liberalism for Adam Smith's *Wealth of Nations*.

Britain and the Industrial Revolution

In the eighteenth century, the banner of economic and cultural leadership passed from the Netherlands across the narrow seas to England, which, despite a relatively small population, was for over a century certainly the richest and probably the strongest nation on earth, the leading state of its system, much as Athens once led among the Greeks. London was the financial center of the world and the British navy was stronger than any other. Modern industrialization based on power-driven machinery took its start in England almost a century before other nations followed. England also deserves most credit for inaugurating scientific agriculture. Behind these achievements lies a scientific-utilitarian intelligence; England has contributed more than any other nation to the rise of modern science. At the same time, English literature is second to none; and in no branch of arts, philosophy, or learning has the English achievement been slight.

The English advancement became conspicuous in Tudor times, as English merchants and mariners took over trade previously handled by Italians and Hanseatics. Under Elizabeth and James I, economic expansion was marked. Cottages of brick and stone replaced wattled, chimneyless huts, glass windows became common, and carpets replaced rushes. The national wealth increased over 4 percent yearly, tripling from 1558 to 1584. England also grew strong rapidly. Privateers brought home silver and fed the national pride. The navy was much enlarged and improved. The defeat of the Armada in 1588 was exhilarating, the humiliation of the mightiest and proudest power by a small nation that had hardly guessed its own strength. In all the sea fighting of these decades, while Spain lost hundreds of ships England lost but one, which stood up against the whole Spanish fleet.

At the end of the sixteenth century, colonization and trade seemed to offer boundless opportunities. As never before, foreign writings of all kinds were translated into English (F. Hill, 1965). A flood of foreign novelties in fashions and literature, new Italian influences, and the revival of classic learning all came together to stimulate the imagination. The Renaissance burst upon Elizabethan England at the same time as the marvels of distant lands, exotic products, and knowledge of strange peoples. Italian literature gave a new sense of pleasure in language, and the Greek spoke to the individualism of the age, but the most influential writings were Hakluyt's and others' tales of far travels.

After the defeat of the Armada, this stimulation ignited the mixture of nationalism and individualism to produce an outburst of imaginative drama and poetry. The first public theater was not opened until the middle of Elizabeth's reign; but there was soon a troop of dramatists, many of whom would be better known had they not stood in the shadow of Shakespeare. In the plays of the latter, as in those of Marlowe and others, are explicit the interests of the age: the heroism of antiquity, the wonders of worlds newly discovered, and the glories of English history. The great narrative poem, Spenser's *Faerie Queene,* may be read as an allegory of England's wars; and the New World gave a setting for Thomas More's *Utopia.*

The Elizabethan age of poetry continued into the reign of James I. Then, as the novelty of discovery wore off and optimism gave way to internal dissension, the exhilarating sense of omnipotence was replaced by questioning of the social-political order and the divine way. For a generation or more, as confidence waned, the quality of literary works declined, and enthusiasm gave way to escapism. However, there was great faith in education as a means to prosperity and happiness (Davies, 1959). The Bible translation of King James's scholars fed Puritan thought, and individual study meant individual interpretation and suggested independent worship. A host of new religious groups arose, many with strange ideas and new prophets; when the floodgates were opened by the defeat of Charles I, there was a veritable torrent of diverse religious writings, many reaching out to novel interpretations, some rejecting even basic ideas of Christianity. Of the sects of the age, almost all have disappeared, except the Baptists and Quakers. Quakerism, which spread with great rapidity, was most expressive of the new urges in its rejection of all ritual and churchly authority, making everyone a priest, communicant with the divine. The controversy between crown and Parliament and the unsettling of old institutions in the time of the civil war and Commonwealth also produced a flood of political thinking, equalitarian, communistic, republican, or authoritarian, inquiries into rights and property such as had hardly been known before in the West. The two most famous writers, Harrington and Hobbes, represent tendencies almost completely opposite.

Restoration England was weary of (and stifled) religious and political controversy. Minds turned to practical questions and antidogmatic science (Feuer, 1963). But here also there was a background of achievement. In Elizabethan times there had been a good deal of scientific writing, more the work of practical men, mostly Puritans, than of the conservative universities (C. Hill, 1965), and Gilbert and Harvey made notable discoveries in magnetism and physiology. Early in the seventeenth century Francis Bacon wrote of the need for experimental science, and English astronomers were fairly well abreast of

Galileo. But English science became broadly influential when issues of faith receded after the civil wars. In 1662, Charles II extended his patronage to an informal discussion group and the Royal Society began to discuss "experimental philosophy." Its greatest president was Newton, who was born in 1642, the year of the overthrow of Charles I, and made his chief discoveries in 1665-1666; he did not have to argue with the past but was honored as a prince of learning. The English showed themselves more eager than any other nation (except the Dutch) to apply to practical affairs the scientific knowledge then burgeoning. Many merchants and manufacturers assisted the Society in its studies of mechanic arts, natural resources, and manufacturing methods; and the Newtonian intellectual revolution spread through British society with extraordinary speed. Science was also stimulated by the knowledge brought from strange lands, the collections of plants and animals that directed curiosity to nature, and the need for studies of geography and navigation.

In the eighteenth century the movement took shape whose effects are more obvious today than those of all political cataclysms together, the combination of technology, business, and ultimately science in the industrial revolution. This was truly a revolution in that it transformed British society. At the beginning of the eighteenth century, four fifths of the people were engaged in agriculture, at its end less than half; in a brief time, England became a land of factories. To date the beginnings of the industrial revolution, one might point to 1785, when a steam engine was first installed in a cotton mill, or to 1769 when Arkwright patented a machine for drawing and twisting thread. But inventions were continuous and improvement was steady since the Restoration. The industrial revolution was the British evolution.

England was ready for it. The land had long been wealthy. When early in the seventeenth century crown prince Charles went to Spain to seek a bride, his party, although sympathetic to Spain, wondered at the barrenness of the fields and the misery of the inhabitants. Other English travelers professed to be shocked by the poverty of the lower classes of France and Germany of this time. And during the seventeenth century, despite civil war and confusion, both population and standard of living rose substantially. Improved agricultural practices also prepared the way. In the seventeenth century, the Royal Society investigated the treatment of soils; there were experiments with clover and other cover crops and fodder crops, and the average yield of wheat rose about 50 percent. The drainage of the Fens, helped by Dutch ideas of reclamation and Dutch engineering, added considerably to arable land. Progress was most marked in animal husbandry; animal breeding was systematized, and weight of marketed sheep and cattle doubled during the century. Better crop rotations were found. A beginning was made toward mechanization, with such devices as a seed drill, improved plows, and a threshing machine.

Industry had likewise long been building up. From the fifteenth century technological progress had been notable in machinery of many kinds, bookkeeping, metalworking, and printing. The sixteenth century brought numerous inventions; coal came widely into use as an all-around fuel (wood becoming scarce). Under Elizabeth, most wool, formerly exported raw, came to be woven in England. Mining of iron and other metals was much expanded; an attempt was made to reduce iron with coal instead of charcoal. The arms industry was thriving; Elizabeth's seamen complained that they were hit by English bullets from English guns. During the seventeenth century money-making schemes became the fashion and the English acquired a reputation for inventiveness. For example, in 1632 a process was found for casting brass buckles so that one man could produce as many as ten before; but this was prohibited lest it cause unemployment. During this century, coal output increased fourteen times to 3 million tons. From about 1600 (and for nearly three centuries thereafter) England led all nations in heavy industry.

In the eighteenth century, innovation became explosive. In 1711 Newcomen introduced a steam pumping engine, effective enough to be used widely in mines. The growing economy led to the construction of roads and a network of canals, which in turn enlarged markets. In 1733 came the fly shuttle, one of the first of a long series of improvements in the textile industry, as new machines enormously raised productivity first of spinning and then of weaving. Ocean ships grew larger and better; during the century the tonnage of ships clearing British ports increased nearly tenfold. Thanks to a new cannon-boring machine, James Watt was able to make cylinders sufficiently precise for his efficient steam engine. It was learned to smelt iron by the use of coal from which the fumes had been driven; iron became much cheaper and replaced wood in the construction of machinery. Coal production tripled in the century. In 1815 England had several thousand steam engines in operation; France, her nearest rival, had only fifteen small ones. By the end of the eighteenth century England was entering the age of iron, coal, and steam, a generation ahead of the Continent (Robertson, 1939) and ready for the massive industrialization of the nineteenth century, when coal output grew twenty times over. Through about 1860, England had close to half the world's industrial production.

There are many reasons for this leadership into modernity. Geography invited the English to become mariners and traders; the land was admirably situated as an entrepôt. Contacts across the seas are educational, and it is difficult for a nation that knows the world to keep its mind closed, while the economy that depends upon foreign markets must be oriented toward production. Many foreigners, Flemings, French Huguenots, and others, brought their talents and ideas to England as a haven of relative peace and toleration. A rather large market was needed that innovations should pay; and if France or China potentially offered larger markets, their masses were too poor to buy much more than the cheapest necessities. Countries such as Holland and Switzerland, like England relatively affluent and unrestrictive, were handicapped by smallness and lack of natural resources. Coal was vital, and England was fortunate to possess accessible deposits. But the most striking series of inventions was in the weaving, by hand or waterpower, of cotton imported from Asia, and in pottery, suitable clays for which are found in almost every land. The industrial revolution resulted mostly from the application of ingenuity in a land possessing a practical mentality, capitalistic organization, capital, and ready entrepreneurs.

English society had been favorable for commerce and enterprise for centuries. Free trade within England came early in the Middle Ages as a fruit of national unity, and traders enjoyed prestige practically since the beginnings of the kingdom. By the fifteenth century land was freely for sale and class distinctions were becoming less rigid. In the time of Elizabeth, capitalists were getting away from guild restrictions by setting up works outside the towns, while the Statute of Apprentices opened the crafts to all who fulfilled the requirements of training. While the bulk of the population of most continental countries was more or less tied to the land, Englishmen were free to move and improve themselves. There were many restrictions and monopolies, as generally in Europe, but lack of means of enforcement made many of them ineffective; early in the seventeenth century there were calls for open competition and full freedom of trade. The civil war was in part a protest against the official monopolies, and it ended most of them except the temporary patents given as an incentive for invention. The Puritans stood for social-spiritual success that respected not birth or position but probity, diligence, and ensuing prosperity. New towns arose in northern England free of guild restrictions. Free traders took most foreign commerce from the chartered companies. From the Restoration onward, economic individualism and doctrines of freedom of enterprise took hold, despite mercantilist regulation of foreign commerce; attachment to "natural liberty" was quite as strong in economic as in political affairs. A century before Adam Smith, writers claimed that by serving his self-interest a man served the community; and in 1702 Parliament declared, "Trade ought to be free and not restrained."

British government was as good as any of the age, stable and effective yet limited and unoppressive. Typically, London had a reliable penny post with frequent deliveries early in the eighteenth century (George, 1953). Credit was well developed from Elizabeth's day. In the eighteenth century the soundness of the banking system contrasted markedly with the chaos of French finances, and Frenchmen complained that their English competitors had unfair advantages of easy credit and adequate capital. Monopolies were unimportant, taxation was moderate, the share of national wealth going to the church was relatively small, wages were uncontrolled. The government encouraged invention by protective patents and rewards, and to be an inventor was a good way to rise in social status (Bowden, 1965).

Much less than in most lands was success in England equated with official position, and property brought influence rather than the reverse. The middle class was very large and merged indistinguishably into its betters and inferiors, and men of the best families could honorably enter business (Henderson, 1969). Wealthy persons invested their capital more productively than in patents of nobility, French style. Fortunes were to be made in business, not in milking the state, and England became business-minded. There developed logical-empirical attitudes. As British philosophers have insisted on the necessity of concrete evidence, producers have felt free to question customs and seek improvements.

Intangible factors were indispensable. The credit system could not prosper without mutual trust. Accumulation of capital required frugality and willingness to invest in productive enterprise (Briggs, 1959). The industrial revolution could come to England not only because men were invited to help themselves but because they took pleasure in improvement. It was a token of the civic spirit that England in the eighteenth century, unlike continental countries, accepted public responsibility for the maintenance of the disabled, poor, and aged. Adam Smith argued that it was enough that men look to their self-interest in order that society should gain, and this became the economic philosophy of liberalism. But it was necessary that many should strive beyond rational calculations of their own profit; hundreds wrestled with the problems for every name that is remembered (Bowden, 1965). The great inventions came out of countless losing speculations. Many failures are forgotten while a few successes are remembered, but even the latter usually incurred losses before they were perfected or made profitable. A whole series of spinning machines proved impractical before a successful one was patented in 1770. Few innovators reaped riches. Like explorers of new continents, they pushed forward, garnered more adventure than money, and prepared the way for men after them to enrich themselves. They had to be inspired not chiefly by an urge for profit but by a spirit of improvement, a restless desire to do things better in new ways; they practically dedicated themselves to a cause, often at the expense of their peace of mind, family life, fortune, or career. A disproportionate number of them were Dissenters, descendants of the Puritans; and when they were successful, they commonly lived frugally, enjoying not material luxury but the satisfaction of achievement, feeling that their plants were theirs to manage for the best, but that their wealth was a trust. At least a little such spirit has always been necessary for the increase of human productivity.

8 The Nation-state System: Interaction and Development

Competition

Because of heterogeneity and dimensions, the Western state system is inherently more complex than its predecessors. Moreover, its interactions have been more strongly conditioned by rapidly evolving technology. The principles stated for earlier state systems remain evident, however, in the complicated history of the West: the effects of competition, of the relative openness of societies, of movement among states, of variety, and of size, have been much the same in the long experience of the West as in classic Greece and other parallel systems.

The open and uncertain international order implies tension and striving among states, often deadly and always engaging, which fosters innovation, raises the stature of intellectuals, improves performance, and enlivens. Competition of individuals and groups is a major stimulus to effort, perhaps the biggest reason for exertions beyond the minimum, whether to swim faster or to climb the corporate ladder. On the state level, such competition is often burdensome if not dangerous, as in the matching of armed forces; but it has been in many ways stimulating for civil accomplishments. The very arts of destruction have nourished material progress. Just as in the dawn of civilization men found it more urgent to develop metalworking for weaponry than for farming, in Renaissance days the need to direct the flight of cannonballs was an irrefutable argument for the study of motion. Galileo put arguments into the mouths of arsenal workmen, mixing the study of projectiles with the improvement of mechanics (Feuer, 1963). The wars of the eighteenth century, like others before and since, gave incentives not only for invention but for increased production and so helped nurse the industrial revolution in England (Plumb, 1957). France was driven by the Napoleonic wars to promote manufacturing; not only was there a powerful stimulus of demand but the emperor offered, in the effort to meet the British challenge, many large prizes for inventions (Henderson, 1969).

In less violent ways Atlantic states were led to overseas exploration, first by the urge to challenge the Italian monopoly of Oriental trade, then by the desire to get ahead of rivals in the treasure hunt. Rivalry with Frederick the Great led Maria Theresa of Austria to reform her state, modernizing laws and administration. Economic rivalry has also propelled nations; the English, for example, measured themselves by their successful Dutch cousins. A seventeenth-century tract on economic improvement was entitled, "How to Beat the Dutch without Fighting" (Coleman, 1961, p. 45).

Culture has also profited directly. Princes and republics have long vied in the brilliance of their capitals and have lured painters, sculptors, architects, writers, and so on, for whom material appreciation supplements divine inspiration. Many a university has been founded or improved because of the shame and loss that the young men went abroad to study; and competitive pride has been midwife of academies, museums, and laboratories. Competition has also made education seem a political necessity since the eighteenth century (Roach, 1969) and has given it a practical and scientific content. The Swedish Academy of Sciences was founded in 1739 on English, French, and German models to promote economic power (Stomberg, 1931). From the time of Napoleon, states have patronized science for strength, outstandingly in power-minded Prussia and Germany. French education was reformed after the defeat of 1871. A German scholar, Adolf von Harnack, insisted in 1910 that Germany must spend more to keep up preeminence in science or suffer political disaster (O. Hale, 1971). Even Asiatic peasants are stirred to modernization by ideas of nationalistic glory (Foster, 1962).

More critical than the generation of ideas is their acceptance. Few societies really encourage change, which is probably a threat to established position; even in relatively free and competitive nations, inventors commonly spend much more effort on securing support for application than on the actual invention (Barnett, 1953). However, "in peace," as Gibbon wrote of his late eighteenth-century Europe, "the progress of knowledge and industry is accelerated by the emulation of many active rivals; in war, the European forces are exercised by temperate and indecisive conflicts" (*Decline and Fall,* chap. 38, II). The never-relaxed contention for power and position, for status, glory, and security in an insecure world, generates, as nothing else can, an atmosphere propitious to improvement. Those who have responsibility—and the freer the society, the larger number of persons responsible—should continually be spurred by the need to improve, even at a cost to comfort. Every advancement of a rival is a goad;

and the more intimate and competitive the international system, the more forceful the prodding. Insecurity jolts one out of routine. It was part of the greatness of Florence that it was chronically in crisis, beset by a sense of urgent need in foreign and domestic policy, and this made life interesting and actions important (Brucker, 1962).

International competition is a supreme reality principle. Independent states in the multisided contest can disregard facts at their peril. They are constantly under pressure toward rationality, a guidance the more necessary for larger states of bureaucratic-hierarchic organization. In the contentious community, there are always blows to pride or interests that demand new responses. Foreign complications have regularly triggered major changes; among many examples, the English, French, and Russian revolutions (of 1905 and 1917) were set in motion by involvements abroad that the rulership was not able to handle. For this reason, true conservatives—in Sparta, Prussia, Russia, or elsewhere—are not aggressive but isolationist, fearful of foreign complications.

The contest of nations, flavored by the spice of violence, vitalizes civic endeavors and gives meaning to activity in every sphere. As an old song ran:

> So long as flashes English steel
> And English trumpets shrill,
> He is dead already who doth not feel
> Life is worth living still
> (Russell, 1936, p. 205

As Shakespeare had it, on the eve of the battle of Agincourt, "Now all the youth of England are on fire,/And silken dalliance in the wardrobe lies." On the battlefield, his Henry V cries out:

> We few, we happy few, we band of brothers;
> For he to-day that sheds his blood with me
> Shall be my brother; be he ne'er so vile
> This day shall gentle his condition;
> And gentlemen in England, now a-bed
> Shall think themselves accursed they were not here,
> And hold their manhoods cheap
> (*Henry V*, II, chorus, 1-2, and *IV*, iii, 60-66).

Emotions associated with the contest of nations could be overwhelming. Treason was held the most despicable of crimes, and patriotism was at times the strongest of feelings; *pro patria,* as for nothing else, it has been held to be sweet and proper to die or kill. The needs of the polity overrode all other values. Not very long ago, William James (1911, p. 275) called war "the romance of history," and stated as the common view, "If war had ever stopped, we should have to reinvent it, in this view, to redeem life from flat degeneration."

Foreign affairs engross the attention and give purpose to the elite, whose example largely makes the morale of society; in the shared cause the commonfolk find dignity and a worthy place. As Montesquieu wrote, "What I call virtue in the republic is the love of the *patrie*, that is to say, the love of equality" (Cobban, 1963, p. 102). People make their own the struggles of present and past, and of their neighbors and fellow citizens. Nothing so well as the contentions of the sovereign community builds respect for law while making sacred authority unnecessary. As an Elizabethan poet wrote, "Had all been virtuous men, There never had been princes upon earth" (C. Hill, 1965, p. 267).

Discipline of primitive groups arises from exigencies of dealing with outgroups, internal comradeship being correlative to external hostility (Stonequist, 1937). Legality, democracy, and openness of society all depend upon a shared will; and common objectives are a substitute for a strong political apparatus. The ethical sense of a people reflects and is reflected in their political life; as the Florentines observed, the spirit grows in contact with the commonwealth (Baron, 1955). From the individual's selfish point of view, it does not pay to be a very good citizen (Almond and Verba, 1963); but in some societies, everyone has known that he could ordinarily count upon his neighbor to be fair in his dealings, to help in case of need, and to act according to law and conscience. As a result of such cohesiveness, small competitive states have been able to stand up against large empires. Peoples of well integrated small nations, such as the Greeks, Catalans, Swiss, Flemings, and Swedes, have often made excellent fighters even far from home and in poor causes.

Success in the striving of the powers, unless it is complete enough to lead to complacency, is energizing. Pride of standing, competition for the leadership of the world, and the sense of power over destiny give confidence and spur to achievement. Thus the Greeks were uplifted by victory over Persia. So were the Florentines by their successful defense of liberties at the beginning of the fifteenth century; like the Athenians, they associated intellectual leadership with military valor (Baron, 1955). Shattering the pretensions of Spain in the sixteenth century helped inspire Elizabethan poetry and drama. Defeat, too, may usher in an efflorescence of art, as in France after 1871 (Kavolis, 1972).

Better than victory, defeat brings home needed lessons; war, as Thucydides said, is a "violent teacher" (Glover, 1926, p. 71). Communal troubles and shared stress, as psychologists have pointed out, make a society healthier; the British, for example, found under bombardment in World War II a novel sense of community and an entirely new inspiration in the national cause (Tanner, 1976). Many nations, perhaps all of which have long histories, have been at some time reinvigorated and rejuvenated by the loss of battles or wars, which have positive results as long as there remains a fundamental confidence that bars resignation and a conviction that difficulties can be overcome. People are shocked into admitting change. In nineteenth-century China, superstitious hostility prevented erection of telegraph lines; when war with France came, opposition to them vanished (A. Smith, 1907). After a disastrous and humiliating defeat by Napoleon, the Prussian king said, "The state must make up in intellectual force what she has lost in physical" (Gillespie, 1969, p. 127). It did so successfully enough to more than recover physical force as well. France, after defeat in 1871, enjoyed a national revival; the victory of 1918 was followed by lassitude and stagnation.

It was extremely useful to Russia to be beaten in the Crimean War; made aware of its backwardness, the regime proceeded to the emancipation of the serfs and other liberal measures preparing the way for the remarkable economic progress of the last decades of the century. As a Russian journalist, Pogodin (Lederer, 1962, p. 77), put it:

> The common danger, the personal sorrow, sympathy for the fate of children and relatives, the sense of national honor, the hatred of foreigners, contempt for ungrateful allies, the offended pride caused by the enforced retreat—all these have awakened our spiritual energies. A host of questions that were not even thought of earlier is being discussed everywhere. New ideas germinate and gain in content as they are being exchanged. Wishes and hopes arise. Songs fill the air, the imagination is at work.

When governments and societies grow stale, the patriot might well pray for defeat.

The Open Society

Competition curtails power (Knorr, 1973). The victory of a political order is not complete unless it is universal. The coexistence of states in tension means that across the borders there is always potential support for dissidents, and it is difficult fully to liquidate an opposition morally and materially abetted from outside. As long as dissidents can look to a source of sympathy and support and a possible haven of safety, no rule can be quite monolithic; with an opposition ever present across the borders, there is always at least a potential opposition at home. It is not necessary that the views of the foreign state coincide with those of the local nonconformists; Realpolitik may decree encouragement for deviants. The autocratic Richelieu, fomenting revolt in Catalonia, called for the establishment of a republic (Merriman, 1963). The Russian tsar supported a liberal revolution in Greece in the 1820s because of enmity for Turkey. Imperial Japan aided Socialist-Revolutionaries during the Russian revolution of 1905, and imperial Germany financed the Bolsheviks in 1917 in order to weaken the Russian war effort.

An outside pressure may be conservative. For example, subsidies from Louis XIV helped Charles II do without Parliament. The Holy Alliance after the Napoleonic wars aimed at the preservation of legitimacy and monarchy; Alexander of Russia and Metternich of Austria attempted for years to act as gendarmes of Europe, suppressing revolutionary movements wherever they might arise on the Continent. French money helped the Prussian monarch get the better of his estates in the seventeenth century and helped the tsar to ride out the Revolution of 1905.

But in active international rivalries, the effect of foreign meddling has more often been liberal or at least destabilizing and antitraditional. The dynamics of international rivalry in the latter part of the nineteenth century brought Russia and Austria into an opposition fatal to traditional autocracy in both. Foreign powers appeal to the dissatisfied, those poorly treated by their governments. So far as international politics are more contention than cooperation, help is usually given to rebels, probably more in need of material support than regimes. Desire to avenge defeat in the Seven Years' War and to restore the balance of power induced royalist France to assist republican American colonies against England. Dutch trade rivals of the English also assisted the Americans financially (Ward, 1968). As a result, the colonies became independent, George III's attempt to restore the kingly power was ended, and the French monarchy was fatally undermined. Earlier, French support had helped the Swiss cantons to stand against the Holy Roman Empire (P. Martin, 1949). Foreign troubles of Spain made possible the Portuguese recovery of independence in 1640. The cooperation first of French Huguenots, eager to assist coreligionists, and then of Elizabethan England, desirous of weakening Spain, was indispensable for the Netherlands' difficult struggle for independence (Geyl, 1964). The spirit of Polish resistance could hardly have survived more than a century of foreign occupation without support and encouragement in the West. English capital financed Latin American revolt against Spain, and it suited England and the United States to guarantee the republics against suppression. Nineteenth-century Russian tsars, fearful of revolutionary movements, supported uprisings in the Turkish empire; to enlist popular support, they gave Balkan peoples progressive constitutions that caused envy in the Russians.

The international contest gives reasons for loyalty, obedience, and paying taxes and makes coercion less necessary. Interest and enthusiastic involvement in political affairs are libertarian; from the eighteenth century, the word "patriot" had had connotations of freedom (Huizinga, 1959). As a French *philosophe* wrote, "There is no *patrie* under the yoke of despotism" (Cobban, 1963, p. 102). Concern for the community gives the citizens a better claim to a share in the state and makes more workable the republican or democratic system. Without a strong civic consensus, the constitution of the democratic polis would have been entirely unworkable. Representative government requires a consensus sufficiently firm that the state can at the same time represent varied opposing interests and yet function with fair harmony. It presupposes a sense of the nation that representatives should be not merely advocates of special interests but spokesmen of the whole, prepared to speak unpleasant truths such as an emperor never hears.

The needs of the community supersede personal and ascriptive relations and require that positions be open to ability; the freedom to rise not only brings talent to high places but encourages ambitions. When all feel superior to or at least set off from foreigners, there is less urge to assert social superiority and to keep domestic inferiors in their place. In the pride of Athens, nobles like Solon and Pericles promoted democracy, and aristocrats mingled with slaves in the streets. National pride is also an antidote for corruption and extortion, which support arbitrary power. Officials who feel they must show performance are resistant to both flattery and bribes (Tullock, 1965).

Rulers in a competitive world probably claim and need firm authority. Discontents may be diverted to the foreign cause, internal divisions may be overridden, and the common emergency justifies extraordinary discipline and demands. Yet in competitive states the leadership, perhaps most of all, are drawn to serving the general cause; and there can be no republicanism unless the elite are loyal to the republic. Oppression eases as concern for real achievements grows. If those around the ruler are more moved to serve the state than to please him, they will condition their support on approval of his policies. The Catalonian parliament assumed power in 1462 not only because a king infringed traditional rights but because he alienated lands to France; the struggle for rights mingled with the national struggle (Merriman, 1936).

In an insecure realm, autocracy is contained by demands of rationality and the need to win cooperation; and popular participation brings popular control. The need for consent requires discussion, and discussion implies equality. If war is useful only for an elite, it may be a motive or pretext for repression; but the struggle that represents a felt collective need is likely to be liberalizing in effect. Castilian kings gave concessions and autonomy to towns to secure cooperation in the wars of the Reconquest, withdrawing them when it was finished. It was mostly the need of money for campaigns that rendered medieval kings dependent on parliaments. Kings of Aragon lost standing at home when they spent energies and resources in foreign adventurings (Merriman, 1936). Medieval English kings or Holy Roman emperors sacrificed much of their authority when they chased glory in France or Italy and were forced to purchase cooperation with the only thing they had to give, political concessions. The French Estates General gained most authority in the worst times of the long war with England in the fourteenth century; it then, as never afterward until 1789, came forward as a popular body, calling for virtually democratic rights and substantial control over the government.

In more recent times, the democracy of Holland was at its best during the war for independence. Foreign troubles forced the early Stuarts to call the parliaments that clipped their wings. Difficulties of foreign policy led the Swedish nobility to admit commoners to high office in 1723 (Lindsay, 1957). To encourage recruiting during the American war, the British government made concessions to Catholics, which had to be extended to Protestant dissenters (Ward, 1968). The personal power of George III was ended both by the disgrace of the American defeat and by the need to get money from the commercial classes to pay for the war. Britain did not waver from democracy when standing alone against the German-dominated continent in 1940; the ordeal brought a marked leveling of British society; nor did modern Israel compromise democracy through decades of war and danger from surrounding Arab lands. In Russia during the Napoleonic wars the tsar was popularized to counter French promises to free the serfs (Cherniavsky, 1961). A century later, the tribulations of World War II brought some humanization of Stalinism. Ideology was displaced by patriotism, censorship was relaxed, political indoctrination was neglected, and the doors of the governing party were opened. When victory brought back security, writers were purged and doctrinal purity was reasserted (Ulam, 1974).

The mentality of international affairs carries over to the domestic political atmosphere. The community of competing states, with the balance of power, shifting alliances, and the acceptance of equals, makes an atmosphere of toleration, rationality, and legality. Moors were well-treated in Aragon-Catalonia because that kingdom wanted friendly relations or alliances with emirates of Africa (Merriman, 1936). When Spain felt itself atop the world, they were expelled. The study of international law in the seventeenth century helped divorce domestic law from theology (Grimm, 1954). In the game of power politics, ideology is a burden; necessity has often brought monarchist and republican, Catholic and heathen, into a common cause.

The existence of free states is contrary to the absolutist view of order. The monarch of the world lacks perspective and proportion, with little to remind him that he is not divine, as the courtiers chant and the people believe. In omnipotence, there is no realistic political sense. Absolutism is clouded by the existence of equals. Mere awareness of the size of the world in the sixteenth century deflated the pretensions of the Holy Roman Empire (Butler and Maccoby, 1928). If there is no foreign opposition, neither should there be any at home. When states admit balancing powers with the necessity of compromise and adjustment among equals externally, they are harder to deny domestically. The foreign political world is to a degree mirrored in the domestic. Where a single state is all-powerful, men accept the autocratic ruler; where states are balanced, internal political forces usually prevent total concentration of authority.

The political thinking of open societies is complex and diverse; the ablest expositors of authoritarianism, such as Plato and Hobbes, have written in unusually free societies. But the idea of the balance of power in government, the accommodation of independent forces offsetting each other for the protection of freedom, could hardly have been conceived without its prototype, the balance of power on the international stage. The constitutional regime, like the state system, requires consideration for opposing views and respect for different powers confronting each other, none of which can wholly dominate the others. Its politics, like civilized international relations, proceeds within a framework of accepted relations, a struggle for advantages, not annihilation or total dominion.

So far as there is communication among states of a system, ideas of right and wrong are generalized, and political values are subject to imitation like architecture and literary forms. The states also share a great deal of general culture; their problems and means of meeting problems are to a degree similar.

For this reason, certain political forms seem to be normal for certain eras, a common style toward which the majority gravitate. The polis apparently answered the needs and mentality of the small Mediterranean states of antiquity, and city-states seem to have been remarkably similar over a wide area and in somewhat dissimilar conditions. Autonomous towns of medieval Europe, from Russia to Spain, had much in common; communes on the Baltic and the Adriatic were of the same genus, and they had points of resemblance to the ancient polis. Fairly strong monarchy was taken for granted in the Europe of the seventeenth and eighteenth centuries. In the nineteenth century Europe seemed to be moving toward parliamentary government; almost everywhere, even in Russia, the trend seemed to be toward ministries responsible to elected chambers. It may be, too, that the political process influences thinking. Thus, the Socratic approach to truth by dialogue may be seen as an echo of the wrangling Athenian assembly, while Western scientific inquiry is the counterpart of parliamentary politics.

Whatever the specific institutions, the essence of the state system is the limitation of political power; and freedom is almost equivalent to variety, variation, innovation, and discovery. So far as the interactions generate slackness of authority and toleration of diversity, they permit and promote creativity, new ideas and ways that add up to what has been called progress. In the arousal of an uncertain world, capacities are heightened (Berlyne, 1966). When reasoning is in demand and answering questions and learning give emotional satisfaction, the capacity to learn is raised; involvement with a cause that needs and rewards intelligence is the best means of increasing it. Stimulating surroundings, attitudes, expectations, and culture can frequently raise the measured intelligence quotient of a child about twenty points, perhaps as much as thirty (Bernard, 1962). Psychologists have found that boys in an autocratically run school showed more hostility, while those in a democratic climate were more constructive and cooperative and did better work (Heidenreich, 1967). It may be surmised that open societies, where the atmosphere conduces to criticism and inquiry, have a substantially higher level of effective intelligence than static, traditional, and authoritarian societies, bound to obedience and habit.

The progressive societies have evoked not only intelligence but genius, which is the fullest realization of potential. It is the ability to grasp the truly new, and this is possible only where innovation is welcome. The creative personality is necessarily deviational (Rogers, 1962). Impatient with convention and routine, careless of others' opinions, and uninterested in personal relations, he is a misfit who disturbs comfortable patterns and settled organization. Genius, like madness, means a tension between the individual and his surroundings, which leads away from convention and security. The way of the original artist, writer, or scientist has usually been hard even under the most favorable conditions (Thompson, 1962). Only the loose or half-anarchic order of free activity and urge to improvement (Barnett, 1953) gives courage and strength to inquire deeply into the secrets of the universe or to create novel beauty, giving permanent and universal significance to the ephemeral and local.

Movement and Comparison

Division of the world also signifies some degree of freedom because from each polity there is access to an outside, to lands where the writ of the local authority does not run. Where there is no alternative, brutal oppression evokes more fawning than rebellion. If a man even knows of the existence of civilized lands where he might laugh at his rulers, awe must be less blind. Yet no member of a state system could shut out foreign intercourse and the flow of ideas without excessive cost and ultimately weakening itself; the idea might occur to a Russian tsar but hardly to a ruler in a state system. A Calvin is needed to govern a Geneva despotically. Nor can competing states fully concert any policy of general repression or political control, because they can never agree. But if merchants, pilgrims, scholars, curiosity-seekers, and officials can travel, they inevitably see differences and compare ways at home and abroad. So far as power leans upon beliefs, as ripe despotism always does, different currents of ideas undercut authority, weaken indoctrination, encourage disaffection, and probably soften the will of the rulers themselves. For the real tyrant, hardly any measure of security is more pressing than to raise barriers, psychological and political, to fence in his realm.

Plurality means choice; and even if all states were despotic, it would be a useful freedom to be able to choose among them. Serfs who can defect to another lord are half free. It was a long step into the Muscovite autocracy when boyars in the sixteenth century lost the traditional right to change masters. In recent days, the Communist government of East Germany gained stability when it halted the flight of its citizens by erecting the Berlin Wall in August 1961. Wherever civilized states have lived in close contact, from ancient Greece to this day, countless political thinkers and leaders have found refuge abroad and there continued their work or at least saved their skins, possibly to return one day to their homelands. Florentines sentenced to death regularly fled the city. Nearly a hundred thousand Dutch sought safety in England during the war of Netherlands independence, and their ideas and temper helped shape the forces that hurled down the Stuarts. Hundreds of upper-class Englishmen fled from the repression of Mary Tudor; returning to England, they gave strength and direction to the reversal of policy (Dickens, 1964).

About two hundred thousand Huguenots were scattered to England, Holland, Prussia, and America after Louis XIV revoked the Edict of Nantes. Some of them went back to France, carrying English ideas, including the first powerful attacks on the monarchy (Grimm, 1954). John Locke perfected his empirical philosophy in Holland. Descartes was so impressed with the diversity of beliefs he encountered among the Dutch that he resolved to accept only what could be proved and made this the basis of his philosophical method. Voltaire, in his three-year exile in England, was struck by constitutional government, toleration, and the prestige of learning. In the latter part of his life he lived in a Swiss town near the French border. Many French thinkers found refuge in Switzerland before the Revolution; by a reverse twist, after the French repressed democracy in Geneva in 1782, many radicals, headed by Necker, took refuge in France and contributed not a little to the shaping of the French Revolution (Oechsli, 1922).

Recognizing such possibilities, Tsar Nicholas in 1853 feared that the dismemberment of the Turkish empire would produce small republics to serve as asylum for "Kossuths, Mazzinis and other revolutionaries of Europe" (Jelavich, 1964, p. 115). Herzen, publishing in London his *Bell*, gave heart to many in Russia and helped educate the tsar himself, who found it more informative than the muzzled Russian press. In the 1970s, Soviet dissidents can most easily spread their message by smuggling manuscripts to the West, from which they are returned to the Soviet land by radio broadcasts.

It was part of the political flux of seventeenth-century England that most eminent Englishmen of that time traveled abroad (Clark, 1940), whether they became acquainted with the liberties of Holland or the beaten peasants and gilded nobility of France. Artists have long traveled to different lands to improve themselves, from the Greek artists who worked on the temples of many poleis, to the peripatetic scholars of the Renaissance and the painters who used to flock to Paris. When Europe discovered new worlds, thinkers found much to admire in the very different cultures of China, Persia, or Siam; odd or admirable customs provided a starting point for criticizing the home society, as in Montesquieu's *Persian Letters*. Even moving within a country is stimulating, as it makes one aware of limitations, falsities, and inconsistencies of the regime, that one could hardly perceive as such if he sat only in his own village. Autocrats often seek to limit their subjects' travel, requiring permits or otherwise discouraging movement. The finance minister of Nicholas I of Russia opposed the building of railroads lest they increase the restless spirit (Pushkarev, 1963).

States learn from one another. The Greeks studied constitutions of fellow city-states. One Italian republic would build on the experience of others. Medieval French communes sent for copies of charters to use as models and to cite as precedents; Flemish and German towns borrowed each other's legal institutions and codes. Englishmen under the early Stuarts studied and admired the republican constitution of Venice (C. Hill, 1965). As Britain rose to leadership, its Parliament became the model for representative bodies all over Europe. To mitigate the corruption of autocracy by foreign influence, Maria Theresa banned the teaching of English in Austrian universities (Cowie, 1964). Foreign influence was especially striking in the liberalization of French thinking prior to the Revolution. Although England was a national rival, English influence was increased by admiration for its progressive agriculture, modern industry, and science. When everything English—clothes, carriages, chinaware, and so on—was fashionable (Cowie, 1964) men came easily to admiration for the relatively orderly and efficient British political processes. Montesquieu derived from the British example not only the idea of mixed government but confidence in the possibility of freedom. Voltaire attacked the French regime through praise of

English ways, expounding English ideas better, or at least more forcefully, than the English did.

Movements arouse international reverberations. Victories of Flemish democrats sent tremors through feudal Europe in the fourteenth century. In the seventeenth century, revolutions in Catalonia, Portugal, Naples, England, France (the Fronde), and the Netherlands, all directed in the first instance against illegal taxation, showed a contagion of ideas in widely varying national conditions. Dutch toleration of Spanish Jews encouraged England and Denmark to admit Jewish refugees in the seventeenth century. Calvinism came to the Low Countries via France and energized revolution against Spanish rule. The Netherlands was held up as living proof that a government could be at once free and stable; the success of the Dutch not only gave confidence to English opponents of absolutism but taught them tactics, such as attacking ministers rather than royalty, withholding taxes, and basing opposition on natural law and ideas of contract (C. Hill, 1965).

The American Revolution hastened the decay of European absolutism. Idealizing American liberties, European liberals saw the struggle as theirs and its success as an augur of their own (Gershoy, 1944). The issue seemed to be a simple one of bravery, liberty, and equality against power, exploitation, and pride; discussing it, the discontented criticized their own government in defiance of censorship. The French studied the American government and admired the successful republic with its rational constitution, no hereditary aristocracy, and no established church. Republican and democratic ideas took hold where monarchy had previously been taken for granted. Germans wrote poems and erudite tracts on America; English reformers used the American example of toleration; George Washington was a hero to Russians, Poles, and Italians. Conspirators in Ireland, the Netherlands, and Finland modeled themselves after the Americans (Ward, 1968). The first Russian to raise an intellectual protest against autocracy, Alexander Radishchev, read Benjamin Franklin (Palmer, 1968).

French revolutions of 1789 and 1830 echoed across the Continent. The fall of the Bourbons in 1830 led to the independence of Belgium and an unsuccessful Polish uprising and was followed by the reforms of the British Parliament. Revolution in Spain in 1820 ignited insurrections in Naples, Portugal, Piedmont, and Greece, and began the end of the post-Napoleonic system. The victory of the liberal Swiss cantons in 1847 encouraged revolution in Naples at the beginning of 1848; magnified by a radical French revolution, the wave spread and shook almost all governments between Russia and Britain. In this century, the Russian revolution of 1905 was an inspiration for reformist movements in India and Turkey and for the founding of the Kuomingtang in China. Kemal Ataturk's modernization of Turkey shook the Islamic world although, unlike the Russian Revolution of 1917, it made no effort to proselytize (Emerson, 1960). Gandhi and the Indian National Congress became models for a host of anticolonial parties. The colonial empires collapsed after World War II almost simultaneously everywhere, despite great disparities of conditions, because what one ex-colony obtained others felt entitled to demand.

There are contrary effects. Political influences often have authoritarian results, especially when coming from the more to the less powerful; and rulers learn lessons of power and of dangers to their station. Russian nobles of the sixteenth century were enchanted with the liberties of Poland; Ivan the Terrible, with no yen to become like an impotent Polish king, decimated them. In 1968 and after, Soviet oligarchs increased the severity of controls over Eastern European vassals because of the example of the Czech effort to democratize communism. While opponents of monarchy in early seventeenth-century France were heartened by victories of English parliamentarians, the royalists were shocked by the execution of Charles I and determined to avoid the fate that befell him and his ministers (Hassall, 1902). The illiberal ideal may sway as well as the liberal. Many a prince found himself excused in Machiavelli; Hobbes was appreciated in the milieu of Louis XIV (Bailly, 1946). Rulers have often copied instruments of control while scorning institutions that reduce the powers of leadership.

Withal, the net effect of the interchange of ideas is libertarian. Despotism does not gain by confrontation of different institutions but thrives on isolation; autocrats do not like political comparisons. Nicholas I forbad the study of foreign constitutions (Pushkarev, 1963). Where different ways can be compared, the pragmatic can better prevail over the stereotyped, the rational over the mythical, the practical over the traditional; and autocracy often suffers from critical examination.

In the divided world any tyranny is limited; no one can burn the books of more than the territory he rules, and book-burning is ineffective if the undesired works and ideas can live elsewhere. As Hume remarked, in "Of National Character," large states make uniform customs; small ones, as the Greek, bring variety. Not only do multiple foci of development stimulate one another; division gives areas freedom to evolve and change without being held back by the laggards. Athens went ahead despite the conservatism of Sparta and the sluggishness of Thrace and Boetia. Italy in the Middle Ages became the center of European learning and teacher of most of the Continent. In the seventeenth century Holland was a model for the economic development of England, which became in and after the industrial revolution the tutor of Europe.

There being some correlation of freedom with progress and creativity, free institutions have recommended themselves by success. In the wars of the latter part of the seventeenth century, the French were led to imitate the freer economic institutions of the Dutch, despite hatred for them, because of the much greater success of the latter in supplying their armies (Nef, 1950). The English saw from the Dutch example that toleration was good for trade (Clark, 1940), and associated the Netherlands prosperity with their republicanism (Gooch, 1959). In the eighteenth and nineteenth centuries, continental Europe was much influenced by British liberty and constitutionalism; and this influence mounted with the British industrial revolution, victory over Napoleon, and subsequent commercial and naval supremacy. Even in authoritarian Germany and Russia, men were strongly drawn toward British economic and political liberalism, because England pointed the way to wealth and power. When rulers, as in tsarist Russia, wished to exclude liberal ideas, those concerned for national greatness would nonetheless take them up.

It is possible to see political virtues that hardly exist. French democrats of the eighteenth century, viewing England in the light of their own aspirations, saw more liberty and democracy than that constitutional but aristocratic country possessed. Similarly, modern radicals have been more influenced by the claims of the Bolshevik revolution to new dimensions of freedom than by contemplation of its reality. People often do not understand what they see at a great distance. But most important is the idea that elsewhere the state may be better organized. The pervasiveness of the better example led Gibbon in 1781, when absolutism was still nearly universal, to state, "The abuses of tyranny are restrained by the mutual influences of shame and fear. Monarchies have imbibed the principles of freedom or at least of moderation, and some sense of honor and justice is introduced into the most defective constitution by the general manners of the time" (*Decline and Fall,* chap. 38, II).

Commerce

The movement of goods among independent polities is no less important than the movement of ideas and persons, although many of the effects of the former are indirect. Trade is an indispensable foundation for the state system. It is the first reason for amicable relations among states, as previously noted; and it creates an influential class interested in security of transportation and a pacific and orderly international stage. War may help some producers, but it is commonly disastrous for merchants, who fear reprisals, confiscations, uncertainty, and disruption of markets. The historical record clearly shows that more commercial nations are less aggressive (Stratton, 1929; Melko, 1973). As a German militarist lamented, "The [trading interests] believe that peace is the essential condition of commerce" (Bernhardi, von, 1914, p. 11).

Trade, moreover, is tolerant by nature, as material advantage overrides political prejudice. Trade requires trust and comity. As Montesquieu said, "Commerce is a cure for the most destructive prejudices, for it is almost a general rule that wherever we find agreeable manners, there commerce flourishes; and that wherever there is commerce, there we meet with agreeable manners" (*Spirit of the Laws,* book 20, chap. 1). The inscription over the old Antwerp bourse was, "For the use of all men of whatever land or language." The fairs of the Middle Ages were havens of liberty and toleration.

The exchange of goods also broadens mental horizons. Men traveling with their wares or studying markets, seeing and comparing, have frequently wished for themselves the opportunities or freedoms that they observed abroad. Not rarely, they have transported subversive literature; thirteenth-century German merchants who went to Italy for business carried back pamphlets and ideas of the commune, and tsarist Russian merchants sometimes included illegal newspapers in their shipments. In seventeenth-century England, foreign merchants imported forbidden books and spread antimonarchic doctrines (Dickens, 1964). The ports supported the parliamentary cause against the Stuarts while the hinterland was royalist.

So far as boundaries are permeable, international division gives freedom to private wealth. Although frontiers are beset with controls and tariffs, this handicap is compensated for by the merchants' ability to deal with competing overlords and by the fact that wealth is transferable. Smuggling is facilitated by the frequent venality of officials; and taxes and controls are moderated by the awareness that they frighten capital, which even extreme measures, including censorship of mails, can only partially seal in. On the other hand, concessions are offered to lure investments. A despot who has to cultivate foreign trade is much less of a despot. While Asiatic emperors have been quick to despoil riches as soon as they become tempting, European kings have been able to do so only under some restraint and at considerable ultimate cost to their power. Although they laid tolls on trade and fleeced their bankers often enough, they could hardly forget that they might need to borrow again and that trade could dry up or flow elsewhere. The decline of Spain in the sixteenth century and after was much accentuated both by the ruinous sales tax and by bad credit ratings; after various repudiations of debts, Spanish kings could no longer raise money for their soldiers, who fought excellently only for good pay. The bulk of Spanish trade fell to foreigners, in part because they could deal more advantageously with authorities than could Spanish subjects (Renard and Weulersee, 1926).

The empire that is a world unto itself can squeeze its subjects to exhaustion; and all such empires seem to have done so, taking ordinarily half or more of the produce of the soil and taxing to the limit any politically unprotected enterprise prosperous enough to attract attention. But when power is split, the ability to appropriate is far less. Dues of Greek city-states were trivial on commerce and modest (5 to 10 percent) on agriculture. The Italian republics taxed lightly; when, as in fourteenth-century Florence, economic difficulties led to raising assessments, people emigrated.

If medieval kings could not raise taxes without the consent of a parliament, including representatives of the towns, it was less because of respect for rights than because money could take flight and the kings could hardly clutch it without the consent and cooperation of the merchant class. When Charles I was trying to collect ship money, a worrisome number of persons of wealth were departing to escape taxation and tyranny. Peter's authoritarian Russia suffered as capitalists sent their funds to London or Amsterdam for safety (Grunwald, de, 1956).

Insofar as political power is scattered or decentralized, economic power can come into its own. In all state systems, commercial interests have been very influential, even in India and China of the times of contending states, not to speak of the Greek or Italian congeries of city-states, where they were often supreme. In medieval and early modern Europe international banking and trading houses, from the Fuggers to the Rothschilds, had princely or kingly wealth and carried much weight in the highest councils. In modern Europe, bankers and industrialists, cartels and combines, have been powerful enough that political leaders have sometimes been called their puppets. Recently there has been more scope for private enterprise in smaller nations, as the Low Countries and Switzerland, than in such as England and France, more given to controls and governmental planning if not operation of industry. Relative size may have something to do with the fact that in some smaller Marxist-Leninist states, such as Yugoslavia and Hungary, there has been much more pressure for economic liberalization than in the giant Soviet Union. For basically the same reasons, federal systems have been favorable for private wealth, as in federal Germany and the United States. States cannot squeeze businesses too severely when they can emigrate to a more favorable jurisdiction. Economic freedom also permits outsiders to play an important part in the community, such as metics in classic Athens, Jews in premodern Europe, and Dissenters in Britain. Such persons have commonly contributed disproportionately; for example, most of the inventors and innovators of the industrial revolution in England were Nonconformists or Scots (Reid, 1954).

When economic power is more important, part of sovereignty in effect falls to it, narrowing the field of the state and permitting an opener society. Individualism, a vice in the authoritarian state, becomes a virtue. It is far from ideal that status be based on wealth, but this is at least as rational as ancestry, control of instruments of force, or the favor of a potentate. Wealth is not so exclusive a title to position as landholding or aristocratic origin; commerce is a loosener of social rigidities, tending to break down traditional class distinctions. As Samuel Johnson said, "Gold and silver destroy feudal subordination" (Briggs, 1959, p. 15). A rising middle class is receptive to new ways and ideas and becomes a revolutionary force in a hierarchic social order. Needs of commerce break down collectivist ways, and monetary relations are freer than political. Aristocrats of the Old Regime preferred to regard peasants as too childish to work for money (Ward, 1968), but the commutation of feudal duties to money dues improved the status of peasants of the Middle Ages. Monetary relations are less demeaning than obligations of service. From the viewpoint of aristocratic or universalistic values, the commercial society, where wealth counts more than birth and performance more than person, is crude and uncultivated. Monopolizers of power and holders of special privileges are averse to the market economy because it bespeaks rewards and status for effort. Business deals with rootless, impersonal, nonideological values; it is essentially rationalistic and seldom tradition-bound as long as competitive.

A society with a large middle class and flexible stratification can evolve more rapidly than one with a feeble middle class (Henderson, 1969), and the bourgeois milieu encourages talent and ambition to rise through science (Gillispie, 1960).

Economic freedom to manage one's property has historically been closely related to intellectual freedom to manage one's thoughts (D. Hill, 1911). Fears for loss of trade have done more than all theories to bring about religious freedom. Sixteenth-century Dutch merchants stood empirically aside from the disputes of Catholics and Calvinists (Wilson, 1968). No other pressure against the traditional order gives so much force to abstract claims for liberty.

All governments must take account of the productive forces of their countries, and as long as production is privately and competitively controlled there must be a substantial degree of freedom; the self-managed economy requires and sustains limited government. Private wealth can finance a variety of political movements, back an opposition, and exert pressure against the government. London merchants, for example, supported Puritan preachers and schools under the first Stuarts (Dickens, 1964). When British newspapers became financially independent in the nineteenth century, their political influence grew enormously (Roach, 1969). Private wealth may, in its anarchy, support ideas of any brand, even those unfriendly to itself; capitalism subsidized the studies of Karl Marx and many no less radical.

The business community rests on legality. Progress from status to contract is from authority to freedom with law. Politics implies inequality, command, or a threat of coercion; commerce in open markets means dealings on a basis of formal equality, according to recognized rules and by mutual consent. The mentality of the market is of precision and objectivity (Frost, 1961). Business needs evoked a spirit of exact calculation in medieval Italy (Mayer, 1939). The middle classes, seeking security for property and person, freedom to produce and enjoy wealth, want limited government with fixed rules, in a spirit of rationalism and accountability. A British cleric of Restoration times characterized "men of trade" as "generous, sober, and charitable" (Clark, 1940, p. 35), one might say, good republicans. It was the merchants of the Netherlands above all who found Spanish imperial rule unbearable. The rising mercantile interests of prerevolutionary France, the wealthiest of whom were engaged in foreign trade (Barber, 1955), made possible the new ways of thought that eroded the absolutist regime (Roustan, 1926).

It has been said of the Anglo-Saxons that they will suffer any government that gives security of trade, but only a constitutional regime does this. The mercantile interests need a negotiated contract, with balanced claims and fixed procedures; and a republic is a contract between equals. The elaborate checks and allocations of functions of such mercantile states as Athens and Florence, and the emphasis on rule of law in England were in the spirit of commerce. The essence of the revolution of 1688, which set the pattern of modern English government, was the idea of contract, by breach of which the crown was forfeit (Acton, 1930).

The middle classes want a government subject to their influence or control; this means a republic. Through the Middle Ages, "republic" was virtually synonymous with merchant-dominated polity. Even the government-affiliated semimonopolistic combines, or Zaibatsu, of prewar Japan favored representative government. Usually the rule of the merchants is fairly sound and sensible by comparison with that of hereditary kings, military captains, palace cliques, or sundry bosses. Those who make money need more practical sense than courtiers, generals, or nobles; they expect it of the government, and are prepared to furnish it. A result may be plutocracy, but this softens into democracy more easily than does aristocracy. Respect for law implies equality before the law. Rights of property by extension become the rights of man; open doors for new wealth, ambitions, and enterprise become open doors for everyone. Many a time, as in Athens, in medieval Florence, in the France of 1792, in Puritan and twentieth-century England, the claims of the middle classes have been taken up by the lower class and advanced to equalitarian demands. But democracy has often suited the economic elite as well as any other form of government. In Florence the aristocrats preferred election to sortition, because the voters ordinarily chose the leading citizens as their leaders.

In ancient Greece as in medieval Italy (Hale, 1960), the relative prestige of merchants as against military or landed interests has been proportional to the republicanism of government. In Italy republican government lasted longest in Florence and Venice, where the commercial interest ruled; especially in the latter city, which lacked a hinterland, the merchant princes had no competition from landed nobles. In Holland, flourishing commerce went with political freedom. British constitutionalism would have been impossible without dedication to trade; it was a virtue of the British aristocracy to mix landholding with a readiness to go into business. The prestige of the commercial class in eighteenth-century England was amazing to continentals. The democratic colonial America that led the struggle for independence was more commercial than agrarian.

The commercial, economically oriented pluralistic society, moreover, is more productive than the politically oriented, more absolutist, controlled, and monistic society. Commerce brings hand and brain together, as noted by Needham (1953), who saw the weakness of the merchant class in imperial China as the chief cause of the inhibition of science. Indeed, political freedom has been closely associated with economic progress; the breakdown of feudal controls in the eighteenth and nineteenth centuries was cause as well as result of the economic upswing that led to modern industrialization. The sometimes cynical Machiavelli wrote that "experience shows that cities have never increased in dominion or in riches except when they have been at liberty ... as soon as tyranny is established over a free community ... they no longer go forward and no longer increase in power or in riches." And, "Riches multiply in a free country to a greater extent, both those that come from agriculture and those that come from industry, for each man gladly increases such things and seeks to gain such goods as he believes, when gained, he can enjoy. Thence it comes that men in emulation give thought to private and public advantages; and both kinds keep marvelously increasing" (*Discourses on the First Decade of Titus Livius*, 2.2).

Rule of law, predictability of relations, and respect for private interests are commonly joined with the so-called "bourgeois" virtues of prudent calculation, thrift, industry, and honesty. Without a sense of honor, trade is difficult; as Montesquieu noted, "The spirit of trade produces in the mind of man a certain sense of exact justice" (*Spirit of the Laws,* book 20, chap. 2), the opposite of that produced by domination. The Athenian grain trade was carried on by the good faith of parties (Calhoun, 1926). Commercial nations like England and Holland have become famed for honesty; the bankers knew that reputation of probity was a major asset (Wraith and Simpkins, 1964). Medieval German merchants had a reputation for honor and integrity while the nobles were known as perjurers and robbers (King, 1914).

Where private wealth making is respected, there must be respect for work and incentives for achievement that the hierarchic society usually lacks. The seventeenth-century Dutch, like English Puritans, made self-denial, thrift, sobriety, hard work, and correctness in their dealings a religious and moral duty. In eighteenth-century England, Quakers especially throve because they were meticulously reliable (Wraith and Simpkins, 1964). Reliability enables people to work together effectively, and the prime asset of such countries as Switzerland, the Netherlands, and Scandinavian lands, relatively rich despite scanty natural endowments, has been the ability of their peoples to cooperate.

As remarked by Hume, republics have the rule of law and hence security, which gives incentives for improvement and science (*Essay* xxvii). Middle classes are receptive to improvement while elites committed to a traditional structure are apprehensive of change and depressed classes are inert or fearful of departures from the known (Foster, 1962). In republican Italy, the medieval, feudal will to power over men gave way to the will to commercial and intellectual power, to power over the material world. Man became less an object of domination and more an active dominator of nature (Martin, von, 1966). The fact that the smaller, freer states have been more productive and generally capable than the more imperial societies has made possible the existence of state systems.

Nonsovereign Divisions and Federalism

Divisions other than that of the states in a state system, so far as they bring about interactions similar to those between sovereign states, must have some of the same effects. Sovereignty is not strictly definable and, like all political concepts, is relative. Only the state living quite alone, if this were possible, would be totally free; and sovereignty then would lack meaning. The autonomy of every state is limited by the power of others, and the powerful are in effect more sovereign than the weak. There are also all manner of bonds restricting the freedom of nations, from informal understandings through alliances of mutual convenience to alliances, like those with Rome, that could be broken only by an act of rebellion, outright protectorates, loose confederations, federal systems, and states with some local autonomy, to thoroughly centralized regimes in which subdivisions exist only for administrative convenience.

Of these, federal systems are of special interest because they represent at their best an attempt to retain some of the benefits of the freedom of states while securing advantages of broader unity. They have ordinarily arisen from needs for common defense of small states within a state system, as in the cases of the Greek federations, the league of Swiss cantons, and the alliance of provinces that grew into the loose Netherlands republic (Wilson, 1968). There are other advantages in association, and the functions of the central administration are likely to increase with modernization, as they have grown in Switzerland and the United States. But it is characteristic of federalism that defense and foreign relations are the prime functions of the federal authority while ordinary housekeeping is left to the component states. Thus, the federal systems have more or less the nature of a compact among equals; a federation implies a constitutional order making an agreed and permanent allocation of powers, with respect for rights and liberties at least of certain entities. Only state systems make federalism possible.

The relation of federalism to political freedom is well known; federalism has often combined with oligarchy but is incompatible with despotism. The attachment of such countries as Switzerland and the Netherlands to their liberties has had much to do with the strength of local units within them. It can hardly be doubted that federal division is vital for the maintenance of representative constitutional government in the United States. In the many strains that this country has suffered, it is easy to imagine that, without the institutions of the federal system and the customs attached thereto, at some time power must have become sufficiently concentrated for a party or individual to eliminate the opposition.

The divisions of a federal system provide support for competing powers within the government and society, a plurality of political springboards, training grounds, and bases of operations for political competition; they furnish channels for pressure from below on the central authority. Limited government accustoms people to managing their own affairs and insisting on their own rights. Until overtaken by modern centralization and mass communications, the smaller units have usually been closer to the people and more democratic than the large; they have thus provided models and exerted pressure toward general democratization. Federal relations foster a mentality of adjustment and compromise rather than one of domination. Under federalism, there is no omnipotence; all have to operate within a framework of agreement.

The relation between internal political division and freedom is broad; it has been characteristic of free communities that they have left much authority to smaller units of government. The Greek polis was divided and subdivided into self-governing tribes and demes. The communes of the Middle Ages, from Italy to Russia, were aggregates of partly autonomous sectors or guilds. In Britain the supremacy of Parliament has been theoretically absolute, but local self-government has long been firmly implanted; and areas of differing background—Scotland, Northern Ireland, and, to a lesser extent, Wales—have many autonomous institutions and clamor for more.

Federalism is not easily copied where the basis is lacking, because it is difficult to endow local authorities with legitimacy that they did not previously possess. The synthetic federalism of such countries as Mexico, Brazil, and Nigeria has been ineffective. But so far as the federal system is a reality, it does much more than provide a support and framework for constitutionalism. When men are attached to local powers, these contribute to a competitive and individualistic spirit. Federal division shelters diversity and improves opportunities for mutually beneficial interchanges. Under a federal system, censorship and control of opinion are more difficult. Control of the economy is also restricted, so far as the states are sovereign in this area while goods and wealth are free to flow among them. The weakness of a federal system may be its rigidity, since the fixed allocation of authority, protecting local institutions, consecrates a set of vested interests. The best example is that of seventeenth- and eighteenth-century Poland, the libertarian constitution of which ultimately brought oligarchy by a few families and paralysis of the sejm through the liberum veto.

Something like a federal system may be produced by a de facto division of powers among many small potentates. An example is the loose Germany of the eighteenth and early nineteenth centuries, where the coexistence of over three hundred nearly sovereign units and as many as three thousand semisovereign ones (Bruford, 1952) permitted a considerable degree of freedom although each small state was autocratic. Under these circumstances, censorship of books and newspapers was feeble, if not self-defeating. When the censor refused to pass the books of a senior Austrian official, the latter noted with pleasure that prohibited books, printed outside the country, had a bigger sale at higher prices (Hertz, 1962). Some princes were always more tolerant and readier to welcome intellectuals made uncomfortable elsewhere, political criticism was acceptable as long as directed at the neighboring statelet, and fanaticism was correspondingly reduced. Since the Peace of Westphalia, there was some religious toleration, as subjects had the right to emigration if they would not conform to the creed of their prince (Gebhardt, 1955). Thereafter, differences being sanctioned, fanaticism and intolerance declined.

Need for trade weakened controls in Germany, as did extensive travel. It had long been customary for students to make a tour of the many universities on the conclusion of their education, and travel became fashionable for young gentlemen entering the world. Even artisans would wander to learn how their trade was done elsewhere (Steinhausen, 1933). Such travel was the more enlightening because of the independence and individuality of the universities and towns, each with its own style and traditions (Bianquis, 1958).

Rivalry of princes led them to patronize artists and to establish art galleries, scientific institutions, and universities, of which there were thirty-seven by 1780. Compulsory schooling was inaugurated in several states, beginning with Hesse in 1619, at a time when Richelieu believed the people should remain untaught to make passive subjects and patient soldiers; and the practical requirements of the state made education practical (Steinhausen, 1933).

The German achievement was primarily the work of the bourgeoisie, those who had means and education but who were left outside the feudal structure. They were the professors and scholars for whom knowledge was improvement (Bianquis, 1958). They were the exponents of such national feelings as existed and the solid citizens who cherished economic virtues and made an atmosphere in which no one would pluck apples from a tree planted by the public path (Staël-Holstein, de, 1958). In the atmosphere of formality and rank-consciousness, they cultivated an emphasis on personal effort, rationality against superficiality, and utilitarian spirit and individualism that culminated in the romantic passions of *Sturm und Drang*. Their dynamic religious movement was pietism, the heart of which was an optimistic striving for improvement of the individual soul (Pinson, 1954); all the great poets and philosophers were Protestants, that is, men of an outlook alien to the imperial tradition (Hertz, 1962). With few exceptions, such as Charles Moses and Wilhelm von Humboldt, they were not disposed to question the superior political order; but their thoughts soared in speculative freedom.

The world knows the host of great names of this period, from Leibnitz, philosopher of optimism, to Goethe, a polymath like Leonardo. But the geniuses were only the pinnacles of the cultural uplift. There was a strong interest in nature and mechanics, a broad urge to useful knowledge, a passion for collecting and learning (Steinhausen, 1933). There was an explosion of literature; the 2,000 listed writers of 1760 rose to 11,000 in 1806; even the butcher and baker often had literary aspirations. Every town had its library (Staël-Holstein, 1958). In Hanover, a town of twenty thousand, there were six or seven bookstores, and the peasants had a reading society (Hertz, 1962).

This situation brought an intellectual flowering comparable to that of ancient Greece, which became the German ideal of beauty and harmony, or perhaps more comparable to that of medieval Italy, the freedom of small states being somewhat overshadowed by a higher power. By contrast, united Bismarckian Germany, despite its scientific prowess, suffered in the opinion of some a "desolation of the spirit" (Steinhausen, 1933, p. 665).

Inferior and Superior Powers: Imperial States

The essence of the state system is the interaction of offsetting powers and dealing among equals. But some always swell stronger while others remain relatively weak, and relations are correspondingly distorted. Even among the Greek city-states a few felt called to empire while a flock of midget or weak states clustered around, many compelled to cling as clients or resigned to subjection. Superior and subordinate powers—especially a single dominant power and its clients—form not a competitive group but a power structure, and the results of their interaction are antithetical to those of relations between near equals. Domination may be cultural, economic, or political, but these have usually run together. Whether paternalistic and mild or crudely exploitative and brutal, it is a negation of sovereignty. This introduces into state systems themes of empire.

Hierarchic relations between states and peoples promote hierarchic relations within them. The lord of a Javanese plantation surrounded by lackeys and slave girls was quite a different person from the Dutchman who fought against odds for freedom of commerce, faith, and nation (Cady, 1964). European colonial expansion after the fifteenth century led to the revival of slavery, which had practically disappeared from Europe from about 1000 A.D. (Burns, 1954). Even the equalitarian Swiss cantons, becoming masters of subject territories, began to regard themselves as successors of the feudal lords and, although more respectful of legality, behaved as lords (P. Martin, 1949).

Various reasons why mastery of foreign peoples strengthens political differences have been remarked in preceding pages. Prestige of domination brightens the aura of rulers, and successful use of force abroad legitimizes its use at home. Not only tribute from conquered lands but any economic advantages of superiority free kings and elites from dependence on good will at home and from the need to consult their people. Administrators of dependent peoples are natural supporters of autocracy; men of liberal sentiments usually develop an authoritarian outlook in colonial posts (G. Lewis, 1963). The real or supposed benefits of superior position make for a mentality of privilege, and inequality abroad makes the inequality of elite and masses more acceptable. Superiority has to acknowledge no need for improvement. The holding of advantages makes change seem inherently undesirable.

Spain is perhaps the best example. During the trying wars against the Moors, it rose to real prosperity; as a great master of empire, it sank back to bleakest poverty. Manufacturing came to a height under Ferdinand and Isabella (Renard and Weulersee, 1926), and bullion beginning to flow under Charles V gave a flush of prosperity. Yet soon the royal revenues had to be mortgaged to foreign bankers; the collection of taxes was in the hands of Genoese, and the German banking house of the Fuggers farmed the revenues of the military orders and important mines (Hume, 1931). With a huge fenced-off market, Spanish industry declined; the textile industry in particular, strong at the time of unification, became ever less able to meet the demand. Early in the sixteenth century, Seville had some sixteen thousand looms; a century later, only two hundred remained. Charles resorted to price fixing, prohibition of exports, and total regulation of overseas trade. Finding taxes shrinking in value while his treasury was emptied by incessant wars, he struggled to collect more money, through sundry new taxes and also by the sale of rights and offices (Merriman, 1925).

When imports were banned to avoid competition with high-priced Spanish goods, smuggling became general. In a century, trade with the Indies declined by three quarters. Toward the end of the seventeenth century perhaps a tenth of the goods exported from Spain to the colonies were of Spanish manufacture, and only 5 percent of Spanish trade with the colonies was in the hands of Spaniards (Regla, 1961). The debts of the state were several times repudiated, and forced loans were imposed on nobles and burghers. Goods of merchants were confiscated; those who protested were imprisoned. Offices and indulgences were sold, taxes were raised, and the currency was debased.

In the next century, Spain became a very poor nation even as it continued, so far as able, to profit from an enormous American empire. There was an extreme shortage of precious metals, although their export was forbidden (Coleman, 1961). The chief business of the bureaucracy came to be the collection of taxes, but the treasury was always empty, and late in the century even the soldiers were unpaid. People were hungry, but much of the land was idle; peasants abandoned their holdings because of taxation. Englishmen in Spain on a royal mission in 1623 laughed, as noted already, at the barren lands, bad inns, and ragged people of the land that pretended to dominate the world (Trevelyan, 1930). Despite stringent protection, by the end of the century, manufacturing had declined to insignificance. Swarms of idlers and bandits, thieves and sharpers, infected town and countryside.

The commonfolk thought they should be monks or soldiers—good ones, to be sure; the Spanish continued to excel in the profession once associated with their glory. But the army had so many generals as to arouse the mirth of foreigners. The Spaniards were said to be characterized by pride, ceremoniousness, love of titles, superstition, and improvidence (Ogg, 1925). A patent of nobility was ample excuse for doing nothing; a host of nobles hung around the court or depended on official or ecclesiastical position. A remedial decree of 1680 made it permissible for nobles to own factories, provided they did not manage them. As much as a fifth or a quarter of the population held religious posts of some kind, which gave exemption from taxes and legal responsibilities, while not far from a tenth were employed by the state (Crow, 1963; Kohn, 1955).

The wave of Spanish invention lasted roughly from the mid-fourteenth to the early sixteenth century (Sorokin, 1957). The golden age of art—the time of Murillo, Velasquez and El Greco, of Cervantes, Lope de Vega, Calderon, and many others—came later, lasting well into the seventeenth century. But these geniuses of imperial times excelled more in ornament than in depth, like court artists, with tendencies toward the ornamental, rhetorical, and bombastic. The appeal of the deeper writers was a pessimism of decay and the vanity of existence, a melancholy contrasting, as in *Don Quixote,* of reality and ideal. Innovation was considered bad in principle. A Spanish lexicographer wrote in 1611 that "characteristically [novelty] is dangerous because it sullies traditional usage" (Foster, 1962, p. 65). There was correspondingly little science or philosophy but, rather, pride in unyielding credulity and in the fanaticism of a formalistic religion, a blending, it appeared to foreigners, of hypocrisy and superstition. Mathematics, not to speak of experimental science, came to be held sinful. A typical movement was Quietism, which found sanctity in passivity and internal peace unruffled by external activity or urge to improvement (Regla, 1961). When a canal was needed, a committee of theologians was called to consider the project; they decided that if God had desired rivers to be navigable, He would have made them so (Elliott, 1964).

The flowering of French arts and literature under the glow of the Sun King has been cited as a counterexample, evidence that prosperity and great art are consonant with despotism. The age of Louis XIV is remembered for elegant works and brilliant names; it became the classical age to which France looks back and upon which is based much of the frequent French assumption of cultural superiority. Its decorative elegance has hardly been excelled, from Sèvres china to chiseled dramas. It is testimonial to the ability of an intelligent monarch, using academies to guide and support the arts and paying generously for approved production, to evoke something of an artistic golden age.

The reality is less flattering to monarchic principles. The literary works, formal and rather impersonal, shone more for polish than for penetration. Writers had to contend with a court atmosphere, in which naturalness was tabu (Bouvier, 1853), and a refined court language, so far as possible separated from the speech of the vulgar. The prevailing mode was obscure allusions and fanciful expressions.

Louis, moreover, deserves little credit for the accomplishments of the age. The plays of Corneille and Molière were used to fill interludes in the pageants that he preferred, and he had little appreciation for the leading talents (Aubry, 1947). By the time of his personal government (1661), Descartes, Corneille, and Pascal had done their work, and Racine, Molière, La Fontaine, La Rochefoucauld, and Boileau had reached maturity. After them, literature was reduced to a court exercise (Duby and Mandrou, 1958). The Academy had a near monopoly of patronage of painting, but an independent school led by Watteau did more memorable work than the court painters. Original thinking was not encouraged. Aristocrats at court confined their conversation to trivialities because of the many informers (Nicolson, 1962). Louis shut bookstores, closed half the presses of Paris, and had his police watch the rest. It was forbidden to give a performance for more than four persons without official permission. Some of the greatest men of the day went abroad; Pierre Bayle, precursor of the Enlightenment, followed Descartes to Holland. In the atmosphere of political artificiality, attempts to apply knowledge for practical uses were apt to be regarded as misguided (Nef, 1950). Non-Aristotelian philosophy was (ineffectually) prohibited (Duby and Mandrou, 1958). Although there was much erudition in the study of the past and science was officially supported, the France of Louis XIV contributed nothing to the spectacular scientific progress of the age of Newton, Huygens, Leibnitz, and many others, especially in England and the Netherlands.

There were marked parallels between Louis XIV and Philip II of Spain: intolerance, the persecution of the Huguenots corresponding to the expulsion of the Moors; efforts to control the Catholic Church; exaltation of the king;

unwillingness to trust ministers; expansion of the bureaucracy; cultural brilliance decaying to ornamentation. These regimes were also alike in the economic price of the imperial state. Richelieu had been afraid that the people would be unruly if permitted to be prosperous; under Louis there was no such risk. As the extravagance of the court grew and the wars ate up reserves, taxes became extremely heavy, the more ruinous as they were raised where production increased. Economic policy was sacrificed to political, as in the repression of the Huguenots; industry declined under the depredations of officials; and there was little incentive to production (Renard and Weulersee, 1926). The royal corvée was stiffened. Compulsory military service was introduced, the peasants being taken by lot. There could never be enough money, for, after the failure of Colbert's efforts to cleanse and regularize finances, only about a third of tax revenues reached the treasury (Prestwick, 1957). Tax farmers and military contractors grew very rich while real wages sank. La Bruyère described the peasants as half animals dwelling in caves and eating roots. An Englishman touring in France in 1660 found the people "distinguished from the inhabitants of other countries by thin cheeks, canvas clothing and wooden shoes," a poverty that he attributed to the parasitism of "idle drones" (Trevelyan, 1930, p. 368). During Louis's most glorious years, from 1660 to 1680, the economy contracted; thereafter it went down more radically. Hardship at times caused disorders and peasant risings, even while Louis kept up appearances at court. In the half century up to the end of his reign, while much of Europe was growing steadily, the population declined by a fifth (Gooch, 1956). Causes included the wars and the exodus of the Huguenots; but most important, in the fertile land of France, was hunger brought by taxation. The grandeur of Louis brought France some snatches of territory but left it sick.

Unequal relations are more broadly contrary to the essence of the state system. Inferiority reduces responsibility and demoralizes the state, since it loses autonomy (Vital, 1967). Those who see the decisions being made by superior powers tend to lose the capacity for independent thinking (Foster, 1962). Imitation is taken for granted, independent effort is discouraged, and politics lose dignity. The "traditional" rural community, as described by Banfield, Foster, and many others, is not really traditional but dominated, contrasting markedly with rural communities of well integrated premodern states—Greek, Swiss, Dutch, Swedish, and so on. The reputed amorality of Renaissance Italy may be ascribed at least in part to the loss of autonomy from the latter decades of the fifteenth century; later, under Spanish sway, social decay was striking. In a somewhat different way, Japan, always overawed by China although never politically dominated, made no inventions of consequence and showed little artistic originality. The shadow of American power over Latin America, even though it were exercised with selfless benevolence, would suffice to explain much of the failure of the Latin republics to make more political and economic progress during this century.

Size

It is essential for a state system that a number of states be fairly equal in size or power; others, enabled to maintain independence by the reciprocal offsetting of the greater, may be smaller and feebler. Those of more modest size are generally more prone to republicanism. While Sweden and France have both oscillated, Swedish absolutism was never so thorough as the French, despite Sweden's much greater exposure to authoritarian influences, and Swedish freedom came earlier and was more consistent. The Swiss attachment to liberty rose not within a national state but from many small cantons, just as the Netherlands drew its traditions from the autonomous towns and districts. The smaller medieval towns inclined toward democracy or at least a broadening of oligarchy; in the larger towns, narrower rule or tyrrany more commonly prevailed.

The principle is general. The larger and more centralized organization is regularly more bureaucratic and less innovative (Wesson, 1967). The unification of French universities under Napoleon led to neglect of research and scholarship and suffocation of provincial institutions; French science fell far behind that of decentralized Germany (Cardwell, 1963). Big company bureaucracy similarly discourages radical new ideas; and major innovations, from the diesel locomotive to xerography, have often come from outside large established industry (*Business Week,* 1976). Individual inventors and small companies are much more productive of inventions (Kaufman, 1970).

As a state expands, it is likely to become more authoritarian, profiting by the reduction of independencies much as a central regime strengthens itself by drawing to a single head the authority of local bodies. When Italy had several scores of free communes, they were republican; when they had become consolidated to a handful, tyranny was the rule. The Spanish nobles knew in the fifteenth century that the union of Castile and Aragon would strengthen monarchy (Merriman, 1936); in fact it exceeded their expectations, degrading not only the middle classes but the nobility. On the edges of the Greek state system Thrace and Macedonia, although essentially Greek in background and culture, were politically of a different genus. Vast Russia, although racially akin to Europe and Christianized well before much of the Baltic area, has for centuries remained at least half alien to the Western community. This was not true of moderate-sized, pluralistic pre-Mongol or Kievan Russia, which was fairly well up to the Western level. It has been noted how towns of northwest Russia in particular shared the liberal development of medieval Europe. But the unified, centralized, and much expanded imperial Muscovite state that emerged after the expulsion of the Mongols has been somewhat apart from and hostile to the Western state system, perennially lagging technologically, distrustful, and alien. This was hardly from lack of communication. From the time of Ivan the Terrible (1533–1584), the Russian government has made efforts far beyond those of any

Western power to import technology, and that monarch did not consider it out of the way to propose marriage to an English lady. But in 1767 the British ambassador found the Russians to be the least virtuous and ingenious, as well as the most autocratic, nation of Europe (Putnam, 1952). Through most of the nineteenth century the Russians found themselves falling farther behind, apparently chiefly because the immensity of the land required or permitted a political system that hindered progress.

In the present day the size of Russia—the Soviet Union—may cease to be a handicap and may conceivably become advantageous. There is doubtless an approximate optimum size for cultural development at any technological level. The city-states of Sumeria and later those of classic Greece were surely near the optimum for their times. Classic culture, however, outgrew the city-states; and intellectual and economic as well as political leadership passed in Hellenistic times to larger polities, such as Syracuse, Rhodes, Pergamum, and Ptolemaic Egypt. In the Middle Ages the progressive units again were towns, at first quite small ones; by the Renaissance, fairly sizable city-states came to the fore. The nation-states that superseded them may have been at first rather too large; their rise apparently dampened progress for a time. France in 1300 seemed too big to be governed as a single country (Mattingly, 1955). The leading state of the seventeenth century, the Dutch republic, had less than 2 million inhabitants when England had about 6 million and France 20 million (Wilson, 1968). Since the seventeenth century the nation-states, especially middle-sized ones such as England and the Netherlands, have functioned well. Now they—or at least the smaller ones—are in danger of becoming obsolete. It has become impossible for a country the size of Greece to give itself first-class modern educational and research facilities, nor can it provide a sufficient market for very modern and productive industry. Small states that have entered this age with outstanding capacities and unsurpassed cultural backgrounds, such as the Low Countries and Scandinavia, seem to be fairly well able to maintain their standing; but they must depend on borrowings of science and technology from more massive states. (Kohr, 1957, emphasizes and overemphasizes the virtues of smallness of states.)

Larger size is more favorable for technology and science, so far as they require specialization and equipment, than for art. The Greek city-states were artistically more original than the larger Hellenistic states, but these left their predecessors far behind in natural science. The towns of the Middle Ages excelled more in art, the succeeding larger states more in science.

The advancement of technology, on the other hand, favors the enlargement of the state. Opportunities increase for the larger organization at the higher level of complexity and technological potency. Economic development, improvements of communication and organization, increased possibilities for specialization and scientific professionalization, the need for greater investments, and the like all make size more productive. In the more highly civilized society there is need for giant economic organizations and centers of learning, and so for states that can support them and provide them a field. The advantages of scale increase directly with the level of technology. For technical progress, it is evidently desirable that the state be as large as compatible with freedom of inquiry and the competitive ethos that make science possible and desirable.

Some inventions, especially those available only or chiefly to the state and useful for compulsion, are instruments of political authority. Artillery, for example, was most helpful for the consolidation of absolutist monarchy in early modern Europe. But such inventions seem to have been outweighed by those that increase interactions among people and the ability of larger groups to forward a common purpose. The states of Europe have been growing smaller in terms of transportation time since the fourteenth century (Mattingly, 1955). Trade has gained importance, and the more complex economy has become harder to manage arbitrarily, with technical rationality raised in importance against political will. The need for trained people and a higher level of general education restrains arbitrariness of power, intensity of communications being the strongest socioeconomic correlate of political development (McCrone and Cnudde, 1967). Improved communications provide means for rulers to know the needs of those below and channels through which the people can make their wants known and learn about the government, making possible a state that is at once integrated and responsible.

The importance of printing stands out; probably more than anything else, the cheap multiplication of written information has made possible the progressive community of substantial nation-states that in turn brought about the scientific-industrial age. The governor of Virginia in 1642 lamented, "For learning has brought disobedience, and heresy and sects into the world; and printing has divulged them and libels against the government. God keep us from both" (Hohenberg, 1971, p. 27). The printed word more than anything else universalizes experience. The earliest newspapers, in seventeenth-century England, were filled mostly with foreign news (Davies, 1959). In recent times, political journalism has virtually made the liberal-democratic state. For example, in eighteenth-century England the manifold enlargement of the informed public by pamphlets, newspapers, and the subsequent reporting of debates and votes in Parliament made manipulation ever more difficult and led to both widening of the franchise and professionalization of administration (Wraith and Simpkins, 1964).

Along with complications and dangers, technological development may bring about fuller and more equal opportunities, erosion of arbitrary power and advantages, and broader political participation. Better communications are relatively more helpful for free and horizontal than for authoritarian and hierarchical relations. Despotic states may be quite large at a low level of technology. For example, the Achaemenid Persian empire extended from India to Europe and Upper Egypt, and the Inca empire, without writing, wheeled vehicles, or riding animals, stretched from northern Ecuador to central Chile. But it was felt in classic Greece that a free polis should not be too large for the citizens all to gather and hear a single orator.

Thanks to improved communications, it has been possible for the size of open, pluralistic societies to increase hundreds or thousands of times from the ancient city-states to huge but more or less democratic and free-minded powers of today. For progress this is fortunate, indeed indispensable. However, improvement of arms and of means of communication and administration invites the consolidation of states, and as bigger units become more useful, the conditions that enabled a number of interacting states to preserve independence are ended unless a larger balance can be found.

State Systems

In a few times and places, there have arisen political units of suitable size able to function in close interaction without destroying one another through many generations, sufficiently large and strong to dominate their world yet small enough or divided enough to permit limited government. Then there can be effective pluralism, unity with diversity, partition of power with interaction, and sufficient anarchy to permit freedom, individualism, and belief in the possibility of improvement, yet not so much as to prevent progress, and enough moral and political order to maintain communication and permit the necessary organization for innovation and cultural accumulation. The state system is an unsettled world, with no overall guidance and no agreed directions, but with unceasing change and opportunities for improvement. It is a world of insecurity; the West has always been dissatisfied with old ways and truths.

In the open societies of state systems, humans have been overtaken by distrust of the past; to lack firm political authority is to lack a firm hitching-post for belief. Life has been filled with contrasts of good and bad, hopeful faith and heresies, doubts and irreligion, morality and immorality, as in Buddhist India, Hellenistic Greece, or the modern world. In the medieval French Midi, glorification of love, even courtly lasciviousness, mixed with the extreme asceticism of the Catharine Perfects. Such times have challenged and disturbed; filled with unquiet change in contrast to the usually complacent, custom-bound world, they have perhaps brought as much discontent as satisfaction. Customs turn fluid; styles of clothing in fourteenth-century Flanders changed from year to year, almost as in modern Paris (Meeüss, de, 1962).

Whatever tends to check political power and so reduces the ability to control minds or makes an opener, more pluralistic and individualistic society frees human energies for many purposes; and various states have excelled in various directions. The Italians were especially outstanding in decorative arts, the Netherlanders in science and painting. The English of Elizabethan times made their mark in poetry, their descendants in science. But generally excellences run together. The people of the leading states have been not merely the most gifted writers and artists but the best soldiers and sailors. They have been the most efficient traders and farmers as well; it is commonly forgotten that commercial communities from classic Greece and Carthage to Florence, Flanders, and eighteenth-century England have greatly improved agricultural practices. The competitive societies have also been the best ordered and devoted to virtues sometimes regarded as old-fashioned in the new age. Within nations, it may not be that the rich are exceptionally virtuous; but among nations it has been broadly true that the virtuous were rich. Wealth has been for the people, too. In the typical grand empire, especially in its labored decadence, the common folk are deemed practically cattle. In the pluralistic system, especially in smaller states, society is less composed of rulers and ruled and more of people together. The state system, generating pluralism, sets all of society in motion. Political institutions and productivity grow together with science, philosophy, literature, and art. To become genius-rich, a society has only to inspire the brilliant minds that are usually wasted.

For the West, cumulative stimulation has culminated in wholly unexampled output in virtually all realms, above all in the mastery of natural forces and in the appropriation of the earth. But, having mastered the earth, the peoples of the state system do not know what to do next.

Part Three

From the Old to the New World

9 The Passing of the European System

Nineteenth-century Indian Summer

The golden age of the Western European-centered nation-state system was the eighteenth century prior to the French Revolution, a time when, in the nostalgic view of a more distraught later age, life was interesting but uncomplicated and the world was in its place as never since. Then, as seldom in history, the sovereign powers formed a well functioning and outwardly stable community. Generally similar in economic development, cultural level, and politics, they were desirous of preserving the social, political, and international status quo. Diplomacy was at its height and was highly international; diplomats of all nations formed an aristocratic community. The ruling elite was also to an unusual degree international in spirit, sharing values and literally speaking a common language, French, especially in Central Europe, in preference to divisive national tongues. The balance of power was respected as the norm of statecraft. It was ordinarily followed in practice and upheld in pretense even when states were seeking selfish advantages. The existence of all important powers seemed assured. The principal infraction of national sovereignty, the partition of Poland, was possible only because of quite exceptional circumstances, was moved mostly by a power (Russia) only partly in the European system, and was much reprobated. In classic balance-of-power style, alliances were easily made and unmade and any member of the community was considered a suitable partner, present enemies being potential future allies. War was limited in objectives and consequently in means and intensity, ordinarily sparing civilians, an acceptable and fairly rational means of political action.

This was also a time of optimism, when a new light seemed to be flooding over humanity. Intellectual confidence was at its height, uplifted by the conviction that man, maker of civilization, could reduce nature to mathematical law and seek freedom by reason (A. Weber, 1948). The expansion of knowledge was assumed automatically to produce human betterment. The scientific breakthroughs of the seventeenth century had generated an enthusiastic awareness of the potentials of intelligence for solving problems: it was a springtime of knowledge. There were countless little inventions and improvements, and life was becoming steadily easier and materially better equipped; there seemed no reason that progress could not go forward indefinitely.

But this very trend of inquiry and improvement was making the comfortable world of the Old Regime obsolete at the zenith of its prosperity. Currents of skepticism arising from the contradictions between the new nationalism and traditional institutions were undermining the faith on which much of the consensus of the family of states was based. The moral foundations of the supposedly benevolent despotism of the age were rotting, not only because its legitimacy was corroded by intellectual criticism but because the old elites were increasingly artificial and corrupt. Meanwhile new classes were growing to claim a share of the power.

There were new populist tendencies, such as those exemplified by the American Revolution and its Declaration of Independence. Journalism was becoming a power; the number of papers in England, for example, grew from 90 in 1750 to 264 in 1800 (Palmer, 1968). Presumably because of improved hygiene and better diets, resulting from improvements in agriculture, the population of Europe began to rise sharply, growing about 50 percent during the century; Europe was becoming more crowded and more urban. For such reasons, the old genteel style of warfare was already worn out; a French tactician, Comte de Guibert, in 1773 envisioned a more ruthless combat by bigger armies when governments learned to mobilize their people (*Encyclopedia Britannica*, 1974).

The obsolescence of the Old Regime was shown by the ease with which French absolutism tumbled. The greatest liberating revolution of history then undertook to inaugurate a new age. The French Revolution overthrew feudalism, enthroned popular sovereignty, gave new powers to the nation-state, and nearly led to the downfall of the state system. It consecrated a new principle, the equality of persons, quite inconsonant with the stability of the old ways, and accordingly challenged the legitimacy of all traditional governments. It opened a series of fearful wars for unprecedented ideological causes. Mobilizing the masses, it created much larger armies than eighteenth-century princes could sustain, citizen armies which, being conscripted and commanded to fight for the fatherland, were much cheaper than the hired mercenary forces of the Old Regime, but which had to be inspired by a new passion of violent enmity. Ideologized war was deeper and fiercer; defeat now meant no minor adjustment of the frontier or transfer of a colony from one monarch to another but a change of social order, the overthrow of a ruling elite, perhaps the subjection or loss of identity of a nation. It might mean impoverishment, because Napoleon made victory profitable. Nationalism thus graduated into imperialism and a new effort to overthrow the balance of power, an effort based not on the mere accumulation of lands, as in previous reachings toward hegemony, but upon the new forces of the age.

The conservative powers were victorious, thanks to the inability of Napoleon to wrest seapower from England or to subdue Russia. The victors did their best to restore the old system by the settlement of 1815, consciously striving to patch up the balance of power, at a time when the incipient industrial revolution was introducing into international relations a dynamic uncertainty that would destabilize any fixed equilibrium. France, in the old style, was not crushed but shorn of some border territories and invited to resume its place in the councils of Europe. The negotiators of the peace also tried to revive monarchic legitimacy, repressing the republican and democratic institutions encouraged by the French Revolution.

They were remarkably successful in restabilizing the international order. In the first half of that century it was fairly well accepted that no power should seek unilateral advantages (Craig, 1960). International law reached its highest level. Overall, it was a time of faith—somewhat less naïve than before the French Revolution but more widespread—in the steady and indefinite improvement of the human condition thanks to science, enlightenment, the productivity of the burgeoning industrial age, and the improvement of manners. Around 1860 Europe reached the acme of its material supremacy over the rest of the world.

The state system seemed to have come into new life. But in reality it had only entered its Indian summer. The victors of 1815 were much more successful in drawing boundaries than in reaffirming the monarchic principle, which had made the eighteenth-century style of genteel international relations possible; and the populist-democratic tendencies could be only temporarily pushed out of view by the defeat of revolutionary France. The leading powers, forming the self-anointed Holy Alliance, tried to repress liberal movements (such as the 1820 revolutions in Spain and Italy), but the league of autocrats could not restore the old fixity; the French Revolution and material changes brought the form of government everywhere permanently into question (Hawgood, 1960). Every few years there were new blows to the old order, until the revolutionary wave of 1848 fairly well broke it up in central Europe; and democratization rather steadily gained ground through the century. Journalism, too, came into its own, mobilizing a growing public opinion. No longer could an elite make foreign policy at its convenience. Nationalism superseded the erstwhile international community of the aristocracy. The principle of nationality also came increasingly to undermine that of sovereignty where the two conflicted in Central and Eastern Europe (Bury, 1964). Differences of economic and political development destroyed the homogeneity of regimes and turned diplomatic issues into philosophic conflicts. Foreign policy was called upon to preserve or restore the unity being undermined by growing social conflict, and the mingling of foreign and domestic politics made balance-of-power politics impossible. Nations had to devote themselves to more passionate causes than the equilibrium of Europe.

War became still less appropriate as an instrument of policy and adjustment of the international order. After 1830 there was rapid improvement of methods of warfare, and power became ever more dependent on scientific-industrial progress (Liddell-Hart, 1964). In the democratizing age, universal conscription was generalized, and this meant that there had to be a universal engagement of emotions. Unlike democratic city-states, democratic nation-states, in which the individual was submerged and the mass was unmanageable, could not fight with restraint. Industrialization also gave more and better means of destruction while greatly increasing potential losses of both wealth and lives. Railroads helped make possible general mobilization of men and materials and reduced the difficulties of overland conquest. At the same time, the population of Europe was increasing faster than ever, more than doubling in the nineteenth century and contributing to strains and tensions.

In view of the justified fears of war, the Concert of Europe was called upon to supplement the balance of power in keeping the peace; and the frequent congresses and conferences functioned rather well through most of the century. But no gathering of diplomats could avail against the fact that heightened nationalism brought together most of the German mass that had been kept immobile by the old Holy Roman Empire (formally dissolved, 1806). A united Germany, potentially much the strongest power of Europe (Russia not being fully on the scene and relatively feeble in its backwardness), made impossible a flexible European balance of power. The situation was worsened because of the rapidity of technological development; industrialization after 1870 pushed Germany ever farther into the lead. German nationalism was late and unsatisfied—there were no clear boundaries of the German nation, short of all more-or-less Germanic territories, including Switzerland, the Netherlands, and Austria. Hence it took on an especially virulent character, claiming as its due more than the more mature powers were prepared to admit. European diplomacy in the last decades of the peaceful century faced an overwhelming problem, the adjustment of Germany to the international system in which the dominance of the old leaders of the West, Britain and France, was increasingly hollow.

It was also an ill omen that Prussian and German national goals were achieved by Bismarck's "blood and iron," thereby making military force an acceptable, indeed valued, means of national improvement. His three short and successful wars—against Denmark, Austria, and France—seemed to demonstrate the possibility of lucrative victory and led to false optimism at a time when weapons were becoming deadlier than ever. At the same time, they made universal military service an apparent necessity for security; only Britain refrained. The power of Germany and the lessons of the wars also led to the replacement of the Concert of Europe by newly permanent and inflexible military alliances; France and Russia, seconded by Britain, lined up against Germany and decadent Austria, trailed by an unwilling Italy. Concern for the preservation of the balance of power had yielded to concern for the preservation or overthrow of the old order (Craig, 1960).

It was also misleading that military force continued to be apparently useful as a tool of imperialism overseas after expansion on the European Continent had apparently become outdated. Partly, it seems, because of a growing sense of insecurity of the powers (Field, Keohane, and Nye, 1972) in the latter part of the century, the European system was extended to assert dominion over most of the world (chiefly Africa) that had thus far escaped. This provided some relief from tensions, and it was a late expression of the confidence of the Western powers in their superior civilization. It was still possible for Europeans to believe, in the manner of sixteenth-century Spanish conquistadors, that they were doing a service to the peoples whom they undertook to administer and guide.

But this shouldering of the "white man's burden" was a last fling of confidence by the Western system, and a rather hesitant one. Imperialist states acted only against militarily impotent peoples, generally of low cultural level. By the end of the century, empire building was subsiding, although some feeble moves were still being made; the Italians tried to catch up by appropriating African territories, and several powers staked out spheres of influence in China. But the Italian acquisition of Tripoli was compensation for failure to take Ethiopia, and the powers in China showed far less imperial drive than a century and more earlier in India.

At the same time, power was flowing to new centers, both in Europe and outside it. By 1900 the United States had substantially more railroad mileage than all of Europe; after 1890, the United States was the leading industrial nation. On the other side, the Japanese began after the Meiji Restoration (1868) to show that the secrets of technological power could be appropriated by nonwhites. Japan, obsessed by the need to show itself equal to the West, modernized so rapidly and effectively as to join the scramble for colonies (as did the United States) and to defeat a rival imperialist, semi-European Russia, in their war in 1904 (Lockwood, 1954). The Japanese victory over Russia and the resultant Russian Revolution of 1905 echoed across Asia, causing stirrings in Turkey and Persia; nationalists were excited to offer the first serious challenge to British rule of India, the crown jewel of the empire.

Well before these distant events it was becoming evident, as the nineteenth century progressed, that cracks and fissures were appearing in the wholeness of European civilization. On the one hand, it was a century of phenomenal material progress, the time of coal and iron industrialization supplemented by new mastery of electricity and the beginnings of electrical and chemical industry, the firm establishment of biology as a science, and the beginnings of modern thought in the study of society. On the other hand, the political and social framework of Western society was losing coherence. The advanced form of the state, parliamentary government, was clearly declining in authority, and nationalism no longer sufficed to restore it (Wallace, 1924). Industrialization increased wealth but failed to reduce inequality and to satisfy ever-growing expectations. There arose a new set of social conflicts, not yet fully resolved. Marxism raised a broad protest against the bases of the state system, the "capitalist" order, attacking its values and proposing an alternative form of society. John Locke in a simpler age looked for truth and freedom in the Western tradition. Marx sought power to overturn the Western tradition. At first an almost unheard voice, Marx became widely influential posthumously in the 1890s (Wesson, 1976). The Paris Commune of 1871 was the opening flareup of a new kind of radical politics.

Marx proposed a political materialism; Darwin gave a scientific basis for a materialistic interpretation of humanity. Darwinism, setting man in a new and at first sight cruder relation to nature, cast doubt not only on the established churches but upon all faith that claimed a spiritual content. Late in the century, antirational philosophies became popular; Nietzsche's assault on conventional values, Christian, humanitarian, and democratic, became immensely popular about the time Marxism was becoming a force. Many seemed to welcome the argument that Western society was decadent and thereby demonstrated that it was on the way to being so. Other prophets of the irrational followed, extolling intuition over intelligence, the primitive or barbaric over the conventionally civilized, and proclaiming the failure of liberalism (O. Hale, 1971). In the first years of the twentieth century, Georges Sorel exalted will, irrationalism, and violence, and Sigmund Freud was maturing his powerful attack on the cherished tabus of European society, finding respectability a cover for repressed sexuality. He popularized ideas that would have seemed wholly abhorrent to an earlier day. Turning middle-class virtues upside down, he diagnosed thrift, for example, as evidence of anal attachment.

Art also bespoke breakdown. In the first half of the nineteenth century, the Romantic movement in literature, music, and art exalted the emotional side of life over the rationalism of the eighteenth century, in part reflecting the popular-democratic trend and the cult of the "natural man." The old orderliness faded away increasingly as the century ripened, until there developed the "fin de siècle" mood, which was almost a "fin du monde" melancholy. Literature was falling into decadence in terms of the basic traditions and values of the West since the Renaissance, leaving behind the idea of creative certainty and the sense of art mirroring or interpreting nature, turning to "art for art's sake" and rejecting responsibility for truth. Emotion was elevated over reason, and pessimism became modish (Thorlby, 1970). Writers raised more questions than they offered answers. Poetry became esoteric, intentionally more or less obscure. Music sought an often-difficult purity. Debussy and Stravinsky replaced Beethoven and Brahms. Painting dallied with Impressionism and Expressionism, and ultimately fell into such a degree of abstraction as to invite the viewer to guess meanings. Lacking any particular message or definite purpose, many artists toyed skillfully with their materials. Sorokin (1942) with some reason saw "sensate" culture painfully dying, having become sterile, superficial, unheroic, and incoherent. Along with the older faith that helped to make its community—religion having practically ceased to be a positive intellectual force—the state system lost many of the pressures and drives that guided life, in a striking parallel to Hellenistic times.

Time of the Wars

In the first years of this century, the sovereign state in Europe, it may well be averred, was absurd (A. Weber, 1948). This was evidenced by two antithetical trends. On the one hand, there was much internationalism, rapidly growing trade, economic, scientific, and cultural exchanges and cooperation. There were many more international organizations; from 1815 to 1900, 164 had been founded, and 304 in the short time from 1900 to 1914 (Gay and Webb, 1973). There were disarmament conferences and an important peace movement. Labor had its international, which seemed a powerful force against war. Norman Angell (1933) maintained, sanely but prematurely, that the nations were too intertwined financially and economically to go to war, and that if they did all would be losers. On the other hand, the decline of old values, new ones not yet being strong, was reflected in a newly ruthless Realpolitik and accentuated militarism. An arms race, with corresponding fears and tensions, gripped the Continent; military costs per capita tripled from 1870 to 1914 (O. Hale, 1971). Kipling extolled the glories of combat, and shortly before the beginning of the Great War, it was possible for leading Germans to scoff at the pernicious world peace (Vyvyan, 1968). On the one hand, there was optimism resulting from scientific and material progress—Einstein, Planck, Max Weber, and others made their significant contributions during these years, while the automobile, airplane, radio, and many other inventions were appearing, and industrial prosperity was at last spreading widely through society. On the other hand, there was a foreboding about the effects of irrationality in statecraft, a fear of a coming general war.

The state system was thus inwardly decadent, lacking in moral basis, and without means of absorbing and compensating change, both within states and among them. Internal tensions grew, especially in Central Europe, as economic and social modernization raced forward while political structures stood still (Gordon, 1974). The shifting of power relations because of uneven economic growth strained the rigid system. Nationalism, previously supportive of the nation-states, became destabilizing. The idea, generated by the European nation-state system, that a language group was entitled to its own sovereign state, contributed to stability in Western Europe; romanticized, identified with liberation, and transplanted to the territories of the old Austrian and Turkish empires, it opened a hornets' nest of discord. In the East, nations were not clearly defined and separated; the attempt to apply the nation-state principle of nationality could hardly be accomplished without violence. War, although no longer a suitable extension of politics, was in a sense necessary. There was a mood of desperation, a feeling that the stakes of conflict were apocalyptic because the equilibrium no longer supported the general freedom. In the German motto, *"Weltmacht oder Untergang"*; it appeared necessary to reach for the highest rank or to be resigned to insignificance. The degree to which the atmosphere had degenerated, even before the violence of the world war poisoned the European mind, was shown by the fact that enemy ships, allowed freely to depart after the beginning of the Crimean War and the Russo-Japanese war, were seized in 1914 even before the formal opening of hostilities.

World War I—which was not truly worldwide but practically a European civil war, unlike the succeeding phase—began from the desperate effort of the rickety Austro-Hungarian empire to stem the solvent growth of nationalism among its Slavic minorities by crushing independent Serbia—an attempt to stem the historical tide. At the outset it was widely hoped that the war would be short and relatively harmless, like the small wars that had occurred since 1815—lessons of the American Civil War were overlooked—but it soon appeared that the stakes were higher. The overrunning of neutral Belgium, an act long integral to German strategic planning, was a transgression hardly admissible in a civilized system. Passions were aroused and the commitment to victory was deepened by such acts and by the propaganda that seemed necessary to elicit the required spirit of sacrifice; the losses that began mounting could be justified only by complete victory in a transcendent cause. The conflict quickly became more total than any since the Thirty Years' War (1618-1648). Germany, pressed between hostile France and Russia, felt that it had to break out and secure its place in the world; France and Britain feared that defeat would mean not a readjustment of relations but permanent subjection to militaristic German hegemony, the practical end of their career as nation-states.

The disaster was many times greater than anyone could have foretold, and deeper than could be guessed even by surveying the wreckage at the end. It was the war of annihilation of the passing state system, in which a large fraction of a generation was slaughtered and whole populations were given to mutual ruination. But it was even more a psychological and moral disaster. Ruined cities could be repaired, and losses to manpower could be made good eventually; but the blow to European self-confidence and ideals of freedom, rationality, progress, rule of law, and laissez-faire economics was irreparable. International law and practices were abused, if not forgotten; in a sense Europe reverted to barbarism. The late nineteenth-century attack on rationalism and Western ideals seemed substantiated by the senseless struggle; and the aftermath was demoralization, a sense of hopelessness and disorientation expressed in such movements as Dadaism and surrealism (Gay and Webb, 1973).

The incapacity of the old state system was shown by the fact that only the entry of an outside power, the United States, prevented German victory and presumably indefinite German hegemony. Partly because the United States had always distrusted and stood apart from the balance of power, partly because the old order was discredited, the peace of Paris departed from the tradition upheld at previous settlements from Westphalia (1648) through Vienna (1815), and made no effort to restore a balance in Europe. Instead it was based upon the destabilizing, populist principle of self-determination of peoples. It punished the losers far more severely, however, than any previous European settlements, imposing indefinitely huge obligations to pay reparations for war damages and forcing them to admit moral guilt—a move made necessary by the moralization of the conflict but a cause of new bitterness. To replace the balance of power, a League of Nations was erected, at the instance of the non-European power that stood over the negotiations, a universalization and formalization of the old Concert of Europe.

The war also gave impetus to the spread of power away from Europe, a tendency growing for some decades but inconspicuous until accelerated by the cataclysm. While productive capacities were hurt in Europe, elsewhere they were swelled by exceptional demand. European industrial production fell 23 percent from 1913 to 1920; American production rose 22 percent (Briggs, 1968). The United States came out of the war with more industrial plant than all of Europe and became at the same time the world's creditor while Europeans lost or liquidated most foreign holdings. It was only by virtue of the anomalous return of the United States to political isolationism that the European powers could see themselves playing the old power games in the interwar period. Japan also boomed during the war years, laying the basis for its subsequent challenge; and in many countries, from Latin America to India, wartime shortages and unfillable demand stimulated new industrial growth. The old Europe-centered world economy was dead (Fischer, 1948).

Weakening and discrediting colonial powers, the war did much to loosen the European hold on empire. There were stirrings in China, the Netherlands Indies, and India, stimulated by Wilsonian ideas of self-determination and the weariness of the belligerents. In 1920 a French observer foresaw that equality and national self-determination could not be denied indefinitely to colonial peoples, predicting that the League of Nations would come to be dominated by colored nations (Demangeon, 1920). Even in tropical Africa, in the 1920s, Britain began heading down the road to abandonment of empire by yielding ever more slivers of authority to Africans. Indians saw their troops fighting in Europe as equals of Europeans, and wondered why they had to be governed from a country half a world away. From 1919 the independence movement progressed rather steadily, the British yielding step by step until compelled to grant full independence after World War II. The white dominions, long self-governing, achieved independence by the Statute of Westminster, in 1931; and they slowly drifted away from the mother country.

The lands of the Western state system thus, in the aftermath, suffered a grave loss of power and leadership in several ways. Economic and political power was shifting away from Europe as many countries, led by the United States, built up productive capacity on the European model. The political dominion of European empire lost legitimacy and became decreasingly profitable, politically and economically, as subject peoples began to apply to themselves European, especially British, ideas of rights and human dignity. To these attacks on the European position was joined another, Bolshevism, which achieved power in a desperate, half-beaten disillusioned Russia.

The Leninist Bolshevik or Communist movement amounted to a bitter broadside assault on all aspects of the Western world of a character quite new to history. Its intellectual inspiration derived from the reaction inaugurated by Marx within the Western world against the morally and socially disturbing success of the industrial revolution. The Marxist socialist movement was largely deradicalized by the first part of this century, thanks to the fact that the industrialization, instead of dividing society into a few rich owners standing over the ever more impoverished working masses, raised the general welfare (Wesson, 1976). But the disturbance of the war, the discredit of existing institutions, and revulsion against traditional values brought socialism to the fore in most countries of Europe and gave it intellectual and political standing. In Russia, the lack of a basis for Western-style liberal representative government enabled the most radical of the major parties, the extremist wing of Russian Marxism, to seize power in the near anarchy following the decapitation of the state by the overthrow of the tsar.

Mixing Western-derived Marxist concepts and slogans with Russian political ways and traditions, Lenin and his followers called for the utter overthrow of the traditional society, the state system and its values. Theirs was a new universalism based nominally on the Marxist class struggle, in effect, upon Russian imperial messianism. They did not conceive of themselves as revolutionaries within the state system world, but as leaders into a new world order. They regarded the nation-state as inherently evil, a creation of the hated capitalist order, and set themselves the task of destroying it.

The Western state system thus faced a declared and dedicated opponent that it did not understand and with which it was not prepared to deal. The Soviet Russian state was much enfeebled, however, when its revolutionary, that is, anti-Western fervor, was most intense; and its dedication to the overthrow of the Western "bourgeois" order diminished roughly in proportion as its strength grew with reconstruction and then rapid industrialization in non-Western style. But a major power now had an interest in international instability. In a spirit quite opposed not merely to the balance of power, but to accepted international comity, the Soviet Union sought to subvert even those states with which it had for practical reasons good working relations. For example, in the early 1920s the Soviet state was developing trade with Germany, seeking credits, and cooperating in the training of the Reichswehr in ways forbidden by the Treaty of Versailles while encouraging, guiding, and subsidizing a revolutionary movement to overthrow the liberal German state.

In effect, the Russian revolutionaries blamed the West—which had long been intruding economically, culturally, and to some extent politically into the Russian empire and humiliating if not injuring its character—for Russia's sorrows; and in reaction they struck out to turn the tables and seek vengeance. They backed or launched anti-Western movements wherever they could in the colonial world and in due course made anticolonialism more violent and turned it away from Western political channels and parliamentary democracy (Ulam, 1974). They split off, inspired, and supported an anti-Western sector of the leftist or socialist movement, wedded it to violence of language and tactics, and raised political tensions wherever they touched. They attacked the economic foundations of the Western world as immoral, backward, and oppressive and offered, in their ideologically conditioned approach, an alternative, not only for the dissatisfied of the West but for non-Western nations that wished the power of modern industry but could not or would not follow the Western pattern. It is a sign of the weakness of the West that it was morally on the defensive and half inclined to accept as just this onslaught of impoverished and backward Russia, an attack that, if the West had had the self-assurance of an earlier generation, would have been rejected as barbarism.

At the end of the 1920s came another severe blow to the old system. The Great Depression showed that the traditional economic dispensation was outworn. The effects were worst upon international trade. While industrial production in leading countries shrank by 20 percent to as much as 50 percent, international trade all but disappeared, declining to as little as 10 percent of earlier values. Economic competition in the former style of the sovereign states was no longer sufficient; there was need for a wide measure of cooperation and mutual restraint in trade and monetary affairs, such as was developed after World War II.

Economic troubles, coming after the trauma of the war, heightened the mood of antirationalism and pessimism epitomized by Oswald Spengler's *Decline of the West*, published 1918-1922 but most popular in the early 1930s. Spengler prophesied the coming of an age of caesars; and would-be caesars did, indeed, appear in large numbers, beginning with Benito Mussolini, who gained power in Rome in 1922. The first result of the victory of the Allied powers over the more militaristic-authoritarian Germany—a victory gained in the name of freedom and popular government—had been a general triumph of democratic institutions across Europe west of Russia. This briefly seemed to be the new wave, thanks in large part to the example and influence of the United States. But it was only a wave, not a tide, and it began to recede soon after the United States pulled away from European involvement and back into complacent isolationism. The idea of popular sovereignty, based on universal suffrage, could prosper only by general acceptance of the political ideals of law and reason; against these, political movements borrowing more or less of the approach and methods of Bolshevism but rejecting its social goals raised banners of heroic emotionalism and militarism. Peoples seemed to accept strong leaders as the touted alternative to anarchy. One by one, the infant constitutional-democratic states of Central and Eastern Europe and the Balkans were replaced by autocracies more or less in the new style, until by 1938 only Czechoslovakia held out. Democracy was replaced by demagogic mass-party dictatorship, and nationalism was perverted to chauvinistic hypernationalism or racism.

The inventor of the new style of tyranny was the pompous, sawdust caesar Mussolini, a one-time socialist who mixed populist motifs with nationalistic authoritarianism (Ebenstein, 1939). An outgrowth of the nihilism that had been growing in the West for half a century, fascism was a reaction against the Western tradition and a repudiation of the ideals of decency, freedom, and reason in favor of force and megalomania. Where it took power, intellectual life was suffocated as it had not been for many centuries in Europe. The widespread admiration that the basically fraudulent fascist movement encountered in Europe testified, like the ambiguous response to Bolshevism, to the moral weakness of the age (Gay and Webb, 1973).

A stronger movement of primitivistic political violence, anti-Bolshevik yet in many ways akin to Bolshevism, was that of Adolf Hitler and German National Socialism. It was a reaction of disillusionment and injured pride. Not only was Germany deprived of territories, charged for the costs of the world war, and branded as culpable; unlike losers in previous contests, Germany was not promptly reintegrated into the state system but was kept in the status of an international pariah, approximately until the 1925 Locarno settlement. Inflation wiped out middle-class savings in the 1920s; and in the early 1930s Germany was battered by the Depression more harshly than any other power. As a result, Germans were ready to accept Hitler's mythology of Germanic superiority and mobilize behind him in an emotional revolt against the international system and its values, somewhat akin in spirit to that of Lenin but more chauvinistic-retrogressive in its doctrines of race and glory.

The response of the Western democracies, France and Britain, to the new danger was also discordant with the spirit and axioms of the nation-state system. Renouncing political ambitions, they rebelled against the horrors and futility of war by turning pacifist, to a degree even antinational. Stamina and national will seemed to have been washed out by World War I. Elite youth took a position that would have seemed treasonous to an earlier generation. Many in France became Communist—that is, Moscow-bound—or secretly or openly sympathized with the Hitlerites. The feelings of English intellectuals were expressed by the Oxford Union, which in 1933 carried by a large majority the proposition, "This House will under no circumstances fight for its King and Country" (Gay and Webb, 1973, p. 1045).

Parliamentary government proved ineffective and uninspiring in Britain, while the French Third Republic appeared as a scandal-prone charade. Only hesitantly rearming, the democracies instinctively tried to avoid trouble by yielding ground, thereby encouraging the power-bent dictatorships to demand more. Germany, Italy, and Japan, raising against the old leaders of the West the claim of "have nots" against "have" powers (Simonds and Emeny, 1937)—a foreshadowing of the demands of the Third World forty years later—joined in a general attack on the sated and lethargic West. Inspired by hatred of the old order, proclaiming ideological warfare on the principles of moderation, respect for nationhood, and "bourgeois" values, they turned first to political, then to military aggression. When in 1939 the two great rebels against the state system, Nazi Germany and Stalinist Russia, joined hands to carve up Eastern Europe, chronic crisis was converted into open hostilities.

In the first part of the war, Britain and France hoped to avoid serious fighting and failed to mobilize effectively. The national contest no longer sufficed to galvanize the popular will. But the conflict turned into a struggle for survival, a war of annihilation, as befits the closure of a historic era. Even more than during World War I, the code was savagery. Mass slaughter became the rule, by maltreatment of civilians, by carpet bombardment of cities, and even as organized policy. Defeat, especially for peoples of Eastern Europe, meant plunder, enslavement, and murder, as though at the hands of Genghiz Khan.

World War II was decided even more than its predecessor by extra-European powers, and the outcome confirmed and reinforced the eclipse of Europe. In reality, the posturings of the Nazis and the maneuverings of the Western European nations in the interwar period had been rather empty, made possible only by the abstention of the United States from European diplomacy. In the aftermath of World War II, not only had basic strength shifted drastically away from Europe; all major states of Europe came out of the war humbled and shaken by defeat, except Britain; and even Britain, having rallied when it stood alone, in victory sank back to apathy with neither spirit nor strength to play a major role in the new world. Proud states of Eastern Europe became subject to Soviet domination, while those of Western Europe had to look to the help of the United States for economic recovery and to its military power for their security.

Nationalism was blackened not only by the tragedy of war but by association with Nazism and racial murder, concentration camps and gas ovens. War between leading powers, the traditional instrument of the state system, was declared criminal by the Nuremberg and other war crimes trials, whereby retribution was visited upon the leaders of the vanquished, a reversion to primitivism in reaction to barbarism. Moreover, in the last gasp of the conflict the United States put into play the superweapon that deprived war among strong states of whatever sense it may have retained and made the idea of hostilities within the cramped European theater suicidally ridiculous.

Thus World War II marked the end of the nation-state system not only by sealing the shift of power away from the formerly dominant states, in the way that the victory of Philip ended the Hellenic state system. It also showed the obsolescence of the residual means of interaction—war. Consequently, it cleared the way for a new system of a fundamentally different nature.

10 The New World System

Emergence

If the pattern of the past had prevailed after World War II, a larger outside state would have stepped in to gather up the wreckage of the shattered state system, unite the whole sphere, and establish a new universal empire, appropriating the civilization of the defunct states to its new order.

Instead, two large states stood over the ruins of Europe, neither of them quite nation-states in the old tradition, but rather cosmopolitan-universalist in outlook and multinational in origins (Field, 1972). Russia was too war-devastated to press forcefully; facing the opposition of the United States, it could only extend its sway over the states on its western marches. The United States, although much stronger economically and in military potential, with sole possession of nuclear weapons, was unprepared to establish more than the loosest kind of dominion, its economic hegemony being accepted easily because of needs of reconstruction. Hence the direction of world politics fell into the hands not of a single power, but of two that had previously been largely outside, Russia self-excluded by ideological choice, and the United States superiorly unwilling to involve itself in Old World politics. These, the so-called superpowers—a new name for a new brand of sovereignty—sharply contrasted in philosophy and manners. There arose the curious situation wherein the power with the will to bring the world within its political framework was checked by another with the potential but without the will to subdue the globe. The latter was concerned mostly with maintaining its own kind of world, a world with room for pluralism, economic free enterprise, and independence of smaller states.

The magnitude of the change was not realized at first. It was assumed that American forces would be withdrawn soon from Europe, and that the Russians, having established friendly regimes in Eastern Europe, would be preoccupied with reconstruction. The British, who were treated as semiequals of the United

States and the U.S.S.R., looked to a revival of French and German strength to help check Russia in Europe. But by 1947 the dominant fact of world affairs was the duel of the two giants, which came to be called the "cold war." The chief cause of the confrontation, beyond political and systemic rivalry, was that no one knew where the boundaries of the spheres of the superpowers were to be drawn or what kind of international system was to take shape in the new world.

It was a new kind of outwardly ideological struggle, concerned not so directly with improvement of the national position as with the shape and goals of society—that is, ideology. In it, the United States assumed that the only real problem of international relations was aggressive Communism, a total evil with which there could be no compromise. Soviet ideology, on the other hand, interpreted the conflict as one of irreconcilable class enemies. Bipolarity was tense and seemingly very dangerous, as any gain for one side seemed to mean a threatening loss for the other; yet through a generation of uncertainty and crises, the superpowers never seriously injured one another and repeatedly pulled back from a showdown. At worst, the standoff led to limited war, another historical novelty, a sort of half war made possible by the inadmissibility of total and potentially decisive war. Limited wars, as in Korea and Vietnam, were justified by the global ideological contest; but they were fought on the territory of third states, without use of the ultimate weapons, and without even breaking diplomatic relations between the superpowers. They were, like the cold war itself, a substitute for real wars.

Through the long inconclusive contest the two superpowers came to recognize, at least partially, the realistic limits of their spheres and capacities. So far as limits were accepted, the result was a reduction of basic tensions and of the dangers of a new war. At the same time, the American and Soviet-led groupings of states tended to loosen. On the one side, a recovered Western Europe felt less need for American aid and guidance, and Charles de Gaulle led France in an atavistic effort to reassert national power and glory. On the other, the least firmly bound Communist states, Yugoslavia and China, broke away from the Soviet alliance and left world communism in disarray.

Despite their rivalry, the United States and the Soviet Union, as nonmembers of the old state system, both worked to hasten the shaking loose of formerly colonial peoples from European dominion, the liquidation of a leftover of the old supremacy. Communists, so far as they could, stimulated and aided anticolonial "liberation movements"; overseas empire was less practical in the face of a very strong power determined to undercut and sabotage it. The United States more genteelly and discreetly exerted pressure for European powers to grant independence to colonies as rapidly as practical. In 1956, the United States and the Soviet Union stood firmly together to frustrate the Anglo-French effort to revive gunboat diplomacy in the Near East—the last effort of European powers to assert power in the old way.

Other factors, however, were more basic in the almost total retreat of European political power from the non-Western world in a mere twenty years—

power built up over centuries and apparently secure as late as the mid-1930s. Military operations expelled European authorities from Southeast Asia and adjacent lands; none of the colonies occupied by the Japanese could be more than briefly repossessed. Having aspired to democracy in the face of Nazi totalitarianism and having vaunted their dedication to freedom, democratic countries lacked the will to govern ruthlessly; and ruthless government was necessary if the peoples of former colonies were to accept a renewed status as inferiors. Independence for the largest colony, India, long restive and too populous for Britain to hold if the Indians really wanted to be free, came in 1947, only a little delayed by the difficulty of sorting out the Moslem and Hindu populations. France let Algeria go, despite a substantial European population, after a costly guerrilla war. The British, French, and Belgian colonies of sub-Saharan Africa, however little prepared for independent statehood, followed; nearly all of Africa became independent from 1957 (Ghana) to 1963 (Kenya and Zambia). As a result, the international system became numerically non-Western. In 1925, 48 of 55 nations of the League were of the Western tradition; in 1974, only 43 of 138 members of the United Nations could be placed in the category of "Western."

The transfer of power to the newer nations—and to older states of the non-Western world—was not completed by the granting of independence. Only slowly did the so-called Third World states come to realize that they could challenge old powers and old assumptions with impunity. An early move toward fuller independence was the ostentatious assumption of a stance of neutrality between the United States and the Soviet Union, in defiance of the Stalinist position that it was impossible to be neutral in the class struggle and of the feeling of such Americans as Secretary of State Dulles that it was immoral to be neutral in the contest between right and wrong. "Positive neutralism," directed mostly against the stronger of the superpowers, was consecrated at the Bandung Conference of 1955. In that same year, Egypt began receiving arms from the Soviet Union, thus beginning the Soviet penetration that enabled the Near East to act more and more in defiance of the wishes of Western powers. The United Nations, in the General Assembly of which small and very poor preindustrial states voted equally with France or the United States, provided a forum where the Third World states learned to wield influence. Pushing their own interests with little consideration of the wishes of the industrial nations, supported by the Soviet bloc and China, and easily dominating world conclaves with their numbers, they began more self-confidently to scold the richer nations, raise claims on them, seize properties of their corporations, or in some cases collude to raise prices of raw materials.

The sovereignty of the weaker states hence seemed to acquire more reality than in the first postwar years, while the granting of independence to small colonies raised the number of states toward 150, a number reminiscent of the multiplicity of sovereignties in Europe prior to the consolidation of nation-states. Somewhat paradoxically, whereas nationalism declined markedly in

Europe, where countries of the West joined in the European Economic Community and those of the East enjoyed limited sovereignty under the Soviet aegis, the new nations cultivated a nationalism violent perhaps in proportion to their psychological insecurity.

The very number of often strident voices of the Third World tended to undermine the bipolarity of the cold war years, approximately 1947-62, since most states put forward demands of small interest to the superpowers and so pushed the issue of communism and Soviet expansionism toward the background. Bipolarity also eased because of the decreasing commitment of the superpowers to change and their growing willingness to cultivate mutually advantageous relations. The United States from the mid-fifties, if not earlier, seemed to give up any idea of ejecting Soviet power from Eastern Europe; and after a dozen years of fruitless engagement in Vietnam it lost interest in anti-Communist crusading anywhere. The Soviet Union, on the other hand, seemed increasingly to value trade relations, with large-scale technological imports from the West, even at some political or ideological sacrifice. Issues causing friction between the superpowers were mostly uncertainties coming out of World War II and the dissolution of the European empires. Those in the former category, such as the settlement of boundaries in Germany and Korea, were one by one more or less settled. The power vacuums left by the retreat of European empire lost most of their explosiveness as it became evident that Third World states had little interest in either side in the Soviet-American confrontations.

Concurrently, the relative strength of the superpowers was diminished by the faster growth of other centers. In the military dimension, the Big Two continued nearly as dominant as ever despite the construction of modest nuclear deterrents by France and China. Economically, however, they lost ground, as the American growth rate continued well below the world average and the Soviet ceased to be exceptional. Japan raised its productive capacity at an unprecedented rate to become by the 1970s an economic giant, with foreign trade two and a half times that of the Soviet Union. Even more remarkably, in a sense, the old nations of the West revived and rose to new prosperity. World War II did not so shatter European morale as did the First. The struggle, seen as the necessary overcoming of a great evil, did not seem so senseless as the earlier more strictly nationalistic combat. Victory appeared not as the mere return to a discredited past but as an opening of new horizons (Gay and Webb, 1973). In affirmation of this hope, the major European powers were able to form an economic union in 1957 (joined by Great Britain in 1973), retaining their essential freedom but permitting their industries to operate on a continental scale. By this adaptation, the peoples of the old state system were able to raise themselves to levels of productivity approximating, and in some cases surpassing, that of the United States.

For these reasons, the bipolarity of the first postwar years and of the cold war were outworn by the time when, in 1971, the United States moved to regularize relations with both China and Russia within a framework of mutual acceptance. Ideology was relegated to the background; and diplomacy, not only between the superpowers but among those of second rank, took on a flexibility not seen since the rise of fascism. The partial settlement was reached by no positive agreement, but by virtue of the fact that there was no feasible way to change the basic situation in which all had to live. Thus, Soviet-American relations ceased to dominate international politics, which was agitated by a multitude of currents and controversies swirling among a multitude of states of the greatest diversity.

The World Divided

MARXIST-LENINIST STATES

It may reasonably be assumed that an international system can function smoothly so far as its components are similar in economic level, culture, and political philosophy, sharing outlooks and facing similar needs. In this regard, the contemporary international order is highly defective. An important group of states, expanded since World War II from Russia to some fifteen states with close to a third of world population and industrial production, purposefully set themselves apart from and in principle reject the prevalent world system as inherently wrong. They claim to follow a new gospel, Marxism-Leninism, and to represent a transition to a new and better social form. A much larger, although less powerful, set of states of non-Western heritage are so remote in economic capabilities from the dominant industrial powers that they belong virtually to another world.

The division between the less developed countries and the industrial West is not clearcut, but the Marxist-Leninist states are self-defined. The original purpose of Lenin's 1917 revolutionary coup in Russia was the overthrow of the state system in its entirety through seizure of power everywhere, in the name not of a state but of the working class led by its ideologically tempered vanguard, the party. (To this day, the preamble to the Rules of the Communist Party of the Soviet Union states, "The Communist Party of the Soviet Union is an integral part of the international communist and working-class movement.") Within months, however, the revolutionary regime found itself compelled to behave like a state, dealing with other states as equals and accepting peace with them. The civil war and blockade by Western powers intervened to isolate Bolshevik Russia during its formative period, up to 1920-1921, but since then the Soviet Union has always suffered ambivalence between usually increasing acceptance of normal and mutually profitable international relations and usually decreasing but propagandistically useful hostility to the conventional Western-dominated state system (Wesson, 1974). World revolution was virtually given up as a practical consideration after 1924; that same year also saw Soviet Russia's breakthrough to recognition by leading Western powers. Stalinist transformations, 1928 and after, again intervened to set Russia farther apart as a strange world; but World War II gave a national cause and brought Russia into close contact, into an alliance of sorts, with the Western powers. In the time of peril, the Stalinist system became prudent and realistic in dealing with the independent world outside. In the cold war, Stalin reemphasized the specialness of Russia and its newly acquired sphere; but since his departure the trend has been toward assimilation, albeit gradual, of Russia to the world system (Kennan, 1961).

The attack on capitalism, which nearly amounts to an attack on the state system, continues in principle. The Soviet state still cultivates the ideology of contest to assure its legitimacy and stability. But the Russian proverb, "Our land is rich, but there is no order," and the fixing of order within the Russian domain seems to imply more or less verbal and emotional, to some extent practical, rejection of the alien international system. The unchanging essence of Soviet and other communism is the offensive defense of imperial-authoritarian principles and fundamental political institutions against the Western onslaught.

The Soviet government and the governments of other Marxist-Leninist states endeavor to control the passage of information across the borders, to isolate the people from cosmopolitan influences, and to limit travel by Soviet citizens far more strictly than any Western government and the generality of non-Western governments. Foreign trade is strictly controlled and supposedly limited to essentials. Participation in international organizations is closely restricted. No Communist state has really close or cordial relations with any non-Communist state.

But in order to keep up economically, trade is essential for the Marxist-Leninist states, whose ability to invent and innovate is low despite heavy investment in science and in the promotion of technology (Sakharov, 1975). Since 1959 Soviet dependence on trade with the West has grown steadily (Goldman, 1975). The importation of technology, even of technicians, must be fostered to escape stagnation. The flow of information cannot be blocked or even fully scrutinized; ever more people must be permitted to risk contamination abroad. Credits are avidly sought from the supposedly long-decadent capitalists, who are invited to finance socialism. In order to maintain its thus compromised integrity, the Soviet system must ever reassert its fundamental creed of moral and historical superiority, promoting Communist parties abroad, using every opportunity to drive wedges into Western society, and taking up all the anti-Western outcries of the less developed world.

Controls and propaganda hold the system in place, but they cannot keep it youthfully vigorous. The would-be dynamic creed loses emotional effect in the increasingly fixed and conservative society. The revolution becomes a new established order, as revolutionaries pass from the scene and their children settle down to the delights of power. Ideology ceases to be an important motivation; managers are rewarded by material benefits, status, and security. The perquisites of the rulership and the omnipresent, ever growing corruption erode the remnants of idealism (H. Smith, 1976). Coercion is still needed and used, but it becomes less effective because less reinforced by convictions. Totalitarianism is a temporary phenomenon, lasting only until the rationale of thorough repression wears thin and various groups learn to protect themselves from the domination of the center and acquire their own status and permanence.

In these circumstances, it seems predictable that the Soviet state and even more so the more westernized states of Sovietized Eastern Europe, will become more dependent on technological imports because of the stiffness of controls and will perhaps become rather less of an alien group in the international system as they continue to interact with growing intensity with the developed countries of the West. The Soviet upper class dress after Western styles, listen to Western broadcasts, and watch foreign movies (H. Smith, 1976). The erosion of dissimilarities has been the overall tendency of Communist evolution, with numerous ebbs and flows, ever since the respective revolutions. The Communist system is subject to the shared international environment, and its peculiarities probably will continue to blur unless new conflicts and opportunities for expansion should make for a reassertion of separateness. To maintain the Communist genus of social control requires not only the dogmas of Marxism-Leninism, sanctifying the rule of the party in the name of the working class, but the myth that there is no contradiction between individual and collective interests. It is of the essence of the state system to permit and recognize partial and by extension individual interests. In it, absolutes are vulnerable and institutions and men are on their own.

Yet the aging Communist state becomes more like a decadent imperial society than a pluralistic member of a state system. The Communist order is tightly structured, with the ruling apparatus, political structure, instruments of coercion, and ideology all interdependent and mutually reinforcing; and it is well designed so that everyone in a position to influence policies has a vested interest in maintenance of the edifice. There is no significant basis of support for movements of change, and careers are to be made only within the norms of the system and largely by virtue of conformity to them. Even the desire for foreign travel becomes a means of control, because coveted permission to go abroad is given as a reward for dedication to the Soviet way.

So far as they continue to maintain their distinctive approach and ideological commitment, the Marxist-Leninist states present difficulties for the state system that the nation-states never quite know how to handle. Despite increased pragmatism and flexibility, they introduce rigidities into the network of relations. The countries of the Soviet sphere are not free to maneuver independently, to some extent because of ideological reasons: Soviet domination and the compulsory ideological view of the world require that they maintain special political relations with the Soviet Union. It is clearly the Soviet purpose to maintain the forms of sovereignty but to empty them of content. The idea of limited sovereignty subject to an overriding "proletarian internationalism" is alien to the Western tradition and the ways of the state system. Even Communist states that are more or less opposed politically to the Soviet Union, Yugoslavia, Albania, and China find it ideologically obligatory usually to take an anti-Western, particularly an anti-United States stance.

The ideology of struggle between classes implies disturbance of international relations; Marxism-Leninism is the only extant ideological justification for war. Questions of armament and disarmament are much more difficult to treat with Marxist-Leninist states than they would be with opener states because of difficulties of securing information (only partly solved by satellite observation) and because of inherent xenophobia; any extension of arms control into the Communist state represents an abridgment of the system. In regard to broader economic problems, such as questions of world resources, food supplies, or population control, fruitful agreement becomes difficult so far as the Marxist-Leninist states insist on treating the matter within their ideological and political framework. Soviet and Chinese cooperation in meeting world food problems has been limited to denunciations of the "imperialists"; they do not even compromise secrecy to the extent of permitting a forecast of their needs on the world market. Difficulties confronting humanity become issues to use against the West rather than problems to be solved. Any good functioning of the world economic and monetary system represents a political setback for the Communist states, thus far only secondarily offset by their commercial interests.

There is not likely to be real trust between Marxist-Leninist states and leading Western powers until one side or the other undergoes deep change, because the basic thrust of Marxism-Leninism is anti-Western or anti-state system. Marxism in its inception was anticommercial and anti-industrial, universalistic, authoritarian, and anti-individualistic, a reaction evoked by the overthrow of the feudal order and the institution of the new reign of industrial production and economic, "bourgeois" power. Marxism began as a protest of technological laggards, of German philosophy against British capitalism (Marx saw Germany as ready for communism because of its philosophy and its backwardness) (Lichtheim, 1969), and of groups more or less injured by the social and economic transformation—the "idyllic" values of feudalism, lamented in the *Communist Manifesto* (Marx and Engels, 1959)—as well as workers sucked from the countryside into the new factories and exploited in proportion to their defenselessness. It grew to greatness not in the leading but in late-coming capitalist states, particularly Germany, and still more so in Russia, an imperial land of mentality basically hostile to the progressive West and the so-called bourgeois ideals—the ideals of states favorable to individualism and private property that endangered the Russian empire.

The age-long dilemma of the Russian empire, since it became a multinational state in the first part of the sixteenth century, was the contradiction between the need to rule in the fashion of a universal-type empire and the need to take over and apply the technology of the pluralistic Western system. The two requirements were fairly well met through the eighteenth century by selective borrowing under state control, the importation of technology while political and philosophical ideas subversive of autocracy were largely excluded. Difficulties grew in the nineteenth century, however, for several reasons. The rate of development of technology multiplied in the West as the industrial revolution flowered in England and spread eastward on the Continent, making it ever harder for Russia to keep abreast. The standard of living in the West rose more than in Russia, making the former ever more attractive as a model, while industrial development gave Western states ever increasing military power that the transit government was hard pressed to match. At the same time it became less practical, in view of the growing ease of travel and communications, to check the flow of undesirable ideas.

The reaction of Nicholas I to the first serious manifestation of subversive Western politics, the 1825 Decembrist uprising, was to draw something like an iron curtain around Russia and concentrate on maintaining the status quo. The futility of this endeavor was shown by the rottenness and weakness revealed by the Crimean War (1854–56). It was imperative to open the doors for the sake of material progress. But this led to the growth of a class of educated persons who did not fit into the imperial society, the intelligentsia, and to a burgeoning of political thinking and debate.

It seemed evident to the Russian intellectuals of the latter nineteenth century that things were going badly and should be drastically changed. There were two chief currents of opinion. One held that the answer was for Russia simply to take over Western ways and institutions, that is, systematically and thoroughly to modernize. Not only was this humiliating, but it also failed to answer the question of how the non-Western empire was to be ruled, how Russian greatness was to be sustained. The alternative was to stress native virtues, as the Slavophiles understood them, in contradiction to the supposedly immoral and decadent West, to strengthen Russia basically by purifying it—a soul-satisfying, if rather romantic, position.

Marxism in effect synthesized the contrary approaches by offering a Western social theory that promised a pure collectivist society with all the virtues attributed to the Russian popular peasant soul but free of all the bourgeois vices. Marxism hence became a vehicle of the Russian intellectuals' aspirations, especially around 1890 to 1905, to reaffirm the basic values of their society, order and collectivism, in a modern fashion.

Lenin, as leader of the extremist or nativist wing of Russian Marxism, reshaped the creed and its practice to make it suitable for Russian political needs, partly through turning it into the doctrine of an elitist party, the counterpart of the authoritarian bureaucracy that governed the tsarist realm, partly by shifting the focus from the exploitation of the working classes to that of the subjected colonial peoples. He put old Russian motifs of violent change, conspiratorial organization, anticapitalism, and anti-Westernism in Marxist dress.

This amounted to refurbishing earlier expressions of protest against Western bourgeois culture such as the Slavophilism of the mid-nineteenth century, which impugned the more liberal societies as morally bankrupt and rejected liberalism and constitutional government in favor of supposed native virtues. In the latter half of the nineteenth century, pan-Slavism foreshadowed Bolshevism by calling on the poorer and more backward but purer Slavic nations (like a Marxian proletariat) to unite against the corrupt West and to march to world supremacy (world revolution) under the leadership of Russia.

Marxism as reshaped by Lenin was too unorthodox to have broad appeal in normal times. But it was raised to be the offensive-defensive dogma of the Russian empire in its hour of distress in 1917, without an effective government and facing a losing war. It represented an attempt to pull away, to cry shame on the war of contending states (Lenin's biggest appeal was the demand for immediate peace), and to try to turn the war from a contest of skills and technology to a contest of political ideals and organization (in which Russia supposedly excelled). Subsequently, the tight Soviet political order rationalized by Marxism-Leninism was able, using the ideology of conflict as a barrier, to erect and maintain a screen between itself and the dangerous outside, that is, to keep the huge Russian-Soviet state as nearly as possible in the condition of a universal empire. Just as Peter the Great imported Dutch and English designs for ships and artillery to defeat Western opponents, Lenin borrowed Western political tools to restore the autocracy that had decayed under the tsars because of inflexibility. Marxism-Leninism in effect reflected the struggle of the Russian empire, refurbished by Lenin, to survive and counterattack in the inimical world dominated by the Western powers, an affirmation of the imperial-unitarian against the pluralistic principle.

As a Marxist believer, Lenin at first looked to revolution in the West to come to the rescue of his revolution. But as soon as it appeared that Europe was restabilizing and that European workers generally rejected the Russian version of liberation, the Leninists turned to their natural allies and aligned their version of Marxism with the discontents of the non-Western world. They looked first and most strongly toward the Asian areas of historic high civilizations injured and embittered by Western intrusion or dominance. "Socialist revolution," that is, became virtually equivalent to anti-imperialism or anti-Westernism, the proletarian class, virtually nonexistent in the colonial world, being a dispensable ornament. The effort to raise the East was unrewarding for the first decades, but World War II and the Soviet army brought Marxist-Leninists to power in a number of areas that, like Russia, had suffered degradation or humiliation in their relations with the West—poorer parts of Eastern and southern Europe, including Yugoslavia and Albania, where Communists achieved power by their own efforts, and China.

In the postwar period, the Communist powers have continued to play, so far as possible, on the conflicts of the Third World with the West, a peasant guerrilla movement having become an adequate surrogate for a proletarian revolution.

Governments, too, have become increasingly acceptable to the Soviet Union and China, regardless of their treatment of local Communists, so far as they are anti-Western in world affairs. The antagonisms between the powers of the bourgeois West and the Third World are much more important to Soviet and Chinese propaganda than the oppression of the workers under capitalism. The Chinese in particular have gone to great lengths to present themselves as champions of the poor peoples of the earth, who are as much the majority of mankind as Marx thought factory workers should become. The concern of Marxism-Leninism is no longer the proletarian revolution that Marx predicted, or the pseudoproletarian revolution that Lenin accomplished, or even the industrialization and modernization of Stalinism, but the moral counterattack of the non-Western world.

Communism thereby seems to merge, so far as it remains a vital creed, with the protest and demands of the Third World; its nature becomes more openly what it has always been in essence, that of a shield for weaker societies and cultures against aggressive Western penetration—political, economic, and cultural. In the cold war the Soviet Union was anti-American not because of any mission of social change (which did not appear) or from fear of American attack (for which there was no evidence) but partly from resentment that America was rich and globally powerful while the Soviet Union was poor and cramped despite its heroic sacrifices and glorious victories, and more from fear that the ideas and way of life of the pluralistic Western nation-state system might prove too solvent for the Soviet type of multinational empire.

Communism loses dynamism as Communist states become subject to the same vices that have afflicted other tightly ruled conservative societies. But Communist states, after a slackening, repeatedly swing back to reassert ideology and their differences from the West, Stalin's Second Revolution and Mao's Cultural Revolution having been only the most spectacular of many instances. It is well known that economic and cultural productivity would be much increased by easing controls, and many times Communist states have moved toward relaxation, especially in industrial management. But as soon as it appears that relaxation in any way menaces political supremacy of the established apparatus controls are restrengthened. It would seem that the system is basically stable so long as the rulership gives priority to political power.

Lenin's synthesis of Western forms and authoritarian substance is politically useful and hence persistent; it has never yielded any territory in which it has once become well established. Hence, even as Communist states become accustomed to large-scale dealings of many kinds with the pluralistic industrialized states, their soul, so to speak, remains faithful to the universal-imperial way.

POOR VERSUS RICH

Rather special circumstances, including major war and a thorough shakeup of society, seem to be required for the imposition of the radical discipline of

Leninist Communism. The large majority of non-Western states make no claim to represent a superior society in rebellion against the world establishment, nor do they usually try to institute the fullness of controls that Marxist-Leninist powers find necessary. For the most part, they are simply anxious to enjoy a larger share of the benefits of the present system. By their economic level, however, they belong to a different world, with inevitably different problems and mentality. In consequence, they, especially the intellectuals among them, are more or less embittered and anti-Western, frequently tinged with Leninism or nativist passions defensive of self-respect and traditional values. That the international system is divided not by political, cultural, or religious differences but by economic inequality is historically unprecedented; more backward states were formerly simply outside the community. But now, when the state system claims universality, the most fundamental antithesis in the world is not between Communist and anti-Communist or "socialist" and "capitalist," but between the West of the old state system (plus states that have managed to join the community, particularly Japan) and the many non-Western states, mostly former colonial territories, which lack comparable productive capacities. As the Secretary-General of the United Nations, U Thant, said in 1962, "The present division of the world into rich and poor countries is ... much more real and much more serious, and ultimately much more explosive, than the division of the world on ideological grounds" (Rossi, 1963).

The shape and dimensions of the problem are new, and have been growing steadily more acute in recent years. But the basic situation, the separation of peoples of more advanced technology from those less well equipped, is age-old. The nineteenth century took it for granted that there were modern, civilized peoples and others less fortunate who required modernization or civilization. For five hundred years or more the West has enjoyed marked superiority in most material ways, especially in the convincing sphere of military power. Earlier, the Greeks and Chinese looked down on the less advanced peoples surrounding their world, and one may assume that the Sumerians saw their land as something of an island of material achievement. Wherever there has been an area of successful innovation, from paleolithic times onward, there must have been peoples with material advantages, better tools and hence better weapons, more material wealth and the means to more cultural development.

The differences are persistent, because the area in the lead has psychological and organizational advantages over those called upon to catch up. This is particularly true of rapidly evolving Western civilization. Since the fifteenth century, large numbers of European adventurers and traders have been circulating to all corners of the earth, displaying their achievements and in effect challenging all other peoples to copy them or suffer humiliation and exploitation, possibly enslavement. In 1444, a Greek ruler was urged to send his young men to learn Western technology—from the manufacture of textiles and arms to metallurgy and the use of waterpower—for use against the Turks (White, 1962), and in the middle of the sixteenth century Ivan IV began the importation of

Western artisans and inventions to Russia (Tompkins, 1940). By the nineteenth century, some Western countries, especially the United States and Britain, had developed something of a missionary complex. Except in the Americas, Europeans were slow to establish their political dominion over backward lands but at first sought advantages for commerce; native states of Africa and Asia had some generations of freedom in which to bestir themselves to meet the threat. Yet of all the peoples who were amazed, baffled, menaced, and injured by Western intrusions, only the Japanese really awoke to the situation and purposefully modernized; and they did so very late, after two centuries of ostrich-like isolation, when change was violently thrust upon them. For four or five centuries, during which the less progressive lands have had every incentive to catch up, they were generally falling farther behind.

The division of the world became sharper after the middle of the eighteenth century when machine-driven factory production became important, first in Britain and subsequently in continental Europe and the United States. The disparity of real incomes began to grow from a ratio of three or four to one to ten, twenty, or even a hundred to one. In the postwar period, the situation has continued to deteriorate despite a large-scale, multiform transfer of technology to the needier nations. This has been successful enough that the relative disparity of incomes has increased little or not at all, on the average, despite rapid population growth in the needier countries, and some less developed countries have shown very high growth rates. But the problem has become more severe because of awareness and conscience. The less developed countries can no longer feel satisfied with their independent cultures and largely isolated economies. All have been brought into a single interacting system, with vaunted independence and sovereignty of all, and all peoples have been given to understand that they are free and equal and have equal rights to the pursuit of happiness—or to happiness itself. If the less fortunate, who are the large majority, see themselves as weak, hungry, and largely deprived of the supposed benefits of material civilization, they must believe (as the West has taught them) that this is an unnatural condition, a gross injustice.

But the remarkable fact is not backwardness but progressiveness, the historical circumstances that enabled the Western world to generate exceptional innovative capacities. Modern scientific-industrial civilization is a high-flown product of perhaps unique conditions, and there is no reason to expect that it should be readily transferable to quite different societies—or, for that matter, that it should endure indefinitely among the peoples who originated it. The broadest explanation of the poverty of the less developed world is simply that it lacks the social and political structures that enabled the West to advance in the first place, and the circular effects of poverty and weakness make it difficult to catch up.

More specifically, the lag of the less developed countries may be analyzed in various aspects. There are economic ruts. Poverty, ignorance, and disease all make it harder to attack poverty, ignorance, and disease, especially when healthy reproductive instincts convert a slight improvement of material standards plus a modicum of modern hygiene and preventive medicine into unprecedented runaway population growth. Simple conservatism also plays a negative part; social change means a shift of elites, and elites seldom willingly relinquish status. The West may have retarded social change while thrusting massive material change upon weaker societies. It is certainly doing so now, less by conscious purpose than by largely excluding war and violence, than which nothing more compels a reordering of society.

Social structures are inhospitable to modernization; in the hierarchic society—less developed societies are generally authoritarian and hierarchic—position is more important than achievement, and the more effective ways of getting ahead are nonproductive. For example, in many countries, especially in Latin America, huge amounts of land are kept out of production in order to keep labor in surplus and support the social system (Adie and Poitras, 1974). Waste and parasitism of various varieties weigh on production. The gap between elite and masses is enormous, and the less idealistic members of the elite feel no urge to reduce their height of privilege by trying to improve the condition of those below (Wraith and Simpkins, 1963; Andreski, 1969). Backwardness, with ignorance, apathy, and the psychological burdens of helplessness, makes bad government; and bad government makes backwardness. The political forms of the modern West were devised for nation-states. But many of the new nations lack the ordinary elements of nationhood—a national language, national culture, a historical tradition, and whatever else lends distinction to belonging to a particular political community. (On difficulties of political order, see Heeger, 1974.)

According to Communist doctrine, there is a "law of uneven development" in capitalism. This is true so far as capitalism is associated with the loose, pluralistic society. Where there is little artificial leveling, freedom in large-scale societies means freedom for some, by craft or merit, to push their own fortunes and to take advantage of the innocence, weakness, ignorance, or lack of comparable ambition of others. Freedom means inequality. This is equally true among the states. Wealth produces wealth (if well handled), and in the open state system wealth and power tend to flow to wealth and power, even if the stronger take no unfair or forcible advantage—the fact of being richer and stronger is advantage enough within the rules of the game.

Thus, among the Greeks, a few cities, headed by Athens, garnered much more than their share, for reasons unclear except in that those getting a headstart tended to widen their lead until overtaken by some misfortune (as, in the case of Athens, the war with Sparta). A few towns without important visible advantages, such as Milan, Florence, and Venice, forged ahead in medieval Italy, although the location of many others was not apparently inferior. Presumably, as one town prospered a bit more, merchants favored it; as it became an outstanding mercantile center, it could better support crafts, productive enterprise, banks, and so on, and thereby drew more masters and journeymen. Transportation to the budding center is improved, it becomes known far afield, its coinage gains acceptance, and merchants can handle business more expeditiously by drafts on its banks. It acquires self-confidence, and its people enjoy the intangible but real advantage of feeling themselves superior to other people.

Such effects become stronger in the more fluid and more complex world of our day. Wealth is a basis for producing more wealth and for educating to skills. Brains draw brains and make possible better education; intelligent people become more productive in contact with other intelligent and informed people. The centers enjoy prestige; from them come the important directions and significant ideas, and what they export is assumed to be superior.

The handicap for the less developed nations is particularly clear in the emigration of highly qualified personnel. Doctors or engineers can earn in India only a small fraction of what they may earn in Europe or America; Argentine scientists transferring to the United States not only can enjoy a materially better life but superior research facilities and a more stimulating milieu (*Brain Drain*, 1974). The more advanced the technology, the worse the situation. Not only is it impossible for a less developed land to dream of an autonomous computer industry; not even major European powers can support real competition for IBM, which spends on research and development more than the total revenues of all European computer producers. If fusion power becomes practical, it will be a boon for the few states that can afford the enormous capital costs.

On the other hand, the less favored countries are under severe psychological as well as material handicaps. They suffer all the effects of inferior position, including those mentioned earlier, plus a pervasive demoralization. There are propensities to authoritarianism and dogmatism. Less developed countries may try to progress by "mobilization regimes," but these are only briefly successful before succumbing to the general rot of overcontrol and abuse of power; to assimilate political forms that release productive capacities seems very difficult. They are singularly weak. Long ago Adam Smith (1937, p. 669) remarked:

> In ancient times the opulent and civilized found it difficult to defend themselves against the poor and barbarous nations. In modern times the poor and barbarous find it difficult to defend themselves against the opulent and civilized.

The poor majority of nations are far more disadvantaged, economically and culturally, as well as militarily, than they were two hundred years ago. Feelings of helplessness and dependency discourage effort; foreign cultural and economic domination looms over independent thought and enterprise. The contradiction between the reality of inferiority and the pretense of equal sovereignty causes chronic political instability (Kling, 1964). The pall of insignificance hangs over all.

Frustration, along with material deprivation and hunger, is a human tragedy for the large majority of mankind and a burden on the conscience of the more affluent. The cleavage between those who are poor, as most of mankind has usually been throughout history, and those who are phenomenally rich by the standards of the past, is also a burden on the state system. The large majority of the non-Western states suffer, in their poverty and weakness, an overwhelming grievance, for which there is no better explanation at hand than that they have been misused and maltreated. Third World states were not quick to realize that they could safely defy the one-time masters of earth; but as they came to this realization, encouraged by the equalitarian intellectual currents of the West itself, they were certain to raise their demands. Thus there comes a new ferment; the modern accusation is not of material aggression but of subtle economic exploitation, "neocolonialism," and cultural imperialism—in effect, of the gap in wealth, power, and influence.

It is not true that most of the world is in a revolutionary or prerevolutionary condition; most countries of the Third World are basically more conservative than Western Europe or the United States. But they react, as the West loses the ability and even more the will to coerce them, against the old Western-dominated state system and its values. They have a common set of attitudes, and their scores of foreign ministers, assembled in international gatherings, speak from a platform of shared injury. They are united not only by poverty but by resentment against the economic and cultural intrusion of the alien West, which they can exclude only at the price of further backwardness, but which they blame for the hunger of their peoples and the decay of their cultures. Contrary to former ways, their nationalism is not usually directed against their neighbors (once boundaries have been sorted out) with whom they probably have few dealings and few quarrels, and whom they are hardly permitted to fight in any case. On the contrary, nationalism is primarily anti-Western, mostly anti-United States, and their grievances are not so much individual as a broad discontent with the world order. They cannot combine, militarily, in the manner of the old balance of power, to check the strongest power; but they join to beg, clamor, and berate, exerting a moral pressure new in world affairs, especially through the guilt-burdened intellectuals of the West. Their weapon is the equalitarian ethos plus threats of disorder if they are driven to desperation.

The gap between rich and poor roils and weakens the international order. It needs a general conviction of justice, but there is none. The poor are primarily concerned with a redividing of the world's wealth, hardly with planning for the future. It is not easy to perceive how the richer states can satisfy the needs and demands of the poorer, or how they can be ignored. Equalitarian claims grow without the corresponding idea of the duties of all. Agreement on matters of increasingly critical importance, such as control of nuclear weapons, rules governing trade and investment, population growth, and regulation of use of the oceans, demand a consensus of many independent states; and this consensus breaks down in the face of the radically different needs of the affluent and the starving. It is questionable how well a prosperous center can go forward, with the requisite confidence and conviction, surrounded by a world of discontent. It is equally difficult to guess how the disparities can be overcome while states retain their sovereignty. An unmanageable economic gap implies an unmanageable political and ideological division.

The World as State System

The present international system differs from past state systems in some respects while falling into the traditional pattern in others. Unlike its predecessors, it is not a cultural-political island; there is no longer an outside of barbarian (or at least alien) peoples to whom the more progressive peoples of the state system can feel superior or at whose expense they can expand. Potential frictions are accentuated by racial dissimilarities as well as deep differences of historical and cultural background. Productive levels are absurdly disparate.

Yet modernization has overlaid these differences, and the globe is permeated by a technological civilization that drives nations in common directions whether they like it or not. Broadcasting and the airplane, both developing steeply from the 1920s, have brought about a communications and travel revolution of this century fully as profound as that of the fifteenth. In terms of spread of news and ease of movement, the modern world is more a community than was ancient Greece. Travel and commerce prosper, both in absolute and relative terms. The number of persons crossing national boundaries doubled each decade after World War II, as did world trade (in current dollars). If some states, such as China or Burma, would still keep their peoples insulated from the outside, it is at a large economic sacrifice; their way appears to belong to the past, not the future. International trade, steadily growing more rapidly than production, pushes as in the past toward opening doors; and trade spreads ideas and styles. Although some have applied scientific-industrial knowledge much more widely and effectively than others, all states seem to desire to march, and with varying success do march, in similar directions.

The linguistic diversity of the world is counteracted by the ease with which messages are translated and reproduced. Moreover, there is virtually a new world lingua franca; English has no competitor as a general means of communication. English was perceived to be on the way to global ascendancy in the latter part of the nineteenth century (Field, 1972), and it has only expanded since then. In the decline of the Europe-centered state system, French and German, close rivals to English before World War I, have receded to regional languages. The only language with a full technological vocabulary, English is the preferred second language of education around the world and is practically a necessity for really advanced education anywhere. It is the medium of a large majority of international business. It is the official language or an administrative language of about half of the countries of the world and chief language of the UN; statesmen everywhere use it to communicate with the world. A Thai minister can hardly speak to a Pakistani except in English (L. Brown, 1972).

Ease of communication brings cultural homogenization. In the latter part of the nineteenth century, technology was reversing the isolating effects of rising nationalism, and literature, art, and music were increasingly shared across Europe (Field, 1972). This tendency accentuated markedly in this century, carried forward by the press, radio, motion pictures, television, and the transistor radio, so that most of the world shares not only a "high culture" of sophisticates but considerable "low culture" of entertainment. Partly because of the advantages of a few centers, chiefly in the United States, partly because of the prestige of the advanced industrial world, local cultures are more than ever being submerged. Whatever is special or national, whether Japanese, Brazilian, or Nigerian, comes to seem parochial, quaint, or peasantish, a tourist attraction perhaps, but of limited interest for the sophisticated unless it can perchance win international recognition. Only a few large states, especially Russia nd China, can sustain a fair degree of cultural autonomy; even in Russia, intellectuals and youth are avidly receptive of Western modes. Defensive measures only underline the problem; requiring, for example, that theaters show a certain percentage of local products downgrades the native and makes the imported more desirable.

An important aspect of cultural homogenization is the general acceptance of political values of democracy and equality. In the nineteenth century, new states would take a king from a European royal family as their badge of nationhood; but monarchy, the traditional form of the nation-states, was practically erased by the world wars (Ensor, 1960). This means of political stability being obsolete, the democratic ideal is *de rigueur,* and the advanced industrial states are remarkably uniform in their adherence to constitutional and representative government with universal suffrage. The less developed almost all make obeisance to democratic mythology and probably, like the Soviet Union, have more or less democratic forms because this is the accepted way. For many reasons, however, their reality is generally oligarchy or dictatorship. Hence, pseudo-democracy is the prevalent and perhaps characteristic form of government of the age. The mode is also equalitarian and humanitarian. In South Africa and Rhodesia regimes based on racial discrimination have come under almost irresistible pressure. In the spirit of the age, capital punishment has become almost defunct in the industrial countries; the state has virtually renounced the ultimate right over its subjects.

Becoming more democratically minded, Western society—and following it at varying distances the rest of the world—has become more respectful of rights and abhorrent of violence. On the international scene this implies respect for sovereignty and repudiation of the use of force except for self-defense. Long before the world wars dramatized the fact, even a century and more ago, war had ceased to be a suitable means of action among modern nations. By the Kellogg-Briand Pact (1928) outlawing war, nearly all states agreed to what was logically imperative. History did not follow the logic of civilization, but the need for restraint is now overwhelming.

Atomic weapons, first fission and then fusion with roughly a thousand times greater explosive power, have in effect done what the Kellogg-Briand Pact tried to do—outlaw war. The superpowers are sufficiently frightened of the possibility of war between themselves, since they have most to lose, that they strongly desire to keep conflicts with and between less powerful nations under control. Nuclear arsenals, it is true, grow beyond measure and out of proportion to possible utility. Already in 1954, the *New York Times* was warning of the pileup of nuclear weaponry bringing less security (Herz, 1959), and destructive power has increased about a thousandfold since then. But strategic armaments serve chiefly to make strategic arsenals useless, and, by their very existence, inspire caution. Navies are perhaps most useful mostly for show; thus, American exercises in the Persian Gulf may—or may not—suggest to Arab rulers that it might be impolitic to raise oil prices. They also elicit angry charges of intimidation and planned aggression. There seems little inclination to make physical use of them. If there were ever a call for gunboat diplomacy, it would be to secure indispensable petroleum supplies at moderate prices from the Near East, but it does not seem to have been seriously considered. Such a course would be excessively dangerous, would outrage world opinion, would bring into question the entire international system favored by the United States, and would very likely fail.

The use of violence is less attractive because not much is to be achieved thereby. In the cost-benefit analysis of the politics of aggression, the cost has soared and the benefits have shrunk. No state starting a major war in this century has won (Stoessinger, 1974). The aggressor states of the 1930s were atavistically obsessed with the idea of territorial expansion or empire, but their defeat meant repudiation of the idea. Now it is generally recognized that force has lost acquisitive and retained punitive value (Schelling, 1966). Aggrandizement is not likely to bring security but the reverse, and the prospects for economic gain by acquisition of subject lands are much less than those to be expected from domestic investment. Hence there is a unique absence of territorial claims among advanced states; among the less developed there are few, and those mostly not serious.

As never before, the sovereign states seem to be secure within their boundaries; not a single one has been extinguished, while they have proliferated by scores, in the postwar period—a very large number of states is usual in the early stages of state systems, but their numbers have ordinarily shrunk rather steadily. Somewhat surprisingly, in view of ideological commitment, the Soviet Union even refrained from inviting Communized states of Eastern Europe to join the Union. Long ago it came to be the unwritten law of the nation-states that major powers were not to be annexed; in the new day practically no change of boundaries brought about by force (unless, as in the case of Bangladesh, it can be called a liberation) is to be countenanced. Except for a very few unsettled areas, most importantly in relation to Israel, there is little for states to fight about. Hence the postwar period has been, by historical standards, phenomenally peaceful; and the conflicts that have occurred, virtually all in the Third World—in Korea, Vietnam, Nigeria, Sudan, India-Pakistan, Near East—have been concerned with sorting out the consequences of World War II and the liquidation of overseas holdings of Europe—quarrels, that is, of transition to the new world system. The result is a curious anomaly. Modern states, even the strongest, have become militarily indefensible, and the state (except for the very few most capable) has virtually lost its classic function of national defense (Herz, 1959). Yet by virtue of this very danger, the territorial state is more secure within its boundaries than ever. Many small states and such great ones as Japan live with insignificant military strength of their own in approximately as much security as the most heavily armed states.

By extension, major powers would seem to have little interest in intervening in the internal affairs of others. The principle of noninterference, like democracy and equality, is generally accepted as virtuous. The next-to-top powers for the most part seek simply to do business with Communist, non-Communist, democratic, or authoritarian powers alike, and in most of them the military tradition seems to be disappearing (Knorr, 1975). Such self-denial is more difficult for the superpowers. During the years of most intense rivalry with the Soviet Union, the United States took a mission of halting not merely Soviet expansionism but also something called "Communism," believed dangerous to American values. Unrewarding exertions in Vietnam led to questioning of the necessity for such preoccupation, and to more or less normalization of relations with China and the Soviet Union. Neither superpower has abandoned the habit of mind, however. The United States is sensitive to whatever may be interpreted as Communist advances. The Soviet Union continues to assert a right of helping "socialism" within an undefined "socialist commonwealth" and anywhere else it may see fit to assist "class" or "people's liberation" struggles.

Nonetheless, the decline in the usability of violence and general respect for the sovereignty and integrity of states imply fundamental changes in interstate relations, primarily their depoliticization. There is more fear of nuclear war than of a specific enemy. Foreign policy has in part shifted from its old preoccupation with security and strength, the prime mover of the old nation-state system, to concern for other, especially economic issues. The superpowers and a few engaged in particular quarrels, such as Greece and Turkey or Israel and its Arab neighbors, remain engrossed with military affairs; but for most others foreign policy is concerned largely with commerce and economic advantages. The alliances built up for the cold war remain formally in existence, but they receive less attention and may be in part moribund.

There is a new fluidity of international relations, somewhat in the manner of the classic balance of power, after the rigidity of bipolarity; but this does not represent a new balance of power because there are no powers to balance in the old sense. It represents, rather, the nonutility of power or the emergence of new kinds of power. There are new problems quite different from that with which the balance of power should cope, that is, the prevention of accumulation of too much power by any member of the system.

As foreign relations become less political, it becomes less clear whether states have a foreign policy or a set of more or less interrelated foreign policies concerning different issues in the world. They probably agree with one set of states in regard to nuclear policy, with another in maritime affairs, and so on; only exceptionally, as in the case of Israel, is a special interest likely so to prevail as to form the basis of an integrated foreign policy. Domestic problems become increasingly interwoven with external demands and problems; correlated with the shift of emphasis in foreign policy from security and power to economic needs is the shift of focus of the state from defense to welfare.

There are two corollaries. One is that verbal aggression becomes a surrogate for physical, and the once-genteel language of diplomacy seems obsolete, as insults and affronts are hurled across the international scene. For contrast, it may be recalled how France went to war in 1870 because of an implied snub in Bismarck's reworded account of a meeting of the Prussian king with the French ambassador. An adjunct of verbal aggression may be the refusal or breaking of diplomatic relations, a way for smaller powers to slap big ones or vice versa, such as Iceland against Britain or Arab states against the United States, or the United States against Cuba—not used, it may be noted, between the major powers, for whom it might increase dangers of mutual destruction.

The other corollary is that, since welfare is an increasingly important object of foreign relations, the interests of states are more cooperative and less competitive. In the power arena, the gain of one is the loss of another; in economic affairs, the prosperity of one probably contributes to the prosperity of others. The states in general, primarily but not only the modern industrialized states, share an interest in the expansion of trade, in economic and monetary stability, in the checking of inflation, and so on. They are all to some degree threatened by international disorder, from plane hijacking to narcotics traffic; and problems of resources and environment require general agreement for the general benefit. There is some tendency, moreover, for states, at least the wealthier, to accept some responsibility for the well-being of the needier; they do not feel comfortable when people are starving in large numbers anywhere.

In the reduced utility of force, means of action change. Economic pressures are still usable and are seemingly acceptable, especially when used by non-Western nations. There may be intrigues and deceits, major or minor. The Soviet Union manages at once to procure cheap grain and to roil Western markets; Arab and African nations logroll in the UN to the detriment of Israel and South Africa. But most prominent is the increased importance of psychological factors and persuasion (Herz, 1959). Propaganda has come into its own as an instrument of national policy, while the world climate of opinion acquires a novel importance. Foreign policy is a matter of values, and the accepted values are those of the global village, largely determined by the most powerful states. If these treat land grabbing as a vital interest, others will do likewise; if they show more willingness to renounce use of force, weaker states can be expected to follow. For many years, nuclear testing in the atmosphere was accepted as a matter of course; public opinion led to moves toward ending it by both the United States and the Soviet Union, and brought about a treaty in 1963. The French, who had done very much less to poison the air than the superpowers, held out; but they too in 1974 pledged to hold no more atmospheric tests. Similarly, the Japanese, after much hesitation, at length bowed to the feelings of nature lovers and promised to limit whale harvests, in the worlds of the Japan Whaling Association, to "give reassurances to the conservationists and others on Japan's desire for global cooperation" (*Christian Science Monitor*, 1974).

So far as statesmen become better educated and aware of world opinion, they are more influenced thereby; leaders everywhere, following events through the international media and feeling themselves members of the general community, take note of the expectations of civilized society. So far as the planet is informationally integrated, they must think of their actions in some degree in planetary terms. Demands are also raised on them. It would have been inconceivable before World War II that a Japanese premier would have been toppled by the example of accusations against an American president, as Kakuei Tanaka was brought down in 1974 by perceived analogies between his conduct and that of Richard Nixon.

Finally, since violence is less at issue, international affairs become less of a state monopoly and more the province of nonstate actors, semigovernmental and private organizations, nonpolitical international bodies, multinational corporations and individuals (S. Brown, 1974). The state holds the monopoly of legal force; but commerce, charitable assistance, cultural affairs, health protection, and a hundred other important and probably growing activities may be carried on as well, possibly better, by nonpolitical bodies. The number of nonprofit international organizations, shooting up after World War II, reached about three thousand by 1970, many very small but others large and powerful, such as the International Air Transport Association (Skjelsbaek, 1972; Keohane and Nye, 1972). Vested interests and international bureaucracies grow up, with their special outlooks partly or largely divorced from the nation-state. International law, having lost its former primary function of regulating combat, expands into innumerable understandings of commerce, communications, and so on. The new state system becomes an infinitely complex network of interactions, most of them different from those that have formed the chief substance of international relations in the past.

Problems of the New World Order

MORALE

It is unclear whether the present international system is capable of meeting and resolving the problems bequeathed to it by the nation-state system that made science and technology but that, like others, was made obsolete by its success. Questions arise chiefly in three areas: the morale, cohesiveness, and motivation of society; the institutions of government; and the management of the international system itself.

Morale comes into question because of the fading of competitive drives. War, the threat of war, and the ability of the state to defend itself or possibly to impose its will upon others served to stimulate and energize state systems. The measuring of strength with others, especially among the contestants for leadership, brought realism to the fore, increased the value of knowledge and concrete achievement, and strengthened social bonds. As Francis Bacon opined, "No body can be healthy without exercise, neither natural body nor politic; and certainly to a kingdom or estate, a just and honorable war is the true exercise... for in a slothful peace, both courages will effeminate and manners corrupt" (*Essays*, "Of the True Greatness of Kingdoms"). Shortly before World War I, Friedrich von Bernhardi (1914) expressed strongly the desirability or necessity of war for the health of the nation, for the elimination of the unfit and the growth of the stronger nation. As he saw it, in peacetime, "all petty and personal interests force their way to the front during a long period of peace. Selfishness and intrigue run riot, and luxury obliterates idealism. Money acquires an excessive and unjustifiable power, and character does not obtain due respect" (p. 19). In war, on the contrary, "great personalities take their proper place; strength, truth, and honor come to the front and are put into play" (p. 26). Such forthright sentiments have been something of a Germanic specialty in modern times, but Douglas MacArthur (1927) expressed himself similarly after World War I: "A warlike spirit, which alone can create and civilize a state, is absolutely essential to national defense and national perpetuity." More recently, a semiserious American book (Lewin, 1962) found the horrors of an assured peace to exceed even those of war.

International conflict may still have a little of its traditional invigorating effects. The cold war seemed to solidify American society and to give it purposefulness as long as people believed in it; and in the first part of the Korean War, Americans were glad to see themselves repelling a tyrannical aggression. In the Arab-Israeli war of 1973, when the Arabs for the first time scored some impressive victories over their long-time antagonists, it suddenly became a matter of pride to be an Arab. Syrians and Egyptians claimed to have erased the shame of earlier defeats. The governments made a big show of the victories, real or exaggerated, and the people responded with self-respect and assurance. "It is as if a new wind blew through all our hearts," said a Syrian woman of letters (*Christian Science Monitor,* 1973). The performance of Arab armies, and of their societies, was vastly better in 1973, thanks to the lessons of 1948, 1956, and 1967. There was a new realism, sobriety, and willingness to work. "There is indeed a new Arab man," exulted a Jordanian writer (*New York Times,* 1973). The reshaping of Egyptian and Syrian society was barely begun, and poverty remains a fearful incubus; but a generation of tensions with Israel, especially since the conflict became dangerous to everyone by virtue of bombing, did something to change the semifeudal landlord-fellah society toward ways of the competitive state system.

But the world can hardly permit itself much such stimulation in the future. War between major powers can no longer be contemplated; the nuclear holocaust is in the same category as a possible superearthquake or comet striking the earth, pure calamity beyond imagination. In World War I, there was still some glory and heroism, or at least an attempt to glorify and find heroics, despite filthy trench warfare and the impersonality and mechanization of butchery. In World War II, there was much less; it was a nasty thing to be gotten over without romancing. Nowadays, to be militantly patriotic, when the national strength is expressed in megatons capable of destroying tens of millions of people, is to be inhumane and unmodern. Power has become a dubious quantity, as much a danger as a shield.

If relations between states are no longer really competitive, involving few or no dangers or dangers that are only fatalistically to be contemplated, the sovereign states will settle down to something like the stagnant tranquility of the universal empire. The nation-state, having largely lost its function as defender of the community, has lost the principal basis of its legitimacy. Only a few can seriously think of self-defense; the vast majority of states face no visible threat of invasion from their neighbors, and national security depends primarily on the general acceptance of the status quo and the unwillingness of the big powers to permit fighting or aggrandizement by force. Without an enemy at the gates, internal dissensions come to the fore, as in the demands of Scots and Welsh for autonomy in Britain, and of Bretons in France, or the upsurge of a counterculture in the United States (Field, 1972). The nation-states grew out of war and the needs of dangerous competition; if war among them is no longer acceptable, there is no point to structures that may be too centralized for their minorities and too divided to meet the broader needs of the age. Basques, Catalans, Corsicans, Scots, Welsh, and others ask why they should not have a state of their own instead of forming parts of outmoded units.

The modern intellectual belongs to the world and is superior to any particular nation. The nation-states, except for a few of the biggest, have shrunk to something near insignificance. Patriotism was one of the strongest feelings, a powerful stimulus and inspiration; in the new age the idea of giving one's life for his country seems rather silly. There is no longer a danger to the community, or the danger is of madness or fate. For the modern sophisticate, national feeling is not only weak; it is seen as narrow, positively bad, a menace to peace and international understanding. All conflict between states is degraded. Confrontation foreign policies, a surrogate for a genuine international contest, divide as much as they unite. Even the past loses its inspiring glow; great national victories and quondam military glories are forgotten if not deprecated by the sophisticated.

We must have peace, but peace is tedious and dull. The environment of struggle, softened but never ended by the influences of community, made modern civilization; the blander age of general security threatens psychological vacuity and social dissolution. It was not mere political rhetoric when Jimmy

Carter said in his acceptance speech, "We feel that moral decay has weakened our country, that it's crippled by a lack of goals and values." George F. Kennan wrote gloomily of the West "succumbing feebly, day by day, to its own decadence, sliding into debility of its own self-indulgent permissiveness: its drugs, its crime, its pornography, its pampering of the youth, its addiction to its bodily comforts, its rampant materialism and consumerism" (*Wall Street Journal*, 1976).

The whole catalog of social troubles of the modern states, from rising crime rates and the fading of the work ethic to poorer education, may be associated with this outwearing of old drives. Everything summarized by the apathy, demoralization, and indiscipline of contemporary society would seem curable if people felt themselves part of a group engaged in serious competition for the right to exist. The commonly rejected "middle-class" values are those generated by the competitive state system; from the 1950s, the value of competition as the heart of the "Protestant ethic" of thrifty, hard-driving America was being obviously replaced by the "social ethic" of getting along with other people (Whyte, 1956, pp. 16-17). The adolescent rebellion, conspicuous in the 1960s well before American society was torn by a war felt as useless, was an attack on the older respectability, on the success symbols of the achievement society, such as neatness, monogamy, and the future ethic. Self-indulgence became a positive value (Quigley, 1966). Youths maturing in the directionless society felt lonely and unneeded, and it was the tragedy of millions not to know what to do with their lives, while improvisations, from drugs to communes, proved empty. (On the internal tensions and contradictions of contemporary America, see Bell, 1976.) Ripening directionlessness, like the anomie of the folk brought from a tribal society to a metropolitan slum, is perhaps most conspicuous in America, the leading state of the Western world; but it has its counterparts in the bored bourgeois of Sweden, the effete intelligentsia of England and Holland, and the rootless youth of the whole Western world.

In this situation, it no longer seemed so important to reward effort or talent as to distribute more evenly the goods of society. The competitive states are equalitarian because everyone is valuable; the new age is equalitarian because everyone has a claim to a proper share. In the absence of external reason to accept deprivations or suffering, everyone is considered entitled to demand a full quota for himself. A major function of the government, its single most expensive operation, above defense and the keeping of order, became the transfer of resources—a development reminiscent of latter-day Greece, in which likewise the competition of the polities was outmoded.

In the nonachievement society the idea that technology and the earnest application of intelligence could bring real good was left behind. In the midst of its most wonderful accomplishments, science lost luster. People looked, rather, for the warts; and many, especially intellectuals, opposed such engineering wonders as nuclear energy and supersonic transportation with a fervor contrasting with the possibly naïve enthusiasm of an earlier generation for dramatic technological innovation. The ideas—some would say myths—that objectivity and the accumulation of data and understanding are values per se, and that technical information can solve our problems, have seemed to be giving way to subjectivity and intuitionism, with the downgrading of individual achievement. The psychic energy of America has entered a palpable decline (Gimpel, 1976).

A drive to understanding, helped along in the United States by post-Sputnik competition with the apparently quickly rising Russians, crested in the later 1960s; since then appropriations for scientific research slackened. Support for basic research declined, in real terms, by 13 percent from 1968 to 1974; expenditure per working scientist decreased 30 percent (*Science*, 1977). In 1973 for the first time there was a drop in the rate at which Americans patented new ideas and institutions (Marina, 1975). Praise of science in the world wars for producing better weapons has been replaced by dispraise for increasing the dangers of annihilation in collaboration with the military-industrial complex. In the words of a writer in *Science* (Thackray, 1976, p. 248), "We are less certain than we used to be about both the power and the virtue of 'the modern mentality.' We hesitate over whether science is anything but a fiction that has outlived its usefulness." Restrictions on research proliferate, and scientists themselves have become more self-critical and doubtful of their mission. It is questionable whether Americans would have been disposed to send astronauts to the moon if the question had arisen a decade later.

The feeling grows that science, to be meaningful, must relate to social needs. The problem has become less how to advance technology than how to live with it. Today's questions are social—how to manage the economy, population problems, international frictions, control of the environment, and so on—in short, how to manage what we already have to bring more happiness or to forestall disaster. The questions are ethical—what is good, how to live, what of the family, not how to achieve. They are questions asked by philosophers of empires rather than by the inquisitive thinkers of flourishing state systems, like the Roman inquiry into justice after the Greek inquiry into the nature of things. It is less important to dig into the secrets of nature than to probe the mysteries within and learn the truth about oneself.

Disillusionment with technology and science has been accompanied by widespread resort to new-old faiths, from astrology to variants of Oriental religions of contemplation and mysticism, hoary occultism, tales of extraterrestrial "aliens," novel cults, and alternative life styles, in a manner faintly parallel to the flooding of Near Eastern cults into the Greek world in decline. Some become nostalgically past-oriented, a tendency especially visible in England, the present of which is so much less glorious than bygone days. The sense of apartness or nonidentification with the prevalent order and its values is also reflected in the self-flagellation common among the intellectual elite and the antinationalistic acceptance of responsibility for the world's ailments.

Demoralization seems to have notably progressed in Britain, long a proud leader of the nations (Haseler, 1976). With no more national glory and with security dependent on the United States, there seems to be little national purpose. In class conflict and bitterness, there is little urge to produce more for the community. During recent years, the productivity of British labor has increased hardly at all; that is, the steady stream of technological improvements in means of production has been almost entirely absorbed by social frictions and waste. By the early 1960s, the productivity of labor in Britain was lower than in most Western European nations, and it has continued steadily to lose ground (Koestler, 1964). A British steel worker produces only a third as much as his Japanese counterpart. The British share of world trade, still a respectable 22 percent on the eve of World War II, was approximately 6 percent in 1974. With little idea of national purpose, with no humiliation of defeat to get over, with no shakeup of institutions forced upon them, the British feel little incentive to reshape old structures. Extreme reluctance to change ways is accompanied by strong desire for "social justice," or fulfillment of traditional expectations. Stability is preferred to efficiency, and workers are automatically suspicious of bosses (Shanks, 1964; Quigley, 1966). In the lassitude, it is not considered necessary really to exert oneself even in athletic training. As a Londoner remarked, "It's not like the war, when we had a common enemy we could stand up against. It's just depression and backsliding and gloom. Maybe there won't always be a Britain" (*New York Times*, 1974). The British social order has become in many ways suggestive of a Third World nation (Moss, 1977). Social causation is infinitely complex, but the most obvious reason for the British lassitude is that Britain, alone of major European powers, was spared revivifying defeat but lost its empire from causes beyond its control: the heroic fight brought no positive reward.

In short, the new world has an identity crisis. Barring a threat of interplanetary warfare, it is questionable whether societies not subject to serious competitive challenge can hold together and function well enough to meet the grave but mostly intangible needs of the modern day. The traditional answers to the question why one should not merely seek his own pleasure have been moral law from without, religion or the dictates of an earthly or supernatural ruler, or the needs of the community. But intellectual skepticism has largely emptied religion of content for at least the leadership, while the most important community, the state, has morally failed.

It is questionable whether the competition of national power can be replaced by another of comparable effect. The "class struggle" that the Marxist-Leninist states evoke lacks persuasiveness in the modern context. Cultural competition among states is hardly inspiring; most at any event have little distinctiveness, and it is difficult to convince intellectuals that the heritage is worth much struggle. Economic growth has served as an inspiration and vindication for Japan in the postwar era, a more modern way of national self-assertion than violent empire building; and Marxist-Leninist states have made much propagandistically of their real or claimed achievements. But this has limited utility, and new preoccupations intervene; some view economic growth beyond a certain level as a positive sin against world environment and resources. At best exponential growth must fairly soon slow down, to the disillusionment of those dedicated to it.

Nations, in any case, do not compete because of the (nonexistent) awareness of the value of competition, but because they desire certain rewards of supremacy. These rewards hardly exist in the postindustrial world. The nations instead need and seek order and harmony, which rather conduce to passivity. There are ample general and cooperative causes, desirable or necessary for the well-being of humanity, from the protection of environments to the elimination of gross poverty; but such noncompetitive causes are not very engaging and lack political support. Few are deeply stirred for something so abstract; the moving cause is an exciting human opponent. Few are indifferent to the national fight; the future of mankind is less compelling. William James (1911) long ago sought a "moral equivalent of war"; the search goes on. As Soviet dissenter Andrei Amalrik put it, "I believe that everyone who values freedom is confronted by the problem of creating a new ideology which will transcend both liberalism and Communism and make its central issue the indivisible rights of man" (*New York Times,* February 3, 1977, p. 3).

GOVERNMENT

Closely related to the problem of social order is the question of what form of government may prevail and whether it can fill the needs of the new universe. In the past, state institutions have roughly corresponded to the international order. Bureaucratic despotism has been the rule for the continental empires. The classic polis, the medieval commune-republic, feudal monarchy, absolutist monarchy, and parliamentary government have all been characteristic of differing state systems. The expanded system of today shows two trends, to publicitarian-plebiscitarian democracy, as in the United States, or to pseudodemocracy, with oligarchic or dictatorial rulership with engineered consent or appearances of consent, the archetype of which is the Soviet Union. Virtually no respectable opinion is overtly contrary to democracy as an ideal, albeit ill defined, while equality as a theoretical desideratum seems to take precedence over prosperity or strength. Nearly all pay at least lip service to those twin values, however little they are realized in most of the world.

There is practically no alternative basis of legitimacy and authority. Democratic consent remains theoretically sacrosanct when other sources of legitimacy, from hereditary right to racial superiority, are cast down. Only the values of the people's will and rights resist, thus far, the acid of rationalism. The growth of the democratic ethos fully corresponds to the rule that technological improvement and greater ease of spreading opinions usually leads toward liberalization as long as the size of political units is not increased. In this generation not only has there been no consolidation but small states have multiplied (with less effect, to be sure, because of their extreme weakness); and the small, weak states, however undemocratically ruled, see in the ideology of popular rights a guarantee of their own position. Outright tyranny has become unmodern.

It is to be remembered, however, that an atmosphere of international contention has in the past been congenial, possibly essential for popular government. The rise of modern democracy was closely associated with the growth of modern nationalism. The patriotic sense and national feeling of community have been important, perhaps essential, to making inherently rather cumbersome democratic systems workable. The decline of international competition, the erosion of the emotional bonds, and the decreased validity of the nation-state can only hurt democratic morale, making it more difficult to maintain consensus and act decisively contrary to the interests of entrenched groups, as is certain to be necessary.

Democracy cannot function if people simply want the maximum for themselves, and the citizenry in the new age raises claims faster than the state can hope to satisfy them. The essence of political decay in most states is the excess of demands on the state over willingness to serve it. On the other hand, would-be autocratic governments no longer need the cooperation of their citizenry for purposes of national defense. There is a lack of military defeats to renovate institutions and show the need for basic reforms. It is possible as previously only in imperial societies for elites of authoritarian countries—Marxist-Leninist, militarist, or simply dictatorial—to dedicate themselves entirely to the preservation of their own power.

The modern technological age seems to call for nondiscrimination, awareness of feelings and needs of people, and the legitimacy of consent. But the concentration of control over means of communication may raise doubts as to the real meaning of the democratic order. In some ways, the ordinary citizen becomes more helpless in the face of the computer bureaucracy and the intellectual elite; and it can hardly be doubted that the old American liberalism has faded in a "crisis of authority" (Lowi, 1969, p. 49), leaving the name to proponents of government intervention for welfare.

Decreased commitment to the commonwealth places the mass man on the margin of political life; at the same time, lack of tensions plus easy travel and communications make coercion less feasible in the pluralistic society. People are less in a position to defend their rights, but the state has difficulty in repression. Conceivably, freedom and democracy might diverge. The Soviet Union, for example, might permit a great deal more freedom of movement and of speech while retaining control of means of mass communication and becoming very little more democratic. Some Communist countries, such as Hungary, and many states of the Third World interfere rather little in the lives of their citizens, as long as these do not aggressively engage in politics; yet the levers of authority are tightly held.

Democracy is in most places unacceptable in practice. Western culture has been extended superficially, not deeply, to the basically authoritarian non-Western world. Many, perhaps most, of the states of the world lack the confidence and coherence necessary for the successful operation of democratic institutions. They would find the free contention of opposing parties unbearably divisive and a guarantee of paralysis (Mehden, von der, 1969). For the Soviet Union, effective representation for the non-Russian half of the population would be an invitation to dissolution. Many another state is similarly fissured. Moreover, in the lack of strong drives toward general improvement, democracy seems to invite retrogressive, divisive, or parasitic interests to claim whatever they can. The bureaucratic apparatus may become (as in Uruguay and Brazil before the military took over the state) the foremost pressure group within the state, seeking to maximize its rewards and minimize its exertions. Elites exclude benighted masses from any real share of power.

The pressure group that most commonly takes charge of the state, however, is the military. Where there is no alternative basis for authority, force readily prevails. Paradoxically, in a situation of minimal danger of invasion by neighboring powers, the armed forces become not less but more politically potent. They serve as symbol of the sovereignty of weak states; in imitation of the military forces of great powers and of history, they are a badge of prestige for states that have little to boast. With low morale for lack of realistic purpose, they turn to police functions, the support of the ruling elite. Rulership is thus associated with possession of the instruments of force, and it does not matter greatly whether generals actually stand at the head of the state or not. Perhaps half of the world's governments are military based, and in many of the remainder the military has an effective veto.

For such reasons, the world sees much undemocratic democracy—"guided democracy," "one-party democracy," or "people's democratic republics"—wherein the will of the people is expressed through the pronouncements of the rulers, dictatorship putting on modern democratic forms and boasting total dedication to the welfare of the masses. The Marxist-Leninist states stand our for congratulating themselves on being democratic while most effectually concentrating power in a small, irremovable, and self-selected leadership. Democratic forms in such cases are helpful to the monopolistic authority rather than a restriction on it. The façade serves propagandistic purposes, deceiving some and confusing the opposition; the regime is harder to attack when it has preempted the vocabulary of liberal government and can point to institutions for popular participation, however unrealistic these may be.

Pseudodemocracy, however, is not promising. It may get over some of the problems of unity and direction thhat arise to trouble more candid authoritarianisms. But it rests ultimately on the ability to apply coercion and violence, which are unmodern. It requires, in more developed states, an ideological rationale; but this becomes threadbare as contradictions show through, promises are defaulted, and intellectuals move to skepticism or to more or less open dissidence. The modern dictatorial regime, leaning on pretenses, lacks the legitimacy to permit criticism of its actions without rejection of the system, and can hardly permit examination and appraisal, which are essential to correction of defects.

The pretense of democracy means that any constitution is more or less fraudulent; and the nonconstitutional regime has no way to check abuse of power, especially the use of authority by leaders to perpetuate or strengthen their positions. Without external dangers to propel reforms—defeat repeatedly taught tsarist Russia, for example, to mend its ways and spurred it to catch up with the West—it is the more necessary for a closed society like the Soviet Union to have means for change built into the political system and the more difficult to achieve this. For these reasons, pseudodemocracy portends immobility, demoralization, and corruption. The usual result has been an irregular alternation between dictatorship, marked by abuse of power and corruption, and oligarchy, marked by corruption and stagnation.

Unrestricted power seems invariably to lead, in the longer term, if not in the shorter, to the progressive stifling of the economy. An obvious key to the productivity of the West is competition, the struggle to advance in a world where each is free to apply his abilities; as a late eighteenth-century Chinese reformer, Yen Fu, surveying the calcification of the imperial bureaucratic regime, found, "Unity and progress result from diversity and competition" (Gasster, 1972, p. 23). But to this day China has found no good way to incorporate diversity and competition into the command structure.

A viable state system needs to find, in internal political life as well as on the international scene, a workable balance between freedom and order, rights and duties. Most of the world lives under highly arbitrary rulership more or less dressed up for decent appearances. Nor is there an intensive search for such a balanced order. In the absence of strong competitive pressures, it becomes the more necessary purposefully to design adequate institutions; but the modern world strikingly lacks capacity for political innovation. Even the revolutionaries seem to have renounced the blueprinting of the desirable organization of society; they would make their revolution and hope that, with revolutionaries in charge, something better should emerge. Perhaps it is impossible to design a new politics, just as it seems to be impossible to design a new state system.

INTERNATIONAL ORDER

The contemporary world system is a ridiculous product of accident, marked by extremest inequality in the face of nominal equality. The two strongest powers have practically all strategic capability, while the European Economic Community, the world's biggest trading power, has neither coherence nor military strength, and Japan, an economic giant, has neither military capacity nor political will. China is a superpower only in terms of ant-like numbers. The majority of states are hopelessly weak militarily, economically, and in terms of modern culture; and their formal sovereignty is insubstantial, eroded in practice however upheld in principle (Sprout and Sprout, 1971). Yet even the small, feeble states, many representing only the haphazard dissection of colonial empires, seem more secure than ever. They possess the legal shield of sovereignty, a principle to which all are attached; the smallest and poorest cannot be annulled by force without a symbolic threat to the security of all. To exclude violence as a means of international action it is necessary to guarantee the independence of all states.

The principle of the freedom of states is also indispensable because it represents the foundation of freedom everywhere. The vital and basic freedom lies not in any particular economic or political arrangements but in the fractioning of power, the sovereignty of numerous political units. It is with a just perception that the United States has for many generations made support for the independence of states a cardinal point of its foreign policy. Security for this pluralism makes a climate for pluralism within the nation also. The system of multiple sovereignties provides focal points for decentralization in a world much subject to centralization, the logical result of homogenization.

Yet the freedom of states leads to complications. Force and compulsion by the stronger powers are unacceptable, and small states are of necessity pacific; but rivalries and antagonisms persist among the great, a perennial contest for prestige and position rationalized in terms of defense of the state and its ideals. Normal people, especially those directing strategy, enjoy the confrontations of power, the military-diplomatic games, the scheming to gain an advantage or frustrate the enemy, our team against theirs, an engagement of masculine, possibly even boyish, spirits (Yost, 1972). Only on this account is it understandable that an American president has himself aroused from sleep to be briefed on minor developments in an intrinsically unimportant Cyprus crisis, or that John Kennedy should spend the largest fraction of his time during the first two months in office on the composition of the government of Laos (Wildavsky, 1971).

Two major states of different outlook, such as the Soviet Union and the United States, or the former and China, find ample reason to be dissatisfied with one another's actions. So for that matter can the United States and India or France, so far as their attention is not preempted by stronger antagonisms. Such confrontations are mostly verbal; neither side thinks seriously of using major force, and probably neither cares to forego the benefits of trade and other relations, nor does anyone become angry enough to break diplomatic relations and so make adjustments more difficult. Yet lower-scale force, which implies little or no danger of nuclear war, may be used here and there in international relations. It is for this reason that American presidents decline to renounce the use of subversion, although its returns are slight in comparison with costs in world opinion, that the Communist states insist on the right to support guerrillas, that Third World nations refuse to forswear terrorism, and that all feel free to indulge in slanderous rhetoric.

Much international controversy is thus about very little, mostly prestige—that is, pride, self-esteem, a striving not for true national security but for image security and for an image of strength in the international community. The first part of the cold war had the serious purpose of defining the limits of postwar Soviet expansionism; but after Stalin's death it shifted away from the Soviet periphery and became more rhetorical-political, a largely symbolic duel, with a characteristically fluctuating degree of intensity. When dangers and costs rose, the contestants would back away; if détente seemed to make it safe to be more truculent, basic rivalries came to the fore.

Such waves in the cold war were several, but the longest arose over Vietnam. The United States felt that prestige, to compensate for the loss of North Vietnam to communism, required that South Vietnam be made an anti-Communist success story. As the struggle turned into an American war, the Johnson administration presented it as necessary to stop Soviet-backed Communism and at the same time kept it as detached as possible from American-Soviet relations in order to prevent it from becoming really dangerous. Although costs climbed out of proportion to possible gains, the leadership felt that withdrawal would be cowardly and too much of a blow to the American image and presumably their own self-image. But in the general and congressional opinion, the adventure showed all too clearly the drawbacks and futilities of anti-Communist interventionism. Hence moves by the Nixon administration toward better, potentially even quite friendly relations with China and the Soviet Union were greeted with enthusiasm. But as fears and Vietnam losses receded in memory, the warts of détente reappeared; it again became respectable to criticize Soviet injustices and call for putting a stop to Communist expansion, taken as surrogate for Soviet imperialism.

Such contests, of varying earnestness and peril, seem endemic to the international system, wherein foreign policy must be viewed less in terms of material national objectives, more in terms of psychological rewards for decision makers. The biggest cold war, or unfriendly peace, naturally goes on between the strongest powers. But China and Russia seem to take pleasure in confrontation, and both would doubtless feel freer to indulge their dislike of the United States if they detested each other less. Arabs and Israelis carry on a standoff in which each side continually menaces the other yet both usually refrain from the risks and costs of actual combat. Many states take pleasure in abusing another verbally, sometimes a neighbor, more often the nation that most injures the self-esteem of the weak and poor, the United States.

Seldom, however, do such latter-day international contests have much unifying value. They are often essentially hollow, and are so perceived, a game not really of nations but of leaders and their pride. Thus the American public came to feel, for the most part, that it had no real stake in the Vietnam war; and the war, far from bringing Americans together in a common cause, divided them more bitterly than anything since the Civil War, turned them away from competitive values, and engendered unprecedented cynicism. Earlier, Korea had divided the nation, although less deeply; and the 1956 excursion of Britain and France to Suez split those countries. From the point of view of sophisticated observers, international antagonisms are false, the work of self-serving politicians, and only a hindrance to the solution of real problems.

But the rivalries, however bloodless, are excuse enough to pile up super-arsenals of strategic weapons on both sides far beyond any reasonable calculation of use—arsenals that always represent a risk that someday leaders, out of some compulsion or because the powers levered themselves into a situation of unavoidable escalation, might make use of the apocalyptic potential at their fingertips. Apart from the possibilities of such a dramatic denouement, the waste is huge, a major diversion of badly needed resources. There is a political waste, too, as national leaderships spend a large fraction of their energies dealing with unreal problems. And there is a political burden, as alleged needs of national security are made a major excuse for repression in many countries and for doubtful or illegal acts in the United States.

Not only the biggest powers but the smaller are free, within the broad limits set by the nuclear overhang, to be irresponsible in pursuit of whatever they may conceive to be their interests. In the exercise of their unimpeachable sovereignty, states can do many things dangerous or harmful to other states, which may or may not be able to protect themselves. There is nothing to prevent a score of states from making nuclear weapons and targeting others with missiles sufficient to make cities uninhabitable. A state may find it convenient to deal carelessly with nuclear material for peaceful reactors, to leak poisonous wastes into the ocean or atmosphere, to pollute a neighbor's seas or air, or to steal its rain. States, especially the richer and stronger, can clandestinely aid terrorists or parties of rebellion, and some Mideast and Communist countries seem to do so almost as a matter of principle. Perhaps with appropriate secrecy and disguises, states may help their balance of payments by supplying drugs to the international underworld. So far as producers of essential materials can come to agreements, they can charge whatever the traffic will bear for oil, aluminum ore, or a score of other materials available in limited quantities.

The need for international cooperation in the regulation of the common resources of mankind is much beyond the ability of sovereignties to come to agreement. Formerly the rivers and oceans were able to digest what little was cast into them; now free use would mean turning them eventually into cesspools. Yet agreement seems hard to reach and might be equally hard to enforce; a few recalcitrants can hold up many an excellent international initiative. Likewise, it seems necessary and impossible to put together a workable and equitable world system of monetary and trade regulations to protect all sides and forestall disruptions. It has also been impossible to agree on equitable rules governing foreign investments and multinational corporations. Nor does there appear to be any likelihood of agreement for the most rational exploitation and conservation of exhaustible resources.

Not less important, the nations are free to breed themselves into global slums in a world where the more fortunate cannot remain untouched by the misfortunes of others. Progress has been possible in the past only because war and disease kept numbers from growing more rapidly than productivity. Only in conditions of relative scarcity of people and abundance of resources were there sufficiency and leisure to encourage experimentation, innovation, and nonutilitarian art and science. Thanks to chronic conflict and plagues, average peasant holdings in the Middle Ages were about sixty acres (Thompson, 1932). Very few countries know comparable abundance today, as Western civilization has given the peoples of the world the opportunity to procreate up to the limits of famine.

The richer nations seem to face the dilemma of trying to prevent starvation by sharing or attempting to cut themselves off to preserve their relatively high material standards. (For a statement of the problem, see L. Brown, 1974). Neither answer promises a livable world. Projections based on recent trends that the world population will double well before 2000 A.D. can hardly be fulfilled; starvation, because of waste and corruption as much as lack of production, will certainly prevail long before. Already some states seem poised on the abyss. Thus Bangladesh struggles to keep alive with a population growing at the rate of 3 percent yearly; it has rice yields among the lowest in Asia, along with unemployment of 35 to 50 percent, a per capita income of about $60, and a bankrupt and incompetent government. Its neighbor, India, is not far behind; and many a country can see in Bangladesh the image of its future unless overcrowding is halted in ways now unforeseeable. Malthus' timetable was faulty but his syllogism was impeccable: a population growing exponentially will eventually be checked by nature if not by man.

These incapacities and incongruities of the contemporary international system suggest that it may not last very long in this world of rapid flux. There are obvious tendencies to breakdown and political disorder, both on the world stage and within countries rich and poor. If problems grow more rapidly than the ability to cope with them, as many doomsayers predict (such as Meadows, 1974), degradation may become self-generating, or some madness or desperation may bring nuclear war. The international system would then break down in anarchy or dictatorship or both, perhaps with a government of the world, so far as it remained governable.

It may be, on the other hand, that civilization will continue to adjust much as it has in recent decades, hardly solving basic problems but keeping them from exploding. Then, if trends continue, the world may be expected to become a little like a defective federal system, the effective power of the territorial jurisdictions limited not by a central government—the UN, unrealistically dominated by the numerous small, weak states is not a step toward world government but an impediment to it—but by the interdependent environment in which they must operate, with their existence shielded by the overriding fear of violence and recognition of its nonutility. Even the greatest powers can hardly make major decisions of international politics in isolation in the eighteenth-century manner (Keohane and Nye, 1972). While jealously guarding the forms and symbols of sovereignty, the states become locked into more and more interrelations from which it is costly or difficult to withdraw. No less important, the world has become something of a psychological community, in which leaders are concerned with what others think and say about them; the obverse of the general concern for face or prestige is a responsiveness to what may be vaguely called civilized opinion. Nearly all states take some pride in observing international norms, even when material interests might indicate taking quite legal, although disapproved, actions. Thus, in the postwar period states have generally abstained from competitive devaluations and have followed the rules in handling gold stocks. Mavericks, such as Muammar Kaddaffy of Libya and Idi Amin of Uganda, are few; and they are subject to more or less reprobation by those by whom they would measure themselves, other Arab or African presidents.

Loyalties withdrawn from nation-states, the functions of which become less compelling, may be transferred partly to groups within the states, partly to international or regional organizations, as states, from convenience or necessity, abdicate responsibilities to functional bodies more capable of handling them. Sovereignty, then, is likely to be reduced, especially for the smaller and more dependent states, to a thin legalism, a national flag and rights of local administrations, while important decisions are made by regional, international, or transnational private and public organizations, which would grow to fill the needs.

In either case, one may see ahead the end of the long road that began, so far as we know, with the Sumerians. The territorial polity will no longer be able to serve as the integrating competitive unit of social existence, the chief conditioner of human behavior and values. If humans are to go forward with what has been proudly called civilization or even are to maintain the present level of relative affluence and high population, it will be necessary to construct new structures to provide new orientations, new political institutions supplementing or supporting the sovereign state as the basic vehicle of pluralism and the open society. The competition of territorial societies is no longer sufficient.

Epilogue

Selectivity, some kind of sieve of survival and growth for some, disappearance for others, has been the rule of generation of new order since life began. Early humans, we may assume, were driven to improve their tools, institutions, and means of communication not only to kill the wily and powerful mammoth but to defend their hunting grounds and themselves from other humans. As soon as mankind had raised itself well above the capacities of animals, the chief yardstick of performance became the competition of other humans and the chief stimulus to improvement was the need to surpass them.

Through history, the most important vehicle of competition has been the sovereign state, the supreme organization of society, the great and enduring culture-creating group with which large numbers can identify. Discovery, innovation, productivity, social discipline, and political order have flourished when the sovereign units, small enough to arouse feelings of participation yet adequately large to permit the application of available techniques, have been in competition sufficiently strong to engage emotions yet not so desperate as to destroy the rivals.

Yet progress is inherently self-limiting because it does away with the conditions that make it possible. The state systems, by virtue of their inventiveness, have made themselves obsolete. Only that of the West managed to hold out for a millennium by expansion and metamorphosis. Now the Western nation-state system is worn out. It can expand geographically by extending the recognition and forms of Western sovereignty to the remainder of the world despite military and economic weakness and cultural gaps. But the ultimate potential means of competition, military power, is both far too concentrated and unusable. Competition, the nourishment of state systems, is left to little more than such trivia as Olympic Games.

But competition is the chief reality principle of the life of states, just as it is of the economy. Unless there is a measuring of peoples and ways, reward and stern punishment, it is easy to sink into stagnation and lethargy. If firms or countries do not suffer consequences of poor performance, incentives to improvement or even maintenance of standards are feeble; and without stimulation there is rot.

The critical question thus seems to be whether humanity can learn, in effect, to compete on a higher level, not for power of one group over another but for the solution of major problems facing technological civilization, for welfare and general improvement. If this can be brought about by reeducation, it will represent a triumph of reason to make pale the dreams of philosophers of the Enlightenment.

References

ACTON, J. 1930. *Lectures on Modern History.* New York: Macmillan.

ADAMS, R. 1966. *The Evolution of Urban Society.* Chicago: Aldine.

ADCOCK, F., and MOSELY, D. 1975. *Diplomacy in Ancient Greece.* New York: St. Martin's Press.

ADIE, R., and POITRAS, G. 1974. *Latin America, The Politics of Immobility.* Englewood Cliffs, N.J.: Prentice-Hall.

ADY, C. 1936. "Florence and North Italy, 1414-1492." In *Cambridge Medieval History*, vol. 8. Cambridge, Eng.: Cambridge University Press.

AGARD, W. 1942. *What Democracy Meant to the Greeks.* Chapel Hill, N.C.: University of North Carolina Press.

ALDRED, C., in Piggott, S., ed. 1961. *The Dawn of Civilization.* New York: McGraw-Hill.

ALEXANDER, P., ed. 1963. *The Ancient World: To 300 A.D.* New York: Macmillan.

ALMOND, G., and VERBA, S. 1963. *The Civic Culture: Political Attitudes and Democracy in Five Nations.* Princeton, N.J.: Princeton University Press.

ALTAMIRA, R. 1946. *Manual de Historia de España.* Buenos Aires: Ed. Sudamerica.

ALTEKAR, A. 1958. *State and Government in Ancient India.* Delhi: Banarsidass.

ANDREWES, A. 1956. *The Greek Tyrants.* London: Hutchinson University Library.

ANDRESKI, S. 1966. *Parasitism and Subversion, The Case of Latin America.* London: Weidenfeld and Nicolson.

ANGELL, N. 1933. *The Great Illusion,* reissue. New York: Putnam's.

ARTZ, F. 1959. *The Mind of the Middle Ages A.D. 200-1500.* New York: Knopf.

ASHLEY, M. 1961. *Great Britain to 1688.* Ann Arbor, Mi.: University of

Michigan Press.
AUBRY, O. 1947. *Histoire de la France*. Paris: Flammarion.
AVDIEV, V., and PIKUS, N., eds. 1962. *Istoriia drevnei Gretsii*. Moscow: Akad. Nauk.

BAGBY, P. 1958. *Culture and History*. London: Longmans, Green.
BAILLY, A. 1946. *Le règne de Louis XIV*. Paris: Flammarion.
BALASZ, E. 1964. *Chinese Civilization and Bureaucracy*. New Haven, Ct.: Yale University Press.
BANDYOPADHYAYA, N. 1941. *Economic Life and Progress in Ancient India*, vol. 1. Calcutta: University of Calcutta.
BANTI, L. 1973. *Etruscan Cities and Their Culture*. Berkeley, Ca.: University of California Press.
BARAMKI, D. 1961. *Phoenicia and the Phoenicians*. Beirut: Khayats.
BARBER, E. 1955. *The Bourgeoisie in Eighteenth-century France*. Princeton, N.J.: Princeton University Press.
BARK, W. 1958. *Origins of the Medieval World*. Stanford, Ca.: Stanford University Press.
BARNES, H. 1937. *An Economic History of the Western World*. New York: Harcourt Brace Jovanovich.
BARNETT, H. 1953. *Innovation: The Basis of Cultural Change*. New York: McGraw-Hill.
BARNOUW, A. 1940. *The Dutch*. New York: Columbia University Press.
———. 1952. *The Pageant of Netherlands History*. London: Longmans, Green.
BARON, H. 1955. *The Crisis of the Early Italian Renaissance*. Princeton, N.J.: Princeton University Press.
———. 1957. "Fifteenth-century Civilization and the Renaissance." In *New Cambridge Modern History*, vol. 10. Cambridge, Eng.: Cambridge University Press.
BARRACLOUGH, G. 1963. *The Origins of Modern Germany*. New York: Capricorn Books.
———. 1976. *The Crucible of Europe: The Ninth and Tenth Centuries in European History*. Berkeley, Ca.: University of California Press.
BARTHOLD, F. 1909. *Die Geschichte der deutschen Hanse*, 2 vols. Magdeburg: Deubach und Lindemann.
BARY, W. de. 1957. "Chinese Despotism and the Confucian Ideal: A Seventeenth-century View." In *Chinese Thought and Institutions*. Edited by J. Fairbanks. Chicago: University of Chicago Press.
———, ed. 1958. *Sources of Indian Tradition*. New York: Columbia University Press.
BASHAM, A. 1963. *The Wonder That Was India*. New York: Hawthorn Books.
BEARD, M. 1938. *A History of the Business Man*. New York: Macmillan.
BELL, D. 1976. *The Cultural Contradictions of Capitalism*. New York: Basic Books.

BELL, E. 1940. *The Development of Mathematics*. New York: McGraw-Hill.

BENGTSON, H. 1950. *Griechische Geschichte*. Munich: Beck.

BENNET, W., and BIRD, J. 1949. *Andean Cultural History*. New York: Museum of Natural History.

BERLYNE, D. 1966. "Conflict and Arousal." *Scientific American* 215 (August).

BERNADSKII, V. 1961. *Novgord i novgorodskaia zemlia v XV veke*. Moscow: Izd. Akad. Nauk.

BERNARD, H. 1962. *Human Development in Western Culture*. Boston: Allyn and Bacon.

BERNHARDI, F. von. 1914. *Germany and the Next War*. London: Longmans, Green.

BERNSTEIN, E. 1963. *Cromwell and Communism*, reprint ed. New York: Schocken Books.

BIANQUIS, G. 1958. *La vie quotidienne en Allemagne a l'epoque romantique 1795-1830*. Paris: Hachette.

BISHOP, C. 1942. *Origins of Far Eastern Civilizations*. Washington, D.C.: Smithsonian Institution.

BLUM, J.; CAMERON, R.; and BARNES, T. 1966. *The European World since 1815*. Boston: Little, Brown.

———. 1970. *The Emergence of the European World*. Boston: Little, Brown.

BOAK, A. 1943. *A History of Rome to 565 A.D.* New York: Macmillan.

BOAS, M. 1962. *The Scientific Renaissance 1450-1630*. London: Collins.

BODDE, D. 1938. *China's First Unifier*. Leiden: Brill.

BONNARD, A. 1961. *Greek Civilization*. London: Allen and Unwin.

BONNER, R. 1933. *Aspects of Athenian Democracy*. Berkeley, Ca.: University of California Press.

BOSE, A. 1945. *Social and Rural Economy of Northern India, 600 B.C.-200 A.D.*, vol. 2. Calcutta: University of Calcutta.

BOTSFORD, G., and ROBINSON, C. 1939. *Hellenic History*. New York: Macmillan.

BOTSFORD, G., and SHILES, E., eds. 1915. *Hellenic Civilization*. New York: Columbia University Press.

BOUVIER, E. 1853. *Des perfectionnements que reçut la langue française au XVII siècle*. Brussels.

BOWDEN, W. 1965. *Industrial Society in England toward the End of the Eighteenth Century*. New York: Cau.

BOWRA, C. 1957. *The Greek Experience*. London: Weidenfeld and Nicolson.

BOZEMAN, A. 1960. *Politics and Culture in International History*. Princeton, N.J.: Princeton University Press.

BRAILSFORD, H. 1961. *The Levellers and the English Revolution*. Stanford, Ca.: Stanford University Press.

Brain Drain: A Study of the Persistent Issue of International Scientific Mobility. 1974. Washington, D.C.: Government Printing Office.

BRAMFELD, T. 1959. *The Remaking of a Culture*. New York: Harper and Row.

BRANTL, R., ed. 1966. *Medieval Culture: The Image and the City*. New York: Braziller.

BREASTED, J. 1937. *A History of Egypt*. New York: Scribner's.

BRIGGS, A. 1959. *The Age of Improvement, 1783-1869*. London: Longmans, Green.

———. 1960. "The World Economy: Interdependence and Planning." In *New Cambridge Modern History*, vol. 12. Cambridge, Eng.: Cambridge University Press.

BRITTON, R. 1935. "Chinese Intercourse before 700 B.C." *American Journal of International Law* 29 (October).

BROWN, L. 1972. *World without Borders*. New York: Random House.

———. 1974. *In the Human Interest*. New York: Norton.

BROWN, S. 1974. *New Forces in World Politics*. Washington, D.C.: Brookings Institution.

BRUCKER, G. 1962. *Florentine Politics and Society 1343-1378*. Princeton, N.J.: Princeton University Press.

BRUFORD, W. 1952. *Germany in the Eighteenth Century: The Social Background of the Literary Revival*. Cambridge, Eng.: Cambridge University Press.

BRUMBAUGH, R. 1966. *Ancient Greek Gadgets and Machines*. New York: Crowell.

BRUNDAGE, B. 1963. *Empire of the Inca*. Norman, Ok.: University of Oklahoma Press.

BRYCE, J. 1923. *The Holy Roman Empire*. New York: Macmillan.

BULLOCK, C. 1939. *Politics, Finance, and Consequences*. Cambridge, Ma.: Harvard University Press.

BURN, A. 1960. *The Lyric Age of Greece*. New York: St. Martin's Press.

BURNS, E. 1954. *Western Civilizations*. New York: Norton.

BURY, J. 1958. *History of Greece*, rev. ed. New York: Macmillan.

———. 1960. "Nationalities and Nationalism." In *New Cambridge Modern History*, vol. 10. Cambridge, Eng.: Cambridge University Press.

BUSHNELL, G. 1957. *Peru*. New York: Praeger.

BUTLER, G., and MACCOBY, S. 1928. *The Development of International Law*. London: Longmans, Green.

CADY, J. 1964. *Southeast Asia: Its Historical Development*. New York: McGraw-Hill.

CAGGESE, R. 1949. "Italy, 1313-1414." In *Cambridge Medieval History*, vol. 7. Cambridge, Eng.: Cambridge University Press.

CAHEN, L., and BRAURE, M. 1960. *L'évolution politique de l'Angleterre moderne*. Paris: Michel.

CALHOUN, G. 1926. *The Business Life of Ancient Athens*. Chicago: University of Chicago Press.

CANTOR, N. 1963. *Medieval History: The Life and Death of a Civilization*. New York: Macmillan.

CARDWELL, D. 1963. "The Development of Scientific Research in Modern Universities." In *Scientific Change*. Edited by A. Crombie. New York: Basic Books.

———. 1972. *Turning Points in Western Technology*. New York: Science History.

CARRINGTON, R. 1963. *A Million Years of Man*. Cleveland, Oh.: World.

CARY, M. 1959. *A History of the Greek World from 323 to 146 B.C.* London: Methuen.

CARY, M., and HAARHOFF, T. 1940. *Life and Thought in the Greek and Roman World*. London: Methuen.

CHAMOUX, F. 1963. *La civilisation grecque*. Paris: Arthaud.

CHAYTOR, H. 1933. *A History of Aragon and Catalonia*. London: Methuen.

CHERNIAVSKY, M. 1961. *Tsar and People*. New Haven, Ct.: Yale University Press.

CHEYNEY, E. 1920. *An Introduction to the Industrial and Social History of England*. New York: Macmillan.

———. 1936. *The Dawn of a New Era 1250–1453*. New York: Harper and Row.

CHILDE, V. 1951. *Man Makes Himself*. New York: New American Library.

Christian Science Monitor. 1973. 6 November, p. 1.

———. 1974. 29 October, p. 5a.

CHURCH, W. 1959. *The Greatness of Louis XIV, Myth or Reality?* Boston: Heath.

CLAPHAM, J. 1926. "Commerce and Industry in the Middle Ages." In *Cambridge Medieval History*, vol. 5. Cambridge, Eng.: Cambridge University Press.

CLARK, G. 1940. *The Later Stuarts, 1660–1714*. Oxford: Clarendon Press.

———. 1950. *The Seventeenth Century*. London: Oxford University Press.

———. 1960. *Three Aspects of Tudor England*. London: Oxford University Press.

———. 1962. *World Prehistory*. Cambridge, Eng.: Cambridge University Press.

CLARK, G., and PIGGOTT, S. 1965. *Prehistoric Societies*. New York: Knopf.

CLOCHÉ, P. 1931. *Les classes, les métiers, le trafic*. Paris: Les Belles Lettres.

CLOUGH, S. 1953. *The Rise and Fall of Civilisation*. London: Skeffington.

CLOUGH, S., and COLE, C. 1952. *Economic History of Europe*. Boston: Heath.

COBBAN, A. 1963. "The Decline of Divine-right Monarchy in France." In *New Cambridge Modern History*, vol. 7. Cambridge, Eng.: Cambridge University Press.

CODDING, G. 1961. *The Federal Government of Switzerland*. Boston: Houghton Mifflin.

COLEMAN, D. 1961. "Economic Problems and Policies." In *New Cambridge Modern History*, vol. 5. Cambridge, Eng.: Cambridge University Press.

CONNOLLY, W., ed. 1968. *The Bias of Pluralism*. New York: Atherton Press.

COOK, J. 1962. *The Greeks in Ionia and the East*. London: Thames and

Hudson.
COOK, T. 1936. *History of Political Philosophy from Plato to Burke.* Englewood Cliffs, N.J.: Prentice-Hall.
COTTERILL, H. 1915. *Medieval Italy.* London: Harrap.
COTTRELL, L. 1963. *The Last Pharaohs.* New York: Grosset and Dunlap.
COULBORN, R., ed. 1956. *Feudalism in History.* Princeton, N.J.: Princeton University Press.
COULTON, G. 1930. *The Medieval Scene.* Cambridge, Eng.: Cambridge University Press.
COURTILLIER, G. 1945. *Les anciennes civilizations de l'Inde.* Paris: Colin.
COWELL, F. 1962. *The Revolutions of Ancient Rome.* London: Thames and Hudson.
COWIE, L. 1964. *Eighteenth-century Europe.* New York: Ungar.
CRAIG, G. 1960. "The System of Alliances and the Balance of Power." In *New Cambridge Modern History*, vol. 10. Cambridge, Eng.: Cambridge University Press.
CREEL, H. 1953. *Chinese Political Thought from Confucius to Mao Tse-tung.* New York: Mentor Books.
CROMBIE, A. 1953. *Augustine to Galileo.* Cambridge, Ma.: Harvard University Press.
———, ed. 1963. *Scientific Change.* New York: Basic Books.
CROW, J. 1963. *Spain: The Root and the Flower.* New York: Harper and Row.

DAHL, R. 1971. *Polyarchy: Participation and Opposition.* New Haven, Ct.: Yale University Press.
DAHL, R., and TUFTE, E. 1973. *Size and Democracy.* Stanford, Ca.: Stanford University Press.
DAMPIER, W. 1943. *A History of Science and Its Relations with Philosophy and Religion.* Cambridge, Eng.: Cambridge University Press.
DAS, S. 1925. *The Economic History of Ancient India.* Calcutta: Mitra Press.
DAVIDS, T. 1903. *Buddhist India.* New York: Putnam's.
DAVIES, G. 1959. *The early Stuarts 1603-1660.* Oxford: Clarendon Press.
DAWSON, C. 1958. *Religion and the Rise of Western Culture.* Garden City, N.Y.: Doubleday.
DAY, J. 1942. *An Economic History of Athens under Roman Domination.* New York: Columbia University Press.
DEMANGEON, A. 1920. *Le déclin de l'Europe.* Paris: Payot.
D'IAKONOV, I. 1959. *Obshchestvennyi i gosudarstvennyi stroi drevnego dvurech'ia Shumer.* Moscow: Akad. Nauk.
DICKENS, A. 1964. *The English Reformation.* London: Botsford.
DIEHL, C. 1957. *Byzantium: Greatness and Decline.* New Brunswick, N.J.: Rutgers University Press.
DIETZ, F. 1942. *An Economic History of England.* New York: Holt.
DIKSHITAR, V. 1948. *War in Ancient India.* Madras: Macmillan.

DOZY, R. 1913. *Spanish Islam*. London: Chatto and Windus.
DUBY, G., and MANDROU, R. 1958. *Histoire de la civilisation française XVII–XX siecle*. Paris: Colin.
DUN, J. 1965. *The Ageless Chinese*. New York: Scribner's.
DUNHAM, A. 1915. *The History of Miletus*. London: University of London Press.
DUNNING, W. 1905. *A History of Political Theories*. New York: Macmillan.
DUYVENDAK, J. 1963. *The Book of Lord Shang*. Chicago: University of Chicago Press.

EBENSTEIN, W. 1939. *Fascist Italy*. New York: American Book.
EBERHARD, W. 1952. *Conquerors and Rulers: Social Forces in Medieval China*. Leyden: Brill.
EDELSTEIN, L. 1963. "Motives and Incentives for Science in Antiquity." In *Scientific Change*. Edited by A. Crombie. New York: Basic Books.
EHRENBERG, V. 1960. *The Greek State*. Oxford: Blackwell.
EINSTEIN, L. 1902. *The Italian Renaissance in England*. New York: Columbia University Press.
ELLIOTT, J. 1964. *Imperial Spain, 1469–1716*. New York: St. Martin's press.
EMERSON, R. 1960. *From Empire to Nation*. Cambridge, Ma.: Harvard University Press.
EMERY, R. 1941. *Heresy and Inquisition in Narbonne*. New York: Columbia University Press.
Encyclopedia Britannica, vol. 9. 1974. "French Revolutionary Wars." Chicago.
ENSOR, R. 1960. "Political Institutions in Europe: Issues and Political Thought." In *New Cambridge Modern History*, vol. 12. Cambridge, Eng.: Cambridge University Press.

FAIRLIE, H. 1964. "On the Comforts of Anger." In *The Suicide of a Nation?* Edited by A. Koestler. New York: Macmillan.
FAIRSERVIS, W. 1962. *The Ancient Kingdoms of the Nile*. New York: Crowell.
FAN, W. 1958. *Drevniaia istoriia Kitaia*. Moscow: Akad. Nauk.
FARRINGTON, B. 1953. *Greek Science*. Baltimore, Md.: Penguin.
FAY, B. 1966. *The Revolutionary Spirit in France and America*. New York: Cooper Square.
FERGUSON, W. 1911. *Hellenistic Athens*. New York: Macmillan.
FEUER, L. 1963. *The Scientific Intellectual: The Psychological and Sociological Origins of Modern Science*. New York: Basic Books.
FIELD, J. 1972. "Transnationalism and the New Tribe." In *Transnational Relations and World Politics*. Edited by J. Nye and R. Keohane. Cambridge, Ma.: Harvard University Press.
FIGGIS, J. 1934. *The Divine Right of Kings*. Cambridge, Eng.: Cambridge University Press.
———. 1967. *From Gerson to Grotius*. Cambridge, Eng.: Cambridge University Press.

FINLEY, M. 1970. In *Ancient Civilizations 4,000 B.C. to 400 A.D.* Edited by N. Cantor and M. Werthman. New York: Crowell.

FISCHER, E. 1948. *The Passing of the European Age.* Cambridge, Ma.: Harvard University Press.

FISHER, F., ed. 1961. *Essays in the Economic and Social History of Tudor and Stuart England.* Cambridge, Eng.: Cambridge University Press.

FITZGERALD, C. 1950. *China, a Short Cultural History.* London: Cresset Press.

FLACELIÈRE, R. 1959. *La vie quotidienne en Grèce au siècle de Périclès.* Paris: Hachette.

FORD, F. 1976. "Assassination in the Eighteenth Century." *Harvard Magazine* 58 (February).

FORSTER, R., and GREENE, J., eds. 1970. *Preconditions of Revolt in Early Modern Europe.* Baltimore, Md.: Johns Hopkins University Press.

FOSTER, G. 1962. *Traditional Cultures and the Impact of Technological Change.* New York: Harper and Row.

FREEMAN, K. 1950. *Greek City States.* New York: Norton.

FRYE, R. 1962. *The Heritage of Persia.* London: Weidenfeld and Nicolson.

FUNG, Y. 1952. *A History of Chinese Philosophy.* Translated by D. Bodde. Princeton, N.J.: Princeton University Press.

FURET, F., and RICHET, D. 1970. *The French Revolution.* New York: Macmillan.

GADD, C. 1962. "The Cities of Babylonia." Fascicle of *Cambridge Ancient History,* vol. 1, chap. 13. Cambridge, Eng.: Cambridge University Press.

GASSTER, M. 1972. *China's Struggle to Modernize.* New York: Knopf.

GAY, P., and WEBB, R. 1973. *Modern Europe.* New York: Harper and Row.

GEBHARDT, B. 1955. *Handbuch der deutschen Geschichte,* Band 2. Stuttgart: Union.

GEORGE, D. 1953. *England in Transition.* Hammondsworth: Penguin.

GERSHOY, L. 1944. *L'Europe des princes éclairés 1763-1789.* Paris: Fayard.

GEYL, P. 1961; 1964. *The Netherlands in the Seventeenth Century,* 2 vols. New York: Barnes and Noble.

GIDDENS, A., ed. 1972. *Emile Durkheim: Selected Writings.* Cambridge, Eng.: Cambridge University Press.

GILLISPIE, C. 1960. *The Edge of Objectivity.* Princeton, N.J.: Princeton University Press.

———. 1965. "Science and Technology." In *New Cambridge Modern History,* vol. 9. Cambridge, Eng.: Cambridge University Press.

GIMPEL, J. 1976. *The Medieval Machine: The Industrial Revolution of the Middle Ages.* New York: Holt, Rinehart, and Winston.

GLOTZ, G. 1926. *Ancient Greece at Work.* New York: Knopf.

———. 1929. *The Greek City and Its Institutions.* London: Kegan Paul, Trench Trubner.

GLOVER, T. 1926. *From Pericles to Philip.* London: Methuen.

GODECHOT, J. 1969. "The Internal History of France during the Wars, 1793-1814." In *New Cambridge Modern History*, vol. 9 Cambridge, Eng.: Cambridge University Press.

GOLDMAN, M. 1975. *Détente and Dollars.* New York: Basic Books.

GOMME, A. 1962. *More Essays in Greek History and Literature.* Oxford: Blackwell.

GOOCH, G. 1956. *Louis XV, the Monarchy in Decline.* London: Longmans, Green.

―――. 1959. *English Democratic Ideas in the Seventeenth Century.* New York: Harper and Row.

GOODFIELD, J. 1964. "The Tunnel of Eupalinus." *Scientific American* 210, no. 6 (June).

GOODRICH, L. 1951. *A Short History of the Chinese People.* New York: Harper and Row.

GORDON, M. 1974. "Domestic Conflict and the Origins of the First World War." *Journal of Modern History* 46 (June).

GRANET, M. 1952. *La féodalité chinoise.* Oslo: Aschehoug.

GRANT, F., ed. 1963. *Hellenistic Religions.* New York: Bobbs-Merrill.

GRAY, P. 1966. *The Enlightenment,* vol. 1. New York: Knopf.

GREEN, V. 1964. *Renaissance and Reformation.* London: Arnold.

GRIMM, H. 1954. *The Reformation Era.* New York: Macmillan.

GRUNWALD, C. de. 1956. *Peter the Great.* New York: Macmillan.

GUPTA, S. das. 1937. "Philosophy." In *The Legacy of India.* Edited by G. Garratt. Oxford: Clarendon Press.

HABAKKUK, H. 1968. "Population, Commerce, and Economic Ideas." In *New Cambridge Modern History,* vol. 8. Cambridge, Eng.: Cambridge University Press.

HADAS, M. 1959. *Hellenistic Culture.* New York: Columbia University Press.

HALE, J. 1960. "War and Public Opinion in Renaissance Italy." In *Italian Renaissance Studies.* Edited by E. Jacob. New York: Barnes and Noble.

HALE, O. 1971. *The Great Illusion, 1910-1914.* New York: Harper and Row.

HALE, W. 1920. *Ancient Greece.* New York: American Heritage Press.

HALL, A. 1954. *The Scientific Revolution 1500-1800.* London: Longmans, Green.

―――. 1958. "Science." In *New Cambridge Modern History,* vol. 2. Cambridge, Eng.: Cambridge University Press.

―――. 1964. "The Scientific Movement and Its Influence on Thought and Material Development." In *New Cambridge Modern History,* vol. 10. Cambridge, Eng.: University Press.

HALL, D. 1964. *A History of Southeast Asia.* New York: Macmillan.

HALLETT, R. 1970. *Africa to 1875.* Ann Arbor, Mi.: University of Michigan Press.

HAMBLIN, D. 1975. *The Etruscans.* New York: Time-Life Books.

HARDEN, D. 1962. *The Phoenicians*. New York: Praeger.
HASEBROEK, J. 1965. *Trade and Politics in Ancient Greece*. New York: Biblos and Tanner.
HASELER, S. 1976. *The Death of British Democracy*. Buffalo, N.Y.: Prometheus Books.
HASKINS, C. 1927. *The Renaissance of the Twelfth Century*. Cambridge, Ma.: Harvard University Press.
———. 1929. *Studies in Medieval Culture*. Oxford: Clarendon Press.
HASSALL, A. 1902. *Louis XIV and the Zenith of the French Monarchy*. New York: Putnam's.
HAWGOOD, J. 1960. "Liberalism and Constitutional Developments." In *New Cambridge Modern History*, vol. 10. Cambridge, Eng.: Cambridge University Press.
HAWKES, J. 1973. *The First Great Civilizations*. New York: Knopf.
HAWKES, J., and WOOLEY, L. 1961. *Prehistory and the Beginnings of Civilization*. New York: Harper and Row.
HAY, D. 1957. "Introduction." In *New Cambridge Modern History*, vol. 1. Cambridge, Eng.: Cambridge University Press.
———. 1961. *The Italian Renaissance in Its Historical Background*. Cambridge, Eng.: Cambridge University Press.
———. 1958 "Literature: The Printed Book." In *New Cambridge Modern History*, vol. 2. Cambridge, Eng.: Cambridge University Press.
HAYES, C. 1922. "Medieval Diplomacy." In *The History and Nature of International Relations*. Edited by E. Walsh. Freeport, N.Y.: Books for Libraries Press.
HAYES, W. 1953. *The Scepter of Egypt*. Cambridge, Ma.: Harvard University Press.
HAYWOOD, R. 1964. *Ancient Greece and the Near East*. New York: McKay.
HECKSCHER, E. 1955. *Mercantilism*, vol. 2. London: Allen and Unwin.
HEEGER, G. 1974. *The Politics of Underdevelopment*. New York: St. Martin's Press.
HEIDENREICH, C. 1967. *Personality and Social Adjustment: Some Dimensions of Personal Development*. Dubuque, Ia.: Brown.
HENDERSON, W. 1969. *The Industrialization of Europe 1780–1914*. New York: Harcourt Brace Jovanovich.
HERM, G. 1975. *The Phoenicians: The Purple Empire of the Ancient World*. London: Gollancz.
HERTZ, F. 1962. *The Development of the German Public Mind*. New York: Macmillan.
HERZ, J. 1959. *International Politics in the Atomic Age*. New York: Columbia University Press.
HEYDTE, F., von der. 1952. *Die Geburtsstunde des souveränen Staates*. Regensburg: Habbel.
HIBBERT, C., ed. 1974. *The Pen and the Sword*. New York: Weidenfeld and Nicolson.

HICKS, J. 1974. *The Empire Builders.* New York: Time-Life Books.
HILL, C. 1961. "Protestantism and the Rise of Capitalism." In *Essays in the Economic and Social History of Tudor and Stuart England.* Edited by E. Fisher. Cambridge, Eng.: Cambridge University Press.
———. 1965. *Intellectual Origins of the English Revolution.* Oxford: Clarendon Press.
HILL, D. 1911. *A History of Diplomacy in the International Development of Europe.* London: Longmans, Green.
HINSLEY, F. 1963. *Power and the Pursuit of Peace.* Cambridge, Eng.: Cambridge University Press.
HIRTH, F. 1911. *The Ancient History of China.* New York: Columbia University Press.
HITTI, P. 1953. *History of the Arabs.* New York: St. Martin's Press.
———. 1957. *Lebanon in History.* New York: Macmillan.
———. 1967. *The Arabs from the Earliest Times to the Present.* New York: St. Martin's Press.
HODGES, H. 1970. *Technology in the Ancient World.* New York: Knopf.
HOHENBERG, J. 1971. *Free Press/Free People.* New York: Columbia University Press.
HOLE, F. 1966. "Investigating the Origins of Mesopotamian Civilization." *Science* 153 (5 August).
HOLSTI, K. 1967. *International Politics.* Englewood Cliffs, N.J.: Prentice-Hall.
HOROWITZ, I. 1964. *Revolution in Brazil.* New York: Dutton.
HSU, C. 1965. *Ancient China in Transition.* Stanford, Ca.: Stanford University Press.
HUIZINGA, J. 1959. *Men and Ideas.* New York: Meridian Books.
HUME, M. 1931. *Spain, Its Greatness and Decay.* Cambridge, Eng.: Cambridge University Press.
HUNTINGTON, E. 1945. *Mainsprings of Civilization.* New York: Wiley.
HUXLEY, A. 1969. *Brave New World.* New York: Harper and Row.

JACOB, E., ed. 1960. *Italian Renaissance Studies.* New York: Barnes and Noble.
JAMES, W. 1911. *A Moral Equivalent of War, Memories and Studies.* London: Longmans, Green.
JELAVICH, B. 1964. *A Century of Russian Foreign Policy 1814-1914.* Philadelphia: Lippincott.
JESSUP, P., and DEÁK, F. 1935. *Neutrality, Its History, Economics, and Law,* vol. 1. New York: Columbia University Press.
JONES, A. 1957. *Athenian Democracy.* Oxford: Blackwell.
JONES, J. 1956. *The Law and Legal Theory of the Greeks.* Oxford: Clarendon Press.
JONES, P. 1960. "The End of Malatesta Rule in Rimini." In *Italian Renaissance Studies.* Edited by E. Jacobs. New York: Barnes and Noble.

KAGAN, D., ed. 1965. *Sources in Greek Political Thought.* New York: The Free Press.
KAUFMAN, R. 1970. *The Technology Gap.* New York: Praeger.
KAUTSKY, J., ed. 1964. *Political Change in Underdeveloped Countries.* New York: Wiley.
KAVOLIS, V. 1972. *History on Art's Side: Social Dynamics in Artistic Efflorescence.* Ithaca, N.Y.: Cornell University Press.
KENNAN, G. 1961. *Russia and the West under Lenin and Stalin.* Boston: Little, Brown.
KEOHANE, R., and NYE, J., eds. 1972. *Transnational Relations and World Politics.* Cambridge, Ma.: Harvard University Press.
KIENER, F. 1900. *Verfassungsgeschichte der Provence.* Leipzig: Dyksche.
KING, W. 1914. *Chronicles of Three Free Cities: Hamburg, Bremen, and Lübeck.* London: Dent.
KITAGAWA, J. 1966. *Religion in Japanese History.* New York: Columbia University Press.
KITTO, H. 1951. *The Greeks.* Hammondsworth, Eng.: Penguin.
KLEMM, F. 1959. *A History of Western Technology.* New York: Scribner's.
KLING, M. 1964. "Toward a Theory of Power and Political Instability in Latin America." In *Political Change in Underdeveloped Countries.* Edited by J. Kautsky. New York: Wiley.
KLIUCHEVSKY, V. 1913. *A History of Russia,* vol. 3. Translated by C. Hogarth. London: Dent.
KNORR, K. 1973. *Power and Wealth.* New York: Basic Books.
―――. 1975. *The Power of Nations; The Political Economy of International Relations.* New York: Basic Books.
KOESTLER, A., ed. 1964. *Suicide of a Nation?* New York: Macmillan.
KOHN, H. 1955. *Nationalism, Its Meaning and History.* Princeton, N.J.: Princeton University Press.
KOHR, L. 1957. *The Breakdown of Nations.* London: Routledge and Kegan Paul.
KRAEMER, J. 1965. "Tradition and Reform at Al-Azhar University." In *The Contemporary Middle East.* Edited by B. Rivlin and J. Szyliowicz. New York: Random House.
KRAMER, S. 1952. *Enmerkar and the Lord of Aratta.* Philadelphia: University Museum, University of Pennsylvania.
―――. 1956. *From the Tablets of Sumeria.* Indiana Hills, Co.: Falcon's Wing Press.
―――. 1960. "Rivalry and Superiority: Two Dominant Features of the Sumerian Culture Pattern." In *Men and Cultures: Selected Papers of the Fifth International Congress of Anthropological and Ethnological Sciences.* Edited by A. Wallace. Philadelphia: University of Pennsylvania Press.
―――. 1963. *The Sumerians.* Chicago: University of Chicago Press.
―――. 1969. *The Sacred Marriage Rite.* Bloomington, In.: Indiana University Press.
KROFTA, K. 1936. "Bohemia in the Fifteenth Century." In *Cambridge Medi-*

eval History, vol. 8. Cambridge, Eng.: Cambridge University Press.
KROPOTKIN, P. 1903. *Mutual Aid.* New York: McClure, Phillips.

LABAT, R. 1957. "La Mésopotamie." In *Histoire Générale des Sciences.* Edited by R. Taton. Paris: Presses Universitaires de France.
LAFFAN, R. 1957. "The Empire under Maximilian I." In *New Cambridge Modern History*, vol. 1. Cambridge, Eng.: Cambridge University Press.
LANDHEER, B., ed. 1944. *The Netherlands.* Berkeley, Ca.: University of California Press.
LANNING, E. 1967. *Peru before the Incas.* Englewood Cliffs, N.J.: Prentice-Hall.
LARSEN, J. 1955. *Representative Government in Greek and Roman History.* Berkeley, Ca.: University of California Press.
LASKI, H. 1936. "Political Theory in the Later Middle Ages." In *Cambridge Medieval History*, vol. 8. Cambridge, Eng.: Cambridge University Press.
LATOURETTE, K. 1934. *The Chinese, Their History and Culture.* New York: Macmillan.
LATTIMORE, O. 1962. *Inner Asian Frontiers of China.* Boston: Beacon Press.
LAURING, P. 1960. *A History of the Kingdom of Denmark.* Copenhagen: Host.
LEDERER, I., ed. 1962. *Russian Foreign Policy.* New Haven, Ct.: Yale University Press.
LEVI-PROVENCAL, E. 1953. *Histoire de l'Espagne musulmane.* Paris: Maisonneuve.
LEWIN, L. 1962. *Report from Iron Mountain on the Possibility and Desirability of Peace.* New York: Dial Press.
LEWIS, B. 1954. *The Arabs in History.* London: Hutchinson House.
LEWIS, G. 1963. *Puerto Rico.* New York: Monthly Review Press.
LEWIS, O. 1966. "The Culture of Poverty." *Scientific American* 215 (October).
LIANG, C. 1930. *History of Chinese Political Thought.* London: Kegan Paul.
LICHTHEIM, G. 1969. *The Origins of Socialism.* New York: Praeger.
LIDDELL-HART, B. 1964. "Armed Forces and the Art of War: Armies." In *New Cambridge Modern History*, vol. 10. Cambridge, Eng.: Cambridge University Press.
LIJPHART, A. 1968. *The Politics of Accommodation: Pluralism and Democracy in the Netherlands.* Berkeley, Ca.: University of California Press.
LILLEY, S., ed. 1953. *The Social History of Science.* Copenhagen: Munksgaard.
LIMOUZIN-LAMOTHE, R. 1932. *La Commune de Toulouse.* Paris: Didier.
LINDSAY, J. 1963. "The Western Mediterranean and Italy." In *New Cambridge Modern History*, vol. 7. Cambridge, Eng.: Cambridge University Press.
LITTMAN, R. 1974. *The Greek Experiment: Imperialism and Social Conflict, 800–400 B.C.* New York: Harcourt Brace Jovanovich.
LOCKWOOD, W. 1954. *The Economic Development of Japan.* Princeton, N.J.: Princeton University Press.

LODGE, E. 1943. "The Commune Movement, Especially in France." In *Cambridge Medieval History*, vol. 5. Cambridge, Eng.: Cambridge University Press.

LOUGH, J. 1954. *An Introduction to Seventeenth-century France.* London: Longmans, Green.

LOWI, T. 1969. *The End of Liberalism: Ideology, Policy, and the Crisis of Public Authority.* New York: Norton.

LUCAS-DUBRETON, J. 1961. *Daily Life in Florence in the Time of the Medici.* New York: Macmillan.

MacARTHUR, D. 1927. *Infantry Journal*, March.

McCRONE, D., and CNUDDE, C. 1967. "Toward a Communication Theory of Democratic Political Development: A Causal Model." *American Political Science Review* 61, no. 1 (March).

McFARLAND, A. 1969. *Power and Leadership in Pluralist Systems.* Stanford, Ca.: Stanford University Press.

McLEAN, A. 1972. *Humanism and the Rise of Science in Tudor England.* New York: Watson.

MADELIN, L. 1948. *La nation sous l'Empereur.* Paris: Librairie Hachette.

MAHAJAN, V. 1970. *Ancient India.* Delhi: Chand.

MAINE, H. 1905. *Ancient Law.* London: Murray.

MAIR, A. 1908. *Hesiod, the Poems and Fragments.* Oxford: Clarendon Press.

MALLOWAN, M. 1961. "The Birth of Written History." In *The Dawn of Civilization.* Edited by S. Piggott. New York: McGraw-Hill.

MANNERS, J. 1967. *Lectures on European History 1815-1914.* New York: Barnes and Noble.

MARINA, W. 1925. *Egalitarianism and Empire.* Menlo Park, Ca.: Institute for Humane Studies.

MARKHAM, F. 1965. "The Napoleonic Adventure." In *New Cambridge Modern History*, vol. 9. Cambridge, Eng.: Cambridge University Press.

MARTIN, A. von. 1966. "Machiavelli and the End of a Bourgeois Culture." In *Political Theory and Ideology.* Edited by J. Shklar. New York: Macmillan.

MARTIN, P. 1949. "The Swiss Confederation in the Middle Ages." In *Cambridge Medieval History*, vol. 7. Cambridge, Eng.: Cambridge University Press.

MARTIN, V. 1940. *La vie internationale dans la Grèce de cités.* Paris: Librairie Recueil Sirey.

MARTIN, W. 1900. "Traces of International Law in Ancient China." *International Review* 14, no. 1883.

MARX, K., and ENGELS, F. 1848; 1959. "Manifesto of the Communist Party." In *Basic Writings on Politics and Philosophy.* Edited by L. Feuer. Garden City, N.Y.: Doubleday-Anchor.

MASANI, R. 1937. "Caste and the Structure of Society." In *The Legacy of India.* Edited by G. Garratt. Oxford: Clarendon Press.

MASON, S. 1962. *A History of the Sciences.* New York: Collier Books.

MATHIEZ, A. 1962. *The French Revolution.* Translated by C. Phillips. New York: Russell and Russell.

MATTINGLY, G. 1955. *Renaissance Diplomacy.* London: Cape.

MAYER, J. 1939. *Political Thought, the European Tradition.* London: Dent.

MEADOWS, D. 1974. *Dynamics of Growth in a Finite World.* New York: Wiley.

MEEÜSS, A. de. 1962. *History of the Belgians.* Translated by G. Gordon. New York: Praeger.

MEHDEN, F. von der. 1969. *Politics of the Developing Nations,* 2nd ed. Englewood Cliffs, N.J.: Prentice-Hall.

MELKO, M. 1973. *52 Peaceful Societies.* Ontario: CPRI Press.

MERRELL, D. 1962. *Evolution and Genetics.* New York: Holt, Rinehart, and Winston.

MERRIMAN, R. 1925; 1934; 1936. *The Rise of the Spanish Empire,* vols. 1, 2, 3, and 4. New York: Macmillan.

———. 1963. *Six Contemporaneous Revolutions.* Hamden, Ct.: Archon Books.

MODELSKI, G. 1964. "Kautilya: Foreign Policy and International System in the Ancient Hindu World." *American Political Science Review* 58 (September).

MOLLAT, M., and WOLFF, P. 1973. *The Popular Revolutions of the Late Middle Ages.* London: Allen and Unwin.

MOOKERJI, R. 1952. *Chandragupta Maurya and His Times.* Delhi: Rajkamal.

MOORE, S. 1958. *Power and Property in Inca Peru.* New York: Columbia University Press.

MORGENTHAU, H. 1960. *Politics among Nations.* New York: Knopf.

MOSCATI, S. 1960. *The Face of the Ancient Orient.* London: Routledge and Kegan Paul.

———. 1968. *The World of the Phoenicians.* New York: Praeger.

MOSLEY, J. 1974. "Gutenberg's 'Right Worthy Art'." In *Expanding Horizons.* Edited by N. Williams. New York: Newsweek Books (Weidenfeld and Nicolson).

MOSS, R. 1977. "Anglocommunism." *Commentary* 63 (February).

MOSSÉ, C. 1962. *Le fin de la démocratie athénienne.* Paris: Presses universitaires de France.

MUNDY, J. 1954. *Liberty and Political Power in Toulouse.* New York: Columbia University Press.

MUNDY, J., and RIESENBERG, P. 1958. *The Medieval Town.* New York: Van Nostrand.

MURPHY, E. 1972. *History of African Civilization.* New York: Crowell.

MURRAY, M. 1963. *The Splendor That Was Egypt.* New York: Hawthorn Books.

NEEDHAM, J. 1953. "Science and Technology in China." In *The Social History of Science.* Edited by S. Lilley. Copenhagen: Munksgaard.

———. 1960. *Science and Civilization in China.* Cambridge, Eng.: Cambridge University Press.
NEF, J. 1950. *War and Human Progress.* London: Routledge and Kegan Paul.
NEHRU, J. 1946. *The Discovery of India.* New York: Day.
New York Times. 1974. 12 November, p. 4.
———. 1977. 3 February, p. 33.
NICOLSON, H. 1962. *Monarchy.* London: Weidenfeld and Nicolson.
NUSSBAUM, A. 1947. *A Concise History of the Law of Nations.* New York: Macmillan.
NUSSBAUM, F. 1953. *The Triumph of Science and Reason 1660–1685.* New York: Harper and Row.

OECHSLI, W. 1922. *History of Switzerland, 1499–1914.* Cambridge, Eng.: Cambridge University Press.
OGG, D. 1925. *Europe in the Seventeenth Century.* London: Black.
OLDENBOURG, Z. 1959. *Massacre at Montsegur.* London: Weidenfeld and Nicolson.

PALMER, M. 1973. *The Dilemma of Political Development: An Introduction to the Politics of Developing Areas.* Itasca, Il.: Peacock.
PALMER, R. 1965. "Social and Psychological Foundations of the Revolutionary Era." In *New Cambridge Modern History,* vol. 8. Cambridge, Eng.: Cambridge University Press.
PARROT, A. 1961. *Sumer, the Dawn of Art.* New York: Golden Press.
PERELOMOV, L. 1962. *Imperiia Tsin.* Moscow: Akad. Nauk.
PERKINS, J. 1897. *France under Louis XV,* vol. 2. Boston: Houghton Mifflin.
PHILLIPSON, C. 1911. *The International Law and Custom of Ancient Greece and Rome.* New York: Macmillan.
PICKARD-CAMBRIDGE, A. 1914. *Demosthenes and the Last Days of Greek Freedom.* New York: Putnam's.
PINSON, K. 1954. *Modern Germany.* New York: Macmillan.
PIRENNE, H. 1900. *Le soulèvement de la Flandre Maritime.* Brussels: Kiessling.
PIRENNE, J. 1961. *Histoire de la civilisation de l'Egypte ancienne,* vol. 1. Paris: Michel.
PLUMB, J. 1957. *The First Four Georges.* New York: Macmillan.
PONTIERI, E. 1957. *Nei tempi grigi della storia d'Italia.* Naples: Morano.
PORFIDIROV, N. 1947. *Drevnii Novgorod.* Moscow-Leningrad:
PRESTWICH, M. 1957. In *France, Government and Society.* Edited by J. Wallace-Hadrill and J. McManners. London: Methuen.
PREVITÉ-ORTON, C. 1926. "The Italian Cities Till c. 1200." In *Cambridge Medieval History,* vol. 5. Cambridge, Eng.: Cambridge University Press.
PRICE, D. de SOLLA. 1959. "An Ancient Greek Computer." *Scientific American* 200 (June).

PUSHKAREV, S. 1963. *The Emergence of Modern Russia, 1801-1917.* New York: Holt, Rinehart, and Winston.

PUTNAM, P., ed. 1952. *Seven Britons in Imperial Russia.* Princeton, N.J.: Princeton University Press.

QUIGLEY, C. 1966. *Tragedy and Hope: A History of the World in Our Time.* New York: Macmillan.

RADHAKRISHNAN, S. 1958. *Indian Philosophy,* vol. 1. New York: Macmillan.

RADHAKRISHNAN, S., and MOORE, C., eds. 1957. *A Source Book in Indian Philosophy.* Princeton, N.J.: Princeton University Press.

RANDALL, J. 1954. *The Making of the Modern Mind.* Boston: Houghton Mifflin.

RASHDALL, H. 1926. "The Medieval Universities." In *Cambridge Medieval History,* vol. 6. Cambridge, Eng.: Cambridge University Press.

RAWLINSON, G. 1889. *History of Phoenicia.* London: Longmans, Green.

REGLA, J. 1961. "Spain and Her Empire." In *New Cambridge Modern History,* vol. 5. Cambridge, Eng.: Cambridge University Press.

REID, W. 1954. *Economic History of Great Britain.* New York: Ronald Press.

REISCHAUER, E. 1961. *Japan Past and Present.* New York: Knopf.

REISCHAUER, E., and FAIRBANK, J. 1960. *East Asia, the Great Tradition.* Boston: Houghton Mifflin.

RENARD, G., and WEULERSEE, G. 1926. *Life and Work in Modern Europe, Fifteenth to Eighteenth Centuries.* New York: Knopf.

RIEMENS, H. 1944. "The Growth of Netherlands Economy." In *The Netherlands.* Edited by B. Landheer. Berkeley, Ca.: University of California Press.

RITTER, G. 1964. "Origins of the Modern State." In *The Development of the Modern State.* Edited by H. Lubasz. New York: Macmillan.

ROACH, J. 1969. "Education and Public Opinion." In *New Cambridge Modern History,* vol. 9. Cambridge, Eng.: Cambridge University Press.

ROBERTS, J. 1968. "The Italian States." In *New Cambridge Modern History,* vol. 8. Cambridge, Eng.: Cambridge University Press.

ROBERTSON, C. 1939. *England under the Hanoverians.* London: Methuen.

ROBINSON, C. 1950. *Athens in the Age of Pericles.* Norman, Ok.: University of Oklahoma Press.

ROBSON, E. 1957. "The Armed Forces and the Art of War." In *New Cambridge Modern History,* vol. 7. Cambridge, Eng.: Cambridge University Press.

ROGERS, E. 1962. *Diffusion of Innovations.* New York: The Free Press.

ROSENAU, J., ed. 1969. *Linkage Politics.* New York: The Free Press.

ROSSI, M. 1963. *The Third World: The Unaligned Countries and the World Revolution.* New York: Funk and Wagnalls.

ROSTOVTZEFF, M. 1941. *The Social and Economic History of the Hellenistic World,* 3 vols. Oxford: Clarendon Press.

ROUSTAN, M. 1926. *Pioneers of the French Revolution.* London: E. Benn.

RUSSELL, F. 1936. *Theories of International Relations.* New York: Appleton.
RUSSELL, W. 1969. *Man, Nature, and History.* New York: Natural History Press.

SABINE, G. 1961. *A History of Political Theory.* New York: Holt.
SAGGS, H. 1962. *The Greatness That Was Babylon.* New York: Hawthorn Books.
SAKHAROV, A. 1975. *My Country and the World.* New York: Knopf.
SALIN, E. 1944. *Geschichte der Volkswirtschaftslehre.* Bern: Franche.
SANDERS, W., and PRICE, B. 1968. *Mesoamerica: The Evolution of a Civilization.* New York: Random House.
SANSOM, G. 1961. *A History of Japan, 1334-1615,* vol. 2. Stanford, Ca.: Stanford University Press.
SANTILLANA, G. de. 1949. "Greek Astronomy." *Scientific American* 180 (April).
SARBIN, T. 1970. "The Culture of Poverty, Social Identity, and Cognitive Outcomes." In *Psychological Factors in Poverty.* Edited by H. Allen. Chicago: Markham.
SARKAR, B. 1918. "Democratic Ideals and Republican Institutions in India." *American Political Science Review* 12, no. 4 (November).
SCHAPERA, I. 1956. *Government and Politics in Tribal Societies.* London: Watts.
SCHELLING, T. 1966. *Arms and Influence.* New Haven, Ct.: Yale University Press.
SCHEVILL, F. 1936. *History of Florence.* New York: Harcourt Brace Jovanovich.
Science. 1977. 195 (11 March): 939.
———. 1976. 192 (26 April): 248.
SEAL, B. 1958. *The Positive Sciences of the Ancient Hindus.* Delhi: Moti Lal Banarsi Dass.
SEIGNOBOS, C. 1932. *The Evolution of the French People.* New York: Knopf.
SERVICE, E. 1975. *Origins of the State and Civilization.* New York: Norton.
SHAFER, E. 1954. *The Empire of Min.* Rutland, Vt.: Tuttle.
SHANKS, M. 1964. "The Comforts of Stagnation." In *Suicide of a Nation?* Edited by A. Koestler. New York: Macmillan.
SHKLAR, J., ed. 1966. *Political Theory and Ideology.* New York: Macmillan.
SHULL, A. 1951. *Evolution.* New York: McGraw-Hill.
SIMONDS, F., and EMENY, G. 1937. *The Great Powers in World Politics.* New York: American Book.
SINGER, C. 1959. *A Short History of Scientific Ideas.* Oxford: Clarendon Press.
SISMONDI, J. 1860; 1906. *History of the Italian Republics.* Revised by W. Boulting. London: Routledge.
SKJELSBAEK, K. 1972. "The Growth of International Nongovernmental Organization in the Twentieth Century." In *Transnational Relations and World*

Politics. Edited by R. Keohane and J. Nye. Cambridge, Ma.: Harvard University Press.
SMITH, Adam. 1937. *The Wealth of Nations*. New York: Modern Library.
SMITH, Arthur. 1907. *Chinese Characteristics*. New York: Young People's Missionary Movement.
SMITH, G. 1966. *A History of England*. New York: Scribner's.
SMITH, H. 1926. *The Russians*. New York: Quadrangle.
SNELL, B. 1953. *The Discovery of the Mind*. Cambridge, Ma.: Harvard University Press.
SOROKIN, P. 1942. *The Crisis of Our Age: The Social and Cultural Outlook*. New York: Dutton.
———. 1957a. *Cultural Dynamics*. Boston: Porter Sargent.
———. 1957b. *Social and Cultural Dynamics*. Boston: Extending Horizons.
SOROKIN, P., and MERTON, R. 1935. "The Course of Arabian Intellectual Development, 700-1300 A.D., A Study in Method." *Isis* 22, no. 64 (February).
SPAULDING, O. 1937. *Pen and Sword in Greece and Rome*. Princeton, N.J.: Princeton University Press.
SPROUT, H., and SPROUT, M. 1971. *Toward a Politics of the Planet Earth*. New York: Van Nostrand.
SPULER, B. 1943. *Die goldene Horde*. Leipzig: Harrasowitz.
———. 1960. *The Muslim World*. Leyden: Brill.
STAËL-HOLSTEIN, B. de. 1958. *De l'Allemagne*. Paris: Hachette.
STARR, C. 1961. *The Origins of Greek Civilization 1100-650 B.C.* New York: Knopf.
STEINHAUSEN, G. 1933. *Geschichte der deutschen Kultur*. Leipzig: Bibliografisches Institut.
STOESSINGER, J. 1974. *Why Nations Go to War*. New York: St. Martin's Press.
STOMBERG, A. 1931. *A History of Sweden*. New York: Macmillan.
STONE, L. 1970. "The English Revolution." In *Preconditions of Revolt in Early Modern Europe*. Edited by R. Forster and J. Greene. Baltimore, Md.: Johns Hopkins University Press.
STONEQUIST, E. 1937. *The Marginal Man: A Study in Personality and Cultural Conflict*. New York: Russell and Russell.
STRATTON, G. 1929. *Social Psychology of International Conduct*. New York: Appleton.
SYKES, P. 1951. *A History of Persia*, vol. 1. New York: Macmillan.
SYMONDS, J. 1894. *Short History of the Renaissance in Italy*. New York: Holt.
———. 1888. *Renaissance in Italy, The Age of the Despots*. New York: Holt.

TAKEKOSHI, Y. 1930. *The Economic Aspects of the History of Japan*, vol. 1. London: Allen and Unwin.
TANNER, O. 1976. *Stress*. New York: Time-Life Books.
TARN, W. 1936. *Hellenistic Civilization*. London: Arnold.

TATON, R., ed. 1963-64. *History of Science.* New York: Basic Books.
TAYLOR, H. 1938. *The Medieval Mind,* vol. 2. New York: Macmillan.
THACKRAY, A. 1976. "Historiographic Assumptions." *Science* 192 (26 April).
THOMAS, E. 1927. *Chinese Political Thought.* New York: Prentice-Hall.
THOMPSON, J. 1932. *The Middle Ages, 300-1500,* vol. 2. New York: Knopf.
THORLBY, A. 1962. "Literature." In *New Cambridge Modern History,* vol. 11. Cambridge, Eng.: Cambridge University Press.
TILLY, C. 1975. *The Formation of National States in Western Europe.* Princeton, N.J.: Princeton University Press.
TOCQUEVILLE, A. de. 1876. *The Old Regime and the Revolution.* New York: Harper and Row.
TOMPKINS, S. 1940. *Russia through the Ages.* New York: Prentice-Hall.
TOYNBEE, A. 1934. *A Study of History,* vol. 3. London: Oxford University Press.
TRAILL, H., and MANN, J., eds. 1895. *Social England,* vol. 4. London: Cassell.
TREADGOLD, D. 1973. *The West in Russia and China.* Cambridge, Eng.: Cambridge University Press.
TREVELYAN, G. 1930. *England under the Stuarts.* New York: Putnam's.
TRUETA, J. 1946. *The Spirit of Catalonia.* London: Oxford University Press.
TULARD, J. 1974. "Retreat from Russia." In *Age of Optimism.* Edited by A. Palmer. New York: Newsweek Books.
TULLOCK, G. 1965. *The Politics of Bureaucracy.* Washington, D.C.: Public Affairs Press.

ULAM, A. 1974. *Expansion and Coexistence: Soviet Foreign Policy 1917-1973.* New York: Praeger.

VALENTINE, J., and MOORER, E. 1974. "Plate Tectonics and the History of Life in the Ocean." *Scientific American* 230, no. 4 (April).
VILLARI, P. 1888. *Life and Times of Savonarola.* Translated by L. Villari. London: Unwin.
———. 1901. *The First Two Centuries of Florentine History.* Translated by L. Villari. New York: Scribner's.
VITAL, D. 1967. *The Inequality of States.* Oxford: Clarendon Press.
VLEKKE, B. 1945. *Evolution of the Dutch Nation.* New York: Roy.
VYVYAN, J. 1968. "The Approach of the War of 1914." In *New Cambridge Modern History,* vol. 12. Cambridge, Eng.: Cambridge University Press.

WALKER, R. 1953. *The Multi-state System of Ancient China.* Hamden, Ct.: Shoe String Press.
WALKER, T. 1899. *A History of the Law of Nations.* Cambridge, Eng.: Cambridge University Press.
WALLACE, W. 1924. *The Passing of Politics.* New York: Macmillan.
WALLACE-HADRILL, J., and McMANNERS, J., eds. 1957. *France: Government and Society.* London: Methuen.

Wall Street Journal. 1976. 26 August, p. 10.
WALSH, J. 1970. *The Thirteenth, Greatest of Centuries.* New York: AMS Press.
WARD, W. 1968. "The Beginnings of Reform in Great Britain: Imperial Problems: Politics and Administration: Economic Growth." In *New Cambridge Modern History*, vol. 8. Cambridge, Eng.: Cambridge University Press.
WEBER, A. 1948. *Farewell to European History.* New Haven, Ct.: Yale University Press.
WEBER, M. 1958. *The Protestant Ethic and the Spirit of Capitalism.* Translated by T. Parsons. New York: Scribner's.
WESSON, R. 1967. *The Imperial Order.* Berkeley, Ca.: University of California Press.
———. 1974. *The Russian Dilemma.* New Brunswick, N.J.: Rutgers University Press.
———. 1976. *Why Marxism?* New York: Basic Books.
WHILBEY, L. 1898; 1971. *Greek Oligarchies, Their Character and Organization.* New York: Haskell House.
WHITE, E. 1927. *Why Rome Fell.* New York: Harper and Row.
WHITE, L. 1962. *Medieval Technology and Social Change.* Oxford: Clarendon Press.
———. 1963. "What Accelerated Technical Progress in the Western Middle Ages?" In *Scientific Change.* Edited by A. Crombie. New York: Basic Books.
WHYTE, W. 1956. *The Organization Man.* New York: Simon and Schuster.
WILDAVSKY, A. 1971. "The Two Presidencies." In *The Politics of U.S. Foreign Policy Making.* Edited by D. Fox. Pacific Palisades, Ca.: Goodyear.
WILLIAMS, N., ed. 1970. *Reform and Revolt.* New York: Newsweek Books.
———. 1974. *Expanding Horizons.* New York: Weidenfeld and Nicolson.
WILLOUGHBY, W. 1903. *Political Theories of the Ancient World.* New York: Longmans, Green.
WILSON, C. 1957. "The Growth of Overseas Commerce and European Manufacture." In *New Cambridge Modern History*, vol. 7. Cambridge, Eng.: Cambridge University Press.
———. 1968. *The Dutch Republic.* New York: McGraw-Hill.
WITTFOGEL, K. 1957. *Oriental Despotism.* New Haven, Ct.: Yale University Press.
WOODHEAD, A. 1962. *The Greeks in the West.* London: Thames and Hudson.
WRAITH, R., and SIMPKINS, E. 1964. *Corruption in Developing Countries.* New York: Norton.
WU, K. 1928. *Ancient Chinese Political Theories.* Shanghai: Commercial Press.

YOST, C. 1972. *The Conduct and Misconduct of Foreign Policy.* New York: Random House.

ZIMMERN, A. 1931. *The Greek Commonwealth,* 5th ed. Oxford: Clarendon Press.

Index

Achilles, 14, 51, 52
Acragas, 71
Acton, J., 15, 136, 197
Adams, R., 43
Adcock, K., 27, 28, 29, 30, 59
Adie, R., 241
Ady, C., 132, 162
Aeschylus, 69, 71, 74
Agamemnon, 51
Agard, W., 50
Akkadian Conquest, 44
Al Azhar (Cairo), 119
Albigenses, 165
Alcaeus, 69
Aldred, C., 91
Alexander, P., 49
Alexander, the Great, 23, 30, 38, 39, 47, 48, 60, 67, 73, 74, 102
Alexander I, Tsar of Russia, 120, 185
Almond, G., 6, 184
Altamira, R., 137
Altekar, A., 32, 33, 46, 47, 48
Amalrik, A., 255
Amin, I., 263
Amphictyonies, 26, 27
Anabaptists, 141
Anacreon, 69
Anaxagoras, 70
Anaximander, 70
Andreski, S., 241
Andrewes, A., 21, 53, 72
Angell, N., 221
Anglicanism, 110, 113
Antigone, 54, 58

Antiphon, 51
Aphrodite, 50
Apollonius, 76
Aquinas, T., 129, 163
Aratta, 35
Araucarians, 42
Archilocus, 69
Archimedes, 76, 77, 164
Argos, 36
Aristarchus, of Samos, 76, 77, 164
Aristides, 27
Aristophanes, 28, 55, 73, 74
Aristotle, 5, 51, 53, 56, 76, 84, 89, 92, 94, 156
Arkwright, R., 177
Arrian, 47
Arthasastra, 23, 47
Artz, F., 159
Ashley, M., 144, 146
Ashur, 44
Asoka, 66, 74
Athens, 12, 22, 38, 49, 54, 59, 76
Athenian Confederacy, 29
Athenian Constitution, 56, 57
Attica, 49
Aubry, O., 138, 205
Augustus, 83, 103, 104
Averroës, 94

Bacon, F., 168, 176, 250
Bacon, R., 156, 165, 168, 176, 250
Bailly, A., 139, 148, 193
Balazs, E., 97
Bandyopadhyaya, N., 48

Index

Banfield, E., 206
Bangladesh, 262
Banti, L., 25
Baptists, 176
Barber, E., 197
Bark, W., 128, 154
Barnes, H., 106, 155
Barnett, H., 182, 189
Barnouw, A., 173, 174
Baron, H., 109, 124, 164, 184
Barraclough, G., 104
Bartolus, of Perugia, 159
Bary, W. de, 66, 67
Bayle, P., 205
Beard, M., 158
Beethoven, L., 220
Bell, E., 70, 158, 252
Bengtson, H., 60, 75, 76, 77
Berlin Wall, 190
Berlyne, D., 189
Bernard, H., 189
Bernhardi, F. von, 194, 250
Bernstein, E., 146
Bianquis, G., 201, 202
Bismarck, O., 3, 109, 120, 218, 248
Blum, J., 155
Boak, A., 40
Boas, M., 168, 170
Bodde, S., 64
Bodin, J., 136
Boileau-Despreaux, N., 205
Bolshevism, 224
Boniface, Pope, 109
Bonnard, A., 75, 76
Bonner, R., 55, 56
Borgia, Lucrezia, 161
Bose, A., 48
Botsford, G., 22, 30, 31, 39, 49, 50, 59, 70, 74, 75
Bossuet, J., 139
Bouvier, E., 205
Bowden, W., 179, 180
Boyle, R., 171
Bozeman, A., 29, 117
Brahe, T., 170
Brahms, J., 220
Brailsford, H., 146
Braure, M., 145
Breasted, J., 91
Briggs, A., 180, 196, 223
Britton, R., 34
Brown, L., 244
Brown, S., 249, 262

Brucker, G., 42, 163, 164, 166, 183
Bruford, W., 117, 201
Brumbaugh, R., 57, 71, 77
Brundage, B., 90
Bryce, J., 104
Buddha, 47
Buffon, G., 149
Bullock, C., 57
Burke, E., 118
Burn, A., 21, 28, 29, 39, 52, 69, 71, 72
Burns, E., 129, 134, 165, 203
Bury, J., 26, 217
Bushnell, G., 90
Butler, G., 116, 118, 120, 121, 125, 126, 188
Bynkershoek, C. van, 174

Cady, J., 25, 203
Caesar, 83, 102
Caggese, R., 158
Cahen, L., 145
Calhoun, G., 49, 50, 199
Calvin, J., 169
Calvinism, 110, 113
Calvinists, 141
Cambyses, 72
Cameron, R., 155
Canning, G., 127
Cantor, N., 105
Cardwell, D., 207
Carter, J., 252
Carthage, 40, 42
Cary, M., 28, 30, 31, 40, 75
Catalonia, 165, 166
Cathari, 161
Catharine Perfects, 210
Catherine, the Great of Russia, 118
Chaeronea, 38
Chamoux, F., 26, 89
Charlemagne, 102, 104, 110, 112, 113
Charles I, of England, 140, 144, 145, 146, 176, 193, 195
Charles II, of England, 114, 146, 147, 177, 185
Charles V, Holy Roman Emperor (Charles I, of Spain), 102, 109, 112, 124, 127, 136, 137, 159, 203
Charles VIII, of France, 109
Charles XI, of Sweden, 140
Charles XII, of Sweden, 140
Chaucer, G., 157
Cheng, 33
Cherniavsky, M., 188

Cheyney, E., 109, 116, 128, 129, 134
Childe, V., 91
Ch'in, 33, 37
Chou, 37
Chou League, 34
Christ, 104
Chuang Tzu, 46
"Ciompi," 130
Clapham, J., 154, 158, 168
Clark, G., 62, 113, 146, 173, 191, 193, 197
Clearchus, 71
Cleisthenes, 54
Cloché, P., 72
Clough, S., 71
Cnudde, C., 209
Cobban, A., 143, 150, 184, 186
Cola de Rienzo, 160
Colbert, J., 173
Cold War, 260
Coleman, D., 173, 182, 204
Communes, 106, 128, 129
Communism, 224, 232, 238
Confucius, 82, 65
Congress of Berlin, 126
Congress of Vienna, 125, 126
Consolato del Mar, 120
Constantine, 11, 102, 104
Contending States, 24
Cook, J., 69, 70, 86
Cook, T., 109, 129
Copernicus, 77
Córdoba, 94, 95
Corinth, 40
Corneille, P., 205
Cosimo de Medici, 157
Cottrell, L., 91
Coulton, G., 103, 134, 156
Courtillier, G., 48, 67
Cowell, F., 88
Cowie, L., 191
Craig, G., 217, 219
Creel, H., 64
Crimean War, 126, 185
Critias, 70
Crombie, A., 156, 164, 165
Cromwell, O., 146
Crow, J., 137, 204

Dadaism, 22
Da Gama, Vasco, 93
Dahl, R., 6, 81, 82
D'Alembert, J., 150

Dampier, W., 77
Dante, 157, 162
Darius I, 53, 62, 92
Darius III, 73
Darwin, E., 220
Das, S., 48
Das Gupta, S., 33, 68
Davids, T., 23, 48, 66, 67
Davies, G., 145, 146, 176, 209
Day, J., 31
Dawson, C., 159
Deak, F., 42
De Bary, W., 66, 67
Debussy, C., 220
De Flor, R., 166
De Gaulle, C., 229
De Grunwald, C., 195
De Guibert, Comte, 216
Demangeon, A., 223
De Maricourt P., 156
Democritus, 70, 85
Demosthenes, 32, 38, 50, 52
Descartes, 171, 174, 205
De Tocqueville, A., 149, 150
D'iakonov, I., 24, 43, 44
Dickens, A., 116, 170, 190, 195, 197
Diderot, D., 150
Diehl, C., 159
Dietz, F., 173
Dikshitar, V., 33
Diocletian, 103
Diogenes, 78
Dionysius, 26, 38
Dissenters, 147, 180
Domitian, 79
Dozy, R , 95
Dubois, P., 109
Duby, G., 139, 150, 205
Dulles, J., 230
Dun, J., 24, 34
Dunham, A., 52
Dunning, W., 110
Durkheim, E., 3
Duyvendak, J., 27

Ebenstein, W., 226
Eberhard, W., 97
Ecclesiazusae, 55
Edelstein, L., 70
Edict of Nantes, 139
Edward I, of England, 109
Egypt, 90, 91
Ehrenberg, V., 22, 37

Einstein, L., 158, 159, 160, 171, 221
Eixemenes, F., 166
Elizabeth I, Queen of England, 140, 145, 173, 175, 176
Elliott, J., 137, 205
Emeny, G., 227
Emerson, R., 192
Emery, R., 156
Empedocles, 86
Engels, F., 235
Enlightenment, 118
Ensor, R., 245
Erasmus, D., 118, 164
Erech, 44
Erechtheum, 50
Escorial, 137
Estates General, 138, 151
Euclid, 76
Euhemerus, 78
Eumenides, 74
Euripides, 51, 52, 58, 69, 73
European Economic Community, 258
Expressionism, 220

Fairbank, J., 96
Fairservis, W., 91
Fan, W., 44, 45
Farrington, B., 71, 76, 86
Fay, B., 150
Ferdinand, of Austria, 112, 136, 137, 203
Ferguson, W., 31, 39, 59, 74, 75, 77, 78
Feuer, L., 5, 176, 182
Field, J., 219, 228, 244, 251
Figgis, J., 109, 116, 136
Finley, M., 22
Fischer, E., 223
Fitzgerald, C., 34
Flaceliere, R., 49, 73
Flanders, 107, 130
Florence, 157, 158, 163, 164
Fontenelle, B., 171
Ford, F., 112
Foster, G., 182, 199, 204, 206
Fouquet, N., 147
Francis, Saint, 161, 162
Franklin, B., 192
Frederick, the Great of Russia, 118, 123, 125, 182
Frederick Barbarossa, 107
Freeman, K., 52, 71, 72
French, use of, 117, 118, 215
Freud, S., 220
Fronde, 15, 16, 158
Frost, R., 197

Frye, R., 74
Fuggers, 203
Fung, Y., 66
Furet, F., 148

Gadd, C., 35, 44, 63
Galen, 170
Galileo, 164, 167, 170, 177, 181
Gandhi, M., 192
Gasster, M., 258
Gay, P., 221, 222, 226, 231
Gebhardt, B., 201
Genghiz Khan, 227
Genoa, 133
Gentili, A., 121
George, D., 179
George III, 147, 186, 187
Gershoy, L., 118, 143, 148
Geyl, P., 186
Gibbon, E., 4, 142, 149, 182, 194
Giddens, A., 3
Gilbert, W., 176
Gilgamesh, 43, 63
Gillespie, C., 184, 196
Gimpel, J., 253
Glotz, G., 28, 29, 31, 37, 39, 49, 50, 51, 52, 53, 54, 55, 56, 57, 58, 59, 69, 71, 76, 87, 88, 89
Glover, T., 51, 55, 58, 89, 184
Godechot, J., 115
Goethe, J. von, 202
Goldman, M., 233
Gomme, A., 53
Gooch, G., 193, 206
Goodfield, J., 71
Goodrich, L., 97
Gordon, M., 221
Granet, M., 45
Grant, F., 59, 78
Gray, P., 117, 118, 122
Green, V., 165
Gregory, the Great, 102
Gregory I, 103
Gregory VII, the Great, 105
Grimm, H., 188, 190
Grossteste, R., 164
Grotius, H., 120, 121, 174
Grunwald, C. de, 195
Guibert, Comte de, 216
Gupta, S. das, 33, 68
Gustavus Adolphus of Sweden, 113

Haarhoff, T., 28
Habakkuk, H., 143

Hadas, M., 73
Hadrian, 15, 79
Hakluyt, R., 176
Hale, J., 198
Hale, O., 182, 220, 221
Hale, W., 22
Hall, A., 117, 155, 164, 168
Hall, D., 25
Hallett, R., 25
Hals, F., 174
Hamblin, D., 25
Hammurabi, 5
Han dynasty, 11
Hannibal, 75
Hapsburgs, 113
Harappa, 90
Harden, D., 92
Harnack, A. von, 182
Harrington, M., 176
Harvey, W., 171, 176
Hasebroek, J., 30, 49
Haseler, S., 253
Haskins, C., 104, 116, 156
Hassall, A., 138, 144, 193
Hawgood, J., 147, 217
Hawkes, J., 24, 27, 43, 62
Hay, D., 161, 164, 165, 168, 169
Hayes, C., 120
Hayes, W., 91
Haywood, R., 26, 30, 38, 49, 50, 52, 53, 55, 56, 72, 87
Hecataeus, of Miletus, 69
Heckscher, E., 136
Heeger, G., 241
Heidenreich, C., 189
Heliopolis, 91
Hellenistic state system, 23
Henderson, W., 179, 182, 196
Henry IV, 138
Henry VII, 134, 140
Henry VIII, 110, 116, 140, 144
Hephaestus, 50
Heraclitus, of Ephesus, 70, 85, 89
Hercules, 63
Herodotus, 27, 53, 70
Herophilus, 76
Hertz, F., 201, 202
Herz, J., 246, 247, 248
Herzen, A., 191
Heydte, F. von der, 116
Hesiod, 50, 88
Hicks, J., 82
Hill, C., 170, 176, 184, 191, 192
Hill, D., 197

Hill, F., 175
Hinsley, F., 127
Hindu, 23
Hipparchus, 77
Hippodamus, of Miletus, 73
Hirth, F., 65
Hitler, A., 102, 110, 124, 226
Hitti, P., 3, 94, 119
Hobbes, T., 17, 136, 141, 176, 188, 193
Hodges, H., 154
Hohenberg, J., 209
Hole, F., 24
Holsti, K., 24
Holy League, 112
Holy Roman Empire, 103, 104, 105
Homer, 14, 26, 51, 52, 63, 69
Hsu, C., 37, 44, 45, 46
Hsün Tzu, 65
Huan, of Ch'i, Duke, 34
Huang Tsung-Hsi, 66
Huizinga, J., 110, 186
Humboldt, W. von, 202
Hume, D., 156
Hume, M., 149, 158, 193, 199, 203
Huntington, E., 81
Huss, J., 109
Huxley, A., 88
Huygens, C., 174, 205

Iambulus, 78
Iliad, 28, 51, 69
Impressionism, 220
Inca Empire, 42
Indus Valley civilization, 90
Institutes of Manu, 32, 33
Ionia, 54
Ireton, H., 146
Isabella, 136, 137, 203
Isaiah, 92
Isocrates, 27, 38, 73, 89
Ithaca, 51
Ivan, the Terrible, 159, 193, 207
Ivan IV, 239

Jacob, E., 160
Jacobins, 152
James, W., 145, 183, 255
James I, 140, 172, 175, 176
James II, 114, 147
Jason, 38, 73
Jelavich, B., 191
Jessup, P., 42
John, of Salisbury, 129
Johnson, S., 196

Index

Jones, A., 51, 56, 58
Jones, J., 22, 26, 29, 30, 52, 73
Jones, P., 132
Julius Caesar, 15
Justinian, 104

Kaddaffy, M., 263
Kagan, D., 51, 52, 53
Kaufman, R., 207
Kautilya, 23, 108
Kavolis, V., 14, 184
Kellogg-Briand Pact, 245
Kemal, A., 192
Kenna, G., 233, 252
Kennedy, J., 259
Keohane, R., 219, 249, 262
Kepler, J., 171
Kiener, F., 106
King, W., 88, 199
Kipling, R., 221
Kish, 5, 44
Kitagawa, J., 96
Kitto, H., 38, 89
Klemm, F., 154, 155
Kling, M., 242
Kliuchevsky, V., 82
Knorr, K., 185, 247
Koestler, A., 254
Kohn, H., 204
Kohr, L., 208
Koine, 31
Kraemer, J., 119
Kramer, S., 35, 42, 43, 44, 62, 63
Krofta, K., 126, 170
Kropotkin, P., 106
Kshatriya, 47

La Bruyère, J. de, 206
Lacedaemonians, 32
Laffan, R., 135
La Fontaine, J. de, 205
Lagash, 5, 27, 35, 44
Lanning, E., 90
Lao Tse, 65
Laokoon, 75
La Rochefoucauld, F. de, 205
Larsen, J., 22, 60
Laski, H., 129
Latin, use of, 117
Latourette, K., 34
Lattimore, O., 64
Lauring, P., 137
Laws (Plato), 22, 85

Lederer, I., 185
Leeuwenhoek, A. von, 174
Leibnitz, G. von, 171, 202, 205
Lenin, V., 232, 237, 238
Leonardo, 160, 161, 168, 202
Leonardo, of Pisa (Fibonacci), 158
Leonidas, 52
Lorenzo de' Medici, 160
Levi-Provençal, E., 95
Lewin, L., 250
Lewis, G., 203
Lewis, O., 15
Liang, G., 45, 66
Lichtheim, G., 235
Liddell-Hart, B., 218
Lijphart, A., 6
Limouzin-Lamothe, R., 106
Lindsay, J., 142, 187
Li Ssu, 64
Literacy, Greek, 73
Littman, R., 26, 50, 51, 52
Lodge, E., 128
Lodi, Peace of, 108
Locke, J., 174, 190, 220
Lockwood, W., 219
Lough, J., 139
Louis XI, 138
Louis XIII, 136
Louis XIV, 15, 16, 102, 113, 114, 122, 123, 136, 138, 141, 142, 147, 148, 149, 185, 193, 205, 206
Louis XV, 123, 148, 149, 150, 151
Louis XVI, 125, 148, 149, 150
Lowi, T., 256
Lu, 33, 45
Lucas-Dubreton, J., 172
Lucretius, T., 164
Lugalanda, 44
Lugalzagezzi, of Umma, 24, 36
Lull, R., 166
Luther, M., 110, 141, 169
Lutheranism, 112, 113
Lydians, 51
Lysias, 27

MacArthur, D., 250
Maccoby, S., 116, 118, 120, 121, 125, 126, 188
McCrone, D., 209
Macedon, 38, 39
Macedonia, 52
McFarland, A., 6
Machiavelli, N., 2, 23, 38, 42, 109, 160,

161, 162, 193, 198
McLean, A., 168
McManners, J., 142
Madelin, L., 114
Magadha, 32
Magna Carta, 44
Magnus, A., 156
Mahabharata, 32, 47, 48, 66
Mahajan, V., 47
Maine, H., 81
Mair, A., 88
Mallowan, M., 43
Malthus, T., 143, 262
Mandrou, R., 139, 150, 205
Manichaeism, 165
Mantinea, 30
Mao Tse-tung, 238
Maria Theresa, of Austria, 182
Marina, W., 253
Markham, F., 115
Marlowe, C., 176
Marseilles, 106
Marsiglio, of Padua, 129
Martin, A. von, 161, 199
Martin, P., 186, 203
Martin, V., 22, 28, 32, 86
Martin W., 34
Marx, K., 220, 224, 235, 238
Marxism-Leninism, 232, 238
Mary Tudor, Queen of England, 112, 113, 140, 147
Masani, R., 46
Mason, S., 70, 71, 155
Mathiez, A., 148, 150
Mattingly, G., 117, 208, 209
Maurya, 23, 32, 46, 48
Mayas, 42
Mayer, J., 142, 161, 197
Mazarin, J., 139
Meadows, D., 262
Medea, 73
Medici, 162, 163
Meeüss, A. de, 210
Megalopolitans, 32
Megara, 30, 49
Megasthenes, 23
Mehden, F. von der, 257
Melko, M., 194
Menander, 74
Mencius, 46, 48, 64, 65
Menes, 91
Merriman, R., 112, 136, 137, 166, 185, 187, 188, 203

Merton, T., 94
Mesilim, King of Kish, 35
Metternich, of Austria, 185
Michelangelo, 160
Miletus, 30
Milton, J., 160
Modelski, G., 32, 33, 48
Modino, 158
Mohendjo-Daro, 90
Molière, 205
Mollat, M., 129, 165
Mondino, 164
Montesquieu, Baron de, 2, 82, 111, 123, 142, 149, 150, 184, 191, 194, 199
Mookerji, R., 47
Moore, S., 5, 68
Moorer, E., 85
More, T., 176
Morgenthau, H., 121
Morley, J., 169
Moscati, S., 63, 92
Moses, C., 202
Moslem Spain, 95
Mosley, J., 27, 28, 29, 30, 59
Moss, R., 254
Mossé, C., 38, 39, 50, 51
Mo Tzu, 65
Mundy, J., 106, 130, 131, 159
Murphy, E., 25
Murray, M., 91
Mussolini, B., 225, 226

Napoleon, 15, 102, 114, 115, 124, 125, 126, 152
Nazism, 226, 227
Necker, J., 191
Needham, J., 65, 198
Nef, J., 114, 118, 123, 143, 165, 168, 170, 193, 205
Nehru, J., 47
Nero, 79
Newcomen, T., 178
Newton, I., 117, 171, 177, 205
Nicholas, of Autrecourt, 156
Nicholas, of Cusa, 129
Nicholas I, Tsar of Russia, 191, 236
Nicholas Oresmus, 156
Nicolson, H., 139, 205
Nietzsche, F., 220
Novgorod, 130
Nussbaum, A., 120, 154
Nussbaum, F., 167, 171
Nye, J., 219, 249, 262

Odysseus, 50, 51
Oechsli, W., 140, 191
Oedipus Tyrannus, 26, 52
Ogg, D., 122, 135, 136, 139, 167, 170, 171, 204
Oldenbourg, Z., 157
Old Oligarch, 49, 51
Oresmus, Nicholas, 156
Osiris, 91
Ovid, 156

Palmer, M., 8, 148, 149, 192, 216
Panini, 67
Pan-Ionian, 29
Parlement of Paris, 138
Parmenides, 86
Parrot, A., 62
Parthenon, 26
Pascal, B., 205
Pasion, 49
Paterini, 161
Peace, 28
Peace of Utrecht, 125
Peisistratus, 54
Perelomov, L., 45
Pergamum, 75
Pericles, 11, 50, 55, 56, 57, 58, 73, 74
Perkins, J., 150
Peruvian culture, 90
Peter, of Russia, 195
Peter, the Great, 119, 173, 237
Petrarch, F., 157, 160
Philip, of Macedon, 23, 38
Philip II, of Spain, 112, 113, 137, 205
Philip IV, of France, 109
Phillipson, C., 26, 29
Philo, of Byzantium, 77
Phocaea, 49
Phocians, 27
Physiocrats, 143
Pickard-Cambridge, A., 37, 38, 56
Pindar, 22
Pinson, K., 202
Pirenne, H., 91, 130, 173
Planck, M., 221
Plato, 22, 28, 50, 65, 70, 76, 85, 188
Pliny, 84
Plumb, J., 182
Plutarch, 67
Plutus, 55
Pogodin, M., 185
Poitras, G., 241
Politics, 53, 84
Pontieri, E., 167

Porfidirov, N., 130
Poseidonus, 76
Presbyterian, 146
Prestwick, M., 139, 206
Previté-Orton, C., 131, 135
Price, D., 77, 90
Prince, 23
Printing, 168, 169
Protestantism, 113, 141
Pseudodemocracy, 257, 258
Ptolemy, C., 77, 170
Pufendorf, S., 121
Puritan Revolution, 16
Puritans, 144, 145
Pushkarev, S., 191, 193
Putnam, P., 208
Pythagoras, 86

Quakers, 176, 199
Quigley, C., 165, 252, 254

Racine, J., 205
Radhakrishnan, S., 68
Radishchev, A., 192
Ramayana, 66
Randall, J., 141, 155, 156, 164, 165, 174
Rashdall, H., 156
Rawlinson, G., 93
Reformation, 9
Regla, J., 204
Reid, W., 196
Reischauer, E., 96
Rembrandt, R. van, 174
Renard, G., 134, 135, 195, 203, 206
Republic, 28
Richard, the Lion-Heart, 157
Richelieu, A., 15, 113, 138, 185, 201, 206
Richet, D., 148
Riemens, H., 173
Riesenberg, P., 106, 131, 159
Ritter, G., 117
Roach, J., 182, 197
Roberts, J., 167
Robertson, C., 178
Robespierre, M., 152
Robinson, C., 26, 49, 56, 87
Robson, E., 122, 125
Rogers, E., 189
Rosenau, J., 1
Rossi, M., 239
Rostovtzeff, M., 31, 50, 74
Rousseau, J., 7, 82, 118, 149
Roustan, M., 197

Russell, F., 23, 27, 32, 120, 183
Russell, W., 116, 154
Ruysdael, J., 174

Sabine, G., 78, 105, 116, 128, 129
Saggs, H., 27, 43, 44
Sakharov, A., 233
Sakyia Republic, 47
Salin, E., 71
Sanders, W., 90
Sansom, G., 96
Santillana, G. de, 77
Sarbin, T., 15
Sargon, of Akkad, 36
Sarkar, B., 47, 48
Savanarola, G., 157, 161, 162
Schapera, I., 82
Schelling, T., 246
Schevill, F., 157
Seal, B., 67
Seignobos, C., 149
Seleucids, 74
Service, E., 90
Seven Years' War, 186
Shafer, E., 97
Shaftesbury, A., Lord, 117
Shakespeare, W., 75, 159, 176, 183
Shanks, M., 254
Shih Huang-Ti (or First Emperor), 37
Shookra, 48
Shull, A., 85
Shuruppak, 44
Sicily, 72
Signoria, 130
Simonds, F., 227
Simpkins, E., 199, 241
Singel, C., 70
Sismondi, J., 130, 131, 162
Skjelsbaek, K., 249
Slavery, Greek, 50, 51, 78
Smith, A., 143, 175, 179, 184, 242
Smith, G., 140, 145
Smith, H., 234
Snell, B., 69, 70
Socrates, 22, 73
Solomon, 92
Solon, 54, 59, 70, 71
Sophocles, 52, 54, 58, 69, 71
Sorel, G., 220
Sorokin, P., 14, 71, 94, 204, 220
Spain, 203, 205
Sparta, 12, 39, 52
Spaulding, O., 73
Spengler, O., 225

Spenser, E., 176
Spinoza, B., 174
Sprout, H., 258
Spuler, B., 93, 159
Staël-Holstein, B. de, 202
Starr, C., 22, 49
Staling, J., 238
Steinhausen, G., 201, 202
Sterne, L., 123
Stoessinger, J., 246
Stomberg, A., 182
Stone, L., 146
Stonequist, E., 184
Strafford, 144, 146
Strato, 76
Stratton, G., 194
Stravinsky, I., 220
Stuart Restoration, 16
Stuarts, 142, 143, 145
Suleiman, 112
Sulla, L., 79
Sung, Duke of, 34, 35
Surrealism, 222
Swammerdam, J., 174
Sybaris, 30, 71
Symonds, J., 112, 132, 133, 162, 164, 167
Syrians, 51

Takekoshi, Y., 96
Tanaka, K., 249
Tanner, O., 184
Tarn, W., 31, 60, 76
Taton, R., 62
Taylor, H., 129
Ten Thousand, Epic of the, 72
Teutonic Knights, 154
Thackaray, A., 253
Thales, 70
Thant, U., 239
Thebes, 36
Theognis, 52
Theophrastus, 76
Theoric Fund, Athenian, 39
Thermopylae, 52
Thersites, 51
Theseaus, 26
Thomas, E., 65
Thompson, J., 104, 128, 189, 262
Thorlby, A., 220
Tiberius, C., 83
Thucydides, 6, 28, 32, 58, 73, 74, 162, 184
Tilly, C., 134

Thrace, 52
Tocqueville, A. de, 149, 150
Tokugawa shoguns, 96
Tompkins, S., 240
Toynbee, A., 3, 4, 124
Treadgold, D., 13
Trevelyan, G., 204, 206
Trojan Women, 51
Trueta, J., 157, 166
Tudors, 140, 145
Tufte, E., 81, 82
Tulard, J., 114
Tullock, G., 187
Tyre, 92

Ulam, A., 188, 225
Umayyad, 95
Umma, 5, 27, 35
Upanishads, 66
Uruk, E., 35
Urukagina, 44

Valentine, J., 85
Valla, L., 161
Vandals, 102
Vasco da Gama, 93
Vattel, E. de, 118, 121, 125
Vedic songs, 46, 47, 66
Venice, 7
Venetian oligarchy, 132
Verba, S., 6, 184
Vermeer, J., 174
Vesalius, 164, 170
Vico, G., 4
Vikings, 155
Villari, P., 157, 161, 162
Vital, D., 206
Vitoria, F. de, 121
Vlekke, B., 172
Voltaire, F., 118, 149, 150, 190, 191
Vyvyan, J., 221

Walker, R., 24, 33, 34, 35, 44, 45, 64, 82
Walker, T., 116
Wallace, W., 219

Walpole, H., 149
Walsh, J., 155
Ward, W., 186, 187, 192, 196
Washington, G., 192
Watt, J., 178
Watteau, J., 205
Webb, R., 221, 222, 226, 231
Weber, A., 216, 221
Weber, M., 170, 221
Wesson, R., 36, 207, 220, 233
Westphalia, Peace of, 113
Weulersee, G., 134, 135, 148, 195, 203, 206
Whilbey, L., 81, 86
White, E., 75, 83
White, L., 16, 154, 239
Whyte, W., 252
Wildavsky, A., 259
William, of Occam, 129, 156
William, of Orange, 114, 147
William, the Conqueror, 111, 140
Williams, N., 125
Willoughby, W., 70
Wilson, C., 121, 142, 148, 172, 173, 174, 197, 200, 208
Winstanley, G., 146
Wittofogel, K., 43
Wolfe, J., 122
Wolff, P., 129, 165
Woodhead, A., 22, 26, 77
Wooley, L., 27
Wraith, R., 199, 209, 241
Wyclif, J., 109, 169

Xenophanes, 70, 71
Xenophon, 49, 72, 166
Xerxes, 92, 115

Yang Chu, 65
Yen Fu, 258
Yost, C., 259

Zeno, 78
Zeus, 26
Zimmern, A., 28, 49, 50